Advance Praise for
Dōgen's *Shōbōgenzō Zuimonki*

"Shōhaku Okamura's ongoing work of translation and commentary has for many years shaped my understanding of Dōgen's teaching. A deeply devoted Zen priest, his careful scholarship is matched by the modesty, straightforwardness, and thoroughness of his interpretations. Shōbōgenzō Zuimonki is two important volumes in one: part 1 is the Zuimonki itself, Dōgen's informal instructions to his close disciples, freshly translated with lucid comments and notes; and part 2 is the first full translation of Dōgen's waka poems to include extensive Buddhist commentary, referencing a range of Dōgen's other writings. I am thrilled and grateful to have both these important new additions to Dōgen in English; they will give readers a much fuller appreciation of the range of this great master's expression."—Norman Fischer, poet and Zen priest, author of *When You Greet Me I Bow*, *The Museum of Capitalism*, and *Selected Poems*

"I offer profound praise for *Dōgen's Shōbōgenzō Zuimonki* and for this wonderful new translation and commentary by Shōhaku Okumura Roshi. For many Zen students of my generation these inspiring words were our first extensive experience of the writings of Dōgen Zenji. Now we have a fresh translation of this masterpiece, along with insightful commentary, to inspire and guide our practice in the twenty-first century. May Dōgen's Dharma wheel continue to turn for the welfare of this world."—Tenshin Reb Anderson, student of Dōgen

"This translation is not only Dōgen's instructions, handwritten by his successor Ejo and transmitted to us. It's as if the reader were there over and over again with the myriad examples and instructions straight from Dōgen. With the combination of Dōgen's poetry, this gives a light and creative quality. I was struck by the simplicity of Okumura-roshi's presentation, which is the profundity of Zen. This book will stand and speak as a classic—openly shared and digested for the true Zen student." —Jakusho Kwong-roshi, author of *No Beginning, No End*; *Breath Sweeps Mind*; and *Mind Sky*

"This book is a long overdue new translation of *Dōgen's Shōbōgenzō Zui-monki*, his informal Dharma talks, and perhaps his most accessible teachings, as recorded by his disciple Ejō. Shōhaku Okumura brings extensive Zen practice and scholarship to this translation offering footnotes, biographies, and commentary. An added bonus to this book is the addition of Okumura's evocative translations and commentaries on Dōgen's waka poems. If you are a Dōgen fan, this book is a must for your library."
—Shinshu Roberts, author of *Being-Time: A Practitioner's Guide to Dōgen's Shōbōgenzō Uji*

"For those who endeavor to negotiate wholeheartedly the Way of Dōgen Zen, a new work by the incomparable scholar-practitioner Shōhaku Okumura is cause for celebration and gratitude. This superb edition of the *Shōbōgenzō Zuimonki*, based on the 1644 Chōen-ji version of the informal talks that Dōgen's celebrated disciple Ejō recorded after joining Kōshō-ji in 1234, consummately expresses the treasures of the true Dharma eye. Dōgen counsels us only to speak when we have something to say that 'is beneficial to both yourself and others,' and Okumura and his editor Dōju Layton demonstrate that this is a jewel that exceeds all commerce."—Tetsuzen Jason M. Wirth, Seattle University

"Shōhaku Okumura Roshi has produced a tremendously useful and easily understandable translation of this important work about the teachings of Dōgen Zenji. It's accessible and practical. In the *Shōbōgenzō Zuimonki* we get to see a different side of Dōgen from the one Dōgen presents in his own writings. This is Dōgen the way one of his closest students saw him. Dōgen's student, Ejō, asks Dōgen the kinds of questions I would like to have asked Dōgen. The answers are often surprising and illuminating. Having the Japanese text to refer to is a wonderful addition for those of us nerds who like to check the original language."
—Brad Warner, author of *Hardcore Zen* and *Letters to a Dead Friend about Zen*

Dōgen's
Shōbōgenzō Zuimonki

THE NEW ANNOTATED TRANSLATION

Also Including
Dōgen's Waka Poetry with Commentary

Eihei Dōgen

Compiled by Koun Ejō

Translated and Introduced by Shōhaku Okumura

Wisdom Publications
199 Elm Street
Somerville, MA 02144 USA
wisdomexperience.org

© 2022 Shōhaku Okumura

Library of Congress Cataloging-in-Publication Data
Names: Dōgen, 1200–1253 author. | Okumura, Shōhaku, 1948– translator. | Dōgen, 1200–1253. Poems. Selections. | Dōgen, 1200–1253. Poems. Selections. English.
Title: Dōgen's Shōbōgenzō zuimonki: the new annotated translation: Also Including Dōgen's Waka Poetry with Commentary / Eihei Dōgen; translated and Introduced by Shōhaku Okumura.
Other titles: Shōbō genzō zuimonki. English
Description: First. | Somerville: Wisdom Publications, 2022. | Includes bibliographical references and index.
Identifiers: LCCN 2021035855 (print) | LCCN 2021035856 (ebook) | ISBN 9781614295730 (hardcover) | ISBN 9781614295976 (ebook)
Subjects: LCSH: Zen Buddhism.
Classification: LCC BQ9449.D654 S5513 2022 (print) | LCC BQ9449.D654 (ebook) | DDC 294.3/927—dc23
LC record available at https://lccn.loc.gov/2021035855
LC ebook record available at https://lccn.loc.gov/2021035856

ISBN 978-1-61429-573-0   ebook ISBN 978-1-61429-597-6

26 25 24 23 22   5 4 3 2 1

Cover design by Phil Pascuzzo. Interior design by Tim Holtz.

Printed on acid-free paper that meets the guidelines for permanence and durability of the Production Guidelines for Book Longevity of the Council on Library Resources.

Printed in the United States of America.

CONTENTS

Publisher's Acknowledgment

The publisher gratefully acknowledges the generous help of the Hershey Family Foundation in sponsoring the production of this book.

Part One

Shōbōgenzō Zuimonki

Translation and comments by Shōhaku Okumura
Edited by Dōju Layton

EDITOR'S PREFACE

Just as it was to my teacher and his before him, Dōgen Zenji's *Shōbō-genzō Zuimonki* is a personally meaningful text to me. When I first began practicing seriously in my early twenties, I was eager to engage with Dōgen's work. Being mostly unfamiliar with the voluminous lore of Zen, however, I found the more famous *Kana Shōbōgenzō* to be almost completely impenetrable. When I expressed my disappointment in this, someone in my sangha at the Missouri Zen Center recommended *Shōbōgenzō Zuimonki* as a more accessible alternative. Although at first I was skeptical that an approachable text could come from the same author, I was soon surprised at just how down-to-earth it really was. Despite the huge expanse of time, space, and circumstance between me and Dōgen's assembly—I read it for the first time 773 years after its composition, during my commute on an electric light-rail train en route to a biology lab in a city over ten thousand kilometers (over six thousand miles) from Kyoto—I often felt that Dōgen was speaking directly to me.

When my teacher asked me to edit his new translation of *Shōbō-genzō Zuimonki*, I was excited that I would have the opportunity to study the text closely. Thinking back on my time as a perplexed newcomer, I made an effort to ensure that this text included many explanatory notes for those not familiar with the cultural and historical context of Dōgen's time. Several translations of *Shōbōgenzō Zuimonki* already exist, so we felt that providing a bilingual edition with extensive notes would help give the reader a new way of approaching the text. That being said, readers who prefer to have an uninterrupted reading experience will be able to follow the text without a thorough study of the notes. Compared with Dōgen's other well-known writings, *Shōbōgenzō*

Zuimonki usually does not require comprehensive knowledge of allusions to other Zen texts or specialized Buddhist philosophy and terminology.

All translations found in the introduction and in the notes were made by Shōhaku Okumura unless otherwise noted. Brackets in these translations indicate text that does not occur in the original but rather is added to clarify the intended meaning in English, while allowing the reader to see the Japanese context of Dōgen's words. For example, bracketed text is often added in order to demonstrate the unstated subjects or objects of sentences (in Japanese, sentences can be grammatical without specifying a subject or an object). In some cases, the words in brackets are merely a best guess as to the proper interpretation, but notes are provided where inferences are particularly uncertain. Occasionally, brackets are also used to clarify terms without adding a note, as in "just sitting [*shikantaza*]," or "the West [India]."

Japanese transliterations into the Roman alphabet use the Modified Hepburn system. The Japanese text uses the post-1946 "new character forms" (*shinjitai*) rather than the "old character forms" (*kyūjitai*) in which Ejō and Dōgen would have written. The paragraph layout of the English and Japanese texts follows the source text for this translation, *Dōgen Zenji zenshū*. The original Chōen-ji manuscript has the same section divisions used in this text, but it has no paragraphs. The paragraphs were delimited by Ryūshin Azuma, the modern scholar who compiled *Dōgen Zenji zenshū*, based on changes in topic, tone, etc.

We wish to honor the Chinese heritage of our tradition by including Chinese transliterations for specialized vocabulary when appropriate. Chinese characters are given in their traditional form whenever possible, and transliterations use Hanyu Pinyin. Not having any Chinese speakers on this project, I followed Muller's Digital Dictionary of Buddhism (DDB) for Pinyin transliterations whenever possible. Chinese proper names are presented without tone-indicating diacritics, and proper names from any language are not italicized. For Sanskrit words, the International Alphabet of Sanskrit Transliteration (IAST) was used. Words that have entered the English language are typically presented as they would be in English and not in italics. For example, we use "nirvana," instead of *nirvāṇa* as it would appear in IAST. The same holds for words of Japanese and Chinese origin that commonly appear in English—for example, "Kyoto" rather than Kyōto. Japanese proper names follow English ordering conventions of given name first and family name second—for example, Ryūshin Azuma instead of Azuma Ryūshin as it would appear in Japanese.

Buddha is capitalized when it refers to a specific buddha (e.g., the Buddha or Shakyamuni Buddha), but it is otherwise lowercase (e.g., "the buddhas and ancestors"). *Dharma* (and Buddhadharma) is capitalized except when it is used to refer to phenomena (e.g. "the arising of many dharmas"). However, Indic languages, Chinese, and Japanese all lack an uppercase-lowercase distinction, so keep in mind these conventions do not exist in the source languages. When known, birth and death dates are provided for historical individuals, although in many cases these are merely traditionally used dates that are impossible to confirm historically. When these dates are unknown, the abbreviation *n.d.* (meaning "no dates") appears. When *fl.* (meaning "flourished") is used, it indicates the productive years of an individual whose birth and death dates are unknown, and when *d.* is used it indicates the date of death; *ca.* is used for dates that are approximations.

Although I have done my best to present my teacher's translation in a way that is accurate, consistent, and helpful to both students of Buddhism and scholars alike, I am sure I will have missed the mark at times. As is said at the conclusion of the Dharma combat ceremony (法戦式; Jp. *hossenshiki*), "Please forgive my mistakes; they fill heaven and earth, leaving me no place to hide. Friends, if my actions and words have misled you, please wash out your ears in the pure sound of the present and please continue your practice."

Dōju Layton
August 2019

INTRODUCTION

Dōgen's Life and *Zuimonki*

Much is unknown about the details of Dōgen Zenji's life. Today, only a few short descriptions of his life written by his Dharma descendents are available. Examples include *The Record of the Deeds of the Three Great Venerable Masters* (三大尊行状記; Jp. *Sandaison gyōjō ki*), *The Record of the Deeds of the Three Ancestors of Eihei-ji* (永平寺三祖行業記; Jp. *Eihei-ji sansō gōgyō ki*), and a section about Dōgen in the *Record of the Transmission of the Light* (伝光録; Jp. *Denkōroku*) written by Keizan Jōkin (瑩山紹瑾; 1268–1325 CE). We do not even know with certainty who his parents were. The oldest biography of his life, entitled the *Record of Kenzei* (建撕記; Jp. *Kenzei ki*), was written about two hundred years after Dōgen's death by Kenzei (建撕; 1415–1474 CE), the fourteenth abbot of Eihei-ji (永平寺). In the eighteenth century, Menzan Zuihō (面山瑞方; 1683–1769 CE) revised this text, calling it the *Revised and Annotated Record of Kenzei* (訂補建撕記; Jp. *Teiho kenzei ki*) and adding his own interpretations. Until recently, the Sōtō Zen tradition had continued to study Dōgen's life from Menzan's viewpoint. After the second half of the twentieth century, scholars of Dōgen began searching temples throughout Japan for manuscripts that predate the Edo period (1603–1868 CE). Despite the discovery of several of these seemingly less embellished and idealized materials, a decisive biography of Dōgen remains to be written.

Zuimonki is one work available to help us to understand parts of Dōgen's life. It consists of Dōgen's own words, albeit through the filter of his Dharma successor, Koun Ejō (孤雲懐奘; 1198–1280 CE). In this section, I aim to introduce various parts of Dōgen's life that are relevant to *Zuimonki*.

Before Becoming a Monk

Dōgen was born into an aristocratic family in Kyoto in 1200 CE. The *Record of Kenzei* states that his mother died when he was just seven years old. He is said to have aspired to become a Buddhist monk both because it was his mother's wish and because her death awakened him to the impermanence of human life. The *Record* also states that he began to study Buddhism shortly thereafter, and by the age of nine he was reading the *Abhidharma Storehouse Treatise* (阿毗達磨倶舍論; Ch. *Āpídámó jùshè lùn*; Jp. *Abidatsuma kusha ron*; Skt. *Abhidharmakośa-bhāṣya*), Vasubandhu's (fl. fourth or fifth century CE) massive and complex explication of Sarvâstivāda Buddhist philosophy. Dōgen's grandfather on his mother's side hoped to adopt and educate him so that he could become a high-ranking court official. In *Zuimonki*, Dōgen often quotes from Confucian texts and other stories and sayings from ancient Chinese literature and history.[1] His knowledge of non-Buddhist Chinese classics was nurtured through the education he received before becoming a monk.

When he was twelve years old, planning for his coming-of-age ceremony began, and he may have thought that it would be difficult to leave home to become a monk after this rite of passage. Accordingly, he escaped from his grandfather's house in the Kohata (木幡) section of Uji (宇治), then a small town outside of Kyoto, shortly before the ceremony was set to take place. (Incidentally, my teacher Kōshō Uchiyama Rōshi [内山興正; 1912–1988] also lived in this same neighborhood.) Dōgen went to see Ryōken Hōgen (良顕法眼; n.d.)[2]—a Tendai monk living close to Mt. Hiei (比叡山), who was Dōgen's uncle on his mother's side—and expressed his wish to become a monk. Initially, Ryōken advised him to reconsider because his father and foster father would be furious, but when Dōgen stated his solid determination based on his mother's death and her wish for him, Ryōken accepted his nephew's request. Ryōken sent him to a subtemple called Senkō-bō (千光房) in Yokawa (横川) on Mt. Hiei. The next year, 1213, Dōgen received the bodhisattva precepts and became a Tendai monk. The preceptor was Kōen (公圓; n.d.), the abbot of Enryaku-ji (延暦寺),

the head temple of the Tendai sect and a highly significant temple in Japanese Buddhist history.

Aspects of Dōgen's life prior to leaving home are touched on in *Zuimonki*. For example, he says that he loved reading Chinese classics (3-6, 3-9, 5-8) and that he once owned property and other capital (4-7). It is possible he used this wealth to fund his later journey to China. At any rate, we can plainly see that his family was wealthy and that he received the best education that medieval Japan had to offer.

As a Tendai Monk

While he was staying at the monastery on Mt. Hiei, Dōgen studied Tendai teachings, practiced meditation called *shikan* (止観; Ch. *zhǐdàng*; a translation of Skt. *śamatha* and *vipaśyanā*; literally, "concentration and insight"), and possibly also studied Esoteric Buddhism (密教; Ch. Mìjiào; Jp. Mikkyō). However, within a few years he was disillusioned with what he felt were the degenerate conditions at the monastery.

In section 5-7 of *Zuimonki*, Dōgen states that his teachers taught him to study hard to become a well-known teacher so that he could gain fame and profit and ultimately become a teacher to the emperor or other aristocrats. He later read the biographies of eminent monks in ancient China and found that it was deeply mistaken to study Buddhist teaching for the sake of gaining fame and profit. Not only that, on Mt. Hiei there were even soldier monks engaged in fighting with other powerful monasteries, such as Mii-dera (三井寺) and Kōfuku-ji (興福寺). Such was the state of the Buddhist institution on Mt. Hiei during Dōgen's youth. The genuine spirit of the founder of the monastery, Saichō (最澄; 767–822 CE), had been lost, and many sincere practitioners left to find their own way of practice. Such monks were called renunciants, or *tonsei-sō* (遁世僧), literally, "monks who escape from the world." This originally referred simply to those who had renounced a normal life to become monks and enter a monastery. However, in Dōgen's time the Buddhist establishment of the Tendai, Shingon, and Nara schools was supported by the government, the emperor, and powerful noblemen. It was thus closely connected with the political and economic power of the secular world. Therefore, when monks of this time sincerely aroused the mind of awakening, they often felt they had to leave the monastery. There were many such "renunciants" between the end of the Heian era (1185 CE) and the end of the Kamakura era (1333 CE), including Hōnen (法然; 1133– 1212 CE), Shinran (親鸞; 1173–1263 CE), Ippen (一遍; 1234–1289 CE), and Nichiren (日蓮; 1222–1282 CE). They were the driving force that established what scholars call the Kamakura New Buddhism (鎌倉新仏教; Jp. Kamakura Shinbukkyō). The schools they established became some of the largest Buddhist denominations in Japan today. Dōgen and Ejō were also examples of such monks. (See sections 2-15, 3-9, 3-10, 3-12, 4-10, 5-11, and 6-21.)

Not only was Dōgen disappointed by the degenerate conditions at the monastery, but, according to his biographers, he also had serious questions regarding teaching and practice. *The Record of the Deeds of the Three Great Venerable Masters* and *The Record of the Deeds of the Three Ancestors of Eihei-ji* both quote Dōgen as saying:

> The great matter of our [Tendai] school, which is the essence of the dharma gates, is that [all living beings] are originally endowed with the true dharma nature, [and therefore] we are the embodiment of the innate self-nature. Both exoteric and esoteric schools do not differ from this. [If so,] why did all buddhas have to arouse the mind of awakening and practice?[3]

Dōgen visited many teachers to find the answer to this question and to discover someone with whom he could engage in genuine practice. One of the teachers he visited was Kōin (公胤; 1145[?]–1216 CE) at Mii-dera (三井寺; also called Onjō-ji, 園城寺), a Tendai monastery near Mt. Hiei that competed with Enryaku-ji for supremacy within the school. In section 3-5 of *Zuimonki*, Dōgen talks about an admonition he received from Kōin to settle down and study further rather than wandering around in Japan to find a teacher who could give him the answer.[4] Perhaps as a result, Dōgen remained at Enryaku-ji until he was seventeen.

Zen Practice at Kennin-ji

Although Dōgen was not happy on Mt. Hiei and sought an alternative place to practice, he ended up staying at the Tendai monastery for five years. Then, at the age of seventeen, he finally left Mt. Hiei and began to practice Zen with Myōzen (明全; 1184–1225 CE) at Kennin-ji (建仁寺). Myōzen was a student of Eisai (栄西; 1141–1215 CE), the first to bring Rinzai Zen to Japan, and his temple Kennin-ji—although officially part of the Tendai institution—is considered to have been the first Zen monastery in the country. Dōgen practiced with Myōzen at Kennin-ji for six years, from 1217 to 1223. They both decided they should go to Song dynasty China in order to study genuine Chinese Zen. In section 6-13, Dōgen discusses Myōzen's resolution to go to China despite the fact that his first master, Myōyu (明融; n.d.), was on his deathbed and had requested that Myōzen stay with him until his death.

Menzan's *Revised and Annotated Record of Kenzei* states that Dōgen left for Kennin-ji three years earlier, in 1214, and practiced with Eisai until Eisai's death in 1215, only after which did Dōgen begin to practice with Eisai's disciple Myōzen. However, many of today's Dōgen scholars doubt that Dōgen studied with Eisai. Although it might have been possible for Dōgen to have met Eisai while he was visiting teachers in search of answers, it is difficult for me to believe that Dōgen had moved to Kennin-ji before 1215. It is clear from Dōgen's writings that he had gained an extensive knowledge and deep understanding of Tendai teachings and the *Lotus Sutra* (法華経, Jp. *Hokke kyō*), and it is therefore hard to imagine that he studied Tendai for only one or two years. Furthermore, scholars now believe that Edo-era Sōtō historians simply wanted to connect Eisai and Dōgen in order to exalt Dōgen's career. Although Dōgen talks of Eisai with great respect quite a few times in *Zuimonki*,[5] these passages could just as easily be based on what he had heard from others, including Myōzen, while practicing at Kennin-ji.

Practice in China

After a difficult voyage alluded to in section 6-16, Myōzen and Dōgen arrived in China in the fourth month of the Chinese calendar of 1223. Although Myōzen immediately started to practice at a Chinese monastery, Dōgen had to stay on the boat for three months. This may have been because he had not received the Vinaya precepts, which were normally required in order to enter a Chinese monastery, but there is no direct evidence for the cause of his delay. While he was staying there, he met the monk serving as the head cook (典座; Ch. *diǎnzuò*; Jp. *tenzo*), who was from Ayuwang Temple (阿育王寺; Jp. Aikuō-ji) in Ningbo. They shared an important conversation that influenced Dōgen's understanding of the meaning of practice. Dōgen describes this encounter in *Instructions for the Cook* (典座教訓; Jp. *Tenzo kyōkun*).

After the summer practice period ended in the seventh month of the Chinese calendar of the same year, Dōgen finally began to practice with Myōzen at a monastery on Mt. Tiantong (天童山; Jp. Tendō san), located in what is now the city of Ningbo, just south of Shanghai. The abbot of the monastery was a Rinzai master named Wuchi Liaopai (無際了派; Jp. Musai Ryōha; 1149–1224 CE). The abbot died a year or so after Dōgen's arrival. There is no clear evidence if Dōgen left before the abbot's death or in response to it, but around this time Dōgen began to travel, visiting several monasteries[6] in search of a suitable teacher, but it seems he was not happy with any of the abbots he encountered. However, he did meet several practitioners that inspired him whom he did not name, such as the two cooks he discusses in *Instructions for the Tenzo*. He talks about his encounters with other genuine people of the Way in *Zuimonki*—for example, in sections 1-4, 3-7, and 6-2.

By the fifth month of the Chinese lunar calendar of 1225, Dōgen had returned to Tiantong monastery. Shortly after his return, Myōzen—who had stayed behind at Tiantong during Dōgen's travels—died unexpectedly. Soon after he lost his Japanese teacher, Dōgen met the new abbot of the monastery, Rujing (如浄; Jp. Nyojō), and found that this master was the true teacher he had been looking for.

From that point, he studied and practiced with Rujing until receiving Dharma transmission from him in 1227. Dōgen discusses his experiences with Rujing several times in *Zuimonki*, such as in sections 1-1, 2-5, 2-11, and 3-19. Dōgen also recorded his personal conversations with Rujing in what came to be known as *The Record of the Hōkyō Era* (宝慶記; Jp. *Hōkyō ki*). After receiving Dharma transmission, Dōgen returned to Japan. Shortly after Dōgen's departure, Rujing passed away.

Returning to Kennin-ji

Dōgen returned to Kennin-ji with the relics of his deceased teacher Myōzen. He wrote about Myōzen's life and his death in China in the text the *Record of the Transmission of the Relics* (舎利相伝記; Jp. *Sharisōdenki*).[7] In the same year, he likely wrote the first version of "The Universal Recommendation of Zazen" (普勧坐禅儀; Jp. "Fukanzazengi"), a short manual of zazen practice. During his second stay at Kennin-ji, Dōgen observed that the atmosphere had changed from the time before Myōzen and he had left for China. He mentions that the monks had lost their genuine spirit of practice in the period after Eisai's death, which Dōgen discusses in sections 2-14, 4-4, and 5-8. Such conditions were one of the reasons he would ultimately leave Kennin-ji.

According to the section on Ejō in Keizan's *Record of the Transmission of the Light*, Dōgen was visited by his future successor, Ejō, while staying at Kennin-ji. Ejō hoped to learn what had been transmitted to Dōgen during his time in China. After several days of discussion, Ejō decided he wanted to become Dōgen's disciple, but Dōgen asked him to wait until he could establish his own monastery. I will discuss this encounter in further detail in the later section on Ejō's life.

Solitude in Fukakusa

In 1230, Dōgen left Kennin-ji and began staying at a hermitage in Fukakusa (深草). Although today Fukakusa is a part of the city of Kyoto, in the thirteenth century it was well outside of the city limits. While living there alone, or possibly with a few attendants, Dōgen wrote his *Talk on the Wholehearted Practice of the Way* (辨道話; Jp. *Bendōwa*) to express his understanding of zazen practice in which we do not seek to attain anything but simply participate in Buddha's awakening. He also answers some of the questions about Zen practice that he imagined people at his time might have had.

Kōshō-ji

In 1233, Dōgen began to establish the monastery Kōshōhōrin-ji (興聖 法林寺) in Fukakusa, more commonly known by its abbreviated name Kōshō-ji. During the first summer practice period there, he wrote the "Great Perfection of Wisdom" (摩訶般若波羅蜜; Jp. "Maka hannya haramitsu"), which later became the second fascicle of the *Shōbōgenzō*. In the autumn of the same year, he wrote "Genjōkōan" (現成公按) and presented it to a layperson. Ejō joined Dōgen's monastery in the winter of 1234 and began to record Dōgen's informal talks. His compilation of these records later became what we now call *Shōbōgenzō zuimonki*.

Ejō's Life

Ejō's Biography

Biographies of Ejō are found in *The Record of the Deeds of the Three Great Venerable Masters*, *The Record of the Deeds of the Three Ancestors of Eihei-ji*, and a section about him in the *Record of the Transmission of the Light*. According to these texts, Ejō was born in Kyoto into a branch of the powerful Fujiwara clan (藤原氏) in 1198 CE, two years before Dōgen was born. He entered Enryaku-ji on Mt. Hiei when he was young and was ordained by Ennō (圓能; n.d.) in 1218. In Enryaku-ji, he studied basic Buddhist works such as the *Abhidharma Storehouse Treatise* and *The Treatise That Accomplishes Reality* (成實論; Ch. *Chéngshí lùn*; Jp. *Jōjitsu ron*; Skt. *Tattvasiddhi-śāstra*). He later studied Tendai teachings, such as the *Great Cessation and Contemplation* (摩訶止觀; Ch. *Móhē zhǐguān*; Jp. *Maka shikan*) of Zhiyi (智顗; Jp. Chigi; 538–597 CE). When the sincere mind of awakening developed in Ejō, he wished to leave the Tendai monastery like many other sincere monks had, but on the basis of his teacher's advice, he hesitated. He is said to have later visited his mother, who admonished him not to become a high-ranking monk, telling him to instead aim to become a genuine practitioner. Upon hearing his mother's words, he decided not to return to Mt. Hiei.

After leaving, Ejō studied Pure Land Buddhism with Shōku (証空; 1177–1247 CE), a disciple of Hōnen, the founder of the Pure Land school (浄土宗; Jp. Jōdo shū) in Japan. Ejō later moved on and began practicing Zen with Bucchi Kakuan (仏地覚晏; n.d.), a disciple of Dainichi Nōnin (大日能忍; n.d.), the founder of the Japanese Daruma school (日本達磨宗; Jp. Nihon Daruma shū), the earliest school of Zen in Japan (but of questionable credentials). Their practice was aimed at Rinzai-style *kenshō* (見性), in which one has a sort of preliminary awakening experience. According to the *Record of the Transmission of the Light*, while practicing with Ejō at Tonomine (多武; in modern Nara Prefecture, about eighty kilometers [almost fifty miles] south of Kyoto), Kakuan gave talks on the *Śūraṅgama Sūtra* (大佛頂首楞嚴經; Ch. *Dà fódǐng shǒulèngyán jīng*; Jp. *Dai butchō shuryōgon kyō*). When Kakuan mentioned a metaphor from that text in which the emptiness of consciousness is compared to the empty space of a particular pitcher—as well as the phrase "adding emptiness does not increase emptiness, and taking out emptiness does not decrease emptiness"—Ejō was said to have been awakened. It is important to note, however, that the *Record of the Transmission of the Light* provides an awakening story for every person for which a biography is provided. Because of the formulaic nature of this text, the historicity of these accounts of awakening is somewhat dubious.

Ejō's First Meeting with Dōgen

Keizan's *Record of the Transmission of the Light* gives an account of the first encounter between Dōgen and Ejō. In 1227, Ejō heard that Dōgen had come back from China intending to transmit Chinese Zen. Ejō thought to himself, "I have already clarified the essential teachings of the three cessations and three observations (三止三観; Jp. *sanshi sankan*). I have also mastered the essential practice of the Pure Land tradition. Not only that, I have practiced [with Kakuan] at Tonomine and attained the meaning of seeing nature and becoming buddha (見性成佛; Jp. *kenshō jōbutsu*). What else could [Dōgen] transmit from China?"[8]

Despite his alleged skepticism, Ejō, the *Record of the Transmission of the Light* goes on to describe, visited Kennin-ji where he met Dōgen to see what he could learn from him. In the first few days, they talked about the matter of *kenshō* and spiritual intelligence (見性靈知; Jp. *kenshō reichi*), which is what Ejō is supposed to have attained in his awakening experience. Because at first Dōgen did not challenge Ejō's attainment, Ejō was delighted and thought that what he had realized was genuine. After a while, probably because Dōgen saw that Ejō was a sincere practitioner, Dōgen began to discuss his own understanding of practice, which differed from Ejō's *kenshō*-based practice. Ejō was astonished to learn there was more to practice than he had realized. Despite his attempts to counterargue, Ejō understood that Dōgen's insight was completely different from and superior to his own. He aroused the mind of awakening anew and asked Dōgen if he could become his disciple. However, Dōgen rejected his request, saying, "I wish to spread the true Dharma I have transmitted [from Rujing] throughout Japan, and yet I am temporarily living in this temple [Kennin-ji]. I would like to found my own practice place. When I find a place to build a grass hermitage, you can come. You cannot practice with me here."[9] Ejō accepted Dōgen's advice and waited for the proper time.

Dōyū Takeuchi (竹内道雄), a modern biographer of Ejō, suggests that the question-and-answer section in Dōgen's *Talk on the Wholehearted Practice of the Way* could be based on this discussion with Ejō.[10] In particular, the view of a permanent mind-nature (心性; Ch. *xīnxìng*; Jp. *shinshō*) expressed in question ten, which was Ejō's view at the time, was criticized by Dōgen in their first meeting, according to the *Record of the Transmission of the Light*. In Dōgen's *Talk on the Wholehearted Practice of the Way*, this view states: "If you really understand that the mind nature existing in our body is not subject to birth and death, then since it is the original nature, although the body is only a temporary form haphazardly born here and dying, the mind is permanent and unchangeable in the past, present, and future. To know this is called release from life and death."[11]

In the "Talk on the Wholehearted Practice of the Way," Dōgen said such a view is not consistent with the Buddha's teachings at all but rather representative of the fallacious views of the non-Buddhist Senika. Senika is mentioned in a section of the *Nirvana Sutra* (大般涅槃經; Ch. *Dà bānnièpán jīng*; Jp. *Dai hatsunehan gyō*; Skt. *Mahāparinirvāṇasūtra*) that tries to distinguish Buddha-nature and the Brahmanist concept of ātman. There is no direct evidence that Takeuchi's suggestion is correct, but it is true that Dōgen consistently criticized Zen practice centered on attaining *kenshō* experiences. According to *The Record of the Hōkyō Era* and *Dōgen's Extensive Record* (永平広録; Jp. *Eihei kōroku*),[12] Dōgen did not like this form of practice based on the idea of a permanent mind-nature as discussed in the *Śūraṅgama Sūtra*. Shortly before his death, Rujing had told Dōgen that the *Śūraṅgama Sūtra* was not a genuine scripture (which is the opinion of most modern scholars as well).

When Ejō found what Dōgen said to be superior to his own understanding and he decided to become Dōgen's disciple, I am sure he must have felt the need to thoroughly deconstruct and reconstruct his understanding of Zen Buddhist teachings. It may have been this need that led Ejō to record Dōgen's informal Dharma talks for his first three years at Kōshō-ji.

Becoming Dōgen's Disciple at Kōshō-ji

Dōgen first established Kōshō-ji monastery in 1233. Ejō joined the sangha in 1234 and began recording Dōgen's informal talks that year. He continued to do so until 1238. During this period, Ejō received the bodhisattva precepts (in 1235); assisted Dōgen with fundraising and the construction of a monks' hall (僧堂; Jp. *sōdō*); received Dharma transmission; and was appointed the first head monk (首座; Jp. *shuso*), in 1236, for the new monks' hall. He ceased recording Dōgen's informal talks in 1238, perhaps because he felt that he had completely become Dōgen's disciple and thoroughly shared his understanding and practice. At the same time, the Kōshō-ji sangha had developed significantly, and Ejō would have been exceptionally busy with administration and the copying of Dōgen's writings of the *Shōbōgenzō*.

The Remainder of Ejō's Life

After *Zuimonki* had been recorded, Dōgen and his sangha moved to Echizen Province (越前国) to establish Eihei-ji. According to the *Record of the Transmission of the Lamp*, at a certain point Dōgen had Ejō officiate ceremonies in his place. When asked why, he replied, "My life will not be long. You will live longer than I and surely will propagate my Way. Therefore, I value you for the sake of the Dharma." Until Dōgen's death in 1253, Ejō served as his personal attendant (侍者; Jp. *jisha*) even while he was holding other positions.

After Dōgen's death in 1253, Ejō became Eihei-ji's second abbot. He continued to copy Dōgen's manuscripts of the *Shōbōgenzō*, and he compiled volumes 2, 3, 4, and 8 of *Dōgen's Extensive Record*, among other works. He devoted his life to maintaining Dōgen's legacy, including not only his teachings but also his style of practice and lineage, until his own death in 1280. Ejō's only writing was the *Treasury of the Samadhi of Radiant Light* (光明 藏三昧; Jp. *Kōmyōzō Zanmai*), written when he was eighty years old. It has not yet been published in an English translation.[13]

MAIN TOPICS OF DŌGEN'S TALKS IN *ZUIMONKI*

Fundamentally, *Zuimonki* can be read as a highly practical manual of Buddhist practice. Dōgen's words express fundamental aspects of Buddhist practice in terms that are both concrete and straightforward in Japanese society in the thirteenth century. Among the many topics covered, Dōgen especially emphasizes the following points: seeing impermanence; departing from the ego-centered self; being free from greed; giving up self-attachment; following the guidance of a true teacher; and following the practice of zazen, specifically *shikantaza* (只管打坐), or "just sitting."

By and large, these points are the fundamentals of Buddhist teaching. For example, one way Buddhist teachings have been summarized is in the form of the four Dharma seals (四法印; Ch. *sì fǎyìn*; Jp. *shi hōin*). "Seal" here is used in the sense of a stamp that leaves an imprint and certifies something as genuine, as in a "seal of authenticity." In the same way, if we find these four points in a given teaching, we can be sure the teaching is Buddhist. The four Dharma seals are the following: (1) All conditioned things are impermanent (Skt. *anitya*); (2) all defiled things are suffering (Skt. *duḥkha*); (3) all things are without permanent self (Skt. *anātman*); and (4) nirvana is peace.

To me, these are not four separate items but rather one unified message from the Buddha. Impermanence and no-self are the true reality of all things. When we are blind to these truths and live based on the ideas of permanence and a fixed, independent self, everything in our lives becomes suffering. However, when we instead awaken to this true reality, our lives become nirvana.

A different and more well-known way of summarizing Buddhism is the doctrine of the four noble truths (四諦; Ch. *sìdì*; Jp. *shitai*; Skt. *catvāri āryasatyāni*). These are (1) suffering (Skt. *duḥkha*); (2) the cause or origination of suffering (Skt. *samudaya*); (3) the cessation of suffering (Skt. *nirodha*); and (4) the path leading to cessation of suffering (Skt. *mārga*). The "path" refers to the eightfold correct path, which includes right view, right intention, right speech, right conduct, right livelihood, right effort, right mindfulness, and right concentration.

Both summaries cover the same things. The cause of suffering is delusion and the delusive desires of the three poisons of greed, anger, and ignorance. Suffering ends when we instead practice correctly and see the truth. Now, compare the two methods of summarizing Buddhism to the following passage from section 2-2 of *Zuimonki*:

To maintain the way [of Buddhist monks] is to give up self-attachment and follow the guidance of our teachers. The essential point here is to be free from greed. If we wish to put an end to greed, we must first depart from our ego-centered self. To depart from the ego-centered self, seeing impermanence is the primary concern. . . .

For a Zen monk to make progress, the most important thing to keep in mind is that we must just sit [*shikantaza*]. Whether we are sharp or dull-witted, wise or foolish, if we practice zazen, we will naturally improve.

When we read this passage with these basic teachings in mind, we can see the similarity between them and Dōgen's words. We must give up the delusions of self-attachment, as these are the source of suffering, and accept impermanence. In order to let go of the delusive worldview, we should practice zazen so that we can see true reality.

I first read *Zuimonki* when I was a high-school student, shortly after reading a book by Kōshō Uchiyama Rōshi called *Jiko* (自己; meaning "self").[14] I was trying to understand if there was an alternative to the common Japanese way of life at that time, namely the pursuit of money and social status. I was therefore inspired to learn about Uchiyama's wholehearted practice of zazen at his temple, Antai-ji (安泰寺), and the fact that he supported his life by begging (托鉢; Jp. *takuhatsu*). Although I did not understand any Buddhist philosophy at that point, I was encouraged by Dōgen's talks on concrete topics such as living in pure poverty without being pulled by desires for fame and profit. My favorite conversation between Dōgen and Ejō comes at the conclusion of section 3-14:

[*Dōgen*] *instructed*:

Regarding the behavior of patch-robed practitioners, if we mend or patch our old, tattered clothing instead of discarding it, it seems that we are clinging to things. Yet to abandon old clothing and wear new robes shows that we are seeking after new things. Both of these are mistakes. What should we do?

I, [Ejō,] asked, "Ultimately, what should we keep in mind?"

[*Dōgen*] *replied*:

So long as we are free from both greedy clinging and greedy seeking, either is fine. Still, it would be better to mend torn clothing in order to keep it as long as possible and not lust after new clothing.

In the Chōen-ji version of the text, which I translate here, Dōgen first gives instruction to his students in the form of a question. After hearing it, Ejō poses the question back at Dōgen, indicating that perhaps no one had a good answer, and Dōgen then gives his reply. In Menzan's version, the entirety of the first part before "Dōgen replied" is Ejō's question. The opinions of scholars are divided on who was actually speaking which lines in the original version of the text, which is now lost. Yaoko Mizuno (水野弥穂子), a scholar of literature and a translator of Dōgen into modern Japanese, believes the first part before Ejō's question is Dōgen's question to Ejō, as in the Chōen-ji version translated here.[15] Ryūshin Azuma (東隆真)[16] and Rosan Ikeda (池田魯参),[17] two important Sōtō scholar-priests, follow Menzan's version. I will discuss further differences between the Chōen-ji and Menzan versions of the text in the next section.

Dōgen and Ejō were both from aristocratic families. They were also both brilliant people. If they had not become Buddhist monks, they could have easily been high-ranking court officials. If they had not left the monastery on Mt. Hiei, they could have also been high-ranking monks within the Tendai hierarchy. If they had not chosen to become "renunciants" from the Buddhist establishment, they would not have needed to worry about the question of repairing or replacing old robes. Because they left both their homes and their religious institution in order to seek the genuine Way of the Buddha, they lived in poverty, continuing their practice without worrying about the pursuit of material things. I was saved when I learned not only that such people could be found in Japanese history but also that their traditions had continued down to the present through the way of life of Uchiyama Rōshi as well as that of his teacher, Kōdō Sawaki Rōshi (沢木興道; 1880–1965).

The following is a summary of the main points found in *Zuimonki*
and the sections in which they are discussed:

1. Arousing sincere aspiration (the mind of awakening, or
   bodhi-mind):
   1-13, 3-11, 3-16, 6-5, 6-13
2. Seeing impermanence:
   1-6, 1-7, 2-2, 2-8, 2-13, 2-17, 3-6, 3-11, 3-19, 4-2, 4-3, 5-7
   Dōgen connects these first two points in the first section of
   Points to Watch in Practicing the Way (学道用心集; Jp. *Gakudō yōjin
   shū*). He writes that the mind that aspires to seek the Way is the
   same as the mind that sees impermanence.
3. Importance of monastic practice with others:
   1-7
4. Following one's teacher and the Buddha's teachings:
   1-5, 1-13, 1-14, 2-2, 2-5, 2-10, 2-11, 5-1
   To study Buddhist teachings and practice in a concrete way, we
   need to practice with a community of practitioners and receive
   instructions from a genuine teacher.
5. Freedom from personal views:
   1-14, 2-10, 3-19, 5-1, 5-2, 5-6, 6-2, 6-9, 6-14, 6-18
6. Giving up worldly sentiments:
   2-18, 3-1, 3-4, 3-10, 4-9, 6-9, 6-10, 6-14
   When we study under the guidance of a teacher, we need
   to be free from our personal habitual ways of thinking, produced by our karma as members of worldly society. We
   must open ourselves up in order to truly receive Buddhist
   teachings.
7. Parting from egocentric self:
   1-9, 2-2, 2-16, 4-3, 5-1, 5-2, 6-1, 6-2, 6-10, 6-14, 6-18, 6-21
8. Casting aside clinging to body and mind:
   1-2, 1-14, 4-1, 4-3, 6-1
   By seeing impermanence and becoming free from self-
   attachment, we find there is no such thing as a fixed, permanent

self that exists outside of its relation to other beings. Therefore, it does not make sense to attach to our egocentric self.

9. Practice without gaining-mind:
    2-7, 4-3, 4-8, 6-24

10. Living in poverty without clinging to food and clothing:
    1-3, 1-4, 2-13, 3-2, 3-3, 3-6, 3-14, 4-4, 4-7, 4-9, 5-10, 5-11, 6-2, 6-5, 6-22, 6-23

11. Not seeking fame and profit:
    2-13, 2-16, 3-3, 3-12, 4-5, 5-8, 6-15, 6-21

    When we are free from the five aggregates of impure objects of self-attachment (Skt. *pañca-upādāna-skandha*), we can practice, study, and work without gaining-mind.

12. Having compassion or parental mind and working to benefit others:
    1-7, 2-5, 2-9, 2-16, 2-17, 3-2, 4-3, 4-6, 4-7, 6-13

13. Harmony with others:
    2-7, 5-9, 6-7, 6-8, 6-23

    When we see the emptiness of our body and mind (the five aggregates) and become free from self-attachment, we begin to see interconnectedness with other beings.

14. Concentrating on one practice:
    1-10, 2-3, 2-8, 2-11, 3-9, 3-14

15. *Shikantaza*:
    2-1, 2-2, 2-5, 2-11, 3-6, 3-7, 3-11, 3-17, 3-19, 3-20, 4-8, 5-3, 5-10, 6-9, 6-11, 6-16, 6-18, 6-20, 6-24

One of the characteristics of Japanese Buddhism in Dōgen's time, the so-called Kamakura New Buddhism, was that the leading teachers selected one particular practice and focused on it largely to the exclusion of others. Pure Land Buddhists such as Hōnen and Shinran practiced only chanting the name of Amitābha Buddha (念佛; Ch. *niànfó*; Jp. *nenbutsu*). Nichiren focused on chanting the title of the *Lotus Sutra* (題目; Jp. *daimoku*). Dōgen chose the practice of zazen, specifically "just sitting" (*shikantaza*).

In short, seeing impermanence; arousing the mind of awakening; parting from the egocentric self; practicing the Buddhadharma only for the sake of Buddhadharma; concentrating on sitting zazen without thoughts of gaining; living in poverty, free from desire; and working for the benefit of others is the way of life Dōgen urged his disciples to follow in *Zuimonki*.

REGARDING THE TEXT

After Ejō stopped recording Dōgen's informal Dharma talks in 1238, he apparently kept the text for his own private use with no intention to publicize it. However, when Ejō died, one of his disciples found the material and decided to compile and copy it. As it states in the colophon at the conclusion of the text, the collection was given the title *Shōbōgenzō zuimonki* by that compiler after Ejō's death. The manuscript was hand copied over many generations, but Ejō's original manuscript has been lost. The oldest hand-copied manuscript available today was produced some four hundred years after Ejō's death. In the second half of the seventeenth century, the text was published on a few occasions using woodblock printing, and the oldest known printed version dates from 1651. It is unknown what manuscript (or manuscripts) these printed versions were based on.

According to Menzan Zuihō, these woodblock printed versions were not reviewed by an actual Zen monk, which resulted in numerous errors. When Menzan was twenty-seven years old (around 1710 CE), he heard from an old monk who said that while he had been practicing at Eihei-ji, he had once read an old hand-copied manuscript of *Zuimonki*. The monk noted that there were many differences in the manuscript from the woodblock published versions. Menzan was excited at the prospect of studying this text, and he set out to locate it. Later, while Menzan was at Daijō-ji (大乗寺), the abbot there thought he had the text, but they were unable to locate it. After more than ten years, Menzan became the abbot of Kūin-ji (空印寺) and learned that the text had, in fact, been in the possession of Kuin-ji's previous abbot, a disciple of the abbot of Daijō-ji. Comparing this hand-written manuscript with woodblock printed versions, Menzan made corrections and revisions and published his own version in 1770. Because Menzan was a renowned scholar-monk, his version quickly became popular, and consequently it is now called the "popular version" (流布本; Jp. *rufu bon*).

In 1926, the famous scholar and philosopher Tetsurō Watsuji (和辻哲郎; 1889–1960 CE) wrote an article about Dōgen entitled "The Śramaṇa Dōgen" (沙門道元; Jp. "Shamon Dōgen"),[18] which was published in a collection of his essays entitled *A Study of the History of Japanese Spirituality* (日本精神史研究; Jp. *Nihon seishin shi kenkyū*). This book greatly increased Dōgen's popularity among Japanese intellectuals. Watsuji's study of Dōgen was mostly based on *Zuimonki*. In 1929, Menzan's version of *Zuimonki* was revised by Watsuji and published by Iwanami Bunko (岩波文庫), a publisher of classics that uses an inexpensive format similar to American mass-market paperbacks (and actually based on the German Universal-Bibliothek paperback editions from Reclam Verlag). This version gained widespread popularity, and many people outside of the Sōtō school began to read it, as well as the other writings by Dōgen. When I was a university student, I recall that this version of the text cost only fifty yen. I often bought a copy, for example, when I took a train and wanted something to read.

In 1941, the eminent Dōgen scholar Dōshū Ōkubo (大久保道舟; 1896–1994 CE) found an older hand-copied version of *Zuimonki* at the temple Chōen-ji in Aichi Prefecture. This manuscript was one copied by Kido Soe, the second abbot of Chōen-ji, in 1644, and the original manuscript from which it was copied came from Hōkyō-ji monastery in Fukui and dates to 1380. The 1644 manuscript Ōkubo discovered is referred to as the "Chōen-ji version" (長円寺本; Jp. Chōenji-*bon*) after the temple where it was discovered. The Chōen-ji version was published in 1963 by Chikuma Shobō (筑摩書房), a major publisher of literature, with a modern Japanese translation and many footnotes by Yaoko Mizuno. Today, scholars believe the Chōen-ji version is closer to Ejō's original manuscript.

I previously translated Menzan's version of *Zuimonki* into English. This was first published by Sōtōshū Shūmuchō (曹洞宗宗務庁) in 1988, and the translation is still available from Sōtōshū Shūmuchō for free. This new translation is instead based on the Chōen-ji version.

The main differences between Menzan's version and the Chōen-ji version are the following:

1. Although both versions comprise six books, the order is different. Book 6 of Menzan's version is book 1 of the Chōen-ji version. As a result, book 1 of Menzan's version is book 2 of the Chōen-ji version, and so on, until book 5 of Menzan's version takes the place of book 6 in the Chōen-ji version.

2. In section 1-3 of Menzan's version, there is a story of a Chinese Zen master, Fozhao Deguang (佛照德光; Jp. Busshō Tokkō; 1121–1203 CE), who allowed a sick monk to eat meat. This section does not appear in the Chōen-ji version.

3. In section 6-19 of the Chōen-ji version, Dōgen speaks on a quotation from the Confucian classic *The Spring and Autumn Annals* (春秋; Ch. *Chūnqiū*; Jp. *Shunjū*) along with a saying of Zen Master Xuansha Shibei (玄沙師備; Jp. Gensha Shibi; 835–908 CE). This section is not present in Menzan's version.

There are many other minor differences, but most of them do not come through in an English translation. Important differences, however, are mentioned in the notes.

TEXTUAL SOURCES AND ACKNOWLEDGMENTS

The source text for this translation was from Ryūshin Azuma's study of the *Shōbōgenzō zuimonki*, as found in volume 16 of *Dōgen Zenji zenshū* (道元禅師全集). Azuma's work reproduces the original text, provides a modern Japanese translation, and gives extensive commentary. Ryūshin Azuma was a scholar-monk and the abbot of Daijō-ji (大乗寺), an important Sōtō Zen temple in Kanazawa. I also frequently referred to two other Japanese translation-commentaries on the Chōen-ji text, namely Yaoko Mizuno's *Shōbōgenzō zuimonki* and Rosan Ikeda's *Gendaigoyaku shōbōgenzō zuimonki*. When trying to understand difficult passages of the text, I found that the comments and interpretations of all three authors were indispensable. When I had a question about disagreements between their versions, I checked a facsimile of the original Chōen-ji manuscript published by Ikudō Tajima (田島 毓堂) and Yōko Kondō (近藤洋子) in *Shōbōgenzō zuimonki goi sōsakuin*. While working on this translation, I also often referred to the existing English translations. These include Professor Reihō Masunaga's (増 永霊鳳) *A Primer of Sōtō Zen: A Translation of Dōgen's Shōbōgenzō Zuimonki* and Thomas Cleary's *Record of Things Heard: From the Treasury of the Eye of the True Teaching*.

The Japanese text of *Zuimonki* from Azuma's study is also reproduced in this book. I deviated from Azuma's presentation of the text occasionally when I found the text by Mizuno or Ikeda to be more compelling or a better match with the facsimile of the original manuscript provided by Tajima and Kondō. The original manuscript does not include a numbering scheme for the books or sections, so I added these based on Mizuno's and Ikeda's books. I hope that the inclusion of the Japanese text will help those who are able to read some Japanese gain a better understanding of Dōgen's writing.

I have studied *Zuimonki* not only by reading the text itself but also by reading a variety of Japanese books on the topic written by various Dōgen scholars, Zen teachers, philosophers, and others. In addition to the source texts previously mentioned, particular texts that I found helpful included Tetsurō Watsuji's "The Śramaṇa Dōgen," Yaoko Mizuno's *Shōbōgenzō zuimonki no sekai*, Makoto Funaoka's (船岡誠) *Dōgen to shōbōgenzō zuimonki*, and the compilation of essays compiled by Rosan Ikeda entitled *Shōbōgenzō zuimonki no kenkyū*. I would like to express my deepest gratitude to all of these people for their efforts in studying *Zuimonki* or translating it into English.

I made the first drafts of this translation for the Dharma study group at my home temple, Sanshin-ji in Bloomington, Indiana, from

May 2014 to January 2017. Participants of the study group made many corrections and suggestions in order to improve the translation. During that time, regular participants included Seigen Hartkemeyer, Rise Koben, and Dōju Layton. The head monks (首座; Jp. *shuso*) for each summer practice period during that time also participated in the study group while at Sanshin-ji: they included Dōryū Cappelli (2014), Musō Jim Biggs (2015), and Jōshū Judith Toland (2016). Without the interest and support of the study group, this translation would not have been possible. Shunryū Collin Garvey also made many useful suggestions in the process of improving my translation. Finally, I would like to say thank you to my disciple Dōju Layton, who edited this text in its entirety in order to prepare it for publication.

Shōhaku Okumura
July 2019, Bloomington, Indiana

SHŌBŌGENZŌ ZUIMONKI

正法眼蔵随聞記　一

侍者　懐奘　編

1-1

示に云く、

　はづべくんば、明眼の人をはづべし。

　予、在宋の時、天童浄和尚、侍者に請ずるに云く、外国人たり
といへども、元子器量人なり、と云て、これを請ず。

　予、堅く是れを辞す。其故は、和国にきこえんためも、学道の
稽古のためも、大切なれども、衆中に具眼の人ありて、外国人と
して、大叢林の侍者たらんこと、国に人なきが如しと、難ずるこ
とあらん、尤も、はづべし、といいて、書状をもて、此旨を伸しか
ば、浄和尚、国を重くし、人をはづることを許して、更に請ぜざり
しなり。

1-2

示に云、

SHŌBŌGENZŌ ZUIMONKI, BOOK 1

Compiled by the attendant Ejō

1-1

[*Dōgen*] *instructed*:

If you must heed someone, you should heed those with clear eyes.

When I was in Song China, Preceptor Jing[19] of Tiantong invited me to be his personal attendant,[20] saying, "Although Venerable Gen is a foreigner, he is a man of ability."

I firmly declined. The reason for this was that, although it was an important opportunity to become well known in Japan and also for my own practice of the Way, there might have been certain people endowed with clear eyes who would have thought that appointing a foreigner as the abbot's attendant in such a great monastery meant that [Rujing thought] there were no capable people in his country. I had to be very careful about this. I wrote what I thought to the abbot in a letter. Preceptor Jing understood my respect for his country and my concern about such people's feelings, and he did not ask me again.[21]

1-2

[*Dōgen*] *instructed*:

Someone said, "I am sick. I am not a vessel[22] [of the Dharma]. I cannot endure the practice of the Way. I wish to listen [only] to the

有人の云、我病者也、非器也、学道にたへず。法門の最要を
ききて、独住隠居して、性をやしなひ、病をたすけて、一生を終
ん、と云うに、

示云、

先聖必しも金骨にあらず、古人豈皆上器ならんや。滅後を思へ
ば、幾ばくならず。在世を考るに、人皆な俊なるに非ず。善人もあ
り、悪人もあり。比丘衆の中に、不可思議の悪行するもあり、最下
品の器量もあり。然れども、卑下して、道心ををこさず、非器なりと
いつて、学道せざるなし。

今生もし学道修行せずは、何れの生にか、器量の物となり、
不病の者とならん。只、身命をかへりみず、発心修行する、学道の
最要なり。

1-3

示に云、

学道の人、衣食を貪ることなかれ。人に皆、食分あり、命分あ
り、非分の食命を求むとも来るべからず。況んや学仏道の人に
は、施主の供養あり。常乞食に比すべからず。常住物これあり。
私の営にも非ず。菓蓏・乞食・信心施の三種の食、皆是れ清浄食
也。其の余の、田・商・仕・工の四種は、皆、不浄邪命の食なり。出
家人の食分に非ず。

essentials of the Dharma gates,[23] to live alone retiring from the world, to indulge myself, and to tend to my sickness until the end of this lifetime."

[*Dōgen*] *instructed*:

Sages of the past did not necessarily have golden bones; not all of the ancients were superior vessels [of the Dharma].[24] If we consider [the period] after [Shakyamuni's] death, not such a long time has passed. Thinking of [the people] when [Shakyamuni] was in the world, not everyone was endowed with natural talent. There were good people as well as bad people. Among the monks, there were some who did incredibly evil things, while others had the lowest of capabilities. However, none of them demeaned themselves by failing to arouse the mind of awakening; none avoided studying the Way, thinking they were not vessels [of the Dharma].[25]

If you do not study and practice the Way in this present lifetime, in which lifetime will you become a person of [exceptional] capability or a person without sickness? Simply, do not be concerned with your corporeal life, arouse the mind of awakening, and practice. This is what is most essential in studying the Way.

1-3

[*Dōgen*] *instructed*:

Students of the Way, do not be greedy for food and clothing.[26] Each person has an allotted share of food and life. Even if you seek after more than your share, it will never come [to you]. Moreover, for those who study the Buddha Way, there are offerings from benefactors. This cannot be compared with daily begging.[27] There are provisions that belong to the monastery. These are not [the result] of personal activity. Fruits and berries [from the wild], food received through begging, and offerings from faithful believers are the three kinds of pure food. The four occupations of farming, commerce, military service, and craftsmanship all [result in] food of impure wrong

昔一人の僧ありき。死して冥界に行きしに、閻王の云、此人、命分未尽、帰すべし、と云しに、有る冥官の云、命分ありといへども、食分既に尽ぬ、王の云、荷葉を食せしむべし、と。然より蘇りて後は、人中の食物、食することを得ず、只荷葉を食して残命をたもつ。

然れば、出家人は、学仏の力によりて、食分も尽くべからず。白毫の一相、二十年の遺恩、歴劫に受用すとも、尽くべきに非ず。行道を専にし、衣食を求むべきにあらざるなり。

身躰血肉だにも、よくもてば、心も随て好くなると、医法等に見ること多し。況や学道の人、持戒梵行にして、仏祖の行履に、まかせて、身儀をおさむれば、心地も、随て整なり。

学道の人、言を出さんとせん時は、三度顧て、自利利他の為に、利あるべければ、是を言ふべし。利なからん時は、止べし。如是、一度には、しがたし。心に懸て漸々に習べき也。

1-4

雑話の次、示に云、

livelihood.[28] These are not the types of food for [monks] who have left home.

In ancient times there was a certain monk. When he [the monk] died and went to the underworld, King Yama said, "This person's allotted life has not yet been exhausted. Let him return." One of the officers of the world of the dead then said, "Although he has allotted life remaining, his allotted food has already been consumed." The king said, "Then let him eat lotus leaves." After the monk was brought back to life, he could not eat ordinary food in the human realm, and he maintained his remaining life eating only lotus leaves.[29]

Therefore, because of the power of studying the Buddha Way, the food allotted to home-leavers will not be exhausted. The single whorl of white hair [on the forehead of the Buddha] and the blessing of the Buddha leaving us twenty years of his life will never be exhausted, even if we continue to receive it for numberless eons.[30] Devote yourself only to the practice of the Way, and do not seek after food and clothing.

We often read in books on medicine that only when the body, blood, and flesh are well maintained will the mind also be healthy. All the more will people who practice the Way, keep the precepts, uphold the pure practices,[31] and entrust themselves to the activities of the buddhas and ancestors have their minds likewise harmonized.

Students of the Way, when you want to say something, reflect on it three times. If it is beneficial to both yourself and others, then say it. If it is not beneficial, remain silent. This is difficult to achieve immediately. Keep this in mind and gradually put it into practice.

1-4

On one occasion [when Dōgen was speaking] on miscellaneous topics, he instructed:
Students of the Way, do not be concerned about food and clothing.

学道の人、衣食に労することなかれ。

此国は、辺地小国なりといへども、昔も今も、顕密二道に、名を得、後代にも人に知れたる人いまだ一人も、衣食に饒なりと云ことを聞かず。皆な貧を忍び、他事をわすれて、一向、その道を好む時、其の名をも得也。況や学道の人は、世度を捨て、わしらず。何としてか饒なるべき。

大宋国の叢林には、末代なりといへども、学道の人、千万人の中に、或は遠方より来り、或は郷土より出で来るも、多分皆貧なり。しかれども愁とせず、只悟道の未だしきことを愁て、或は楼上、若は閣下に、考妣を喪せるが如くにして、道を思ふなり。

親り見しは、西川の僧、遠方より来し故に、所持物なし。纔に墨二三箇の、直、両三百、此の国の両三十に、あたれるをもて、唐土の紙の、下品なるは、きはめて弱を買取り、或は襖或は袴に作て着れば、起居に壊るるをとして、あさましきをも、顧りみず、愁ず。人、自郷里にかへりて、道具装束せよ、と言を聞て、郷里遠方なり。路次の間に光陰を虚くして、学道の時を失ん、ことを愁て、更に寒を愁ずして、学道せしなり。然れば、大国には、よき人も出来るなり。

伝え聞く、雪峰山開山の時は、寺貧にして或は絶烟、或は緑豆飯をむして、食して日を送て学道せしかども、一千五百人の僧、常に絶えざりけり。昔の人もかくのごとし、今も又如此なるべし。

Although this country is small and remote [from the Buddha's country], among those who are famous in the ways of the exoteric and esoteric teachings[32] and are known to later generations, whether in the past and present, I have never heard of even one among them who had abundant food and clothing. All of them became well known because they endured poverty, were not concerned about other things, and devoted themselves completely to this Way. Moreover, people studying the Way abandon their occupations in society and never seek after [fame and profit]. How could they possibly become wealthy?

Although we are in the final age [of Dharma], in the monasteries in great Song China, there are thousands and thousands of people who are studying the Way. There are some who have come from remote districts or left their home provinces. Most of them are poor. However, they never worry about [food and clothing]. Their only concern is that they have not yet attained realization of the Way. Whether sitting in a lofty tower or in a magnificent hall, they think of the Way [with the seriousness] of having lost their father and mother.

I personally met a monk from Sichuan who had no possessions because he had come from a remote district.[33] All he had was two or three pieces of ink stick. They cost about two or three hundred *wen* in China, which is about twenty or thirty *mon* in this country. He sold them, bought some low-quality Chinese paper that was very fragile, made an upper and lower robe with it, and put them on. Although when he stood up or sat down, his robe tore and made strange noises, he never paid any attention to it and was not bothered. Someone said to him, "You should go back to your hometown and bring some personal belongings and clothing." He replied, "My hometown is far away. I do not want to waste time on the road and lose time [I could spend] practicing the Way." He practiced the Way without any concern for the cold. This is why many good monks have appeared in China.

I have heard that at the time of the founding of the monastery on Mt. Xuefeng, the temple was so poor they sometimes [had no food to cook such that] no smoke came out [of the kitchen chimney], and

　僧の損ずる事は、多く富家よりをこれり。如来在世に、調達が嫉妬を起しししことも、日に五百車の供養より起れり。只、自を損ずることのみに非ず。又他をしても悪を作さしめし因縁なり。真の学道の人、なにとしてか富家なるべき。直饒浄信の供養も、多くつもらば、恩の思を作して、報を思ふべし。

　此国の人は、又我がために、利を思ひて、施を至す。笑て向へる者に、能くあたる、定れる道理也。他の心に随んとせば、是学道の礙なるべし。只飢を忍び、寒を忍びて、一向に学道すべき也。

1-5

一日、示云、

　古人云、聞くべし、見るべし。又云、へずんば、見るべし、みずんば、きくべし。言は、きかんよりは、見るべし。見んよりは、ふべし。いまだへずんば、見るべし。いまだみずんば、聞べしと也。

　又、云、

　学道の用心、本執を放下すべし。身の威儀を改むれば、心も随て転ずる也。先律儀の戒行を守らば、心も随て改るべき也。宋土には、俗人等の、常の習に、父母の孝養の為に、宗廟にして、各集会して、泣まねをするほどに、終には実に泣なり。学道の人

sometimes they had to eat weedy legumes steamed with rice.[34] They lived such a poor life while practicing the Way, yet they always had fifteen hundred monks. People in ancient times practiced in such a way. Today we should also be like this.

The degeneration of monks is often caused by lives of wealth. In the time of the Tathāgata, Devadatta became jealous once he began receiving daily offerings of five hundred cartloads of provisions [from King Ajātaśatru].[35] Not only was wealth harmful to him, but it caused other people to commit evil deeds as well. How can people who truly study the Way become wealthy? Even if a person makes an offering with pure faith, if the offering is especially large, we see it as a debt of kindness and want to repay it.

Also, people in this country make donations expecting some profit for themselves. It is an unchanging principle that people give more to those who approach with a flattering smile. If we do the same in order to curry favor with others, it will surely become an obstacle to our practice of the Way. Just endure hunger, bear the cold, and devote yourselves completely to the practice of the Way.

1-5

One day [Dōgen] instructed:

An ancient said, "You must listen; you must see." He also said, "If you have not experienced, you must look. If you have not seen, you must listen." He meant that we should see rather than listen, and that we should experience rather than see. If we have not experienced, we should see. If we have not seen, we should listen.

[Dōgen] also said:

When practicing the Way, we must be cautious of our deep-rooted attachments and cast them aside. If you change your physical behavior, your mind will change as well.[36] First of all, if you maintain activities according to the precepts based on moral codes and forms, then your mind will also be transformed.[37] In Song China, there is a custom among laypeople. They gather at their ancestral shrine and pretend

も、はじめ道心なくとも、只強て道を好み学せば、終には真の道心も、をこるべきなり。

初心の学道の人は、只、衆に随て、行道すべき也。修行の心故実等を、学し知らんと、思ふことなかれ。用心故実等も、只一人、山にも入り、市にも隠れて、行ぜん時、錯なく、よく知りたらば、よしと云ふ事也。衆に随て行ぜば、道を得べきなり。譬ば舟に乗りて行には、故実を知らず、ゆく様を知らざれども、よき船師にまかせて行けば、知りたるも、知ざるも、彼岸に到るが如し。善知識に随て、衆と共に行て、私なければ、自然に道人なり。

学道の人、若し悟を得ても、今は至極と思て、行道を罷ことなかれ。道は無窮なり。さとりても、猶行道すべし。良遂座主、麻谷に参し、因縁を思ふべし。

1-6

示云、

学道の人は後日を待て、行道せんと思ふことなかれ。只今日今時を過ごさずして、日々時々を勤むべき也。爰に、ある在家人、長病あり。去年の春の比、相契て云く、当時の病、療治して、妻子を捨て、寺の辺に庵室を構へて、一月両度の布薩に逢、日々の行道、法門談義を見聞して、随分に戒行を守りて、生涯を

to cry in order to demonstrate their filial piety toward their fathers and mothers. Eventually, they actually do cry. Students of the Way should do the same. Even if you do not have the mind of awakening in the beginning, if you compel yourself to choose to practice the Buddha Way wholeheartedly, eventually you will arouse the true mind of awakening.[38]

Beginners in the Way should simply practice [the Way] following the other members of the sangha. Do not seek to study in order to gain [extensive] knowledge of the essential points and ancient practices.[39] When you enter the mountains alone or seclude yourself in a city to practice, it is good to understand the essential points and ancient practices without misinterpretation. If you practice following other practitioners, you will be able to attain the Way. For example, when it comes to sailing a ship, if you do not know the ancient practices [of sailing], or even if you do not know how to steer or how the boat sails, if you entrust everything to good sailors, whether you understand or not, you will reach the other shore. Only if you follow a good teacher[40] and practice with fellow practitioners without harboring personal views will you naturally become a person of the Way.

Students of the Way! Even if you have attained realization, do not think that you have reached the pinnacle and stop practicing. The Way is infinite. Even if you have attained realization, continue to practice the Way. Remember the story of Liangsui who visited Zen Master Magu.[41]

1-6

[Dōgen] *instructed*:

Students of the Way! We should not think that we will practice the Way on another day. Do not just spend this day or moment in vain; simply practice diligently day by day, moment by moment. A certain layperson had been sick for a long time. In the spring of last year, he pledged himself to me, saying, "As soon as I have recovered from the sickness I have now, I will renounce my wife and children and build a hermitage near the temple. I will join the repentance ceremony[42] both

送らんと云しに、其後、種々に療治すれば、少しき減気在りしかども、又増気在りて、日月空く過して、今年正月より、俄に大事になりて、苦痛次第に責る呈に、思ひきりて日比支度する庵室の具足、運びて造る呈の隙もなく、苦痛逼呈に、先づ人の庵室を借りて移り居て、纔に一両月に死去しぬ。前夜菩薩戒受、三宝に帰して、臨終よくて終りたれば、在家にて狂乱して、妻子に愛を発して、死なんよりは、尋常なれども、去年思よりたりし時、在家を離て寺に近づきて、僧に馴れて一年行道して終りたらば勝れたらましと、存るにつけても、仏道修行は、後日を待つまじきと、覚るなり。

身の病者なれば、病を治して後に、好く修行せんと思はば、無道心の致す処也。四大和合の身、誰か病なからん。古人必しも、金骨に非ず。只、志の到りなれば、他事を忘れて行ずる也。大事身に来れば、小事は覚えぬ也。仏道を大事と思て、一生に窮と思ふて、日々時々を空く過さじと思ふべき也。

古人の云、光陰莫虚度。若此の病を治んと営む呈に除ずして、増気して、苦痛弥逼る時は、痛の軽かりし時、行道せでと思ふなり。然れば痛を受けては、重くならざる前にと思ひ、重くなりては、死せざる前きにと思ふべき也。病を治するに除をるもあり。治するに増ずるもあり。又治ざるに除くもあり、治せざれば増ずるもあり。これ能々思ひ入るべき也。

又行道の居所等を支度し、衣鉢等を調へて、後に行んと思ふことなかれ。貧窮の人、世をわしらざれ。衣鉢の資具乏して、死

times each month. I will practice daily and listen to your lectures on the Dharma. I would like to spend as much of the rest of my life as possible keeping the precepts." After that, he received various medical treatments and recovered a little bit. But then he relapsed and spent his days in vain. In January of this year, his condition suddenly became critical, and he suffered from increasing pain. Because he did not have enough time to bring the furnishings he had been preparing, nor to build the hermitage, he borrowed someone else's hut to stay in temporarily. Within a month or so, however, he died. The night before [he died], he received the bodhisattva precepts and took refuge in the Three Treasures.[43] He was peaceful on his deathbed. It was better than staying at home and dying in a frenzy, clinging to the bonds of affection for his wife and children. However, I think it would have been better for him if he had left home last year when he had first made up his mind, had lived close to this temple, had become familiar with the sangha, and had ended his life practicing the Way. Considering this case, I feel that we must not defer the practice of the Buddha Way to another day.

If we think that because we are physically sick we will practice better only after we have recovered from sickness, it only shows that we lack the mind of awakening. Because this body is a collection of the four gross elements,[44] who will not become sick? The ancients did not necessarily have golden bones. Only because their aspiration was sufficiently strong could they practice, setting other things aside. We forget trivial matters when an important matter comes up. We must consider the Buddha Way to be the vital matter and be determined to investigate it thoroughly in this lifetime, not wasting even a single day or hour.

An ancient once said, "Do not spend your days and nights in vain."[45] If we receive medical treatments to heal a sickness, but instead of getting better the pain gradually increases, we may think that we should have practiced while the pain was still not so bad. However, when we are in pain, we should be determined [to practice] before our condition becomes critical. And when our condition has become

期日々に近づくは、具足を待て、処を待ちて行道せんと、思ふ呈
に、一生空く過すべきをや。只衣鉢等なくんば、在家も仏道は、
行ずるぞかしと思ふて、行ずべき也。また衣鉢等は、ただあるべ
き僧躰の荘なり。実の仏道は、其もよらず、得来らば、あるに任す
べし。あながちに求ことなかれ。ありぬべきをもたじと思ふべから
ず。わざと死せんと思て、治せざるも、亦外道の見也。仏道には、
命を惜むことなかれ。命を惜まざることなかれ、と云也。より来ら
ば、灸治一所瀉薬一種なんど、用いんことは、行道の礙ともなら
ず。行道を指置て、病を先とし、後に修行せんと思ふは礙也。

1-7

示云、

　海中に龍門と云処あり。浪頻に作也。諸の魚、波の処を過ぐれ
ば、必ず龍と成る也。故に龍門と云也。今は云く、彼処、浪も、他

critical, we should resolve to practice before we die. When we are sick and receive treatment, sometimes the illness passes, and sometimes it gets worse. Sometimes we recover without having any treatment, and sometimes we get worse even though we are being treated. Take this into careful consideration.

Also, we should not think that we will practice only after shelter has been arranged and robes, bowls, and so forth have been obtained.[46] If we are living in poverty, we should not run around [to make such preparations]. While waiting until robes, bowls, and other things have been obtained, can we prevent death from approaching? If we wait until furnishings are ready and our shelter has been prepared before beginning to practice, we could spend our entire lifetimes in vain. Even if we do not have robes, bowls, and so on, we should practice with the resolution that even a layperson can practice the Buddha Way. Anyway, robes, bowls, and other things are simply the ornaments of monkhood. The genuine Buddha Way does not depend on such things. If they are available, we should have them, but do not deliberately seek after them. [At the same time,] we should not consider rejecting them when we can get them. It is a non-Buddhist view to refuse medical treatments because of a desire to die intentionally. In the Buddha Way it is said, "We should not begrudge our lives; we should not fail to take care of our lives."[47] When offered, moxibustion[48] or purgatives will not obstruct our practice of the Way. It is a hindrance to think that we must put aside our practice of the Way and put primary importance on curing our sickness, planning to practice only after we have recovered.

1-7

[Dōgen] instructed:

In the ocean there is a place called the Dragon Gate.[49] [Here] waves constantly billow. Once they have passed through the waves at this place, all fish without exception become dragons. Therefore, this place is called the Dragon Gate. Now I say, at this place the waves are

処に異ならず。水も同く、しははゆき水也。然れども、定れる不思議にて、魚此処を渡れば、必ず龍と成る也。魚の鱗も改まらず、身も同身ながら、忽に龍と成る也。衲子の儀式も、是をもて知べし。処も他所に似れども、叢林に入れば、必ず仏となり、祖となるなり。食も人と同く（喫し、衣も人と同じく）服し、飢を除き、寒を禦ぐことも、同じけれども、只頭を円にし、衣を方にして、斎粥等にすれば、忽に衲子となる也。成仏作祖も、遠く求むべからず。只叢林に入ると、入ざると也。龍門を過ると、過ざると也。

又、云、俗の云、我れ金を売れども、人の買こと無れば也。仏祖の道も如是。道を惜むに非ず。常に与ども人の得ざる也。道を得ることは、根の利鈍には依らず。人々皆法を悟るべき也。只精進と懈怠とによりて、得道の遅速あり。進怠の不同は、志の到ると到ざると也。志の到ざることは、無常を思はざるに依なり。念々に死去す。畢竟暫くも止らず。暫くも存ぜる間、時光を虚すごすこと無れ。

倉の鼠、食に飢ゑ、田を耕す牛の、草に飽ず、と云意は、財の中に有れども、必ずしも食に飽かず。草の中に栖めども、草に飢る。人も如是。仏道の中にありながら、道に合ざるもの也。希求の心止ざれば、一生安楽ならざる也。

道者の行は、善行悪行、皆、をもはくあり。人のはかる処に非ず。昔、恵心僧都、一日庭前に、草を食する鹿を、人をして打ちをはしむ。時に人あり、問云、師、慈悲なきに似たり。草を惜で畜生

not different from those in any other place, and the water is also ordinary saltwater. However, mysteriously enough, when fish pass through this place, they become dragons without fail. Although their scales do not change and their bodies stay the same, they suddenly become dragons. We should know that the way of patch-robed monks is also like this. Although it is similar to other places, if we enter a monastery, without fail we will become buddhas and ancestors. We eat meals and wear clothes just like other people; we satisfy our hunger and ward off the cold just like other people. Still, if we simply shave our heads and reveal its roundness, wear a square robe,[50] and eat gruel for breakfast and rice for lunch, we immediately become patch-robed monks. Becoming a buddha or an ancestor should not be sought elsewhere far away. [Becoming a buddha or an ancestor] depends only on whether or not we enter a monastery; [becoming a dragon] depends only on whether or not fish pass through the Dragon Gate.

Also, there is a saying in the lay world, "Although I sell gold, no one buys it." The Way of the buddhas and ancestors is also like this. It is not that they are stingy with the Way; rather, they always offer it, but people do not accept it. Attaining the Way does not depend on whether our faculties are sharp or dull. Every one of us can realize the Dharma. Depending upon whether we are diligent or lazy, there is slowness or quickness in attaining the Way. The difference between being diligent or lazy is caused by whether our aspiration is firmly established or not. Lack of firm aspiration is caused by not considering impermanence.[51] We die moment by moment. Ultimately speaking, we do not stay [alive] even for a little while. While you are alive, do not spend your time in vain.

There is a saying, "A mouse in a [sealed] granary is starved for food. An ox plowing a field does not satisfy its hunger with grass." This means that even though it is living in the midst of abundance, [the mouse] does not necessarily eat its fill; even though it lives in the midst of grass, [the ox] is hungry for grass. People are also like this.

を悩す、僧都云、我れ若是を打ずんば、此鹿、人に馴て悪人に近づかん時、必ず殺されん。此故に打つ也。鹿を打は、慈悲なきに似れども、内心の道理、慈悲余れること如是。

1-8

一日、示云、

　人法門を問ふ、或は修行の方法を問ことあらば、衲子須実以是答。若は他の非器を顧み、或は初心未入の人、意得べからずとて、方便不実を以て、答べからず。菩薩戒の意は、直饒小乗の器、小乗道を問とも、只、大乗を以て、答べき也。如来一期の化儀も、爾前方便の権教は、実に無益也。只、最後実教のみ、実の益ある也。然れば他の得不得をば論ぜず、只、実を以て答べき也。

　若し此中の人（これ）を見ば、実徳を以て、是をうる事を得べし。仮徳を以て、是をうる事を得べし。外相仮徳を以て是れを見るべからず。

Even though we are in the midst of the Buddha Way, we do not live in peace and joy throughout our lifetime.

All the deeds of people of the Way, whether these actions seem good or bad, derive from deep consideration. These actions cannot be fathomed by ordinary people. Long ago, the Director of Monks Eshin[52] once had someone hit a deer that was eating grass in his garden to drive it away. At the time, someone said to him, "Master, it seems you do not have compassion. You begrudged the grass and tormented the animal." The director of monks replied, "If I did not hit it, the deer would eventually become accustomed to human beings. And when it came near an evil person, it would surely be killed. This is why I had it hit." Although it seems he did not have compassion and had the deer hit, deep in his heart he was filled with compassion in this way.

1-8

One day [Dōgen] instructed:

When someone asks about the Dharma gates[53] or methods of practice, patch-robed monks should without fail answer with the genuine teachings. Even if you believe that the questioner is not a vessel [of the Dharma], or is a beginner who has not yet entered [the Dharma], and that therefore the person is not capable of grasping the meaning [of your words], do not answer with expedient means that are not genuine. In the spirit of the bodhisattva precepts, even if a vessel of the Hīnayāna[54] asks about the Hīnayāna way, we should reply with [the heart] of the Mahāyāna. Among the teaching activities of the Tathāgata during his lifetime, the provisional teachings as an expedient means [, which he expounded before he began to teach the genuine teachings,] are not truly beneficial. Only the final, genuine teaching is truly beneficial.[55] Therefore, without being concerned with whether the questioner is capable of grasping it or not, we should answer only with the genuine teachings.

昔、孔子に一人有つて来帰す。孔問て云、汝、何を以てか来て我に帰する。彼の俗云、君子参内の時、是を見しに、顕々として威勢あり。依て是に帰す。孔子、弟子をして、乗物・装束・金銀・財物等を取り出て是を与き。汝、我に帰するに非ず。

又、云、

宇治の関白殿、有時、鼎殿に到て火を焼く処を見る。鼎殿見て云く、何者ぞ左右なく御所の鼎殿へ入るは、と云て、をい出されて後、さきの悪き衣服を、脱改て、顕々として取り装束して出給。時に、前の鼎殿、遥みて恐れ入てにげぬ。時に殿下装束を竿に掛られて、拝せられけり。人、是を問ふ。我、人に貴びらるるも、我徳に非ず。只、此の装束の故也。愚なる者の人を貴ぶこと如是。経教の文字等を貴ことも又如是。

古人云、言満天下無口過、行満天下亡怨悪。是則言ふべき処を言、行べき処を行ふ故也。至徳要道の言行也。世間の言行は私然を以計らい思ふ。恐らくは過のみあらん事を。衲子の言行、先証是定れり。私曲を存ずべからず。仏祖行来れる道也。

学道の人、各自己身を顧るべし。身を顧ると云は、身心何か様に持べきぞと顧べし。然るに衲子は則ち是釈子也。如来の風儀を慣べき也。身口意の威儀、皆な千仏行じ来れる作法あり。各其儀に随べし。俗猶、服、法に応じ、言、道に随べし、と云へり。一切私を用るべからず。

When a person within [the Dharma] sees [the genuine teachings], he can attain this [teaching] with genuine virtue. [Those outside the Dharma] can attain it [only] with superficial virtue. We should not assess [things] based on external superficial characteristics.[56]

In ancient times, a person visited Confucius to become his student. Confucius asked him, "Why do you want to be my disciple?" This worldly person replied, "Virtuous Worthy One, when I saw you going to court, you looked very dignified and powerful. Therefore, I want to become your student." Confucius then asked [another] disciple to bring his cart, garment, gold, silver, and other treasures and gave them to the [worldly] person. [Confucius] said, "It is not me that you respect."

[*Dōgen*] *also said*:

The emperor's chief advisor of Uji[57] once came to the bathhouse [in the imperial court] and watched the person who was in charge of stoking the fire. The bathhouse worker saw him and said, "Who are you? Why have you come into the court bathhouse without permission?" [The chief advisor] was forced to leave. Then, he took off the shabby clothes he was wearing and changed into magnificent attire. When he appeared [again] dressed up, the worker in charge of the fire saw him from a distance, became frightened, and ran away. Then, the chief advisor put his court dress on the top of a bamboo pole and paid homage to it. Someone asked what he was doing. He replied, "I am respected by others not because of my virtue but because of my clothing." Foolish people respect others in this way. The words and phrases in the teachings of the Buddhist scriptures are venerated in the same way.

An ancient said, "The words [of a statesman] spread all over the land, but there is not a fault on his tongue. The actions [of a statesman] govern the whole country, but there is no one who bears a grudge against him."[58] This is because [the statesman] said what should be said and carried out what should be carried out. These are the "words and actions of ultimate virtue and the essence of the Way."[59] In the mundane world, most people think and make judgments based on their self-centered evaluations. I am afraid there might

1-9

示云、

　当世学道する人、多分法を聞時、先好く領解する由を知られんと思て、答の言の好らん様を思ふほどに、聞くことは耳を過す也。詮ずる処、道心なく、吾我を存ずる故也。只須先づ我を忘れ、人の言はん事を好く聞て、後に静に案じて、難もあり不審もあらば、逐も難じ、心得たらば、逐て帰すべし。当座に領する由を呈せんとする、法を好も聞ざる也。

be nothing but mistakes [in them]. The [proper] speech and deeds of patch-robed monks have been established by our predecessors. We should never hold on to our self-centered views. This is the Way the buddhas and ancestors have practiced.

Students of the Way, each one of us should reflect on our own self. To reflect on our self means to examine how we behave with our own body and mind. Patch-robed monks are already the children of Shakyamuni. We must follow the lifestyle of the Tathāgata. There are codes of dignified conduct regarding the manner of body, speech, and thought[60] that have been carried out by a thousand buddhas. All of us should follow them. Even in the lay world, it is said, "Our clothes should be in accordance with the law; our speech should correspond with the Way."[61] We [monks] must never follow our own [ego-centered] self.

1-9

[*Dōgen*] *instructed*:
Nowadays, when those who study the Way listen to the Dharma, more than anything, they want to [give others] the impression that they understand it correctly, and thus they think about how they can reply with marvelous words. This is why what they hear goes in one ear and out the other. After all, this happens because they do not have the mind of awakening and their [ego-centered] self remains. We should simply forget our self and listen carefully to what the speaker says, then ponder it quietly later. After that, if we find faults or anything questionable, we may make a criticism on another occasion. And if we agree with [the teaching], we should return to the teacher and offer our understanding. When we try to present our understanding immediately, we are not carefully listening to the Dharma.

1-10

示云、

　唐の太宗の時、異国より千里馬を献ず。帝是を得て喜ばずして、自思はく、直饒千里の馬なりとも、独り騎て千里に行くとも、従ふ臣下なくんば、其詮なきなり。因、魏徴を召てこれを問。徴云く、帝の心と同じ。依て彼の馬に金帛を負せて還しむ。

　今は云、帝猶身の用ならぬ物をば持ずして是を還。況衲子、衣鉢の外の物、決定して無用なるか。無用の物是を貯て何かせん。俗猶一道を専にする者は、田苑荘園等を持る事を要とせず。只一切の国土の人を、百姓眷属とす。

　地相法橋、子息に遺嘱するに、只道を専にはげむべし、と云へり。況や仏子は万事を捨て、専一事をたしなむべし。是、用心なり。

1-11

示云、

　学道の人、参師聞法の時、能々窮て聞、重て聞て決定すべし。問べきを問はず、言ふべきを言はずして過しなば、我損なるべし。師は必ず弟子の問ふを待て発言する也。心得たる事をも、幾度も問て決定すべき也。師も弟子に能々心得たるかと問て、云ひ聞かすべき也。

1-10

[*Dōgen*] *instructed*:

During the reign of Taizong of the Tang dynasty, a horse that could travel thousands of miles was presented from a foreign country.[62] The emperor was not delighted by this gift. He thought to himself, "Even if I can travel thousands of miles on this excellent horse, it is useless if no retainers follow me." Then he summoned Wei Zheng and asked his opinion about this.[63] Wei Zheng replied, "I agree with you." Because of this, [the emperor] returned the horse with a load of gold and silk on its back.

Now I say, even the emperor did not keep what was not useful to him and returned it. Furthermore, for us patch-robed monks, besides robes and a bowl, there is absolutely nothing that is useful. Why is it that we store up useless things? Even in the mundane world, those who completely devote themselves to a certain path do not think it necessary to possess property such as rice fields or manors. [Such people] consider everyone in the whole country to be their own people or family.

In his will to his son, the Dharma Bridge[64] Chisō said, "You must exclusively concentrate your efforts on the Way." Needless to say, as children of the Buddha we should give up all other affairs and wholeheartedly devote ourselves to one thing. We must keep this in mind.

1-11

[*Dōgen*] *instructed*:

Students of the Way, when we practice with a certain teacher and listen to the Dharma, we should listen thoroughly again and again until we have attained a definitive understanding. If we spend time without asking what should be asked, or without saying what should be said, it will be our own loss. Teachers give responses to their disciples only when they are asked questions. We should ask again and again to make sure that we have a definitive understanding even about the things we have already understood. Teachers also should ask their disciples

1-12

示云、

　道者の用心、常の人に殊なる事有り。故建仁寺の僧正在世の時、寺絶食す。有る時、一人の檀那、請じて、絹一疋施す。僧正悦て自取て懐中して、人にも持せずして、寺に返て知事に与て云く、明旦の浄粥等に作さるべし。

　然に俗人のもとより、所望して云、恥がましき事有て、絹二三疋入る事あり。少々にてもあらば、給るべきよしを申す。僧正則ち先の絹を取り返して則ち与へぬ。時に此の知事の僧も、衆僧も、思ひの外に不審す。後に僧正自云く、各僻事にぞ思はるらん。然れども、我れ思くは、衆僧面々仏道の志ありて集れり。一日絶食して餓死すとも苦かるべからず。俗の世に交はれるが、指当て事闕らん苦悩を助たらんは、各々の為にも、一日の食を去て、人の苦を息たらんは、利益勝れたるべし。道者の案じ入れたる事如是。

1-13

示云、

whether they have completely understood or not and give them thorough instructions.

1-12

[*Dōgen*] *instructed*:

On some important points, the mental attitude of a person of the Way is different from that of common people. Once while the late superintendent of monks[65] of Kennin-ji was still alive, the temple ran out of food. At the time, a patron[66] invited the superintendent of monks [to his home] and offered him a bolt of silk. The superintendent of monks rejoiced, tucked it under his kimono, and carried it back to the temple by himself, without having his attendant take it for him. He gave the silk to the temple officer in charge and told him to use it to pay for the next morning's gruel, and so forth.

However, a certain layman made a request saying, "An unfortunate thing has happened, and I need two or three bolts of silk. If you have even a small amount, could you kindly let me have it?" The superintendent of monks immediately took back the silk [from the temple officer] and gave it [to the layman]. At the time, the officer and other monks in his assembly were puzzled by this unexpected action. Later the superintendent of monks himself said, "You may think what I did was unreasonable. However, I think that all you monks have gathered together here because of your aspiration for the Buddha Way. None of us would mind even if we run out of food or even starve to death. It is more beneficial to help people living in the lay world who are suffering right now from a lack of something they need. Even for ourselves, it is better to give up one day's food and help others' suffering." Thus is the deep consideration of a person of the Way.

1-13

[*Dōgen*] *instructed*:

仏々祖々、皆本は凡夫也。凡夫の時は、必ず悪業もあり、悪心もあり、鈍もあり、癡もあり。然ども皆改ためて、知識に従がひ、教行に依しかば、皆仏祖と成りし也。今の人も然るべし。我が身、をろかなれば、鈍なれば、と卑下する事なかれ。今生に発心せずんば、何の時をか待べき。好むには必ず得べき也。

1-14

示云、

俗の帝道の故実を言に云、虚襟に非れば、忠言を入れず。言は、己見を存ぜずして、忠臣の言に随て、道理に任せて帝道を行也。

衲子の学道の故実も、又如是なるべし。若し己見を存ぜば、師の言ば耳に入らざる也。師の言ば耳に入ざれば、師の法を得ざるなり。

又只法門の異見を忘るるのみに非ず、又世事を返して、飢寒等を忘て、一向に身心を清めて聞時、親く聞にてある也。如是聞時、道理も不審も明めらるる也。真実の得道と云も、従来の身心を放下して、只直下に他に随ひ行けば、即ち実の道人にてある也。是れ第一の故実也。

正法眼蔵随聞記　一　終

All the buddhas and ancestors were originally ordinary people. While they were ordinary people they certainly did bad things and had evil thoughts. Some of them might have been dull-witted or even fools. However, since they followed their teachers, relied on [the Buddha's] teaching and practice, and transformed themselves, they all became buddhas and ancestors. Today's people should also do the same. We should not disparage ourselves, thinking we are foolish or dull-witted. If we do not arouse the mind [of awakening] in this present lifetime, when can we expect to? If we are fond of [the Way], we will surely attain it.

1-14

[*Dōgen*] *instructed*:

In the lay world, there is a proverb about the way of the emperor: "Unless one's mind is empty, it is impossible to accept loyal advice." This saying means that without holding personal views, [the emperor] should follow the opinions of loyal ministers and carry out the way of the sovereign according to how things ought to be.

The attitude of patch-robed monks practicing the Way should be the same. If we hold on to our personal views, the words of our teacher will not enter our ears. If we do not listen to our teacher's words, we cannot attain our teacher's Dharma.

We should forget not only different views on the Dharma gates but worldly affairs, hunger, and cold as well. When we listen completely purified in body and mind, we can hear intimately. When we listen in this way, we will be able to clarify the truth and resolve our questions. True attainment of the Way is casting aside body and mind and following our teacher straightforwardly. If we maintain this attitude, we will be true people of the Way. This is the primary truth.

The End of the First Book of *Shōbōgenzō Zuimonki*

正法眼蔵随聞記　二

侍者　懐奘　編

2-1

一日、示曰、

　続高僧伝の中に、或る禅師の会に、一僧あり。金像の仏と、又仏舎利とを崇用て、衆寮等にも有て、常に焼香礼拝し、恭敬供養す。

　有時、禅師の云、汝が崇むる処の仏像舎利は、後には汝が為に不是あらん。其僧不肯。師云、是、天魔波旬の付処也。早く是を不捨。其僧、憤然として出づれば、師、僧の後に云懸けて云、汝、箱を開て是を見べし。怒ながら是を開て見れば、果して毒蛇蟠て臥り。

　是を思に、仏像舎利は如来の遺骨なれば、恭敬すべしといへども、又一へに是を仰ぎて得悟すべしと思はば、還て邪見也。天魔毒蛇の所領と成る因縁也。仏説に功徳あるべしと見えたれば、人天の福分と成る事、生身と斉し。惣て三宝の境界、恭敬すれば、罪滅し功徳を得る事、悪趣の業をも消し、人天の果を

SHŌBŌGENZŌ ZUIMONKI, BOOK 2

Compiled by the attendant Ejō

2-1

One day [Dōgen] instructed:

In the *Continued Biographies of Eminent Monks*,[67] there is a story about a monk in the assembly of a certain Zen master. [This monk] worshiped a golden image of the Buddha as well as the relics[68] of the Buddha. Even in the study hall, he always burned incense and prostrated himself in front of them, honoring them and making offerings.[69]

One time, the Zen master said, "The image and relics of the Buddha that you worship eventually will be harmful to you." The monk was not convinced. The master continued, "They are haunted by the heavenly demon Pāpīyas.[70] You should throw them away at once." As the monk was leaving in anger, the master shouted after him, "Open the box and look inside!" Although angry, the monk opened up the box; just as the master had said, a poisonous snake was lying coiled up inside.

As I think of this story, images and relics of the Buddha should [still] be venerated because they are the bones left by the Tathāgata.[71] Nevertheless, it is a mistaken view to think that we can attain realization just by worshiping them. Such a view will cause us to become possessed by demons and poisonous snakes. In the Buddhist teachings, it is said that [veneration of relics] has merit, and therefore it surely

も感ずる事は実也。是によりて、仏の悟を得たりと執するは僻見
也。

　仏子と云は、仏教に順じて直に仏位に到らん為には、只、教
に随て、功夫弁道すべき也。其教に順ずる、実の行と云は、即、今
の叢林の宗とする只管打坐也。是を思べし。

　又、云、
　戒行持斎を守護すべければとて、又、是をのみ宗として是
を奉公に立て、是に依て得道すべしと思ふも、又、是れ非也。
只、衲僧の行履、仏子の家風なれば、従ひゆく也。是れを能事
と云へばとて、あながち是をのみ宗とすべしと思ふは非也。然
ばとて、又、破戒放逸なれと云に非ず。若亦如是執せば、邪見
也。外道也。只、仏家の儀式、叢林の家風なれば、随順しゆく
也。是を宗とすと、宋土の寺院に住せし時も、衆僧に見ゆべか
らず。
　実の得道の為には、只、坐禅功夫、仏祖の相伝也。是れに依
つて一門の同学、五根房、故用祥僧正の弟子也。唐土の禅院に
て持斎を固く守りて戒経を終日誦せしをば、教へて捨しめたりし
也。
　芿公問云、叢林学道の儀式は百丈の清規を守るべきか。
然に、彼に、はじめに、受戒護戒をもて先とすと見たり。亦、今の
伝来相承の根本戒をさづくと見たり。当家の口決面授にも、西来

brings happiness[72] in the human and heavenly realms, just like [venerating] the living body of the Buddha. In general, it is true that if we venerate and make offerings to the realm of the Three Treasures, our faults will disappear and we will gain merit, the karma that leads us to the evil realms will be removed, and we will be born in the realms of human and heavenly beings. However, it is a mistaken view to cling to such activities and say that we have attained the Buddha's realization through these [acts alone].

The Buddha's children should follow the Buddha's teachings. To reach Buddhahood we should make an effort to practice the Way wholeheartedly.[73] The genuine practice of being in accordance with the [Buddha's] teaching is nothing other than just sitting,[74] the essence of our practice in this monastery. We must keep this in mind.

[*Dōgen*] *also said*:

Even though we should protect and maintain our practice based on the precepts and the regulations for eating, it is also wrong to take them as paramount, focusing on them as our only task, and think that we will attain the Way [merely] by living in such a manner.[75] We follow these regulations simply because that is how patch-robed monks behave; this is the family style[76] of the Buddha's children. Although [keeping the precepts] is a good thing, it is wrong to grasp them alone as the essential practice. However, I am not saying that we should break the precepts and become self-indulgent. Clinging to such an attitude is a mistaken view, and [if we do so] we will be outside the Buddha Way. We follow [the precepts] only because that is the standard of the Buddha's family and the family style of Zen monasteries. While I was staying at the monasteries in the country of Song [China], I did not see the monks make them their primary practice.

For true attainment of the Way, the devotion of all effort to zazen alone [is what] has been transmitted from the buddhas and ancestors.[77]

相伝の戒を学人に授く。是、則、今の菩薩戒也。然るに今の戒経
に、日夜に是を誦せよ、と云へり。何ぞ是を誦を捨しむるや。

　師云、

　然り。学人最百丈の規縄を守べし。然に其儀式、護戒坐禅等
也。昼夜に戒を誦し、専ら戒を護持す、と云事は、古人の行李に
したがふて、祇管打坐すべき也。坐禅の時、何の戒か持たれざ
る、何功徳か来らざる。古人の行じをける処の行履、皆、深心あ
り。私の意楽を存ぜずして、只、衆に従て、古人の行履に任せて
行じゆくべき也。

2-2

一日、示云、

　人、其の家に生れ、其道に入らば、先づ、其の家の業を修べ
し、知べき也。我が道にあらず、自が分にあらざらん事を知り修す
るは即ち非也。

For this reason, I taught a fellow student of mine, Gokonbō,[78] a disciple of the late Superintendent of Monks Yōjō,[79] to abandon his strong adherence to the eating regulations and recitation of the *Precepts Sutra*[80] day and night.

Ejō asked, "Regarding the standards of studying the Way in a monastery, should we maintain Baizhang's *Pure Standards*?[81] If so, at their outset we find, 'receiving the precepts and maintaining the precepts are prerequisites.' Also, it seems that the fundamental precepts[82] have been handed down in the tradition that you are transmitting. In the oral as well as the face-to-face transmission of this lineage, the precepts transmitted from the West [India] have also been bestowed. These are the bodhisattva precepts we [are discussing] now. In the *Precepts Sutra* [we are studying] now, it is said that we should recite it day and night.[83] Why would you have us stop reciting it?"

The master [Dōgen] said:

[What you say] is correct. Students, first of all, should maintain the regulations laid down by Baizhang. However, regarding those standards, the precepts are maintained [by doing] zazen, and so forth. "Reciting the *Precepts Sutra* day and night and keeping the precepts single-mindedly" means nothing other than practicing just sitting, in the manner of the ancients. When we do zazen, which precept is not observed? Which virtue is not actualized? All of the activities practiced by the ancients have deep meaning. Without clinging to our personal preferences, we should go along with the assembly and practice, entrusting ourselves to the way the ancients practiced.[84]

2-2

One day [Dōgen] instructed:

If we are born into a certain family and [therefore] enter a certain field, we must first of all receive training in that family business and understand it. It is improper to learn and be acquainted with other things that have nothing to do with our own path or specialty.

今、出家の人として、即仏家に入り、僧道に入らば、須く其業を習べし。其儀を守ると云ふは、我執を捨て、知識の教に随ふ也。其大意は、貪欲無也。貪欲無らんと思はば、先須離吾我也。吾我を離るるには、観無常。是れ第一の用心也。

世人多、我は元来、人に、能と言れ思はれんと思ふ也。其が即、よくも成得ぬ也。只、我執を次第に捨て、知識の言随いゆけば、昇進する也。

理を心得たる様に云へども、しかありと云へども、我は其の事が捨得ぬ、と云て、執し好み修するは、弥、沈淪する也。

禅僧の能く成る第一の用心、祇管打坐すべき也。利鈍賢愚を論ぜず、坐禅すれば自然に好くなるなり。

2-3

示曰、

広学博覧は、かなふべからざる事也。一向に思ひ切て留るべし。只、一事に付て用心故実をも習ひ、先達の行履をも尋て、一行を専はげみて、人師先達の気色すまじき也。

2-4

或時、弉、師に問て云、如何是、不昧因果底の道理。

Now, we are home-leavers, have entered the Buddha's family, and have begun to walk the path of monks. We must study the works of [Buddhist monks]. To maintain the way [of Buddhist monks] is to give up self-attachment and follow the guidance of our teachers. The essential point here is to be free from greed. If we wish to put an end to greed, we must first depart from our ego-centered self. To depart from the ego-centered self, seeing impermanence is the primary concern.[85]

Most people in the world want to have a good reputation and to be appreciated, not only by themselves but also by others. Because of that [defiled motivation], we cannot become better. Just give up self-attachment gradually, keep following the sayings of a master, and you will progress.

If we cling to a certain thing and prefer to pursue it, saying, "[The teacher] speaks as if he understands the truth, and he might be right, but I am not able to give up this thing," we will sink deeper.

For a Zen monk to make progress, the most important thing to keep in mind is that we must just sit [*shikantaza*]. Whether we are sharp or dull-witted, wise or foolish, if we practice zazen, we will naturally improve.

2-3

[*Dōgen*] *instructed*:

It is not possible to study extensively and obtain wide knowledge. We must have the solid determination to stop doing [such things]. Simply focusing on one thing, we must study [proper] mental attitudes and the ancient practices, and investigate how our predecessors practiced. We should concentrate our efforts solely on one practice, and we should not pretend to be teachers or leaders of others.

2-4

Once Ejō asked the master, "What is the meaning of not being blind to cause and effect?"[86]

師云、不動因果也。

云、なにとしてか、脱落せん。

師云、歴然一時見也。

云、如是ならば、果、引起すや。

師云、惣て如是ならば、南泉猫児を截事。大衆已に不道得。即、猫児を斬却了ぬ。後に趙州、脱草鞋、載出し、又、一段の儀式也。

又、云、我、若、南泉なりせば、即、道べし、道得たりとも、即、斬却せん、道不得なりとも、即、斬却せん。何人か猫児を争ふ、何人か猫児を救ふ。

大衆に代て道ん。既に道得す。請、和尚、斬猫児。

又、大衆に代て道ん、南泉、只知一刀両段不知一刀一段。

弉云、如何、是、一刀一段。

師云、大衆、道不得。良久不対ならば、泉、道べし、大衆已に道得す、と云て、猫児を放下せまし。古人云、大用現前して不存軌則。

又、云、今の斬猫は、是、即、仏法の大用、或は一転語なり。若、一転語に非ずば、山河大地妙浄明心とも云べからず。又、即心是仏とも云べからず。即、此一転語、言下にて猫児躰、仏身と見、又、此語を聞て、学人も頓に悟入すべし。

又、云、此斬猫、即是、仏行也。

The master [Dōgen] replied, "Not to drive cause and effect."

Ejō asked, "How can we drop off [cause and effect]?"

The master said, "[Cause and effect] are clearly manifested together at one time."[87]

Ejō said, "If it is like that, how is the effect brought about?"

The master said, "If it is like that, what about Nanquan's cutting of the cat? [No one] in the assembly could speak.[88] [Nanquan] immediately cut the cat. Afterward, Zhaozhou took off his straw sandals, placed them on his head, and left. That was an excellent action."

[Dōgen] also said, "If I were Nanquan, I would have said, 'Even if you can speak, I will cut the cat. Even if you cannot speak, I will cut it. Who is fighting over the cat? Who would help the cat?' On behalf of the assembly, I would have said, 'We have already spoken.[89] Please, master, cut the cat.' I would also say on behalf of the assembly, 'Nanquan knows only the cutting [of the cat] into two pieces with one stroke; he does not know the cutting of it into one piece with one stroke.'"

Ejō said, "What is cutting it into one piece with one stroke?"

The master said, "When the assembly could not speak, and no one answered for a while, Nanquan should have said, 'The assembly has spoken,' and released the cat. An ancient said, 'When the great function manifests itself, there are no fixed rules.'"[90]

[Dōgen] also said, "This 'cutting a cat' is nothing other than the great function of the Buddhadharma, or [nothing other than] 'pivotal words.'[91] If it is not [intended as] a pivotal word, we must not say that 'the mountains, rivers, and the great earth are the wondrous, pure, and bright mind.'[92] Nor should we say that 'the mind is itself Buddha.'[93]

Upon hearing these pivotal words, we immediately see that the cat's body is nothing other than the Buddha's body; also upon hearing these words, students can suddenly enter realization."

[Dōgen] also said, "This cutting of the cat is the action of a Buddha."

[Ejō asked,] "What shall we call this?"

喚で何とか道べき。

喚で斬猫とすべし。

又、云、是、罪相なりや。

云、罪相也。

何としてか脱落せん。

云、別、並具。

云く、別解脱戒とは如是道ふか。

云く、然也。又云、但、如是料簡、直饒好事なりとも不如無。

羿問云、犯戒と言は、受戒以後の所犯を道か。只又、未受以前の罪相をも犯戒と道べきか。

師、答云、犯戒の名は、受後の所犯を道べし。未受以前、所作の罪相をば、只、罪相罪業と道て不可道犯戒。

問云、四十八軽戒の中に、未受戒の所犯を犯と名見ゆ、如何。

答云、不然、彼の未受戒の者、今受戒せんとする時、所造の罪を懺悔する時、今の戒に望めて十戒を授に、犯軽戒、犯すと云也。以前所造罪を犯戒と云に非ず。

問云、今受戒せん時、所造罪を懺悔せん為に、未受の者をして懺悔せしむるに、十重四十八軽戒を教へて、読誦せしむべし、と見たり。又下文に、未受戒の前にして説戒すべからず、と云へり。二度の相違如何。

"We should call it 'cutting a cat.'"[94]

[Ejō] also asked, "Is it a crime?"

[Dōgen] said, "It is a crime."

[Ejō asked,] "How can we drop off [the causality of this action]?"

[Dōgen] said, "[The action of a Buddha and a crime] are different, yet both occur [in one action]."

[Ejō] said, "Is this what is meant by the *Pratimokṣa* precepts?"[95]

[Dōgen] said, "Yes, it is."

[Dōgen] also said, "Though it was a good thing, it is better not to test [an assembly] in such a way."

Ejō asked, "Does the term 'violation of the precepts' refer to violations committed after having received the precepts, or are offenses committed before receiving the precepts also called 'violations of the precepts'?"[96]

The master replied, "The term 'violation of the precepts' applies only to those violations committed after having received the precepts. The offenses committed before receiving the precepts are simply called 'offenses,' or 'offensive actions'; they are not called 'violations of the precepts.'"

[Ejō] asked, "Within the forty-eight minor precepts, there is one that states that violations committed prior to receiving the precepts are called 'violations.' What about this?"[97]

[Dōgen] replied, "That is not correct. What this means is that a person about to receive the precepts should repent of harmful deeds committed in the past.[98] According to the ten major precepts or the forty-eight minor precepts, such evil deeds are [just] called 'violations.' It is not that the previously committed offenses are called 'violations of the precepts.'"

[Ejō] asked, "When people are about to receive the precepts, they should repent of all their past misdeeds. To allow people who have not yet received the precepts to practice repentance, [in the *Precepts Sutra*] we find, 'The master has to teach the ten major precepts and the forty-eight minor precepts and have the student recite them.' And yet,

答云、受戒と誦戒とは別也。懺悔の為に戒経を誦ずるは、猶、是、念経なるが故に、未受の者、戒経を誦せんとす。彼が為に戒経を説ん事、不可有咎。下文には、利養の為の故に、未受の前に是を説くことを修せんとす。最も是を教べし。

問云、受戒の時は、七逆の懺悔すべし、と見ゆ、如何。

答云、実、懺悔すべし。受戒の時、不許事は、且、抑止門とて抑る儀也。又、上の文は、破戒なりとも還得受せば、清浄なるべし。懺悔すれば清浄也。未受に不同。

問云、七逆、既に懺悔を許さば、又、受戒すべきか如何。

答云、然也。故僧正、自所立の義也。既に懺悔を許ば、又、是、受戒すべし。逆罪なりとも、悔て受せば、可授。況、菩薩は、直饒、自身は破戒の罪を受とも、他の為に受戒せしむべし。

in a later section of the *Sutra*, it says, 'You should not preach about the precepts to people who have not yet received them.'[99] Why are there these differences between the two sections?"

[Dōgen] replied, "Receiving the precepts and reciting the precepts are two different things. Reciting the *Precepts Sutra* for the sake of repentance is nothing other than the reading of sutras. Therefore, [even] those who have not yet received the precepts recite the *Precepts Sutra*. It cannot be wrong to explain the *Precepts Sutra* to them. What the later section of the *Sutra* says is that we should not preach the precepts to people who have not received them for the purpose of gaining profit. We should certainly teach the precepts [to those who wish to repent]."

[Ejō] asked, "[In the *Precepts Sutra*] it is said that when we receive the precepts, we should repent of the seven grave crimes. What do you make of this?"[100]

[Dōgen] replied, "We should certainly repent of them. The meaning of the passage 'they are not permitted to receive the precepts' is for the purpose of preventing [people from committing the seven grave crimes].[101] The previous passage means that even if someone violates the precepts, they will be pure when they receive the precepts again. When they repent, they are purified. [Those who have received the precepts but then committed offenses] are different from people who have not yet received the precepts."

[Ejō] asked, "If those who have committed any of the seven grave crimes are permitted to repent, can they receive the precepts again?"

[Dōgen] replied, "Yes. The late superintendent of monks [Eisai] himself insisted on this point. Once [people who have committed one of the seven grave crimes] are allowed to repent, they are also permitted to receive the precepts. The master should allow those who have committed even the seven grave crimes to receive the precepts if they have repented. Even if the master himself violates the precepts

2-5

夜話に云、

　悪口をもて、僧を呵嘖し毀呰する事莫。悪人不当なりと云とも、無左右、悪毀しる事莫れ。先づ何にわるしと云とも、四人已上集会しすべければ、僧の躰にて、国の重宝なり。最、帰敬すべき者也。若は住持長老にてもあれ、若は師匠知識にてもあれ、弟子不当ならば、慈悲心老婆心にて能教訓誘引すべき也。其時、直饒、可打をば打ち、可呵嘖をば呵嘖すとも、毀呰謗言の心を不可起。

　先師天童浄和尚、住持の時、僧堂にて、衆僧坐禅の時、眠を警に履を以て是を打、謗言呵嘖せしかども、僧、皆、被打事を喜び、讃嘆しき。

　或時又上堂の次でには、常に云、我已に老後の今は、衆を辞し、庵に住して老を扶て居るべけれども、衆の知識として、各々の迷を破り、道を助けんが為に、住持人たり。因是、或は呵嘖の言を出し、竹篦打擲等の事を行ず。是、頗る恐あり。然れども、代仏、揚化儀式なり。諸兄弟、慈悲をもて是を許し給へ、と言ば、衆僧流涕しき。

　如是心を以てこそ、衆をも接し、化をも宣べけれ。住持長老なればとて、猥りに衆を領じ、我物に思ふて呵嘖するは非也。況、其人に非ずして人の短を謂、他の非を謗しるは非也。能々用心すべ

by doing so, as a bodhisattva, for the sake of saving them, the master must allow them to receive the precepts."

2-5

In an evening talk,[102] *[Dōgen] said*:

Do not use abusive language to scold or blame monks.[103] Even if they are bad or incapable, do not harbor hatred against them or abuse them thoughtlessly. First of all, no matter how bad they might be, when more than four monks gather together and practice, they form a sangha, which is a priceless national treasure.[104] We should take refuge in [the sangha] and respect it most highly. Even if we are the abbot or an elder, or the master or a teacher, [if monks of the assembly] are bad, we have to instruct and guide them with a compassionate mind and a parental heart.[105] In doing so, even when we have to slap those who should be slapped or scold those who should be scolded, we should not allow ourselves to vilify them or arouse feelings of hatred.

When my late teacher Rujing[106] was the abbot of Tiantong monastery, he would hit the monks of the assembly with his slipper or scold them with harsh words in order to keep them awake while they were sitting zazen in the monks' hall. Yet all of us were thankful to be hit, and we praised him.

Once in a formal Dharma discourse he said, "I have grown old now. I should have retired from the monastery by now and moved into a hermitage to care for myself in my old age. However, I am your teacher, and it is my duty to break the delusions of each of you. As the abbot I must help you attain the Way. To do so, I sometimes have to use harsh language to scold you, or hit you with a bamboo stick, and so forth. I regret having to do this. However, this is the way to enable the Dharma to flourish on behalf of the Buddha. Brothers, please have compassion for me, and forgive me for these deeds." Upon hearing these words all of us shed tears.

き也。他の非を見て、わるしと思て、慈悲を以てせんと思はゞ、腹立つまじき様に方便して、傍の事を言ふ様にて、こしらうべし。

2-6

又物語云、

　故鎌倉の右大将、始め、兵衛佐にて有りし時、内府辺に、一日、はれの会に出仕の時、一人の不当人在りき。

　そ時、大納言にをほせて云、是を制すべし。

　将の云、六波羅にをほせらるべし。平家の将軍也。

　大納言の云、近々なれば。

　大将の云、その人に非ず、と。

　是れ美言なり。この心にて後に世をも治めたりし也。今の学人も其の心あるべし。其人に非して人を呵する事莫れ。

2-7

夜話云、

　昔、魯の仲連と云将軍ありて、平原君が国に有て、能く朝敵を平ぐ。

Only with such a spirit can we lead an assembly and spread the [Dharma] teachings. Even if you are an abbot or a senior monk, it is wrong to govern the community and abuse the monks as if they were your personal belongings. Furthermore, if you are not in such a position, you should not discuss others' faults or speak ill of them. We must be very, very careful. When we see someone's faults, think they are wrong, and wish to instruct them with compassion, we must confront them with skillful means to avoid arousing their anger, and do so as if we were talking about something else.

2-6

[Dōgen] also told the following story:
When Kamakura's late general of the Right Imperial Guard [Minamoto no Yoritomo][107] was beginning his time as the assistant secretary of the headquarters of the Middle Palace Guard,[108] he once attended a special party. He took a seat near the minister of the interior.[109] There was a man who was making a disturbance.

Then, the major councilor[110] asked [Yoritomo] to restrain the person.

The general [Yoritomo] replied, "Give your order to Rokuhara. He is the general of the Taira clan."[111]

The major councilor said, "But you are right here."

The general said, "I am not the person [in charge of this]."

These were admirable words. He was able to govern the country because of such an attitude. Today's students of the Way should have the same attitude. We should not scold others if we are not in a position to do so.

2-7

In an evening talk, [Dōgen] said:
In ancient times, there was a general by the name of Lu Zhonglian. While he was staying in the country ruled by Lord Pingyuan, [Lu] defeated the enemies of the court.[112]

　平原君賞して、数多の金銀等を与へしかば、魯の仲連辞して云、只、将軍の道なれば、敵を討つ能を成す已而。賞を得て、物を取んとには非ず、と謂て、敢て不取と言。魯仲連、廉直とて名よの事也。

　俗、猶、賢なるは、我、其人として、其道の能を成すばかり也。代りを得んと不思。学人の用心も、如是なるべし。仏道に入ては、仏道の為に、諸事を行じて、代に所得あらんと不可思。内外の諸教に、皆、無所得なれとのみ進むるなり。（心を取る。）

　法談の次に示して云、

　直饒我、道理を以て道に、人、僻事を言を、理を攻めて言勝は悪き也。次に、我れは現に道理と思へども、我が非にこそ、と言て、負けてのくも、あしばやなると言也。

　只、人をも言不折、我が僻事にも謂をおほせず、無為にして止めるが好也。耳に聴入れぬようにて忘るれば、人も忘れて、怒らざる也。第一の用心也。

2-8

示云、

　無常迅速也。生死事大也。暫、存命の間、業を修し、学を好には、只、仏道を行じ、仏法を学すべき也。文筆詩歌等、其詮なき也。捨べき道理、左右に及ばず。仏法を学し仏道を修するにも、

Lord Pingyuan praised him and rewarded him with large amounts of gold, silver, and other things, but Lu Zhonglian refused, saying, "I subdued the enemies only because that is the way of a general. I had no intention of receiving a reward." So saying, he did not accept the reward. Because of this incident, Lu Zhonglian is famous for his righteousness and integrity.

Even in the lay world, those who are wise use their abilities and accomplish things solely for the sake of fulfilling their paths. They do not think of receiving rewards. A student [of the Way] should also maintain such a mental attitude. Once we have entered the Buddha Way, whatever practice we do should be for the sake of the Buddha Way. We should not think of gaining something in return. All the various teachings, whether Buddhist or non-Buddhist, encourage us to be without gaining-mind.

(I took down only the essence [of what Dōgen said].)

On the occasion of a Dharma talk, [Dōgen] instructed:

Even when we speak rationally while another person says unreasonable things, it is wrong to defeat the person by arguing logically. On the other hand, it is not good to give up hastily, saying that we are wrong even if we think that we are actually correct. Neither defeat the person nor withdraw by saying we were wrong.

It is best to just leave the matter alone and stop arguing. When we act as if we have not heard and forget about the matter, the person will forget, too, and will not get angry. This is the most important point to keep in mind.

2-8

[Dōgen] instructed:

Impermanence is swift. Life-and-death is the great matter.[113] [Because] the duration of our lives is short, if you wish to learn something and you would like to study something, just practice the Buddha Way and study the Buddhadharma. Literature, poetry, and the like are

尚、多般を兼学すべからず。況や教家の顕密の聖教、一向に擱く
べき也。仏祖の言語すら、多般を好み学すべからず。一事専にせ
ん。鈍根劣器のもの、かなふべからず。況や、多事を兼て、心想を
調へざらん、不可なり。

2-9

示云、

　昔、智覚禅師と云し人の発心出家の事。此師は初は官人也。
誇富、正直賢人也。有時、国司たりし時、官銭を盗で施行す。旁
人、是を官奏す。帝、聴て大に驚き怪む。諸臣皆怪む。罪過已に不
軽、死罪に行なはるべしと定りぬ。

　爰に帝、議して云、此臣は才人也、賢者也。今ことさら此罪を
犯す。若、深心有か。若、頸を斬ん時、悲愁たる気色有ば、速に可
斬。若、其の気色無んば、定めて深心有り、不可斬。

　勅使ひきさりて欲斬時、少も愁の気色無し。返りて喜ぶ気色あ
り。自云、今生の命は、一切衆生に施、と。使、驚き怪で返り奏聞
す。

　帝云、然り。定て深心有らん。此事有るべしと、兼て是を知れ
り。仍て其の故を問。

useless. It is unnecessary to [even] say why we should give them up. Even when you study the Buddhadharma and practice the Buddha Way, do not engage in a variety of extensive studies at the same time. Moreover, we should refrain from studying the exoteric and esoteric scriptures of the teaching schools.[114] We should not be fond of widely studying even the sayings of the buddhas and ancestors. For those of us who are dull-witted and of inferior capacity, it is not even possible to concentrate on a single thing and master it completely. Furthermore, it is not good to do many things at the same time and lose harmony of mind and thought.[115]

2-9

[*Dōgen*] *instructed*:

In ancient times, a person called Zen Master Zhijue[116] aroused the mind of awakening and left home. This master was originally a government official. He was a wealthy, straightforward, and wise man. While he was a provincial governor, he unlawfully appropriated official money and gave it to the people. One of the officials working with him reported this to the government. Upon hearing it, the emperor was astonished and puzzled. All of the ministers also thought it strange. Because the crime was not a minor one, it was decided that he would be put to death.

At that time, the emperor talked the matter over and said, "This officer is a man of talent and wisdom. Now, he intentionally committed this crime, but he might have deeply considered [his actions]. When he is about to be beheaded, if he looks sorrowful and regretful, cut off his head immediately. If he does not show such an expression, he certainly had some profound motivation; do not execute him."

When the imperial messenger brought him out for his beheading, he showed neither regret nor grief. Instead, he looked joyful. He said to himself, "I offer my life in this lifetime to all living beings." The messenger, astonished and beguiled, reported this to the emperor.

　師云、官を辞して命を捨て、施を行じて衆生に縁を結び、生を
仏家に稟て、一向、仏道を行ぜんと思、と。

　帝、是を感じて、許して出家せしむ。仍、延寿と名を賜て可殺
を、是を留むる故也。

　今の衲子も是ほどの心を、一度発すべき也。命を軽くし、生を
憐む心深くして、身を仏制に任せんと思ふ心を発すべし。若、前よ
り、此心一念も有らば、失はじと保つべし。これほどの心、一度不
発して、仏法、悟る事はあるべからず。

2-10

夜話に云く、

　祖席に禅話を覚得故実は、我本知り思ふ心を、次第に知識
の言に随て改めて去く也。仮令、仏と云は、我本知たる様は、相
好光明具足し、説法利生の徳有し、釈迦・弥陀等を仏と知たりと
も、知識、若、仏と云は、蝦蟆蚯蚓ぞ、と云はば、蝦蟆・蚯蚓を、是
を仏と信じて、日比の知恵を捨也。此蚯蚓上に、仏の相好光明、
種々の仏の所具の徳を求るも、猶、情見改まらざる也。只、当時の
見ゆる処を、仏と知る也。若、如是、言に従がつて、情見本執を
改めもて去けば、自、合ふ処あるべき也。然に、近代の学者、自ら
が情見を執して、己見にたがふ時は、仏とは、とこそ有べけれ、

The emperor said, "I thought so! He must have had some deeper motivation. I knew beforehand that he had some justification." Then he asked him what the reason was.

The master said, "I wanted to leave the bureaucracy, offer up my life, and practice in order to form a connection with living beings. I wish to be born in the Buddha's family and wholeheartedly practice the Buddha Way."

The emperor was moved by his aspiration and gave him permission to become a monk. Then the emperor gave him the Dharma name Yanshou, meaning "prolonged life." This was because he had been saved from capital punishment.

Today's patch-robed monks must also arouse aspiration like this at least once. We should arouse the mind that thinks little of our own life, has deep compassion for all living beings, and entrusts our bodily life to the Buddha's teachings. If we have already aroused such an aspiration even once, we should protect it and not lose it. It is not possible to actualize the Buddhadharma without having once aroused such an aspiration.

2-10

In an evening talk, [Dōgen] said:

In the tradition of the ancestors, the true way of understanding a Zen sermon is to follow the teacher's words and to gradually reform the mind that has known and thought [various fixed concepts] since time immemorial. Even if we have previously thought that a buddha has excellent characteristics, is fully equipped with radiant light, and has the virtue of preaching the Dharma and benefiting living beings, like Shakyamuni or Amitābha, we should [nonetheless] believe our teacher if he tells us that a buddha is nothing but a toad or an earthworm. We should give up our former knowledge. If we look for certain excellent characteristics in a toad or an earthworm, [such as] radiant light or other buddha virtues, [then] we still have not reformed our discriminating minds. Just know that what we see right now is buddha. If, in this way, we continually reform our discriminating minds

又、我存ずる様にたがへば、さは有まじ、なんどと言て、自が情量に似る事や有ると迷ひありく呈に、おほかた仏道の昇進無き也。

亦、身を惜て、百尺の竿頭に上て、手足を放て、一歩進め、と言時は、命有てこそ、仏道も学せめ、と云て、真実に知識に随順せざる也。能々可思量。

2-11

夜話云、

人は、世間の人も、衆事を兼学して、何れも能もせざらんよりは、只一事を能して、人前にしても、しつべきほどに、学すべき也。況や出世の仏法は、無始以来、修習せざる法也。故に今も、うとし。我が性も拙なし。高広なる仏法の事を、多般を兼れば、一事をも成ずべからず。一事を専にせんすら、本性昧劣の根器、今生に窮め難し。努々学人、一事を専にすべし。

犇問云、若然、何事いかなる行か、仏法に専ら好み修べき。

師云、

機に随、根に随べしと云へども、今祖席に相伝して専する処は坐禅也。此の行、能、衆機を兼、上中下根等、修し得べき法也。我、大宋天童先師の会下にして、此道理を聞て後、昼夜定坐

and fundamental attachments according to our teacher's instructions, we will naturally become one with the Way. Students of the present day, however, cling to their discriminating minds. Their thinking is based on their personal views that a buddha must be such and such; if what they hear conflicts with their ideas, they say that a buddha cannot be so. Having such an attitude and wandering here and there in delusion, searching for what reinforces their preconceptions, most of them never make any progress in the Buddha Way.

When [their teachers] say, "Climb to the top of a hundred-foot pole, then let go of your hands and feet and advance one step further,"[117] they hold their body dear and say, "I can only practice while I am alive." They do not truly follow their teachers. Consider this carefully.

2-11

In an evening talk, [Dōgen] said:

Even worldly people should focus on one thing and master it thoroughly enough to be able to perform it in front of others, instead of learning many things at the same time without truly mastering any of them. What's more, from the beginningless beginning, we have never learned and practiced the Buddhadharma that transcends the mundane world. Therefore, until now we have been unacquainted with it. Our natures are also inferior. If we try to learn extensively about the many lofty and boundless matters of the Buddhadharma, we will not master even a single thing. Because by nature our capacities are dull and poor, even if we try to concentrate on one thing, it is not possible to thoroughly master that one thing in this lifetime. Students, we should definitely concentrate on one single thing.

Ejō asked, "If that is the case, to which thing or practice of the Buddhadharma should we choose to devote ourselves?"

The master said:

Although it depends upon one's character and capabilities, down to the present day it is zazen that has been handed down and concentrated on in the communities of the ancestors. This practice is suitable

して、極熱極寒には発病しつべしとて、諸僧、暫く放下しき。我、其時自思はく、直饒発病して死べくとも、猶、只、是を修すべし。不病して修せずんば、此身労しても何の用ぞ。病して死なば本意也。大宋国の善知識の会にて修し死て、よき僧にさばくられたらん、先づ結縁也。日本にて死なば、是ほどの人々に、如法仏家の儀式にて、沙汰すべからず。修行して未契先に死せば、好結縁として、生を仏家にも受べし。修行せずして、身を久く持ても、無詮也。何の用ぞ。況や身を全くし病不作と思ふ程に、不知、又海にも入、横死にも逢はん時は、後悔如何。如是、案じつづけて、思切て昼夜端坐せしに、一切に病不作。

如今、各々も、一向に思切て修して見よ。十人は十人ながら、可得道也。先師天童のすすめ、如是。

2-12

示云、

人は思切て命をも捨て、身肉手足をも斬事は、中々せらるる也。然れば、世間の事を思ひ、名利執心の為にも、如是思ふ也。

for people of all capacities. This Dharma can be practiced equally
by those of superior, mediocre, or inferior capabilities. After I heard
this truth while I was in the assembly of my late teacher Tiantong[118]
in great Song China, I sat zazen constantly day and night. When it
was extremely hot or cold, many monks gave up sitting for a while
because they were afraid of getting sick. At that time, I thought to
myself, "Even though I might become sick and die, I should practice
this regardless. If I do not practice when I am not sick, then what is
the use of taking care of this body? Even if I get sick and die, it will
be in accord with my original intention. If I practice and die in the
assembly of an eminent teacher in great Song China and am buried
by such wonderful monks, for one thing it will establish good affinity
[with the Buddhadharma]. If I die in Japan, it will be impossible to
have my funeral service performed by such people or according to
authentic[119] Buddhist ceremonies. If I die while practicing, before
I can accord with the Way, because of this good affinity I will once
again be born into the Buddha's family. Without practice it is meaningless to live long. What would be the use of [such a life]? Furthermore, even if I think I can keep my body healthy and free of
illness, I might drown in the ocean or meet some accidental death.
How regrettable this would be!" I continued to think in this way and
practiced upright, sitting day and night with this determination. In
the end, I never got sick at all.

Now, each of you should practice single-mindedly and wholeheartedly. Ten out of ten of you will be able to attain the Way. This is how
my late teacher Tiantong encouraged us.

2-12

[Dōgen] instructed:

It is rather easy to lay down one's own life, or to cut off one's
flesh, hands, or feet, in an emotional outburst.[120] Therefore, people
might think of doing such things for the sake of worldly affairs or

只、依来る時に触、物に随て、心器を調る事、難き也。学者、命を
捨ると思て、暫く推し静めて、云べき事をも、修すべき事をも、道
理に順ずるか、順ぜざるかと案じて、道理に順ぜば、いひもし、行
じもすべき也。

2-13

示云、

　学道の人、衣粮を煩す事莫れ。只、仏制を守て、心世事に出
す事莫れ。

　仏言く、衣服に糞掃衣あり、食に常乞食あり。何れの世にか、
此二の事、尽る事有ん。無常迅速なるを忘れて、徒らに世事に煩
事莫れ。露命の暫く存ぜる間、只、仏道を思て、余事を事とする
事莫れ。

　或人、問云、名利の二道は、捨離しがたしと云へども、行道の
大なる礙なれば、不可不捨、故に捨是。衣粮の二事は小縁なりと
云へども、行者の大事なり。糞掃衣、常乞食、是は上根の所行、
又、是、西天の風流也。神丹の叢林には常住物等あり。故に其労
なし。我国の寺院には常住物なし。乞食の儀も、即絶たり、不伝。
下根不堪の身、如何がせん。爾らば、予が如きは、檀那の信施
を貪らんとするも、虚受の罪、随来る。田商仕工を営むも、是、邪
命食なり。只、天運に任せんとすれ、果報、又、貧道なり。飢寒来
らん時、是を愁として行道を碍つべし。或人、諌めて云、汝が行
儀、太あらじ。時機を顧ざるに似たり。下根なり。末世也。如是、修

because of their attachments to fame and profit. And yet, encountering various things and situations moment by moment, it is most difficult to harmonize our minds. Students of the Way! We must calm our minds as if giving up our lives and consider if what we are about to say or do is in accordance with the truth or not. If it is, we should act.

2-13

[Dōgen] *instructed*:

Students of the Way! Do not be troubled when it comes to food and clothing. Just maintain the Buddha's precepts, and do not concern yourself with worldly affairs.

The Buddha said, "For clothing, there are robes made of abandoned rags;[121] for food, there is always begging." In what age will these two things ever be exhausted? Do not forget the swiftness of impermanence or be vainly disturbed by worldly affairs. While we temporarily have our dew-like human lives, think exclusively of the Buddha Way, and do not be concerned with other things.

Someone remarked, "Although fame and profit are difficult to give up, because their pursuit is a great obstruction to the practice of the Way, they should be abandoned. Therefore, I will give them up. Although clothing and food are minor things, they are important for practitioners. Wearing clothes made of abandoned rags and only begging for food were practices of superior people. Moreover, that was the custom in India. The monasteries in China have [communal] permanent property.[122] Therefore, they do not need to worry about such things. In the temples in our country, there is no such property. The practice of begging has ceased and has not been transmitted at all. What should inferior people like me who cannot endure [such practices] do? If someone like me tries to gather alms from faithful lay supporters, I will violate the precept that prohibits deceitfully receiving donations [while in fact lacking virtue]. Earning a living as a farmer,

行せば、又退転の因縁と成ぬべし。或は、一檀那をも相語らひ、若は、一外護をも契て、閑居静所にして、一身を助て、衣粮に労事無くして、仏道を行ずべし。是、即、財物等を貪に非ず。時の活計を具して修行すべし、と。此の言を聞と云へども、未信用、如是用心如何。

答云、

夫、衲子の行履は仏祖の風流を労すべし。三国殊なりと云へども、真実学道の者、未有如是事。只、心を世事にいたす事莫れ。一向に道を学すべき也。

仏言く、衣鉢の外は、寸分も不貯。乞食の余分、飢たる衆生に施す。直饒受来るとも、寸分も不可貯。況や馳走有んや。

外典に云、朝聞道夕に死とも可也。直饒、飢死、寒死すとも、一日一時なりとも、仏教に随べし。万劫千生、幾回か生じ幾回か死せん。皆是、如是の世縁妄執也。今生一度仏制に順て餓死せん、是、永劫の安楽なるべし。

何況未だ一大蔵教の中にも、三国伝来の仏祖有て、一人も餓死寒死たるを不聞。世間衣粮の資具、生得命分なり。依求不来、不求非不来。正に任運として心ををく事莫れ。末法也、下根也、と云て、今生に（心を）不発、何れの生にか得道せん。直饒、空生・迦葉の如に非ずとも、只、随分に学道すべき也。

外典云、西施毛嬙に非ざれども、色を好む者は色を好む。飛兎緑耳に非ざれども、馬を好む者は馬を好む。龍肝豹胎に非ざ

merchant, warrior, or craftsman is wrong livelihood[123] [for a monk]. If I trust the workings of the heavens, I will remain an inferior monk as a result of [my] inferior karma. When hunger and cold come, I will be in distress and my practice will be hindered. Someone admonished me, saying, 'Your way of practice is too extreme. It seems you do not reflect on this age and your capacity. Our faculties are inferior, and this is the [degenerate] age of the last Dharma.[124] Such a manner of practice will become causes and conditions for regression [from the Way]. Arrange for support from a donor or get protection from a patron, take care of your body by living in a quiet place without worrying about food or clothing, and practice the Buddha Way peacefully. This is [what it means] not to covet property or belongings. You should practice after having provided for your temporal livelihood.' Although I listened to his admonishment, I still do not believe it. What do you think about such a frame of mind?"

[*Dōgen*] *replied*:

The conduct of patch-robed monks is to strive to carry out the practice style of the buddhas and ancestors. Although [the customs of] the three countries[125] are different, those who truly study the Way never practice in such a manner [as described by this person]. Simply disregard worldly affairs. We should single-mindedly study the Way.

The Buddha said, "Do not store up anything except robes and a bowl. Any extra food you have received through begging should be given away to hungry living beings." Even when you receive [more than enough], do not store it up. Moreover, we should not run after things.

In a non-Buddhist text it is said, "If we hear the Way in the morning, it is fine to die that evening."[126] Even if we might die from the cold or from starvation, we should follow the Buddha's teaching, even if only for one day or one hour. In ten thousand eons and thousands of lifetimes, how many times are we born, and how many times do we die? [This cycle of birth and death] is caused only by such blind clinging to worldly affairs [like that mentioned by this person]. To die of starvation while following the Buddha's teachings in this lifetime would bring about eternal peace and joy.

れども、味を好む者、味を好む。只随分の賢を用るのみ也。俗猶有此儀。（僧）又、如是なるべし。

　況や又、仏二十年の福分を以て、末法の我等に施す。是因て、天下の叢林、人天供養不絶。如来神通の福徳自在なる、猶、馬麦を食して夏を過しましましき。末法の弟子、豈、是を不慕や。

　問云、破戒にして空く人天の供養を受け、無道心にして徒に如来の福分を費さんよりは、在家人にしたがうて、在家の事を作て、命いきて、能修道せん事如何。

　答云、

　誰か云し、破戒無道心なれと。只、強て道心ををこし、仏法を行ずべき也。

　何況や持戒破戒を論ぜず、初心後心をわかたず、斉く如来の福分を与とは見たり。未、破戒ならば還俗すべし、無道心ならば修行せざれ、とは不見。誰人か、初めより道心ある。只、如是、発し難きを発し、行じ難きを行ずれば、自然に増進する也。人々皆、有仏性也。徒に卑下する事莫れ。

　又、云、文選に云、国為一人興、先賢為後愚廃文。言ふ心は、国に賢一人不出来、賢の跡廃也。是を思べし。

However, in the collections of all the Buddhist sutras, I have never read of a single buddha or ancestor who transmitted the Dharma in the three countries who died of starvation or from the cold. As a gift, each person in this world receives, along with an allotted life span, a certain amount of food and clothing. They do not come as a result of being sought after, nor do they stop coming when they are not sought after. Just leave them to fate, and do not trouble your mind about them. If we refrain from arousing the mind of awakening in this lifetime, excusing ourselves on the grounds that this is the degenerate age of the last Dharma, then in which lifetime will it be possible to attain the Way? Even if we are not the equals of Subhūti[127] or Mahākāśyapa,[128] we should practice to our fullest capability.

In a non-Buddhist text it is said, "Even if she is not as beautiful as Xishi or Maoqiang, those who love women will love women.[129] Even if it is not as great as Feitu or Lu'er, those who love horses will love horses.[130] Even if it is not as delicious as dragon's liver or leopard's embryo, those who love flavor will love flavor."[131] We just have to use whatever wisdom we have. Even laypeople have this attitude. Monks must also be like this.

Moreover, the Buddha offered twenty years of his longevity to us living in this degenerate age of the last Dharma. As a result, the offerings and support to the monasteries in this world given by human and heavenly beings have not ceased. Though the Tathāgata had divine powers and virtues and was able to use them at will, he spent a summer practice period eating grain meant for horses.[132] What can his disciples in the age of the last Dharma do but yearn to follow his example.

It was asked, "Rather than vainly receiving offerings from human or heavenly beings while breaking the precepts, or wastefully exhausting the endowment of the Tathāgata without the mind of awakening, would it not be better to live as a layperson, engaging in ordinary family work, keeping ourselves alive, and continuing the practice of the Way?"

2-14

雑話の次に云、

　世間の男女老少、多く雑談の次、或は交会淫色等の事を談
ず。是を以て心を慰とし、興言とする事あり。一旦、心を遊戯し、徒
然も慰むと云とも、僧は尤禁断すべき事也。俗猶、よき人、実しき
人の礼儀を存じ、げにげにしき談の時、出来らぬ事也。只、乱酔
放逸なる時の談なり。況や、僧は専ら仏道を思べし。希有異躰の
乱僧の所言也。

　宋土の寺院なんどには、惣て雑談をせざれば、左右に及ば
ず。我国も、近ごろ建仁寺の僧正存生の時は、一向、あからさま

[Dōgen] answered:

Who said anything about breaking the precepts or being without the mind of awakening? We should simply arouse the mind of awakening forcibly and practice the Buddhadharma.

Moreover, it is said that the legacy of the Tathāgata's blessing is bestowed equally, without regard to whether we maintain the precepts or break them, or whether we are beginners or advanced practitioners. It is not written anywhere that we must return to the mundane world if we have violated the precepts or we must stop practicing if we lack the mind of awakening. Who has the mind of awakening from the outset? If we just arouse what is difficult to arouse and practice what is difficult to practice, in this way we will naturally progress. Each one of us has Buddha-nature. Do not meaninglessly deprecate yourselves.

Also, in the *Selections of Refined Literature*, it is written, "The prosperity of the country is brought about by a single wise person. The Way of the ancients later dies out because of a fool."[133] This means that if a single person of wisdom appears, the country will flourish, and if a single fool appears, the way of the ancients will disappear. Consider this well.

2-14

In a miscellaneous talk, [Dōgen] said:

When engaged in idle talk, men and women in society, both the young and old, often chat about lewd things. In doing so, they amuse their minds and beguile themselves. Although such idle chatter seems to entertain their minds and divert them from boredom momentarily, monks should completely refrain from such talk. Even in lay society, when well-educated and sincere people discuss some serious subject with due courtesy, they do not engage in such talk. They do so only when they are drunk or otherwise unrestrained. Needless to say, monks must concern themselves only with the Buddha Way. Only a few eccentric and immoral monks engage in such indecent talk.

にも如是の言語、不出来。滅後も、在世の門弟子等、少々残留時は、一切に言ざりき。近ごろ、七八年より以来、今出の若人達、時々談也。存外の次第也。

　聖教の中にも、麁強悪業人覚悟、無利の言説は能障正道。只、打出し言ふ語すら、無利言説は、障道の因縁也。況や如然言説ことばに引れて、即ち、心も起りつべし。尤も、用心すべき也。わざとことさらいで、かくなん、いはじとせずとも、あしき事と知なば、漸々に退治すべきなり。

2-15

夜話云、

　世人、多く、善事を成す時は、人に知れんと思ひ、悪事を成時は、人に知れじと思ふに依て、此心、冥衆の心にかなはざるに依て、所作の善事に感応なく、密に所作悪事には罰有る也。是に依て返りて、自思はく、善事には験なし、仏法の利益なし、なんど思へる也。是、即、邪見也。尤も可改。人も不知時は、潜に善事を成し、悪事を成て後は、発露して咎を悔ゆ。如是すれば、即、密々に所成善事には、感応有り、露たる悪事は懺悔せられて、罪、滅する故に、自然、現益も有る也。可知当果。

In the monasteries in Song China, because monks do not engage in idle talk, they never speak of such [lewd] matters. Even in our country, while the superintendent of monks and abbot of Kennin-ji [Eisai] was alive, such talk did not occur at all. Even after his death, while a few of his disciples were still at the monastery, people did not speak of such things. Lately, over the last seven or eight years, the young monks have sometimes indulged in idle talk.[134] This is an unexpected turn of events.

In the sacred teachings it is said, "Though coarse and violent actions may sometimes cause people to wake up, worthless speech obstructs the true Way."[135] Even if it is a word that comes to the lips unintentionally, unbeneficial talk can be a cause and a condition for the obstruction of the Way. Moreover, such lewd talk might cause an [indecent] mind to arise. We must be most careful. Without intentionally forcing yourself not to use such language, realize it is an unwholesome thing and you will be able to reform gradually.

2-15

In an evening talk, [Dōgen] said:

Most people in the world want their good deeds to be known by others when they do good things. When they do wicked things, they want their misdeeds to be hidden from other people. Because this mindset is not in accord with the unseen deities, good things done by [such people] go unrewarded, and their wicked deeds done in secret bring about punishment.[136] Therefore, they privately lament that there are no rewards for good deeds and [there is] no merit in the Buddhadharma. This is a perverted view. We must certainly reform it. While no one is watching, we should do good things in secret. After we have done something unwholesome, we should expose our misdeeds and repent. When you act in this manner, good deeds done in secret will have rewards, and exposed wrong deeds will be repented so that punishment can be dispelled. Therefore, there will naturally be benefit in this present lifetime, and you will [also] be sure of the results in future lifetimes.

爰に有在家人来て問云、近代、在家人、衆僧を供養し、仏法を帰敬するに、多く、不吉の事、因出来、邪見起りて、帰敬三宝、不帰思ふ、如何。

答云、

即、衆僧、仏法の咎に非ず。即、在家人の自誤也。其故は、仮令、人目ばかり、持戒持斎の由、現ずる僧をば貴くし供養し、破戒無慚の僧の飲酒肉食等するをば、不当也と思て不供養。此差別の心、実に仏意に背けり。因て、帰敬の功も空く、感応無也。戒の中にも、処々に此の心を誡めたり。僧と云はば、徳の有無を不択。只、可供養也。殊に、其の外相を以て、内徳の有無不可定。末世の比丘、聊、外相尋常なる処と見れども、又、是に勝たる悪心も悪事もある也。仍て、好僧、悪僧を差別し思事無て、仏弟子なれば、此方を貴びて、平等の心にて供養帰敬もせば、必、仏意に叶て、利益も速疾にあるべき也。

又、冥機冥応、顕機顕応等の四句有る事を可思。又、現生後報等の三時業の事も有り。此等の道理、能々可学也。

Once a certain layperson came and asked, "These days, although laypeople make offerings to monks, and take refuge in and venerate the Buddhadharma, much misfortune occurs. For this reason, evil thoughts have arisen, and people believe they should no longer take refuge in the Three Treasures. What do you think of this?"

[*Dōgen*] *replied*:

This is not the fault of monks or the Buddhadharma but a mistake on behalf of the laypeople themselves. As for the reason for this, for example, they revere and make offerings only to monks who publicly observe the precepts and the eating regulations, but they do not make offerings to shameless monks who break the precepts, drink alcohol, and eat meat, judging them to be worthless. This biased and discriminating mind truly goes against the intention of the Buddha. Because of this, their taking of refuge and reverence is in vain, and there are no positive consequences. Here and there within the precepts, there are admonitions against this frame of mind.[137] You should make offerings to all monks, regardless of whether they have any virtue or not. Most importantly, never judge whether or not they have inner virtue based on their outward appearances. Although monks in this degenerate age look somewhat normal in their outward appearances, they may have much more corrupt minds and do wicked deeds. Therefore, without discriminating between good and bad monks, respect them all simply because they are the Buddha's disciples; make offerings and take refuge with a mind of equality. Then you will surely be in accordance with the Buddha's intention, and you will receive benefits instantaneously.

Also, we should consider the four phrases: "unseen action, unseen response; seen action, seen response [unseen action, seen response; seen action, unseen response]."[138] There is also the principle of karma and its effects in the three periods of time [we receive the effects of karma in the present lifetime, in the next lifetime, or in some later lifetime]. Study these principles very carefully.[139]

2-16

夜話云、

　若、人来て用事を云中に、或は人に物を乞、或は訴訟等の事をも云はんとて、一通の状をも所望する事出来有るに、其の時、我は非人也。遁世籠居の身なれば、在家等の人に、非分の事を謂んは非なり、とて、眼前の人の所望を不叶、臨其時思量すべき也。実に非人の法には似たれども、不有然。捜其心中、猶、我は遁世非人也。非分の事を人に云はば、人、定て悪く思ひてん、と云ふ道理を思て不聞、猶、是、我執名聞也。只、眼前の人の為に、一分の利益は可為からんをば、人の悪く思ん事を不顧、可為也。此事、非分也。悪るし、とて、うとみもし、中をも違はんも、如是不覚の知音、中違ん、何か可悪。顕には、非分の僻事をすると人には見れども、内には我執を破て、名聞を捨つる、第一の用心也。

　仏菩薩は、人の来て云時は、身肉手足をも斬る也。況や、人来て、一通の状を乞ん、少分の悪事を、名聞ばかりを思て、其事を不聞は、我執の咎也。人は、ひじりならず、非分の要事云人かな、と、無所詮、思ふとも、我は、捨名聞、一分の人の利益とならば、真実の道に可相応也。古人も、其義あるかと見る事多し。予も、其義を思ふ。少々、檀那知音の、不思懸事を人に申伝てと云をば、紙少分こそ入、一分の利益をなすは、やすき事也。

2-16

In an evening talk, [Dōgen] said:

Suppose someone comes to talk about his business and asks us to write a letter to solicit something from someone, or to help him in a lawsuit or the like, but we turn down the request, excusing ourselves on the grounds that we are not people [of the mundane world], that we have withdrawn and have nothing to do with worldly affairs, and that it is wrong for renunciants like us to speak about unsuitable things with laypeople. [However,] we must consider the specifics of the situation. Although such an attitude truly seems like the way of a renunciant, it might not be. When we deeply examine our mind, [we can see] that we dismiss the request because we think we are monks who have left the mundane world, and people might think badly of us if we say something improper for a renunciant. This still shows our ego-attachment to fame and reputation. For the sake of the person in front of us, we should do anything that may bring even a little benefit [to them] without consideration of whether others might think badly of us. Even if we become estranged from our friends or quarrel with them because they think we did something improper, it should not concern us to break off [relations] with such unwise people. Although outwardly it may seem to others that we are doing something unacceptable, our primary concern should be to break off the ego-attachment inside of us and throw away any desire for fame and reputation.

When someone comes to ask them for help, buddhas and bodhisattvas cut off even their own flesh, hands, or feet. How much more should we be willing to help a person who asks us to simply write a letter. If we reject the request, being concerned with [the effect on] our personal reputation from a tiny wrongdoing, we are guilty of ego-attachment. Although without careful consideration others may regard us as unworthy renunciants and say inappropriate things, if we throw away our concern for fame and bring even a little benefit to others, we are surely in accordance with the true Way. We find many examples

芽、問云、此の事、実に然なり、但し、善事にて、人の利益とならん事を人にも云伝へんは、さるべし。若し僻事を以て、人の所帯を取んと思ひ、或は、人の為に悪事を云をば、可云伝乎。如何。

師答云、

理非等の事は、我が非可知。只、一通の状を乞へば与れども、任理非、可沙汰、由、云ふ人にも、状にも可載。請取て沙汰せん人こそ、理非をば可明けれ。非我分上。如是の事を、枉理、人に云ん事、又非也。又、現の僻事なれども、我を大事にも思ふ人の、此の人の云ん事は、善悪不違と思ふ程の知音檀那の処へ、僻事を以て不得心の所望をなさば、其をば、今の人の所望をば、一往聞とも、彼状にも、難去申せば、申すばかり也。道理に任て可有沙汰、可云也。一切に是ば、彼も此も、遺恨不可有也。

如是事、人に対面をもし、出来る事に任て能々思量すべき也。所詮は、事に触て、名聞我執を可捨也。

2-17

夜話云、

of the ancient sages who appear to have had the same attitude. I also believe in these examples. It is an easy thing to help a small amount when our supporters or friends ask us to write something for them, even if it is a bit unexpected. We need only a sheet of paper.

Ejō asked, "This is certainly true. Of course it is as you just said if what we write is good and beneficial to the recipient. But what about cases in which someone wants to take another's property by some evil means, or someone tries to slander another? Should we still transmit such a message?"

The master replied:

It is not for us to decide whether it is right or wrong. We should explain to the person who asks us, and also state in the letter, that we are writing it because we were asked to do so, and tell [the recipient] that they should decide whether it is right or wrong to deal with the matter. The person who receives the letter and has to deal with the problem should decide whether it is right or wrong. It is not our business. It is also wrong to ask the person [we write to] to do something that bends the rules [for the person we are writing for] regarding such matters. If we ask a friend or a patron to do something wrong or unacceptable, he might feel compelled to do it because of his respect for us, even though the request was actually made by the person for whom we are writing the letter. In this case, we should write in the letter, "I am writing this letter simply because I have been asked importunately. Please deal with this matter reasonably." If we treat each situation in this way, no one will hold a grudge.

We must consider things like this very meticulously in every encounter with people or situations. The primary concern is to cast aside the desire for fame and ego-attachment in each situation.

2-17

In an evening talk, [Dōgen] said:

In the mundane world today and among those of the monastic world, people want to make sure that their good deeds are known

今、世、出世間の人、多分は、善事をなしては、かまへて人に識れんと思ひ、悪事をなしては、人に不被知思ふ。依此、内外不相応の事出来る。相構て、内外相応し、誤りを悔ひ、実徳を蔵て、外相を不荘、好事をば譲他人、悪事をば向己、志気有るべき也。

問云、実徳を蔵し、外相を荘ざらん事、実に可然。但、仏菩薩の大悲、利生を以て本とす。無智の道俗等、外相の不善を見て、是を謗難せば、謗僧の罪を感ぜん。実徳を不知とも、外相を見て貴、供養せば、一分の福分たるべし。是等の斟酌、いかなるべきぞ。

答云、

外相を不荘と云て、即、放逸ならば、又是、道理にたがう。実徳をかくすと云て、在家等の前に悪行を現ぜん、又是、破戒の甚しき也。只、希有の道心者の由を人に知られんと思ひ、在身失を人に不被知と思ふ。諸天善神及三宝の冥に知見する処を不愧、人に貴られんと思ふ心を誡る也。只、臨時、触事、為興法為利生、諸事を斟酌すべき也。擬して後、言、思て後、行じて、率暴なる事勿れと也。所詮は、一切の事に臨で、可案道理也。念々に不留、日々に遷流して、無常迅速なる事、眼前の道理也。不可待知識経巻教。念々に、無期明日。思当日当時許、後日は甚だ不定也。知り難ければ、只、今日ばかりも、身命の在らん程、可思順仏道也。順仏道者は、為興法利生、捨身命、行諸事、去也。

問云、順仏教勧、可行乞食等歟、如何。

to others, and when they do a bad thing, they try to prevent others from noticing. Because of this, a discordance between their internal [thought] and external [appearances] occurs. We should carefully aspire to make the inner self correspond with outside appearances by repenting of faults, hiding our real virtue, and not being ostentatious; we should offer good things to others and accept bad things for ourselves.

Someone asked, "Surely, we should maintain the attitude of hiding our true virtue and not adorning our outside appearances. And yet, the essence of the great compassion of buddhas and bodhisattvas is to benefit living beings. If ignorant monks or laypeople see our unwholesome external appearances and blame us, they will become guilty of slandering the sangha. Even if they do not understand true inner virtue, if they see good outside appearances, venerate us, and make offerings, they will receive merit that brings about happiness. What do you think of such considerations for others?"

[*Dōgen*] *replied*:

Even if we do not adorn our outward appearances, if we become self-indulgent, it is against the principle of the Way. If we [intentionally] carry out unwholesome deeds in front of laypeople with the stated excuse of hiding our true virtue, this is certainly a gross violation of the precepts. [However,] some monks merely wish to gain fame as rare people with the mind of awakening and want other people not to know their faults. I caution such shameless people who desire to be respected by others: the unseen good heavenly beings, the guardian deities, and the Three Treasures are watching them. We must simply consider all things carefully such that the Dharma flourishes and living beings are benefited in every moment and situation. It is said, "Speak after careful consideration; act after attentive thought; do not act rashly." Ponder over what is reasonable in each and every situation you encounter. [Our life] changes moment by moment and flows swiftly day by day. Everything is impermanent and changing rapidly. This is the reality before our eyes. We do not need to wait for

答云、

　可然、但、是は、順土風、可有斟酌。なにとしても、利生も広く、我が行も進むかたに、可就也。是等の作法、道路不浄にして、着仏衣、行歩せば、可穢。亦、人民貧窮にして、次第乞食も、不可叶。行道も可退、利益も不広歟。只、守土風、尋常、行仏道居たらば、上下の輩、自作供養べし。自行化他、成就せん、如是の事も、臨時触事、思量道理、不思人目、忘自益、仏道利生の方によき様に可計。

2-18

示云、

　学道の人、就可捨世情、可有重々の用心。捨世、捨家、捨身、捨心也。能々、可思量也。

the teaching of masters or scriptures [to see this]. In every moment, do not expect that tomorrow will come. Think only of this day and this moment. Because days to come are very much uncertain and we cannot foresee what will happen, we should resolve to follow the Buddha Way while we are still alive, if only for today. The followers of the Buddhadharma give up their bodily lives and act to enable the Dharma to flourish and bring benefit to living beings.

Someone asked, "According to the Buddha's teachings, should we practice begging for food?"

[*Dōgen*] *replied*:

Yes, we should. However, we have to take into consideration the customs and conditions of each country. Whatever the situation, we should choose what is best for the benefit of living beings and for the progress of our own practice. As for the manners of begging, because roads in this country are dirty, if we walk around wearing Buddhist robes, they will become soiled. Also, because people are poor, it may be impossible to beg without discrimination.[140] [If we cling to such a traditional form,] our practice could regress, and we would be unable to benefit living beings. If we practice in a humble manner following the customs of the country, people of all classes will support us by making offerings of their own accord. Then, practice for ourselves and for the benefit of others will be fulfilled. In each situation, try to choose what is best for the sake of the Buddha Way and for the benefit of others. Do not be concerned with your personal reputation, and forget your own profit.

2-18[141]

[*Dōgen*] *instructed*:

Students of the Way! In giving up worldly passions, we must be very careful in several ways. Give up the world, give up your family, give up your body, and give up your mind. Consider this well.

遁世、隠居山林、不絶我重代家、有思家門親族事。

遁捨家、捨離親族境界、思我身苦事不為、病可発、仏道不行思、未捨身也。

又、不借身、難行苦行すれども、心不入仏道、我心に違く事をば、仏道なれども不為思、不捨心也。

正法眼蔵随聞記　二　終

Even among those who retreat from the world and live secluded in the mountains or forests, there are some who fear that their families, which have persisted for many generations, will cease to exist, and so they become anxious about their family members and relatives.

Although some people depart from their homes and give up family or property, there are those who have not yet given up their bodies. They think that they should not do anything physically painful and should avoid practicing anything that may cause sickness, even though they know it to be the Buddha Way.

Furthermore, even if they may carry out hard and painful practices without clinging to their bodily lives, their minds have not yet entered the Buddha Way. If they resolve not to act against their own minds even if these actions are the Buddha Way, then they have not yet given up their minds.

The End of the Second Book of *Shōbōgenzō Zuimonki*

正法眼蔵随聞記　三
侍者　懐奘　編

3-1

示云、

　行者、先、調伏心、身をも世をも捨事は易き也。只、付言語、付行儀、思人目。此事は悪事なれば、人、悪く可思とて、不作、我、此事をせんこそ、仏法者と人は見め、とて、触事、能事をせんとするも、猶、世情也。然ればとて、又、恣に、任我意、悪事をするは、一向の悪人也。所詮は、忘悪心、忘我身、只、一向、為仏法、すべき也。向ひ来らん事にしたがつて可用心也。初心の行者は、先づ世情なりとも、人情なりとも、悪事をば心に制して、善事をば身に行ずるが、即ち、身心をすつるにて有る也。

3-2

示云、

SHŌBŌGENZŌ ZUIMONKI, BOOK 3

Compiled by the attendant Ejō

3-1

[*Dōgen*] *instructed*:

Practitioners! If we first regulate[142] the mind, it is easy to renounce the body as well as the world. As for our speech and behavior, we only think of how other people view us. We refrain from doing wicked things [only] because these are not good and other people will think ill of us; we do good things at every occasion [only] because others will consider us to be people of the Buddhadharma. These are still worldly sentiments. And yet, if we indulge our desires and do unwholesome things, we are wholly wrongdoers. After all, we should forget our wicked minds and our own bodies and simply do things for the sake of the Buddhadharma. We should be careful [regarding this point] when encountering each and every thing. As for beginners in practice, whether it is worldly sentiment or human sentiment,[143] control your mind, practice good things, and do not do unwholesome things. This is the meaning of renouncing body and mind.

3-2

[*Dōgen*] *instructed*:

　故僧正、建仁寺に御せし時、独の貧人来て道て云、我家、貧にして絶煙、及数日。夫婦子息両三人、餓死しなんとす。慈悲をもて、是を救ひ給へ、と云ふ。

　其時、房中に都て、衣食財物等無りき。思慮をめぐらすに計略尽ぬ。時に薬師の仏像を造らんとて、光の料に、打のべたる銅、少分ありき。取之、自、打折て、束円めて、与彼貧客云、以是、食物をかへて可塞餓。彼俗、悦で退出ぬ。

　門弟子等歎じて云く、正く是仏像の光也。以て与俗人、仏物己用の罪如何。

　僧正答云、実に然也。但、思仏意、身肉手足分て可施衆生。現に、可餓死衆生には、直饒、以全躰与とも、叶仏意。又、我れ、依此罪、縦可堕悪趣、只、可救衆生餓云々。先達の心中のたけ、今の学人も可思、莫忘事。

　又、或時、僧正の門弟の僧云、今の建仁寺の寺敷、河原に近し。後代に応有水難。

　僧正云、我等後代の亡失、不可思之。西天の祇園精舎も、礎計留れり。しかれども、寺院建立の功徳、不可失。又、当時、一年半年の行道、其の功、莫大なるべし。

　今思之、寺院の建立、実に一期の大事なれば、未来際をも兼て、無難様にとこそ可思けれども、さる心中にも、如是道理を被存心のたけ、実可思之。

While the late superintendent of monks [Eisai][144] was residing at Kennin-ji, a poor man came and said, "My family is so destitute that we have had no food to cook for several days. My wife and I and a few of our children are about to die of starvation. With your compassion, please help us."

At that time there was no clothing, food, or other property in the temple at all. Although he turned it over in his mind, he could not think of a plan [to help the man]. At the time there was a small, thin piece of copper to make the halo in the construction of a statue of the Medicine Buddha.[145] He took it, broke it, rolled it up, and gave it to the poor man, saying, "Exchange this for food and relieve your family from hunger." The layman was delighted and left.

[Eisai]'s disciples were surprised and disappointed, saying, "That is nothing less than the halo for a Buddha statue. You gave it to a layman. Is that not a violation of the precept against making personal use of property belonging to the Buddha treasure?"[146]

The superintendent of monks replied, "Yes, it certainly is. However, when we think of the Buddha's intention, he would cut off and offer even his own flesh, hands, and feet to living beings.[147] Even if we gave the whole body of the Buddha to living beings who are actually about to die of starvation, it would be in accord with the Buddha's intention. And also, because of this wrongdoing, even if I have to fall into an evil rebirth,[148] I would [still] simply rescue living beings from starvation." Today's students should reflect on the core of this predecessor's heart. Never forget this.

One time, a monk who was a disciple of the superintendent of monks said, "The current site of Kennin-ji is close to the banks of the [Kamo] river.[149] In the future there could be a disastrous flood."

The superintendent of monks said, "We should not worry about the loss of things in the future. Even at the site of the Jetavana monastery[150] in India, only cornerstones remain. However, the merit of founding a temple is never lost. Moreover, the virtue of practicing

3-3

夜話に云、

唐の太宗の時、魏徴、奏して云、土民謗帝事あり。帝の云、寡
人、仁あつて人に謗られば、不可為愁。仁無して人に褒られば、
可愁之。

俗、猶、如是。僧尤可有此心。慈悲あり道心ありて、愚癡人に
被謗、被譏、くるしかるべからず。無道心にして、人に被思有道、
是を能々可慎。

又、示云、

隋の文帝の云、密々の徳を修して、あくるをまつ。言ふ心は、
能き道徳を修して、あくるをまちて民を厳すると也。僧猶、不及、
尤可用心也。只、内々、修道業、自然に道徳可露外。自不期不望
道心道悳露外被知人。只、専、随仏教順祖道行けば、人、自、帰
道徳也。

此に学人の誤出来る様は、人に貴びられて、財宝出来たるを
以て、道徳彰たると、自も思ひ、人も知也。是、即、天魔波旬の、
心に付たると可知。尤可思量。教の中にも、是をば魔の所為と云

the Way right now, even if only for a year or half a year, is truly enormous."

Now, as I think about this, because constructing a temple was truly a great event in his lifetime, it would have been completely natural [for Eisai] to try to avoid a future disaster. And yet, deep in his heart he [instead] had a noble sentiment such as this. We should consider this carefully.

3-3

In an evening talk, [Dōgen] said:

During the reign of Taizong of the Tang dynasty, Wei Zheng reported to the throne, saying, "Some of the people defame Your Majesty."[151] The emperor said, "As a humble man, if I am benevolent and yet am defamed by the people, I do not worry. I should worry if I were praised by the people despite lacking benevolence."

Even a layperson can have an attitude like this. We monks in particular should have this same mental attitude. If we have compassion and the mind of awakening, we do not need to worry about being slandered by ignorant people. [Only] if they lack the mind of awakening must [monks] be very careful that people regard them as people of the Way.

[Dōgen] also instructed:

Emperor Wen[152] of the Sui dynasty said, "We should secretly cultivate virtue and wait until it is revealed [on its own]." What he meant is that he should nurture virtue until it is naturally expressed and then govern his people with benevolence. If we monks do not yet have an attitude such as his, we should be most careful. Only if we inwardly practice activities of the Way will virtue be naturally revealed outwardly. We should not expect or desire our mind of awakening and our virtue to be expressed and known by other people. If we simply continue to follow the Buddha's teachings and the ancestral Way, people will naturally take refuge in the virtue of the Way.

也。未聞、三国の例、財宝に富、愚人の帰敬を以て可為道徳。道
心と云は、昔より三国、皆、貧にして、身を苦しめ、省約、有慈有
道を、実の行者と云也。徳の顕ると云も、財宝に饒に、供養に誇
るを云にあらず。

　徳の顕に三重あるべし。先は、其の人、其の道を修するなりと
被知也。次には慕其道者、出来る。後には、其道を同行学し、同
行する也。是を道悳の顕るると云也。

3-4

夜話云、

　学道の人は、人情をすつべき也。人情を捨ると云は、順仏法
行也。世人、多、小乗根性也。弁善悪、分是非、取是、捨非、猶
是、小乗の根性也。只、捨世情、入仏道也。入仏道には、善悪を
分ち、よしと思ひ、あししと思事を捨て、我身よからん、我心何と有
ん、と思ふ心を忘れ、よくもあれ、あしくもあれ、仏祖の言語行履
に順ひ行く。

Regarding this point, there is a pitfall for students: others, as well as [we] ourselves, think that to be venerated by people and to amass a large amount of property is the manifestation of our virtue of the Way. We should know that when we think in this manner, we are possessed by the heavenly demon Pāpīyas.[153] We should consider this particularly well. In the teachings, these are also called "the acts of a demon."[154] Among the exemplary [monks] in the three countries,[155] to this day I have never heard that wealth or veneration by ignorant people is [a manifestation of] one's virtue of the Way. Since ancient times, all people with the mind of awakening have been poor, have endured physical pain, have wasted nothing, have been compassionate, and have been led by the Way. Such people are called "genuine practitioners." Manifestation of virtue does not mean we become rich in material wealth or proud of receiving large offerings.

There are three stages in the manifestation of virtue. First, it becomes known [to others] that a person is practicing the Way. Next, those who yearn for the Way come to that person. Then, they study and practice the Way together with that person. This is called "the manifestation of virtue of the Way."

3-4

In an evening talk, [*Dōgen*] *said*:

Students of the Way must discard human sentiment. To discard human sentiment means to practice in accord with the Buddha-dharma. Most people in the world have Hīnayāna nature.[156] They discriminate good from bad, separate right and wrong, and then grasp at "right" things and discard "wrong" things. This is still Hīnayāna nature. If we simply give up such worldly sentiments, we enter the Buddha Way. To enter the Buddha Way, we refrain from making judgments based on discriminative thinking between good and evil and let go of the mind that holds our bodies dear and the worries of our

我心によしと思ひ、又、世人のよしと思事、必よからず。然ば、人目も忘れ、心をも捨て、只、仏教に順行也。身も苦しく、心も患とも、我身心をば、一向に捨たるものなればと思て、苦しく愁つべき事なりとも、仏祖先徳の行履ならば、可為也。此事は能事、仏道に叶たりと思とも、なしたく行じたくとも、仏祖の心になからん事をなすべからず。是、即、法門をも、能心得たる事にて有也。我心も、又、自本習来る法門の思量をばすてて、只、今見処の、祖師の言語行履に、次に心を移しもて行也。如是すれば、知恵もすすみ、悟りも開くる也。元来、所学、教家文字の功も、可捨道理あらば捨、今の義につきて可見也。学法門事は、もとより、出家得道の為也。我所学、多年の功を積めり、何ぞやすく捨んと、猶、心深思ふ、即、此心を、生死繋縛の心と云也。能々可思量。

3-5

夜話云、

故建仁寺の僧正の伝をば、顕兼中納言入道書たる也。其時、辞する言に云、儒者に書せらるべき也。其故は、儒者、元来、忘身幼きより長るまで、学問を本とす。故に、書たる物に、無誤也。只人

minds. Without being concerned with good and evil, we continue to follow the words and conduct of the buddhas and ancestors.

What we think is good in our minds and what worldly people think is good are not necessarily good. Therefore, we follow the Buddha's teachings, disregarding how other people see us and letting go of our own [discriminating] minds. Even if it is hard on our bodies and stressful for our minds, having determined to discard our bodies and minds, we should practice what our venerable predecessors, the buddhas and ancestors, have practiced. Even if we think something is good and accords with the Buddha Way and want to practice it, do not carry it out if it is not in accord with the mind of the buddhas and ancestors. This means that we understand the Dharma gates well. Casting aside both our own minds and our thoughts about those Dharma gates we have studied from the beginning, we should turn our minds toward the words and conduct of the buddhas and ancestors we are studying right now. When we do so, our wisdom will progress and realization will open up. We should even discard our understanding of what we have studied of the writings of the teaching schools[157] when there is reason to do so, and [instead] see things from the perspective [of the teachings we are studying] right now. Studying the Dharma gates is crucial for leaving home and attaining the Way. If, deep in our hearts, we think that what we have accomplished with great effort through many years of study cannot be given up easily, then such a mind is itself bound by life-and-death.[158] We should consider this thoroughly.

3-5

In an evening talk, [Dōgen] *said:*

The biography of the late superintendent of monks [Eisai] of Kennin-ji was written by the Middle Councilor Harukane, a lay monk.[159] [When he was first asked to write the biography,] he declined, saying, "It should be written by a Confucian scholar. This is because

は、身の出仕交衆を本として、かたはら事に学問をするあひだ、自よき人あれども、文筆の道にも、誤出来也。思之、昔の人は、外典の学問も、忘身、学する也。

又云、

故胤僧正云、道心と云は、一念三千の法門なんどを、胸中に学し入て持たるを、道心と云也。なにとなく笠を頚に懸て迷ありくをば、天狗魔縁の行と云也。

3-6

夜話云、

故僧正云、衆、各、所用の衣粮等の事、予が与ると思事無れ。皆、是、諸天の供ずる所也。我は、取り次人に当たるばかり也。又、各々、一期の命分具足す。勿奔走、常にすすめられければ、是第一の美言と覚る也。

又、大宋宏智禅師の会下、天童は、常住物、千人用途也。然れば、堂中七百人、堂外三百人にて、千人につもる常住物なるによりて、長老の住たる間、諸方の僧、雲集して堂中千人也。其外、五、六百人ある間、知事、宏智に訴へ申に云、常住物は千人の分

Confucian scholars forget their own bodies and devote themselves to studying from the earliest part of their childhoods and up through maturity. Therefore, there are no mistakes in their writing. For an ordinary person [like me], serving the government and social intercourse are the primary concerns; we study [only] in our spare time. Although there are some eminent writers of the literary arts among us, our writings can have mistakes." As I think of this [statement], it is clear that the ancients forgot their bodies in order to study even non-Buddhist texts.

[*Dōgen*] *also said*:

The late Superintendent of Monks [Kō]in[160] said, "The mind of awakening is studying the Dharma gates such as 'the three thousand worlds in a single moment of thought'[161] and keeping them in one's mind. This is called 'the mind of awakening.' To meaninglessly wander around in confusion with a bamboo hat hanging around one's neck is called an act under the demonic influence of a *tengu*."[162]

3-6

In an evening talk, [*Dōgen*] *said*:

The late superintendent of monks [Eisai] said, "Monks! Do not think that I give you the clothing, food, and other provisions you use. They are all offered by the various heavenly beings. I merely play the role of distributor. Also, each one of you is fully endowed with an allotted life span. Do not run around seeking after these things." He always encouraged monks in this way. I think these are most admirable words.

Also, in great Song China, Tiantong monastery had enough provisions for one thousand people when the assembly was under the guidance of Zen Master Hongzhi.[163] Thus, they had enough provisions to support seven hundred people inside the monks' hall and three hundred people outside the monks' hall. And yet, because the Elder[164] was the abbot, many monks from all over the country came like clouds to

也。衆僧多集て、用途不足也。枉て、はなたれん、と申しかば、宏
智云、人々、皆、有口、不干汝事、莫歎。云々。

　今思之、人、皆、生得の衣食有り。思によりても不出来、不求、
非不来。在家人すら、猶、運に任せ思忠、学孝。何況、出家人は、
惣て、不管他事。釈尊遺付の福分あり。諸天応供の衣食あり。
又、天然生得の命分あり。不求思、任運として可有命分也。直
饒、走り求て、財をもちたりとも、無常忽に来らん時、如何。故に学
人は、只、宜不余事留心、一向学道也。

　又、或人云、末世辺土の仏法興隆は、衣食等の外護の外に累
なくて修行せば、付其、有相著我の諸人集学せん程に、其中に、
若一人の発心の人も出来べし。故に閑居浄処を構へ、衣食具し
て仏法修行せば、利益も弘かるべし、と。

　今は思に、不然。直饒、千万人、利益につき財欲にふけりて聚
たらん、一人なからん、猶とるべき。悪道の業因のみ自積て仏法
の気分無故也。清貧艱難して、或は乞食し、或は菓蓏等を食し
て、恒、飢饉して学道せば、是を聞て、若、一人も来り学せんと思
ふ人有らんこそ、実の道心者、仏法の興隆ならめと覚る。艱難貧
道によりて一人も無らんと、衣食饒にして諸人聚て仏法なからん
と、只、八両と与半斤也。

　又云、

　当世の人、多、造像起塔等の事を仏法興隆と思へり。又、非
也。直饒、高堂大観、珠を磨て、金をのべたりとも、因是、得道の
者あるべからず。只、在家人の財宝を仏界に入て、善事をなす福

practice, and they had one thousand monks in the monks' hall. Besides that, they had five to six hundred people outside the hall. One of the temple officers reported back to Hongzhi, beseeching him, "We have enough provisions for one thousand people. Because so many monks have assembled, we do not have enough resources to support them. Please take this into special consideration and send the extra monks away." To this Hongzhi said, "Each one of them has his own mouth. It is not your business. Do not concern yourself with it."

Now, considering this, each of us has a certain amount of clothing and food granted from birth. It does not come by worrying about it, nor will it cease to come if it is not sought after. Even laypeople leave such things to fate, being concerned with loyalty [to their lords] or cultivating filial piety [to their parents]. How much more should monks, we home-leavers, be unconcerned with all other things [outside of practice]. Our fortune is given to us by Shakyamuni as his legacy;[165] we also have food and clothing offered by the heavenly deities and arhats.[166] Also, we have the natural share of life we were allotted when we were born. Without chasing after it or worrying over it, we should trust fate that we will receive our allotted portion of life, which is as much as we need. Even if we chase after and secure wealth, what will happen to it when impermanence suddenly comes [and we die]? Therefore, students must not be concerned with extraneous matters; just study the Way single-mindedly.

Also, a certain person said, "In this age of the last Dharma,[167] and in this land far [from where the Buddha lived], we want to make the Buddhadharma flourish. If we could practice easily without worrying about food, clothing, and so on, being supported by a patron, many people attached to outward forms and personal benefit would come together and study. Then, among those people, there might be one person who arouses the mind of awakening. Therefore, find a quiet residence in a clean place, secure provisions such as robes and food, and practice the Buddhadharma. Then this benefit [of one person arousing the mind of awakening] will reach widely."

分也。小因大果を感ずることあれども、僧徒の此事を営は仏法興隆に非る也。只、草庵樹下にても、法門の一句をも思量し、一時の坐禅をも行ぜんこそ、実の仏法興隆にてあれ。

今、僧堂を立んとて勧進をもし、随分に労する事は、必しも仏法興隆と思はず。只、当時、学道する人も無く、徒に日月を送る間、只、あらんよりもと思て、迷徒の結縁ともなれかし、又、当時、学道の輩の坐禅の道場の為也。又、思始めたる事のならずとも、不可有恨。只、柱一本なりとも立て置きたらば、後来も、思ひ企たれども不成鼎と見んも、不可苦思也。

又、或人すすみて云、仏法興隆の為、関東に下向すべし。

答云、

不然。若、仏法に志あらば、山川江海を渡ても、来て可学。其志なからん人に、往向てすすむとも、聞入ん事不定也。只、我が資縁の為、人を誑惑せん、財宝を貪らん為か。其れは、身の苦しければ、いかでもありなんと覚る也。

又云、

学道の人、教家の書籍及び外典等、不可学。可見語録等を可見。其余は且く是を可置。今代の禅僧、頌を作り、法語を書かん料に、文筆等を好む。是、則、非也。頌、不作とも、心に思はん事を書たらん、文筆不調とも、法門を可書也。是をわるしとて見たがらぬ程の無道心の人は、好文筆を調へ、いみじき秀句ありとも、只、言語計を翫んで、理を不可得。我も本と、幼少の時より好み学

Now, as I think about this, it cannot be so. Even if one thousand or ten thousand people get together, if they seek after personal benefit or try to fulfill their desires for material wealth, it is worse than no one having come. This is because only the karma that causes one to fall into the evil destinies[168] would naturally accumulate, and there would be no aspiration for the Buddhadharma. If we remain pure and poor and practice the Way while enduring hardships, begging for food, eating wild nuts or fruits, and enduring hunger, and if a single person hears about us and comes to practice, such a person will possess the genuine mind of awakening. I think the Buddhadharma can truly flourish in this way. To have no [practitioners] because of hardships and pure poverty or having many people gather together because of abundant food and clothing while lacking the Buddhadharma is simply six of one, half a dozen of the other.[169]

[*Dōgen*] *also said*:

Many people today think that constructing images of Buddhas and building stupas can make the Buddhadharma flourish. This is not correct. Even if we construct huge temple buildings adorned with polished jewels and gold, no one will attain the Way [because of such activities]. This is [instead] nothing more than benefit [for] laypeople who put their wealth into the world of the Buddha, thus allowing them to do good. Although they might receive a great result from a small cause,[170] for monks to be involved in such activities has nothing to do with the flourishing of the Buddhadharma. Even within a grass hermitage or under a tree, if we think of one single phrase of the Dharma gates or practice zazen once, this demonstrates the true flourishing of the Buddhadharma.[171]

Currently, I am appealing for donations and working as much as possible to construct a monks' hall.[172] Yet I do not think that this necessarily contributes to the flourishing of the Buddhadharma. Only because there are currently few people studying the Way and because I spend my days leisurely, do I think it better to engage in these activities rather than be idle. I hope this will enable deluded people to form a connection with the Buddhadharma. I am working on this project for the sake of

せん事にて、今もややもすれば、外典等の美言案ぜられ、文選等
も見らるるを、無詮事と存ずれば、一向に捨つべき由を思ふ也。

founding a dojo[173] for zazen practice on behalf of the people studying the Way in this age. I will have no regrets even if what I have wished for and begun might not be realized. I do not mind if but one single pillar is erected as long as people in later generations think that someone had the aspiration to carry out such a project but did not complete it.

A person also came forward and said, "For the sake of the flourishing of the Buddhadharma, you should visit Kantō."[174]

[*Dōgen*] *replied*:

I do not think so. If they aspired to practice the Buddhadharma, they would come and study it even if they had to cross mountains, rivers, lakes, and oceans. If they lack this aspiration, even if I visited them and urged them [to practice], it is uncertain if they would accept it or not. Shall I fool people merely to obtain material support for myself? Is that not being greedy for wealth? Because it would simply tire me out, I do not feel I need to go.

[*Dōgen*] *also said*:

Students of the Way! We should not read the scriptures of the teaching schools, nor study non-Buddhist texts, and so on. We must read [only] the recorded sayings [of the Zen masters] that require study. Put aside all other books for the time being. Zen monks these days are fond of studying literature as a grounding to compose verses or write Dharma words.[175] This is wrong. Even if you cannot compose verses, just write what you think in your mind. Even if your style is not sophisticated, write down the Dharma gates. People without the mind of awakening will not read it if your writing style is not well polished, but even if the style is embellished and there are excellent phrases in it, such people would only play with the words without grasping the principle [behind them]. I have been fond of studying [literature] since my childhood, and even now I have a tendency to contemplate the beauty in the words of non-Buddhist texts. Sometimes I even refer to the *Selections of Refined Literature*[176] or other classic texts. Still, I think it is meaningless, and it should cease immediately.

3-7

一日、示云、

我在宋の時、禅院にして見古人語録時、或西川の僧の道者に
て有しが、問我云、なにの用ぞ。

云く、郷里に帰て人を化せん。

僧云、なにの用ぞ。

云、利生の為也。

僧云、畢竟して何の用ぞ。

予、後に此理を案ずるに、語録公案等を見て、古人の行履を
も知り、或は、迷者の、為に説き聞かしめん、皆、是、自行化他の
為に無用也。只管打坐して大事を明め、心の理を明めなば、後に
は一字を不知とも、他に開示せんに、用ひ不可尽。故に彼の僧、
畢竟じて、何用ぞとは云ひけると。是、真実の道理也と思て、其後
ち、語録等を見る事をとどめて、一向打坐して、大事を明め得た
り。

3-8

夜話云、

真実内徳無して、人に貴びらるべからず。此国の人は、真実の
内徳をば、さぐりえず、外相をもて、人を貴ぶ程に、無道心の学人
は、即、あしざまにひきなされて、魔の眷属と成る也。人にたとび
られじと思はん事やすき事也。中々、身をすて、世をそむく由を以
てなすは、外相計の仮令也。只、なにとなく世間の人の様にて、

3-7

One day [Dōgen] instructed:

While staying at the Zen monastery in Song China, I was read-ing an ancient's collection of recorded sayings. At the time, a certain monk from Sichuan, a person of the Way, asked me, "What is the use [of reading recorded sayings]?"

I said, "I will teach people after I return home."[177]

The monk said, "What is the use [of that]?"

I said, "To benefit living beings."

The monk said, "Ultimately, what is the use?"

Later, I pondered the reason why he said this. Learning the deeds of the ancients by reading the recorded sayings, kōan stories, and so on and explaining them to deluded people is of no use for my own practice nor for the teaching of others. If I devote myself to just sitting [*shikantaza*], and thereby clarify the great matter and comprehend the principle of mind,[178] I will later be able to teach it to others in inex-haustible ways without knowing even one single letter. For this reason, the monk asked, "Ultimately, what is the use?" I thought what he said was true. After that I gave up reading the recorded sayings and other texts, concentrated wholeheartedly on sitting, and was able to clarify the great matter.

3-8

In an evening talk, [Dōgen] said:

Without truly having inner virtue, do not [allow yourself to] be venerated by others. Because people of this country are not able to find true inner virtue, and because they respect people based only on their external appearances, students without the mind of awakening are easily dragged down, becoming the kindred of demons. It is easy not to be respected by others. However, to pretend to have abandoned the body and to have parted from the world is only a matter of out-ward appearances. One who appears to be a common worldly person

内心を調へもてゆく、是、実の道心者也。然ば、古人云、内空くして、外したがふ、といひて、中心は我身なくして、外相は他にしたがひもてゆく也。我身、わが心と云事を、一向にわすれて、仏法に入て、仏法のおきてに任せて、行じもてゆけば、内外ともによく、今も後もよきなり。

　仏法の中にも、そぞろに身をすて、世をそむけばとて、すつべからざる事をすつるは非也。此土の仏法者、道心者を立つる人の中にも、身をす（て）たればとて、人はいかにも見よと思て、ゆゑなく身をわろくふるまひ、或は、又、世を執せぬとて、雨にもぬれながらゆきなんどするは、内外ともに無益なるを、世間の人は、即、是を貴き人、世を執せぬなんどと思へる也。中々、仏制を守て、戒、律儀をも存じ、自行他行、仏制に任て行ずるをば、名聞利養げなると、人も管ぜざるなり。其が、又、我為には、仏教にも順ひ、内外の悳も成也。

3-9

夜話云、

　学道の人、世間の人に、知者、もの知と、しられては無用也。真実求道の人の、一人も有ん時は、我が知るところの、仏祖の法を、不説ことあるべからず。直饒、我を、殺さんとしたる人なり

but goes on harmonizing the inner mind is a person of the true mind of awakening. Therefore, an ancient said, "Being empty inside, following along outside." This means to be without an ego-centered mind on the inside and getting along with others on the outside. If we completely forget our own body and mind, enter into the Buddhadharma, and keep practicing in accordance with the regulations of the Buddhadharma, we will be good both inwardly and outwardly, in the present and in the future.

Even though we have entered into the Buddhadharma, abandoning the self and departing from the world, it is wrong to thoughtlessly abandon what should not be abandoned. In this country, among those who are recognized as people of the Buddhadharma or of the mind of awakening, there are some who do not consider how others see them. They behave badly without any reason, saying they have abandoned the self, or they do things such as getting drenched walking in the rain, thinking they are free of attachment to the world. [Such behavior] is entirely futile, both inwardly and outwardly. Nevertheless, people in the mundane world often consider such people to be venerable and free from attachment to the world. On the other hand, if people maintain the regulations established by the Buddha, keep the restraining precepts,[179] practice for themselves, and instruct others following the Buddha's teachings, others will think that they cling to fame and profit and will not appreciate such people. Yet for us this is the way to follow the Buddha's teachings and cultivate inner and outer virtues.

3-9

In an evening talk, [Dōgen] said:

It is of no value for a student of the Way to be known as a person of wisdom or wide knowledge by people of the mundane world. If there is even a single person who is sincerely seeking the Way, we should not refuse to explain [to them] the Dharma of the buddhas and ancestors, to whatever extent we know it. Even if a person has

とも、真実の道を聞んと、真の心を以て、問はんには、怨心を忘
て、為に是を可説也。其外は、教家の顕密、及、内外の典籍等の
こと、知たる気色して、全く無用也。人来て、如是の事を問に、不
知と答たらんに、一切不可苦也。其を、物しらぬは、わろしと人も
思ひ、愚人と自も覚ることを、傷れて、ものを知らんとて、博、内外
典を学し、剰へ、世間世俗の事をも、知んと思て、諸事を好み学
し、或は、人にも知たる由をもてなす、極めたる僻事也。学道の為
に、真実に無用也。知たるを、不知る気色するも、六借し、やうが
ましければ、かへりて、たうと気色にて、あしき也。もとより不知、
一の事也。

　我、幼少の昔、紀伝等を好み、学して、其が今も、入宋伝法す
るまでも、内外の書籍をひらき、方言を通ずるまでも、大切の用
事、又、世間の為にも、尋常也。俗なんども、尋常の事に思たる、
かたがた用事にて有ども、今、倩思に、学道の碍にてある也。
只、聖教をみるとも、文に見ゆる所の理を、次第にこころえてゆか
ば、其の道理を、えつべきを、先づ文章に、対句韻声なんどを見
て、よき、あしきぞ、と心に思て、後に理をば見也。然らば、なかな
か知らずして、はじめより道理を心ろ得てゆかば、よかるべき也。
法語等を書も、文章におほせて、書んとし、韻声たがへば、被拄
なんどするは、知たる咎也。語言文章は、いかにもあれ、思ふまま
の理を、つぶつぶと書きたらば、後来も、文章わろしと思ふとも、
理だにもきこえたらば、道の為には、大切也。余の才学も如是。

made an attempt to kill us, if the person asks with a sincere mind
to hear the true Way, we must not hold a grudge but expound the
Dharma to them. Except in these cases, it is entirely futile to display
our knowledge of the scriptures of the exoteric or esoteric schools[180]
or of non-Buddhist texts. If someone comes to ‚ask us about these
things, we do not need to feel shame at all in replying that we do not
know. And yet, though we may feel troubled due to being despised
by others for our ignorance, and we might even consider ourselves
foolish, it is nevertheless a terrible mistake if we study the Buddhist
and non-Buddhist classics widely [only] to become a person of wide
knowledge—or to study various things in order to understand mundane things of the world and show off our knowledge. For the sake
of studying the Way, [such pursuits] are truly useless. Because pre-
tending not to know what we know is troublesome and unnatural and
it, instead, creates a respectable image, it is not good. It is best not to
know from the outset.

In my childhood, I was fond of studying classic literature on Chinese history and other texts. Up to that point, reading both Buddhist
and non-Buddhist texts was necessary to [go to China] and transmit
the Dharma, and to become familiar with the local Chinese language.
I thought it was important, and in fact, it was an extraordinary thing
even in worldly society. Laypeople also appreciated it as exceptional
and wonderful. Although in a sense it was necessary, when I reflect
deeply on it now, it was a hindrance to studying the Way. When we
read Buddhist scriptures, if we understand the meaning of the sentences phrase by phrase, we can grasp the principle expressed by the
words. However, people tend to pay more attention to the rhetorical
devices, such as couplets, rhythm, and tone.[181] They judge them as
good or bad and then think about the meaning as an afterthought.
Therefore, it is better to understand the meaning from the beginning
without caring about such things. Also, in writing Dharma words,
trying to write according to the rules of rhetoric or being unable to
write without thinking of rhyming and tone are the fault of having
too much knowledge. Let the language and style develop as they may.

伝へ聞、故高野の空阿弥陀仏は、元は顕密の碩慧なりき。遁
世の後、念仏の門に入て後、真言師ありて、来て密宗の法門を問
けるに、彼人、答云、皆、忘をはりぬ。一事も、おぼえず、とて、答
へられざりける也。これらこそ、道心の手本となるべけれ。などか
少々おぼえでも、有べき。しかあれども、無用なる事をば、云はざ
りける也。一向念仏の日は、さこそ有べけれと覚る也。

今の学者も、この心有べし。直饒、元、教家の、才学等有とも、
皆わすれたらん、よき事也。況や、今学する事、努々有べからず。
宗門の語録等、猶、真実参学の道者は、見るべからず。其余は、
是を可知。

3-10

夜話云、

今、此国の人は、多分、或は行儀につけ、或は言語につけ、
善悪是非、世人の見聞識知を思ふて、其の事をなさば、人あしく
思ひてん、其の事は、人よしと思ひてん、乃至、向後までも執する
也。是、又、全く非也。世間の人、必しも、善とする事あたはず。人
はいかにも、思はば思へ、狂人とも云へ、我心に、仏道に順じた

What is most important is to write down in detail the truth we want to communicate. Even though people in future generations might think that our rhetorical technique is poor, for the Way it is essential to enable them to understand the truth. This is the same for other fields of study as well.

I have heard that Ku Amidabutsu[182] of Mt. Kōya was an eminent scholar of both Exoteric and Esoteric Buddhism. After he renounced the world[183] and entered the Nenbutsu school, a Shingon priest visited him and asked about the doctrine of the esoteric school. He replied, "I have forgotten everything. I do not remember even a single word." Thus, he did not answer the priest's question. This should become exemplary of the mind of awakening. Why did he not remember even a little? Because he did not talk about things he thought useless. I think that people who wholeheartedly practice *nenbutsu* must be like this.

Today's students should also have such an attitude. Even if we used to know about the philosophies of the teaching schools, it would be better to forget them completely. Needless to say, you should not begin studying them now. People of the Way who truly devote themselves to practice should not even read the collections of the recorded sayings of our sect. You should understand this [is also true] of other [books].

3-10

In an evening talk, [Dōgen] said:

In this country today, with regard to actions and speech, most people are concerned with personal fame and reputation. They think [in terms of] good and bad, right and wrong, and believe that if they do one thing, others will think well of them, or if they do something else, others will think poorly of them. They even worry about the future. This is entirely wrong. People in worldly society are not necessarily good. Let people think whatever they may think. Let them even say we are madmen. If we spend our whole lives practicing in accordance with the Buddha Way and refrain from what goes against the Buddhadharma, we need not worry about what people think of us.

らば作、仏法にあらずは、行ぜずして、一期をもすごさば、世間の
人はいかに思ふとも、不可苦。

　遁世と云は、世人の情を、心にかけざる也。只、仏祖の行履、
菩薩の慈行を学、行じて、諸天善神の、冥にてらす処に慚愧し
て、仏制に任て、行じもてゆかば、一切くるしかるまじき也。

　さればとて、又、人のあししと思ひ云ん、不苦とて、放逸にし
て、悪事を行て、人をはぢずあるは、是、又、非也。只、人目にはよ
らずして、一向に仏法によりて、行ずべき也。仏法の中には、又、
しかの如くの、放逸無慚をば、制する也。

　又、云、

　世俗の礼にも、人の不見処、或は、暗室の中なれども、衣服
等をも、きかゆる時、坐臥する時にも、放逸に、陰処なんどをも不
蔵、無礼なるをば、不慚天、不慚鬼とて、そしる也。ひとしく人の
見る時と同く、可蔵処をも隠し、可慚処をも、はづる也。仏法の中
にも、又、戒律如是。しかあれば、道者は、内外を不論、明暗を不
択、仏制を存心、人の不見不知とて、悪事を行ずべからざる也。

3-11

一日、学人、問云、某甲、猶、学道繋心、雖運年月、未有省悟分。
古人多く道ふ、不依聡明霊利。不用有知明敏。しかあれば、我
身、下根劣智なればとて、卑下すべきにも非と聞たり。若、故実用
心の、存ずべき様ありやいかん。

"Renunciation of the world" means being free from the sentiments of worldly people. We should just learn about the deeds of the buddhas and ancestors and about the compassion of the bodhisattvas, repent of our actions in places secretly illuminated by the various heavenly beings and guardian deities, and go on practicing in accordance with the Buddha's regulations. We do not need to care about anything else.

On the other hand, it is wrong to shamelessly indulge ourselves and do unwholesome things, trying to excuse ourselves on the grounds that it does not matter if others think ill of us. Without paying attention to how others see us, we should practice wholeheartedly in accordance with the Buddhadharma. In the Buddhadharma, such indulgence and shamelessness are prohibited.

[*Dōgen*] *also said*:

Even according to worldly etiquette, when changing clothes, when sitting or lying down in places where no one can see us, or when in a dark room, failing to hide what should be hidden and having no propriety is criticized as being shameless before the heavenly beings and spirits. Just as if someone were watching, we should hide what should be hidden and be discreet about what requires discretion. In the Buddhadharma, the precepts speak of the same attitude. Therefore, as practitioners of the Way, we should not discriminate between inside and outside or between bright and dark places. We should keep the Buddha's precepts in mind, refraining from committing unwholesome acts even if no one may see us or notice what we do.

3-11

One day, a student asked, "Although I have been spending months and years aspiring to learn the Way, I have not yet had any realization. Many of the ancient masters said that [the Buddha Way] does not depend on intelligence or sagacity nor require wide knowledge or sharp-wittedness. Therefore, I do not think I should disparage myself for my inferior

示云、

しかあり。不須有智高才、不頼霊利弁聡。実の学道、あやまりて、盲聾癡人のごとくになれとすすむ。全く多聞高才を不用。故に、下々根劣器と、きらふべからず。実の学道は、やすかるべき也。

しかあれども、大宋国の叢林にも、一師の会下に、数百千人の中に、実の得道得法の人は、僅、一二也。しかあれば、故実用心も有るべき事也。今、案之、志之至と与不至也。真実、至志随分、参学する人、又、無不得也。其用心のやう、何事を専にし、其行を急すべしと云事は、次の事也。

先づ、欣求の志の、切なるべき也。たとへば、重き宝をぬすまんと思ひ、強き敵きをうたんと思ひ、高き色にあはんと思ふ、心あらん人は、行住坐臥、事にふれ、をりにしたがひて、種々の事は、かはり来れども、其れに随ひて、隙を求め、心に懸る也。此心あながちに、切なるもの、とげずと云ことなき也。如是、求道志、切になりなば、或は只管打坐の時、或は古人の公案に向はん時、若は知識に向はん時、実の志をもて、なさんずる時、高とも射べし、深くとも釣ぬべし。是れ程の心、不発して、仏道と云程の一念に、生死の輪廻をきる大事をば、如何が成ぜん。若、有此心人は、不云下知劣根、不謂愚鈍悪人、必、悟道す可也。

又、発此志、只、可思世間無常也。此言、又、只、仮令に観法なんどに、すべき事に非ず。又、無事を造、思ふべき事にも非ず。真実に、眼前の道理也。人のをしむ聖教文証道理を待つべから

capacity and lack of wisdom. Is there something about this that has been handed down in the tradition that I should keep in mind?"

[*Dōgen*] *instructed*:

You are right. [Attaining the Way] does not require intelligence or talent, nor does it depend on quick-wittedness or sagacity. [Nonetheless,] in the genuine study of the Way, it is a mistake to encourage a student to become like the blind, deaf, or ignorant. Because having a wide knowledge or great talent is not required, we should not disparage ourselves because of our inferior capacity. True practice of the Way should be easy.

Nevertheless, even in the monasteries of great Song China, among the several hundreds or thousands of monks in the assembly of one master, there are only one or two people who truly realize the Dharma and attain the Way. Therefore, there must be some revered traditions from ancient times [practiced by these one or two people] that we should keep in mind. Now, as I consider this, [attaining the Way] depends on whether one's aspiration is firmly determined or not. Those who arouse true aspiration and study as hard as their capacity allows will not fail to attain [the Way]. We have to be careful to concentrate on and immediately carry out the following practices:

First of all, just maintain the aspiration to earnestly seek [the Way]. For example, people who desire to steal a precious treasure, to defeat a powerful enemy, or to win over a beautiful woman of high nobility will constantly seek an opportunity to accomplish their tasks in any situation or occasion despite [any] vicissitudes because their minds are always occupied with their desire. If they are exceptionally enthusiastic, they will not fail to fulfill their desire. In the same way, if our aspiration to seek the Way is earnest enough when we practice just sitting [*shikantaza*], approach the kōan stories of the ancients, or meet with our teachers, if we act with genuine aspiration, though the target is high, we will hit the mark; though the treasure is deep, we will fish it out. Without arousing such an aspiration, how can we complete the great matter of the Buddha Way in which the saṃsāra of life-and-death is cut off in a single moment? Only if we have such

ず。朝に生じて、夕に死し、昨日見人、今日無き事、遮眼、近耳。是は、他の上にて、見聞する事也。我身にひきあてて、道理を思ふ事を。直饒、七旬八旬に、命を期すべくとも、遂に可死道理有らば、其間の楽み悲み、恩愛怨敵を思ひとけば、何かにてもすごしてん。只、仏道を思て、衆生の楽を求むべし。況や、我れ年長大せる人、半に過ぬる人、余年幾なれば、学道ゆるくすべき。

此道理も、猶、のびたる事也。世間の事をも、仏道の事をも思へ。明日、次の時よりも、何なる重病をも受て、東西も不弁、重苦のみかなしみ、又、何なる鬼神の、怨害をも受て、頓死をもし、何なる賊難にも逢ひ、怨敵も出来て殺害奪命せらるる事もや有ん。真実に不定也。然ればこれ程に、あだなる世に、極めて不定なる死期をいつまで、いきたるべしとて、種々の活計を案じ、剰へ他人の為に、悪をたくみ思ふて、徒に時光を過す事、極て愚なる事也。

此道理、真実なれば、仏も是を衆生の為に説き、祖師の普説法語にも、此道理をのみ説く。今の上堂請益等にも、無常迅速、生死事大を云也。返々も、此道理を、心に忘ずして、只、今日今時許と思て、時光を失はず、学道に心を入る可也。其後、真実に易き也。性の上下、根利鈍、全く不可論。

a determination, without concern for our inferior intelligence or dull faculties, or our ignorance or wickedness, will we surely realize the Way.

Also, once we have aroused such an aspiration, we should think solely of the impermanence of the world. This is not a matter of using some provisional method of [meditative] contemplation. It is not a matter of fabricating something in our minds that does not really exist. [Impermanence] is truly the reality right in front of our eyes. We need not wait for some teaching from others, some proof from some passage of scripture, or some principle. Born in the morning and dead in the evening, a person we saw yesterday is no longer here today; this is what we see with our eyes and hear with our ears. This is what we see and hear about others. We should apply this to ourselves and think of the [impermanent] reality [of all beings]. Though we expect to live for seventy or eighty years, the truth is, we must die in the end. During our lifetime, though we may experience pleasure, sorrow, love for our families, and hatred for our enemies, if we can untie [the entanglements] of our thinking, we can spend [our lifetime] without [being bothered by such things]. We must simply think of the Buddha Way and seek joy for all living beings. For aged people whose lives are already more than half over, [this is true] all the more: How many years still remain? How can we slacken in our study of the Way?

[However,] this attitude is still not aligned with the reality [of impermanence]. Consider [this reality of impermanence] whether it is regarding worldly affairs or the Buddha Way. We may contract some serious disease tomorrow or even in the next moment, or we may have to endure pain so terrible that we are unable to distinguish east from west. We may be suddenly struck dead by some evil spirit, encounter trouble with brigands, or have our life taken by some sworn enemy. Everything is truly uncertain. Therefore, in such an ephemeral world it is extremely foolish to waste time worrying about the various means of earning a living, expecting to live [for a certain number of years], and planning [for the future] when our deaths are so uncertain—to say nothing of plotting evil against others.

3-12

夜話く、

　人多く不遁世、似貪我身、不思我身也。是、即、無遠慮也。
又、是、依不逢善知識也。たとひ思名聞利養、得仏祖名、古徳後
賢、聞是、令悦。たとひ利養を思とも、常楽の益得、龍天の供養を
可得。

3-13

夜話云、

　古人云、朝に聞道、夕に死とも可也。今、学道の人、有此心べ
き也。広劫多生の間、幾回か徒に生じ、徒に死せん。まれに人界
に生れて、たまたま逢仏法時、何にしても死行くべき身を、心ば
かりに、惜持とも、不可叶。遂に捨て行命を、一日片時なりとも、
為仏法、すてたらば、永劫の楽因なるべし。思後事明日活計、不

Precisely because this is the reality, the Buddha preached this [principle of impermanence] to all living beings, and the ancestors taught only this truth in their sermons and Dharma words. In both my formal discourses[184] and instructions, I say that impermanence is swift and life-and-death is the great matter.[185] Reflect on this reality again and again in your hearts without forgetting it. We should remember that we are alive only today; we should wholeheartedly practice the Way without wasting a moment. Other than that, [the practice of the Way] is truly easy. We do not need to discuss whether we are superior or inferior by nature, or brilliant or dull in our capacity.

3-12

In an evening talk, [Dōgen] said:

Those who do not renounce the world seem to hold themselves dear. However, they do not truly think of themselves. They do not consider things from a broader perspective. Moreover, they are this way because they have not met good teachers. Even if they think of fame, they should [aspire to] obtain the fame of the buddhas and ancestors and delight the ancient worthies and future sages. Even if they think of profit, they should [aspire to] obtain the benefit of eternal bliss and the offerings of *nāgás*[186] and heavenly beings.

3-13

In an evening talk, [Dōgen] said:

An ancient remarked, "If I learn the Way in the morning, I would not mind dying in the evening."[187] Today's students of the Way should have this same mental attitude. During eons of life-and-death, how many times have we been born and died in vain? By rare chance, we have been born in the human world and are able to encounter the Buddhadharma. No matter what we do, eventually we must die. Even if, in our mind, our self is dear to us, it is not possible to hold on to it. Giving up our lives, which we must leave behind sooner or later, for

捨可捨世、不行可行道而、あたら日夜を過すは、口惜き事也。只
思切て、明日の活計なくは、飢死もせよ、寒死もせよ、今日一日、
道を聞て、仏意に随て死んと、思ふ心を、先づ可発也。其上に道
を行じ得ん事は、一定也。

　此心無て、世を背き、道を学する様なれども、猶、しり足をらふ
みて、夏冬の、衣服等の事を、した心にかけ、明日明年の、活命
を思て、仏法を学せんは、万劫千生、学すとも、かなうべしとも不
覚。又、さる人もや有んずらん、存知の意趣、仏祖の教には、有べ
しとも、おぼえざる也。

3-14

夜話云、

　学人は、必しも、可死、可思。道理は勿論なれども、たとへ
ば、其言、不思、しばらく先づ光陰を、徒にすぐさじと思ふて、無
用の事をなして、徒に時をすぐさで、詮ある事をなして、時をすぐ
すべき也。其のなすべき事の中に、又、一切の事、いづれか大切
なると云に、仏祖の行履の外は、皆、無用也と可知。

　示云、

the sake of the Buddhadharma, if only for a day or a few moments, will surely be the cause of eternal bliss. It is regrettable to spend our days and nights vainly thinking of our livelihood tomorrow or some later time without casting aside the world that ought to be cast aside, without practicing the Way that ought to be practiced. We should simply make up our mind to learn the Way following the Buddha's intention, even [if] for [just] one day. If we do not have the provisions to keep ourselves alive until tomorrow, it does not matter if we die from the cold or from hunger today. First and foremost, we need to arouse such a resolution. In doing so, we will be able to practice the Way without fail.

Without arousing this mind [of strong resolve], if we outwardly continue to practice the Buddhadharma while internally worrying about things such as clothing for winter or summer and our livelihood for tomorrow or the next year, then despite the appearance of practicing the Way that runs counter to the mundane world, I do not think we will be able to attain the Way, regardless of how many millions of years or thousands of cycles of life-and-death we might practice. There might be such a person, but as far as I know, such an attitude cannot be in accordance with the teaching of the buddhas and ancestors.

3-14

In an evening talk, [Dōgen] said:

Students of the Way! It goes without saying that you must consider the inevitability of death. This principle is certain. Even if we do not consider this [right now], we should resolve not to waste time and to refrain from doing meaningless things. We should spend our time carrying out that which is worth carrying out. Among the things we should do, the most important thing is to understand that all deeds other than those performed by buddhas and ancestors are useless.

[Dōgen] instructed:

3-15

夜話の次に、弉公、問て云、父母の報恩等の事、可作耶。

示云、

孝順は尤も所用也。但し、其の孝順に、在在家出家之別。在家
は孝経等の説を守りて、生をつかふ、死につかふる事、世人皆知
り。出家は棄恩、入無為、無為の家の作法は、恩を一人に不限、
一切衆生斉く父母の、恩のごとく深しと思て、所作の善根を法
界めぐらす。別して今生一世の父母に不限。是、則、不背無為道
也。日々の行道、時々の参学、只、仏道に随順しもてゆかば、其を
真実の孝道とする也。忌日の追善、中陰の作善なんど、皆在家に
所用也。衲子は、父母の恩の深き事をば、如実可知。余の一切、
又、同く重して可知。別して一日をしめて、殊に善を修し、別して
一人をわきて、回向をするは、非仏意歟。戒経の、父母兄弟、死亡
の日、の文は、暫く令蒙於在家歟。大宋の叢(林)の衆僧、師匠の

Regarding the behavior of patch-robed practitioners, if we mend or patch our old, tattered clothing instead of discarding it, it seems that we are clinging to things. Yet to abandon old clothing and wear new robes shows that we are seeking after new things. Both of these are mistakes. What should we do?

I, [Ejō,] asked, "Ultimately, what should we keep in mind?"

[*Dōgen*] *replied*:

So long as we are free from both greedily clinging and greedily seeking, either is fine. Still, it would be better to mend torn clothing in order to keep it as long as possible and not lust after new clothing.

3-15

During an evening talk, Ejō asked, "Should we carry on repaying our debts of gratitude to our fathers and mothers?"[188]

[*Dōgen*] *replied*:

Filial piety and obedience[189] are most important to carry out. Yet there is a difference between laypeople and home-leavers when it comes to performing filial piety. Laypeople keep the teachings in the *Classic of Filial Piety*,[190] and so on, serve their parents while they are alive, and hold services after their deaths. All worldly people know this. Home-leavers abandon their debts of gratitude and enter the realm of nondoing.[191] Within the family of nondoing, the manner [of paying off debts of gratitude] must not be limited to one particular person. Considering that we have debts of gratitude to all living beings just as we do to our own fathers and mothers, we must transmit all the merits of our good deeds throughout the [entire] Dharma world.[192] We do not limit [the dedication of merit] specifically to our own parents and in this [one] lifetime. This is how we do not violate the Way of non-doing. In our continuous day-to-day practice and moment-to-moment study, simply following the Buddha Way is the true fulfillment of filial piety. Laypeople hold memorial services and make meritorious offerings during the period between death and rebirth.[193] As patch-robed monks, we should truly know the depth of the debt of gratitude to our

忌日には、其儀式あれども、父母の忌日には、是を修したりとも
見ざる也。

3-16

一日、示云、

　人の鈍根と云は、志の不到時の事也。世間の人、従馬落る
時、未落地間に、種々の思ひ起る。身をも損し命をも失する程
の、大事出来たる時、誰人も才覚念慮を起す也。其時は、利根も
鈍根も、同く物を思ひ、義を案ずる也。

　然れば明日死に、今夜死可しと思ひ、あさましき事に逢たる
思をなして、切にはげみ、志をすすむるに、悟をえずと云事無き
也。

　中々世智弁聡なるよりも、鈍根なる様にて、切なる志を出す
人、速に悟得也。如来在世の周利盤特は、一偈を読誦する事
は、難かりしかども、根性切なるによりて、一夏に証を取りき。

　ただ今ばかり、我命は存ずる也、不死先に悟を得んと、切に
思て仏法を学せんに、一人も不得は、不可有也。

parents. [However,] we should see that our debts of gratitude to all living beings are as important [as the debt to our parents]. To choose one particular day to practice something especially good and to dedicate its merit to one particular person does not seem to accord with the Buddha's intention. The passage about the anniversaries of the deaths of one's parents and siblings in the *Precepts Sutra* is [only] a temporary [expedient] that applies to laypeople.[194] At the monasteries in great Song China, monks hold ceremonies on the anniversaries of their masters' deaths but not on the anniversaries of their parents' deaths.

3-16

One day, [Dōgen] instructed:

We say someone is dull-witted, but we are dull-witted only when we have not yet aroused thorough aspiration. When people of worldly society fall off a horse, a multiplicity of thoughts arise even before they hit the ground. When some serious thing that may harm one's body or endanger one's life occurs, no one will fail to put all one's resources and intellect to work. On such occasions, regardless of being sharp or dull-witted, all of us will try to discern what is best to do.

Therefore, if we think we may die tomorrow or even this evening, or we are facing a dreadful situation, and we wholeheartedly make efforts and encourage our aspiration, then we will never fail to attain realization.

A person who seems superficially dull-witted but has a sincere aspiration will attain realization faster than a person who is clever in a worldly sense. While the Tathāgata was in the world, there was a monk whose name was Cūdapanthaka.[195] Although it was difficult for him to remember and recite even a single verse, because his aspiration was so earnest he attained verification within one summer practice period.

Our lives exist only in this present moment. If we learn the Buddhadharma and earnestly wish to attain realization before dying, none of us will fail to attain it.

3-17

一夜、示云、

　大宋の禅院に、麦米等をそろへて、あしきをさけ、よきを取て、飯等にする事あり。是を或禅師云、直饒、我が頭を、打破事、七分にすとも、米をそろふる事なかれ、と、頌に作て戒めたり。此心は、僧は斎食等を調て、食事なかれ。只、有にしたがひて、よければよくて食し、あしきをもきらはずして、食すべき也。只、檀那の信施、清浄なる常住食を以て、餓を除き、命をささへて、行道するばかり也。味を思て、善悪をえらぶ事無れと云。今、我が会下の諸衆、此心あるべし。

　因問云、学人、若、自己仏法也、不可求向外と、聞て、深く此語を信じて、向来の修行、参学を放下して、本性に善悪業をなして、一期を過ん、此見如何。

　示云、

　此見解、語与理、相違せり。外に向不可求と云、行をすて、学を放下せば、行をもて所求有りと聞へたり。不求あらず。只、行・学、本より仏法なりと証して、無所求にして、世事悪業等の、我が心に作したくとも不作、学道修行の、懶きをもなして、此行を以て、果を得きたるとも、我心先より求る事無して、行ずるをこそ、外に向て求る事無と云、道理には可叶けれ。南岳の磚を磨して、鏡を求めしも、馬祖の作仏を求めしを、戒めたり。坐禅を制するには非る也。

3-17

One evening, [Dōgen] instructed:

At a Zen monastery in great Song China, they sometimes sifted the wheat, rice, and so on by throwing away the inferior grains and keeping the good ones to cook. This was admonished by a certain Zen master through the use of a verse: "Even if you split my head into seven pieces, do not winnow the rice." He meant that monks should not fuss about arranging fine meals. They should simply eat whatever is available. When they have fine food, they should eat it as it is. When they have only poor food, they should eat it without disliking it. We should satisfy our hunger and provision our lives with the faithful donations from faithful lay supporters and the pure foods provided by temples alone, devoting ourselves exclusively to the practice of the Way. We should not choose good over bad on the basis of flavor. Now, each of us in this assembly should also maintain this attitude.

Someone once asked, "How do you feel about the following view? Upon hearing that one's own self is the Buddhadharma and that it is futile to seek anything outside of oneself, what if students who believed this deeply gave up their practice and studies, and spent their whole lives doing good and bad things according to their personal nature?"

Dōgen instructed:

In this point of view, there is a discrepancy between the person's words and reality. To give up practice and abandon study because of the futility of seeking anything outside sounds as though something is being sought in this very act of giving up. This is not nonseeking. We simply verify that practice and study themselves are the Buddhadharma. Without seeking anything, we should refrain from engaging in worldly affairs and unwholesome actions even if we are inclined to engage in them. We should continue to study and practice the Way even if we have become languid and weary. Even if results are attained, we should just practice wholeheartedly without any expectation in our minds in advance. This attitude is in accordance with

坐、すなわち仏行なり。坐即不為也。是、即、自己の正躰也。此
外、別に仏法の可求無き也。

3-18

一日、請益の次に云、

　近代の僧侶、多く世俗にしたがふべしと云ふ。思に不然。世間
の賢すら、猶、随民俗ことを、穢たる事と云て、屈原の如きは、
皆酔へり、我は独醒たり、とて、民俗に不随して、つひに滄浪に没
す。況や仏法は、事々皆、世俗に違背せる也。俗は髪をかざる、
僧は髪をそる。俗は多く食す、僧は一食するすら、皆そむけり。然
後、還て大安楽人也。故に一切世俗に可背也。

3-19

一日、示云、

　治世の法は、上自天子、下至庶民、各皆、居其官者、修其
業。非其人して、其官をするを、乱天の事と云。政道、叶天意時、
世清、民康也。故に帝は、三更の三点におきさせ給て、治世する
時と、しませり。たやすからざる事、只、職のかはり、業の殊なる
ばかり也。国王は、自思量を以て、治道をはからひ、先規をかん

the principle of nonseeking. Nanyue's polishing of a tile to make a mirror admonished Mazu's seeking to become a buddha.[196] He did not restrain Mazu from doing zazen.

Sitting itself is the Buddha's practice. Sitting itself is not-doing.[197] This is itself the true form of the Self.[198] Aside from this [sitting], there is no Buddhadharma that must be sought.

3-18

One day, when giving instruction, [Dōgen] said:

These days, many monks say that we should follow worldly customs. In my consideration, this is not right. Even in the mundane world, wise people say that it is impure to follow the customs of the people. For example, Qu Yuan said, "Everyone in the world is drunk; only I am sober." He refused to go along with the customs of the people and finally threw himself into the Canglang River and drowned.[199] Moreover, in the Buddhadharma each and every thing is contrary to worldly customs. Laypeople style and adorn their hair; monks shave off their hair. Laypeople eat in abundance; monks eat once a day.[200] Everything is contrary. And finally, [monks] will be people of great peace and joy.[201] For this reason, [the way of monks] should be totally opposed to worldly customs.

3-19

One day, [Dōgen] instructed:

As for the way the world is ordered, from the emperor down to the common people, everyone carries out the functions of their own occupation. If they are not suitable for their position, this is called "putting the world into disorder." When the manner of governance is in accordance with the will of heaven,[202] the world is in good order and the people are at ease. Therefore, the emperor wakes up at the third part of the third watch[203] to do the work of governing the world. This is not an easy job. It is just that the functions and the activities

がへ、有道の臣を求めて、政、相合天意時、是、云治世也。若、是を怠れば、背天、乱世、教民苦也。其より以下、諸侯・大夫・人士・庶民、皆各、有所官業。随其云人也。背其、為乱天事、蒙天之刑也。

然ば、学人も、世を離れ、家を出ればとて、徒に身をやすくせんと思ふこと、暫くも不可有。似有利、後有大害也。出家人の法は、又、其職を収め、其の業を修すべき也。

世間の治世は、先規有道を稽求れども、猶、先達知識の、たしかに相伝したるなければ、自し、たがふる事も有也。仏子は、たしかなる、先規教文顕然也。又相承伝来の、知識現在せり。我に思量あり、四威儀の中にをいて、一々に先規を思ひ、先達にしたがひ、修行せんに、必、道を得べき也。俗は天意に合せんと思ひ、衲子は仏意に合せんと修す。業等して、得果勝れたり。一得永得、大安楽の為に、一世幻化の身を、苦しめて、仏意に随はんは、可在行者心。

雖然、又、すぞろに苦身、不可作事を作せと、仏教には、すすむること無き也。戒行律儀に随ひゆけば、自然に身安く、行儀も尋常に、人目も安き也。只、今案の我見の安立をすてて、一向、仏制に可順也。

又、云、

我、大宋天童禅院に居せし時、浄老住持の時は、宵は二更の三点まで坐禅し、暁は四更の、二点三点より、おきて坐禅す。長老ともに、僧堂裏坐。一夜も闕怠なし。其間、衆僧多く眠る。長老巡

he must carry out are different [from what other people do]. In the case of the emperor, he personally performs the duties of governing with all his intelligence, considering precedents from previous ages, while seeking out ministers endowed with virtue and ability. When his way of reigning is in accordance with the will of heaven, it is called a "well-governed world." If the emperor is negligent in his duties, then he goes against the will of heaven, the world becomes disordered, and the people suffer. From the emperor to the nobility, to the high officials, to the senior officials, to the common officials, and down to the common people, all are in charge of some respective function. As human beings, they must execute their duties in this way. If people go against their duties, they will receive punishment from heaven because they have caused disorder in heaven.

Therefore, you students [of the Buddhadharma], even though you have left home and renounced the world, you should not wish to lead an easy life even for a moment. Although in the beginning it may seem advantageous, later on it will be the cause of great harm. Following the way of monks who have left home, we should fulfill our duties and throw ourselves into our practice.

In governing the mundane world, even if [the emperor] pursues precedents and seeks out virtuous and capable [ministers], because there is no certain way that has been handed down by the ancient sages or past leaders, naturally he might make mistakes. For the children of the Buddha, however, there are definite precedents and scriptural teachings. There are also masters who have received the transmission of such traditions. [Furthermore,] we are capable of thought. In each of the four dignified actions,[204] if we think of precedents and follow our predecessors in our practice, there is no reason to fail in attaining the Way. Laypeople wish to be in accordance with the will of heaven, while patch-robed monks practice to be in harmony with the will of the Buddha. The tasks are the same, but the results [for Buddhists] are superior. This is because the great peace and joy, which is never lost once attained, depends only upon having

行、睡眠する僧をば、或は拳を以て打、或はくつをぬいで打、恥しめ勧めて、覚睡。猶、睡時は、行照堂、打鐘、召行者燃蝋燭なんどして、卒時に普説して云、僧堂裏にあつまり居して、徒に眠りて何の用ぞ。然ば何ぞ、出家入叢林する。見ず麼、世間の帝王官人、何人か身をやすくする。王道を収め、忠節を尽し、乃至庶民は、田を開き、鍬をとるまでも、何人か身をやすくして世をすごす。是をのがれて、叢林に入て、虚く過時光。畢竟じて何の用ぞ。生死事大也、無常迅速也。教家も禅家も同すすむ。今夕明旦、何なる死をか受け、何なる病をかせん。且く存ずる程、仏法を行ぜず、眠臥して、虚く過時。尤愚也。故に仏法は衰へ去也。諸方仏法の、さかりなりし時は、叢林皆坐禅を専にせり。近代諸方坐をすすめざれば仏法澆薄しもてゆくなり。

　如是道理を以て、衆僧すすめて坐禅せしめし事、親く見之也。今の学人も、彼の風を思べし。

　又、或時、近仕の侍者等云、僧堂裡の衆僧、眠りつかれ、或は病も発り、退心も起りつべし。坐久き故歟。坐禅の時尅を、被縮ばや、と申ければ、長老大に諫めて云、不可然。無道心の者、仮名に僧堂に居するは、半時片時なりとも、猶、可眠。道心ありて修行の志あらんは、長らんにつけ、喜び修せんずる也。我若かりし時、諸方長老を、歴観せしに、如是すすめて、眠る僧をば、拳のかけなんとするほど、打せめし也。今は老後になりて、よわくなりて、人をも打得せざるほどに、よき僧も出来らざる也。諸方の長老も、坐

the aspiration to make this phantom-like body follow the will of the Buddha in this lifetime.

Nevertheless, the Buddha's teachings also never compel us to subject our body to meaningless suffering or to do something that should not be done. If we follow the demeanor and behavior prescribed in the precepts, our body will be at ease, our behavior will be appropriate, and we will not disturb others. Therefore, we should abandon any self-centered views we now have and thoroughly follow the Buddha's precepts.

[*Dōgen*] *also said*:

When I was staying at Tiantong Zen monastery in great Song China, while the old master Rujing was the abbot there, we did zazen until the third part of the second watch[205] and got up at about the second or third part of the fourth watch[206] to do zazen. The old master sat with the assembly in the monks' hall. He never took even a single night off. While sitting, many monks fell asleep. The old master walked around hitting them with his fist or his clog, scolding them and compelling them to wake up. If they continued to sleep, he went to the illuminated hall,[207] rang the bell, and called his attendants to light the candles. On the spur of the moment he would give an informal sermon, saying, for example, "What is the use of sleeping in vain while you are gathered together in the monks' hall? Why did you leave home to become a monk and enter this monastery? Do you not see how the emperor and government officials work in the world? Who among them leads an easy life? The emperor righteously administers justice, the ministers serve with loyalty, and so on, down to the commoners who cultivate the rice fields holding their hoes. Who leads an easy life without laboring? You have avoided these labors and entered a monastery, but you now spend your time wastefully. What on earth is the point of it? Life-and-death is the great matter. Everything is impermanent and changes swiftly. The teaching schools and the Zen schools both emphasize this and encourage [us to practice diligently]. You may die this evening or tomorrow morning. [You have no idea] when and how your death may come or what kind of sickness you

を緩くすすむる故に、仏法は衰微せる也。弥々打可也、とのみ、
被示し也。

3-20

又、云、

　得道の事は、心をもて得るか、以身得るか。教家等にも、身心
一如と云て、以身得とは云へども、猶、一如の故にと云。正く、身
の得る事は、たしかならず。今、我が家は、身心倶に得也。其中に

may contract. It is utterly foolish to pass the time while you are alive sleeping or meaninglessly lying down, failing to practice the Buddha-dharma. It is because you practice like this that the Buddhadharma is declining. When the Buddhadharma flourished in monasteries throughout the country, people devotedly did zazen. In recent times, the Buddhadharma is falling into decay because no masters in the various monasteries promote sitting."

I personally saw him encouraging the monks in his assembly with such reasoning and making them do zazen. Today's students should also think of his style of practice.

Also, his lead attendant and others once beseeched him, saying, "The monks in the monks' hall are tired and sleepy. They may fall ill or lose their aspiration because of the long hours of sitting. Please shorten the time of zazen." The old master strictly admonished them, saying, "We must never do that. People without the mind of awaken-ing temporarily staying in the monks' hall would sleep even if we sat for only half an hour or less. Practitioners with the mind of awakening who aspire to practice are happier the longer they are able to sit and, therefore, practice much harder. When I was young, I visited various teachers in different regions. They all encouraged monks in this way and hit them so hard that they almost broke their fists. But since I am now old and weak, I can no longer hit the monks so hard. Con-sequently, no good monks develop. Because the elders at the various monasteries are lenient about sitting, the Buddhadharma is falling into decay. We must hit them all the more!"

3-20

[*Dōgen*] *also said*:

Is the Way attained with the mind or the body? In the teaching schools, it is said that because body and mind are not separate, the Way is attained [not only with the mind but also] with the body.[208] Yet it is not clear that we attain the Way with the body, because they say body and mind are not separate. Now, in my [Dharma] family, the

心をもて、仏法を計校する間は、万劫千生にも不可得、放下心捨
知見解会時、得る也。見色明心、聞声悟道ごときも、猶、身を得
也。然れば、心の念慮知見を、一向すてて、只管打坐すれば、今
少し道は、親得也。然ば、道を得ことは、正く身を以て得也。是に
よりて、坐を専にすべしと覚也。

正法眼蔵随聞記　三　終

Way is [truly] attained with both body and mind. As long as we only think about the Buddhadharma with our minds, we will never grasp the Way, even in a thousand lifetimes or ten thousand eons. When we let go of our minds and put aside our views and understandings, the Way will be actualized. [One person] clarified the mind by seeing the color [of peach blossoms], and another realized the Way by hearing the sound [of a piece of tile hitting bamboo].[209] They attained the Way with their bodies. Therefore, when we completely cast aside our thoughts and views and just sit [*shikantaza*], we will become intimate with the Way. For this reason, the Way is truly attained with the body.[210] This is why I think we should wholeheartedly practice zazen.

The End of the Third Book of *Shōbōgenzō Zuimonki*

正法眼蔵随聞記　四
侍者　懐奘　編

4-1

示曰、

　学道の人、放下身心、一向可入仏法。古人云、百尺竿頭上、猶進一歩。何にも、百尺の竿頭に上て、足を放たば、死べしと思て、つよくとりつく心の有也。其を思切りて、一歩を進と云は、よもあしからじと、思ひきりて、放下する様に、度世の業より始て、一身の活計に至まで、何にも捨得ぬなり。其を捨ざらん程は、何に頭燃をはらひて、学道する様なりとも、道を得こと不叶也。思きり、身心倶に放下すべし。

4-2

或時、比丘尼云、世間の女房なんどだにも、仏法とて学すれば、比丘尼の身には、少々の不可ありとも、何で可不叶と覚。如何、と云し時。

SHŌBŌGENZŌ ZUIMONKI, BOOK 4
Compiled by the attendant Ejō

4-1

[*Dōgen*] *instructed*:

Students of the Way! We should cast away[211] our body and mind and completely enter the Buddhadharma. An ancient said, "At the top of a hundred-foot pole, take one step further."[212] When we have climbed to the top of the one-hundred-foot pole, we certainly think that we will die if we let go of our foothold, and we have a mental tendency to hold fast to the pole. Making up our mind to "take one step further" means [to enter the Buddhadharma]. Having resolved to [take this step] and thinking it cannot be bad, we should give up everything as if casting away [body and mind], from our profession to our livelihood. [And yet,] it is extremely difficult for us to discard these things. Unless we give them up, even if we appear to practice the Way arduously, as though attempting to extinguish a fire enveloping our heads,[213] it is not possible to attain the Way. Make the determination to cast away both body and mind.

4-2

One time, a nun asked, "Even women in lay society study the Buddhadharma. As for nuns [who have left the mundane world], even if we

示云、

此義、不可然。在家の女人、其身ながら、仏法を学で、うるこ
とはありとも、出家人の、出家の心なからんは、不可得。仏法の、
人をえらぶには非ず。人の仏法に不入也。出家在家の儀、其心可
殊。在家人の、出家の心有ば、出離すべし。出家人の、在家の心
有ば、二重の僻事也。用心可殊事也。作ことの難にはあらず。よく
することの難き也。出離得道の行、人ごとに心にかけたるに、似
たれども、よくする人の難き也。生死事大也、無常迅速也。心をゆ
るくすることなかれ。世をすてば、実に世を可捨也。仮名は、何に
ても、ありなんと、おぼゆる也。

4-3

夜話云、

世人を見るに、果報もよく、家をも起す人は、皆正直に、人の
為にもよき也。故に家をも持、子孫までも、不絶也。心に曲節あ
り、人の為にあしき人は、たとひ一旦は、果報もよく、家をたもて
る様なれども、始終あしき也。縦ひ又、一期は、よくてすぐせども、
子孫未必吉也。

又、為人、善事を、為人にして、彼主に善しと被思、被悦と
思てするは、比於悪勝たれども、猶、是は思自身、為人、非実善

have some faults, I feel there is no reason we [unlike laywomen] are not in accord with Buddhadharma. What do you think?"

[*Dōgen*] *instructed*:

[What you said] is not right. Although there are some laywomen who study the Buddhadharma and attain it [as laypeople], home-leavers who lack the mind of home-leaving cannot attain the Way. It is not that the Buddhadharma discriminates among people, but [rather that such] people do not enter the Buddhadharma. There must be a difference in the mental attitude between people in laity and home-leavers. Laypeople who have the mind of home-leaving can be released [from saṃsāra]. [On the other hand,] if home-leavers have the mind of laity, they double their faults. Their mental attitudes should be quite different. It is not that [becoming a home-leaver] is difficult to do. [However,] to do so completely is difficult. It seems that everyone seeks a practice to be released [from saṃsāra] and attain the Way, but those who completely accomplish it are difficult [to find]. Life-and-death is the great matter; impermanence is swift.[214] Do not let your mind slacken. If you renounce the world, you should truly renounce it. I think the provisional names [of "home-leavers" and "laypeople"] are not at all important.

4-3

In an evening talk, [*Dōgen*] *said*:

Among the laity, I see that people who have good fortune[215] and have enabled their families to prosper are all honest and work for the benefit of others. Therefore, they are able to maintain their family prosperity, and their descendents will not die out in later generations. Even if those who are dishonest or those who harm others seem to temporarily receive good fortune and are able to maintain their livelihood for a while, in the end their prosperity will decline. Even if such people seem to spend their lifetimes without trouble, their descendents will not necessarily be fortunate.

Furthermore, when we do good things for others, if we do so because of our desire to be thought well of, or to ingratiate ourselves

也。主には不被知とも、人の為に、うしろやすく、乃至、未来の
事、為誰不思ども、為人よからん料事を作置なんどするを、真に
為人善とは云也。

　況や、衲僧は、是には超たる心を可持也。衆生を思ふ事、親
疎をわかたず、平等に済度の心を存じ、世、出世間利益、都、不
憶自利、不被人知、不主被悦、唯だ為人善き事を、心の中になし
て、我は如是心、もたると、人不被知也。

　此の故実は、先づ須世棄捨身也。我身をだにも、真実に捨離
つれば、人に善被思と云心は無き也。然ども、又、人は何にも、
思はば思へとて、悪き事を行じ、放逸ならんは、又背仏意。唯、
行好事。為人やすき事をなして、代を思に、我よき名を留めんと
不思、真実無所得にて、利生の事をなす。即、離吾我第一の用心
也。

　欲存此心、先づ、須念無常。一期は如夢、光陰易移。露の命
は待がたふして、明るを知らぬならひなれば、唯、暫も存じたる
程、聊の事につけても、人の為によく、仏意に順はんと、思べき
なり。

with others, even though this is better than doing harmful things, such actions are not truly for the benefit of others because we are still thinking of the benefit to ourselves. If we do helpful things for others although they do not notice, or we do beneficial things for future generations without considering whom our acts may benefit, [then] we are truly doing good things for others.

Needless to say, we patch-robed monks should maintain a mind beyond even this attitude. We should have compassion for all living beings without making distinctions based on degree of intimacy and maintain an attitude of saving all beings equally. We should never think of our own personal profit in terms of benefit in either the mundane or transcendent world.[216] Even if we are neither known nor appreciated by others, we should simply perform beneficial actions for others in accord with our own heart and not let others know that we have such a heart.

The ancient practice [for keeping this attitude] is, first of all, renouncing the world and casting aside the self. Only if we have truly thrown away the self will we have no desire to be well thought of by others. However, if we think, "I do not care what others may think," and we act unwholesomely or become self-indulgent, we instead go against the will of the Buddha. We should simply perform wholesome actions and do beneficial things for others. We should not think about the return or expect to gain a good reputation. We should do things truly knowing there is nothing to be gained and work for the sake of benefiting others. This is the primary point to bear in mind in order to achieve release from our ego-clinging.

To maintain this mind [of no desire for gain], we must first of all be mindful of impermanence. One's lifetime is like a dream. Time passes swiftly. Our dew-like lives will disappear even before the dawn. While we are alive for this short time, we must resolve to perform beneficial actions for others and follow the will of the Buddha.

4-4

夜話云、

　学道の人は、尤可貧。見世人、有財人は、先づ瞋恚恥辱の
二難、定て来る也。有財、欲人奪取是、我欲不被取、瞋恚忽に起
る。或は、論之、及問注対決、遂、致闘諍合戦。如是間、瞋恚起、
恥辱来也。貧而不貪時、先免此難。安楽自在也。証拠眼前也。
不可待教文。加之、先人後賢譏之、諸天仏祖、皆、恥之。而、為
愚人、貯財宝、懐瞋恚、成愚人、恥辱の中の恥辱也。貧而、思道
者、先賢後聖之所仰、仏祖冥道之所喜也。

　仏法陵遅し行こと、眼前に近し。予、始、入建仁寺時見しと、後
七八年に次第にかはりゆくことは、寺の寮々に、各々塗籠をし、
持器物、好美服、貯財物、好放逸之言語、問訊礼拝等、陵遅する
事を以て思ふに、余所も被推察也。

　仏法者は、衣鉢の外は、財をもつべからず。何を置かん為に塗
籠をしつらふべきぞ。人にかくす程の物を、不可持、不持、返てや
すき也。人をば殺すとも、人には不被殺なんどと、思ふ時こそ、身
もくるしく、用心もせらるれ。人は我を殺すとも、我は不加報と、
思定めつれば、先づ用心もせられず、盗賊も愁へられざるなり。
時として無不安楽。

4-4

In an evening talk, [Dōgen] said:

Students of the Way should, most importantly, be poor. Looking at people in the mundane world, to start with, those who possess wealth will certainly have two kinds of difficulties: anger and shame. If they have wealth, other people will want to take it. Not wanting [their possessions] to be stolen, anger immediately arises. They would perhaps have arguments regarding the matter [of their wealth being taken] and eventually start a lawsuit or a confrontation that could escalate into a fight or battle.[217] Within such processes, anger arises, and shameful situations may occur. If we live in poverty and lack greed, we are likely to be spared such troubles. We can be peaceful, joyful, and free. The evidence is right in front of our eyes. We do not need to find proof in the scriptures. Furthermore, our predecessors and the worthies to come criticize [having wealth], and the various heavenly beings, buddhas, and ancestors all denounce it. Therefore, to thoughtlessly amass wealth, give way to anger, and become a foolish person is the most shameful of shameful things. Those who are in poverty and yet yearn for the Way bring delight to the buddhas and ancestors and unseen heavenly beings, and are respected by the ancient worthies and wise saints to come.

We can see the decline of the Buddhadharma right before our eyes. [Compared with] when I first entered Kennin-ji monastery, seven or eight years later things had gradually changed:[218] [monks] had built storerooms in each temple building and had a variety of possessions; they liked luxurious clothing, owned property, and indulged in meaningless conversations; they did not care about the forms of greeting one another[219] nor about making prostrations [before the Buddha]. Considering these things, I can only imagine what has happened in other monasteries.

People of the Buddhadharma should not possess anything aside from robes and a begging bowl. What do they need to store when they

4-5

一日、示云、

　宋土海門禅師、天童の長老たりし時、会下、元首座と云僧有き。此人、得法悟道人也。長老にも、こえたり。

　有時、夜、参方丈、焼香礼拝して云、請らくは、師許後堂首座。

　門、流涕して云、我、小僧たりし、未聞如是事。汝、為禅僧、所望首座長老。汝、已に悟道せることは、見先規、超於我。然に首座を望こと、昇進の為か。許ことは前堂をも、乃至、長老をも、可許。余の未悟僧、察之、仏法の衰微、是を以、可知と、云て、流涕悲泣す。

　爰に、僧、恥て、雖辞、猶、補首座。其後、首座、此事を記録して、恥自、彰師美言。

　今案之、昇進を望み、物の首となり、長老にならんと思ふことをば、古人是を恥しむ。只、悟道のみ思て、不可有余事

make storerooms? We should not own anything that we have to hide from others. Rather, when we do not possess anything, we can be at ease. When we are compelled to kill so as not to be killed, we suffer, and our minds are anxious. When we make up our minds not to retaliate even if someone tries to kill us, we need not be on guard or worry about thieves. We will never fail to be filled with peace and joy.

4-5

One day, [Dōgen] instructed:

While Zen Master Haimen[220] was the abbot of Tiantong monastery in Song China, there was a head monk in his assembly named Yuan.[221] This person had attained the Dharma and realized the Way. He had surpassed even the abbot himself.

One night, [before he was head monk, Yuan] visited the abbot's room, offered incense, gave prostrations, and asked, "I request that you appoint me the head monk of the rear hall."[222]

[Hai]men shed tears, and said, "Since the time I was a novice, I have never heard of such a thing. You, as a Zen monk, request [the position of] head monk or abbot. You have already realized the Way. Looking back at previous masters, I can see that you have surpassed me. Do you seek the position of the head monk for the sake of promotion? I would have allowed you to be [the head monk of] the front hall or even the abbot. [From your behavior] I can only imagine how other monks who have not yet realized the Way might be. The decline of the Buddhadharma can be seen from this." Saying so, he shed tears and wept with sorrow.

Although the monk [Yuan] left ashamed of himself and declined the position, [the abbot went on and] appointed him as the head monk. Later, the head monk recorded this conversation, shaming himself and praising his master's excellent words.

Now that I think about this, I see that the ancients put people to shame if [such people] wanted to make themselves important, to become the head of things, or to attain the position of abbot. We

4-6

一夜、示云、

　唐の太宗、即位の後、旧殿に栖給へり。破損せる間、湿気あがり、風霧をかして、玉躰応被侵。臣下、可作造由を奏し鳧ば、帝云く、時、農節也。民、定めて、可有愁。待秋可造。被侵湿気、地に受られず、風雨被侵、天に不叶也。天地に背かば、身不可有。不煩民、自、天地に可叶。天地に叶はば、不可犯身、と云て、終に不作宮、栖古殿給へり。

　況や仏子、受如来家風、一切衆生を如一子可憐。属我侍者所従なればとて、呵責し煩はすべからず。何況同学等侶、耆年宿老等を、恭敬する事、如如来すべしと、戒文文明也。然ば、今の学人も、人には色に出て知れずとも、心中に上下親疎を不別、為人よからんと可思也。

　大小事につけて、人をわづらはし、心を傷すこと不可有也。

　如来在世に、外道多く謗如来、悪くむも有き。仏弟子問云、本より柔和を本とし、慈を心とす。一切衆生等く恭敬すべし。何故にか、如是有不随衆生。仏、言、我、昔衆を領ぜし時、多く呵責羯磨をもて、弟子をいましめて、是に依つて今如是、と、律中に見たり。然ば即、住持長老として、領衆たりとも、弟子の非をただし、いさめんとて、呵責の言を、不可用。以柔和言、いさめすすむと

should just aspire to realize the Way without being concerned with anything else.

4-6

One evening, [Dōgen] instructed:

After his enthronement, Taizong[223] of the Tang dynasty lived in an old palace. Because it was damaged, it became damp, wind and mist entered into it, and the emperor's health was at risk of being harmed. When his ministers made a proposal to build a new palace, the emperor said, "This is the busy farming season. The people will certainly be distressed [if construction begins now]. We should wait until autumn to build. Being afflicted by moisture is due to not being accepted by the earth; being afflicted by wind and rain is due to not living in accordance with heaven. If I go against heaven and earth, I cannot keep my body [healthy]. If I do not cause the people trouble, I will be in accordance with heaven and earth. If [my conduct] is in harmony with heaven and earth, my body will not be damaged." So saying, he did not construct a new palace, and ultimately, he continued to live in the old one.

Furthermore, we as the Buddha's children should maintain the family tradition of the Tathāgata and have compassion toward all living beings as if each of them were our only child.[224] Even if they are our attendants or servants, do not scold them and cause them trouble. Moreover, we should respect and venerate our copractitioners, seniors, and elders as if we were venerating the Tathāgata. This is clearly written in the precepts. Therefore, today's students should also consider doing beneficial things for others without making distinctions between people of the upper and lower classes, or the intimate and unrelated, even if their deeds are not seen and not known to others.

Whether it be a big or small matter, we should not trouble people and hurt their feelings.

While the Tathāgata was in the world, there were many non-Buddhists who slandered him, and some even hated him. A disciple

も、可随は、可随也。況や、衲子、親疎兄弟等の為に、あらき言
を以て、人をにくみ呵責する事は、一向に可止也。能々、可用意
也。

4-7

又云、

　衲子の用心、仏祖の行履を守るべし。第一には、財宝を貪る
べからず。如来慈悲深重なること、喩へを以て推量するに、彼の
所為行履、皆、是、為衆生也。一微塵許、無不為衆生利益。其故
は、仏は是れ、輪王の太子にてまします。一天をも御意にまかせ
給つべし。以財、哀弟子、以所領、弟子をはごくむべくんば、何の
故にか、捨て、自、行乞食給べき。決定、為末世衆生、為弟子行
道、可有利益因縁故に、不貯財宝、乞食を行じおき給へり。然し
より以来、天竺漢土の祖師の由、又、人にも知れしは、皆、貧窮乞
食せし也。

　況や、我門の祖々、皆、財宝を不可畜と、のみ、すすむる也。
教家にも此宗を讃たるに、先づ、是をほめ、記録の家にも、此事

of the Buddha said, "From the beginning, you have been gentle and compassionate in your heart. All living beings should venerate you equally. What is the reason some people do not follow your teachings?" The Buddha said, "In [my] past lives, when I led many people in my assembly, I often admonished my disciples by scolding them and finding fault with them. Because of [these past misdeeds], things like this happen in the present." This conversation can be found in the Vinaya precepts. Therefore, even when we as abbots or elders lead a group of practitioners, we should not use abusive or critical words to admonish our disciples and scold them. If we use gentle words to admonish or encourage them, people who [have the aspiration to] follow will follow. Needless to say, patch-robed monks should never harbor hatred and scold copractitioners using abusive language, whether they are closely related or not. We should be very careful about this.

4-7

[*Dōgen*] *also said*:

To have the mental attitude of a patch-robed monk, we should observe the conduct of the buddhas and ancestors. First of all, we should not be greedy for wealth. As we can surmise from the parables, the Tathāgata had deep and great compassion. Everything he did was for the sake of all living beings. He never did even the slightest thing that was not for the benefit of living beings. What is the reason I say so? The Buddha was the crown prince of the wheel-turning king.[225] [If the Buddha had become king,] he could have ruled the world as he wished. He could have taken care of his disciples with his wealth or fostered them in his fiefdom. Why did he give this up to practice begging on his own? He did not accumulate wealth and practiced begging for food because it was certain to be more beneficial for people in the age of the last Dharma[226] and also for his disciples' practice of the Way. Since then, ancestral masters in India and China as well as well-known practitioners have all practiced begging for food while [living] in great poverty.

を記して讃むる也。未聞富饒財行仏法。皆よき仏法者と云は、或は、布衲衣、常乞食也。禅門に、よき僧と云はれ、はじめおこるも、或は教院、律院等に、雑居せし時も、禅僧の異をば、身をすて、貧人なるを以て、異せりとす。宗門の家風、先、此事を存べし。聖教の文理を待べからす。我身にも、田園等を持たる時も有りき。又、財宝を領ぜし時も有りき。彼時の身心と、此ごろ貧して、衣盂に乏き時とを比するに、当時の心、勝たりと覚ふ。是、現証也。

又云、

古人云、不似其人、莫語其風、と。言心は、その人の悳を不学不知して、其人の失なるを、其人はよけれども、其事あしき也。（あしき）事をよき人もすると、思べからず。只、其人の取徳、莫取失。君子は、取徳、不取失、と云、此心也。

4-8

一日示云、

Furthermore, all of the ancestors in our tradition have emphasized not storing up wealth. Even in the teaching schools,[227] when people praise our school they primarily speak well of this [style of frugality]. The writers of the biographies of monks have also honored [Zen monks] for this [style of practice]. I have never heard of anyone who was rich in material wealth practicing the Buddhadharma. All eminent practitioners of the Buddhadharma have lived only with a patched robe and have always practiced begging. From the time when the Zen school first arose, when Zen monks stayed at the temples belonging to the teaching schools or the Vinaya school, they were considered to be good monks that were different from other monks because they abandoned [attachment to] the self and lived in poverty.[228] Regarding the family tradition of this school, we must primarily remember this point. We do not need to look for written proof within the sacred scriptures. There was a time when I myself owned an estate, and so forth. There was a time when I possessed material wealth as well.[229] Comparing the condition of my body and mind at that time with my present condition of poverty, of possessing just robes and a bowl, I feel that my current state of mind is superior. This is the actual proof.

[*Dōgen*] *also said*:

An ancient said, "Do not speak of a person's conduct if you are not empathizing with them." This means that if we have not perceived and understood others' virtues, we should not criticize them when we see their faults, but rather we should think that they are good and it is just their actions that are bad; even good people do things that seem bad. We should acknowledge only people's virtues, not their faults. The saying "a wise person sees another's virtues and not their faults" means the same thing.

4-8

One day, [Dōgen] instructed:

人は、必、可修陰徳。必、有冥加顕益。たとひ泥木塑像の麁悪
なりとも、仏像をば、可敬礼。黄紙朱軸の荒品なりとも、経教を
ば可帰敬。破戒無慚の僧侶なりとも、僧躰をば可信仰。内心に
信心をもて、敬礼すれば、必、蒙顕福也。破戒無慚の僧なれば、
疎相、麁品の経なればとて、不信無礼なれば、必、被罰也。しか
あるべき如来の遺法にて、人天の福分となりたる、仏像・経巻・僧
侶也。故に帰敬すれば、益あり、不信なれば、罪を受る也。何に希
有に、浅増くとも、三宝の境界をば、可恭敬也。禅僧は、不修善、
不要功徳と云て好悪行きはめて、僻事也。先規、未聞如是好悪行
事。

　丹霞天然禅師は木仏をたく。是こそ悪事と見へたれども、是も
一段の説法施設也。此の師の行状の記を見るに、坐するに必儀
あり。立するに必礼あり。常に貴賓客に向が如し。暫時の坐にも必
跏趺し、又手す。常住物を守ること、眼睛の如くす。勤修するもの
有れば必ず加す。小善なれども是を重くす。常図の行状勝たり。彼
の記をとどめて、今の世までも、叢林の亀鏡とする也。
　しかのみならず、諸有道の師、先規悟道の祖、見聞するに、
皆戒行を守り、威儀を調ふ。たとひ小善と云とも、是を重くす。未
聞、悟道の師の、善根を忽諸することを。故に学人祖道に随んと
思はば、必、善根をかろしめざれ。信教を専にすべし。仏祖の行
道は、必、衆善の所集也。諸法皆仏法なりと、体達しつる上は、
悪は決定悪にて、仏祖の道に遠ざかり、善は決定善にて、仏道の

We should not fail to do good in secret. [If we do good in secret] we will surely receive unseen protection and clear reward. We should venerate Buddha images, even if they are crude, molded statues made of clay and wood. We should take refuge in the teachings of the sutras even if they are written on coarse scrolls made of yellow paper attached to a red rod.[230] We should have faith and respect monkhood even if there are shameless monks who violate the precepts. If we venerate them and prostrate ourselves with faith in our heart, we will surely receive clear blessings. Although we might encounter shameless monks or coarse sutra scrolls, if we do not have faith in them, and treat them disrespectfully, we will certainly receive punishment. Thus, if we take refuge in them and venerate them, we will receive benefit, but if we are faithless, we will receive punishment. No matter how uncommonly crude [some of its aspects] may be, we should venerate the world of the Three Treasures. It is extremely wrong to be fond of committing evil deeds under the pretext that a Zen monk does not need to practice good or seek virtues. By the standards of the past I have never heard of any of our predecessors who indulged in evil deeds such as these.

Zen Master Danxia Tianran[231] burned a wooden statue of the Buddha. Although it seemed to be nothing but an evil deed, his actions were a skillful means of expressing the Dharma. When we read the record of this master's behavior, we find that his sitting was always in accordance with the prescribed standard and while standing he always followed good manners. He always behaved courteously as if he were meeting a noble guest. Even when he sat for a short while, he sat cross-legged, and [when he stood] he held his hands in *shashu*.[232] He protected temple property as though caring for his own eyes.[233] He never failed to offer encouragement when he saw someone practicing diligently. He valued good deeds even if they were small. His behavior in his daily life was excellent. To this day, the record of his deeds remains as a good example in Zen monasteries.

縁となる。可知、若、如是ならば、何ぞ三宝の境界を、重せざらん
や。

　又、云、

　今仏祖（の道）を行ぜんと思はば、所期も無く、所求も無く、
所得も無くして、無利に先聖の道を行じ、祖々の行履を行ずべき
也。所求を断じ、仏果をのぞむべからず。さればとて、修行をとど
め、本の悪行にとどまらば、還て、是、所求に堕し、窠臼にとどま
る也。全く一分の所期を不存、只、人天の福分とならんとて、僧の
威儀を守り、済度利生の行儀を思ひ、衆善を好み修して、本の悪
をすて、今の善にとどこほらずして、一期、行じもてゆけば、是を
古人も、打破漆桶底と云也。仏祖の行履如是也。

Not only this Zen master but all the virtuous masters who have
attained the Way and the ancestors who realized the Way and who
have been respected as our models, all of them maintained the behavior prescribed by the precepts and conducted themselves with dignity.
They appreciated even minor good deeds. I have never heard of any
master of the Way who disregarded good actions. Students of the
Way! If you wish to follow the Way of the ancestors, you should never
make light of good actions. We should wholeheartedly trust the Buddha's teachings. All good accumulates where the Way of the buddhas
and ancestors is practiced. Once you have clarified that all Dharmas
are the Buddhadharma, you should still know that evil is definitely
evil and that it causes us to depart from the Way of the buddhas and
ancestors. Good is always good and connects us with the Buddha Way.
If we know that this is so, how can we not value [all aspects of] the
world of the Three Treasures?

[*Dōgen*] *also said*:

Now, if we wish to practice the Way of the buddhas and ancestors, we should practice the Way of the previous sages and emulate
the conduct of the ancestors [while] expecting nothing, seeking nothing, and attaining nothing. We should cut off our desire for seeking;
we should not expect even the fruit of Buddhahood. Nevertheless, if
we stop practicing and remain engaged in our former evil deeds, we
will be guilty of seeking, and we will remain in our nest.[234] Solely for
the sake of becoming the foundation of happiness for human and
heavenly beings and without having the slightest of expectations, we
should maintain the prescribed manner of conduct, think of acting to
save and benefit living beings, and earnestly perform all good deeds
while giving up our former evil ones. Without stagnating in the good
deeds of the present, we should continue to practice throughout our
lifetime. An ancient called this "breaking the bottom of the pail of
lacquer."[235] The conduct of buddhas and ancestors is like this.

4-9

一日、僧来て、問学道之用心次に、示云、

　学道の人は、先、須貧。財多ければ、必、其の志を失う。在家学道の者、猶、財宝にまとはり、居所を貪り、眷属に交れば、直饒その志ありと云へども、障道の縁多し。古来、俗人の参ずる多けれども、其中によしと云へども、猶、僧には不及。僧は一衣一鉢の外は、財宝を不持、居所を不思、衣食を不貪間、一向に学道す。是は分々皆有得益也。其故は、貧なるが、道に親き也。

　龐公は俗人なれども、僧におとらず、禅席に名を留めたるは、彼の人、参禅の初め、家の財宝を以ちて出でて、海にしづめんとす。

　人、諫之云、人にも与へ、仏事にも用べし。

　対他云、我、已にあたなりと思うて、是をすつ。焉可与人。財は身心を愁しむるあた也。遂に入海了ぬ。而後、活命の為には、いかきをつくりて売て過ぎ髠。俗なれども如是財をすててこそ、禅人とも云はれけれ。何況や、一向に僧は、すつべき也。

　僧云、唐土には寺院定まり、僧祇物あり、常住物等あつて僧の為めに行道の縁となる。無其煩。此国は、無其儀、一向棄置せられても、中々行道の違乱とやならん。如是衣食資縁を、思ひあててあらば、よしと覚ふ、如何。

　示云、

　不然。中々唐土より此国の人は、無理に人を供養じ、非分に人に物を与ること有也。先づ人はしらず、我は此事を行じて、道理を

4-9

One day, on the occasion of a monk visiting and asking about points to watch in practicing the Way, [Dōgen] instructed:

Students of the Way should first of all be poor. If we have much wealth, we will definitely lose the aspiration [to practice]. Those who study the Way as home-dwellers are still bound by their wealth; they greedily indulge in their houses and associate with their families and relatives. Even if they have the aspiration [to practice], they will have many obstacles in practicing the Way. Since ancient times there have been many laypeople who visited [Zen masters to practice]; however, even if they were good practitioners, they could still not be the equals of monks. Because monks do not possess any property at all except for one robe and one bowl,[236] they do not worry about a place to live, nor do they greedily indulge in food and clothing. They single-mindedly study the Way. All those monks attained benefits concomitant with their capacities. This is because to be poor is to be intimate with the Way.

Although Mr. Pang[237] was a layperson, he became well known as an equal to the monks within the community of Zen practitioners. The reason for this is as follows. When he first started to practice Zen, he took all of his family wealth and was about to cast it into the ocean.

People tried to persuade him not to do so, saying, "Why do you not give the property to others or spend it for the sake of Buddhist affairs?"

He replied to them, "I am throwing it away because I believe it is harmful. How can I give it to others? Wealth is a harmful enemy that troubles our bodies and minds." In the end, he threw it into the ocean. After that, he made and sold bamboo baskets to earn his living. Even though he was a layperson, because he threw away all of his property in this way he was considered a person of Zen. Monks, moreover, should give up their property completely.

A monk said, "In China, monasteries have provisions belonging to the community and [communal] permanent property. These can

得たる也。一切一物も、思ひあてがふ事もなくて、十年余、過ぎ送ぬ。一分も財をたくはへんと思こそ、大事なれ。僅の命を送るほどの事は、何とも思ひ畜へねども、天然として有也。人皆有生分。天地授之。我、不走求、必、有也。況や仏子は、如来遺属の福分あり、不求、自、得也。只一向に道を行ぜば、是天然なるべし。是現証也。

又、云、

学道の人、多分云、若其の事をなさば、世人、是を謗ぜんか、と。この条、甚だ非也。世間の人、何とも謗とも、仏祖の行履、聖教の道理にてだにもあらば、依行すべし。世人挙て褒るとも、不聖教道理、祖師も不行ことならば、依行すべからず。

其故は、世人、親疎、我をほめそしればとて、彼の人の心に、随ひたりとも、我が命終の時、悪業にもひかれ、悪道へ趣ん時、何にも不可救。喩へば、皆、人に被謗被悪とも、仏祖の道に、したがふて、依行せば、その冥、実に我をば、たすけんずれば、人のそしればとて、道を行ぜざるべからず。又、如是、謗讃する人、必しも仏道に通達し、証得せるに非ず。何としてか仏祖の道を、善悪をもて、判ずべき。然も不可順世人情。只、仏道に依行すべき道理あらば、一向に依行すべき也。

be helpful to support monks to practice the Way. They do not need to worry [about their livelihoods]. In this country, we do not have such [provisions]. If we completely give up [our property], there will surely be obstacles in practicing the Way. I think it is better to consider some provisioning of clothing and food in advance. What do you think?"[238]

[*Dōgen*] *instructed*:

It is not so. More than in China, people in this country give support that is more than reasonable and make offerings to monks beyond their means. I do not know about others, but I have experienced this and found it to be true. I have spent more than ten years without any possessions, and I have never worried about how to obtain them.[239] It is a great obstacle to think of storing up even a little bit of property. Without having to think of how to gain or store things in advance, we will naturally receive as much as we need just to stay alive. Each person has their own allotted share. Heaven and earth bestow it upon us. Even though we do not run around seeking it, we will receive it without fail. Needless to say, children of the Buddha will receive the blessings that are the legacy of the Tathāgata.[240] We will gain them without seeking. These things will naturally occur only if we wholeheartedly practice the Way. [My own ability to live in this way] is actual proof.

[*Dōgen*] *also said*:

Students of the Way often say that if they do certain things, people in the world will speak ill of them. This is totally wrong. No matter how badly people slander us, we must practice in accordance with the conduct of the buddhas and ancestors or what is taught in the sacred scriptures. Even if everyone in the world praises us, we should neither practice things that conflict with the principles of the sacred teachings nor [practice] those things that the ancestral teachers did not do.

This is because when we face death, no person of the [mundane] world can save us from proceeding toward an evil destiny. We will be pulled by our bad karma, whether they are close [to us] or strangers, whether they praise us or slander us, and even if we follow their opinions. Even if we are reproached and hated by every one of them, if we

4-10

又、僧云、

某甲、老母現在せり。我即一子也。ひとへに某甲が扶持にて
度世す。恩愛もことに深し。順孝の志も深し。依是聊か世に順、
人に随て、他の恩力をもて、母の衣糧にあづかる。若、遁世籠居
せば、一日の活命も、難存。依是、在世間。一向仏道に入ざらん事
も、難治也。若、なほ只すてて、道に入べき道理有らば、其旨何る
べきぞ。

示云、

此の事、難治也。他人のはからひに非ず。只、我れ能く思惟し
て、誠に仏道に志しあらば、何なる支度方便をも案じて、母儀の
安堵活命をも支度して、仏道に入ば、両方倶によき事也。こはき
敵、ふかき色、をもき宝なれども、切に思ふ心、ふかければ、必、
方便も、出来様もあるべし。是、天地善神の冥加も有て、必、成る
也。

practice according to the Way of the buddhas and ancestors, unseen beings will surely help us. For this reason, we should not cease practicing the Way even if worldly people speak ill of us. Also, those who slander or praise us are not necessarily people who have penetrated the Buddha Way and attained verification. How is it possible to judge the Way of the buddhas and ancestors from [the worldly standards of] good and bad? Therefore, do not follow the sentiments of worldly people. If there is a reason for an action to be carried out according to the Buddha Way, then we should carry it out wholeheartedly.

4-10

Also, a monk said, "My aged mother is still alive. I am her only child. She lives relying solely on my financial support. Her affection for me is especially deep. My desire to fulfill my filial duties is also deep. I am somewhat engaged in worldly affairs and have relationships with people; with their kind help I obtain clothing and food for my mother. If I renounced the world and lived in seclusion, I could not expect my mother to live for even one day. For this reason I stay in the mundane world. [On the other hand,] it is also difficult for me not to completely enter the Buddha Way. If there is still a reason for me to abandon [my mother] and enter the Way, what is it?"

[*Dōgen*] *instructed*:

This is a difficult matter. No one else can deal with it for you. After carefully considering it, if you truly aspire to enter the Buddha Way, it would be good for both you and your mother to somehow prepare or find a means to ensure your mother's livelihood before entering the Buddha Way. You will definitely attain what you earnestly wish for. If you wish to defeat a strong enemy, to gain favor with some noble lady, or to obtain some precious treasure, if your desire is strong enough you will surely find some method to attain what you wish.[241] It will certainly be achieved with the unseen help of the beneficent deities of heaven and earth.

　曹渓の六祖は、新州の樵人、たき木を売て、母を養き。一日市にして、客の金剛経を誦するを聞て、発心し、辞母参黄梅。銀、三十両を得て、母儀の衣糧にあてたりと、見えたり。是も切に思ひける故に、天の与へたりけるかと覚ゆ。能々思惟すべし。是、一の道理也。

　母儀の一期を待て、其後、無障碍、入仏道、次第、本意のごとくして、神妙也。不知、老少は、不定なれば、若し老母は、久く止まつて、我は前に去ことも、出来らん時は、支度相違せば、我は仏道に不入を、くやみ、老母は、不許罪に沈て、両人共に益なくして、互に得罪時如何。

　若、捨今生、入仏道たらば、老母、直饒、餓死すとも、一子を放して、道に入れしむる功徳、豈、得道の良縁に非ざらんや。我も、広劫多生にも、難捨恩愛を、今生人身を受て、仏教に遇へる時、捨てたらば、真実報恩者の道理、何ぞ不叶仏意哉。一子、出家すれば、七世のおや、得道すと見へたり。何、一世の浮生の身を思つて、永劫安楽の因を、空く過さんやと云道理もあり。是を能々自はからふべし。

正法眼蔵随聞記　四　終

The Sixth Ancestor of Caoxi was a woodcutter in Xinzhou province.[242] He sold firewood to support his mother. One day at the marketplace he aroused the mind of awakening when he heard a customer recite the *Diamond Sutra*. Then he left his mother and went to Huangmei[243] [to visit the Fifth Ancestor]. It is said that he obtained thirty ounces of silver[244] and used it to supply clothing and food for his mother. I think that was given from heaven because of the sincerity of his aspiration. Ponder this point thoroughly. [If you can find such aid,] this is one reasonable way.

Regarding your mother, waiting until the end of her lifetime and then entering the Buddha Way without any obstacles would seem to be the natural order of events and the ideal way of fulfilling your true aspiration. Yet no one knows what will happen, for there is no certainty that an old person will die sooner than a young person. Your mother may live a long time, and you may die before her. In such a case, because your plan would not have worked, you would regret not having entered the Buddha Way, and your mother would feel guilty for not having permitted you to do so. There would be no merit for either of you, and both of you would have feelings of guilt. Would that be of any value?

If you abandon your present life and enter the Buddha Way, even if your mother had to die of starvation, would it not be better for you to form a connection with the Way and for her to permit her only son to enter the Way? Although it is most difficult to cast aside filial love, even over eons and many lifetimes, having been born in a human body, if you give up [filial love] in this lifetime, when you encounter the Buddha's teachings you will be truly fulfilling your debt of gratitude[245] [to your parents]. Why would this not be in accordance with the Buddha's will? It is said that if one child leaves home to become a monk, seven generations of parents will attain the Way.[246] How can you waste an opportunity for eternal peace and joy by clinging to your body in this uncertain and ephemeral world? Consider this, and ponder these points thoroughly for yourself.

The End of the Fourth Book of *Shōbōgenzō Zuimonki*

正法眼蔵随聞記　五

侍者　懐奘　編

5-1

一日、

　参学の次、示云、

　学道の人、莫執自解。縦ひ有所会、若、又、決定よからざる事もあらん、又、是よりも、よき義もや有んと思て、ひろく知識をも訪ひ、先人の言をも可尋也。又、先人の言なれども、堅く執こと無し。若、是もあしくもや有ん、信ずるにつけても、と思て、勝たることあらば、次第につくべき也。

　昔忠国師の会に、有供奉来れりしに、国師問云、南方の草の色如何。奉云、黄色也。又問、国師の童子の有りけるに問へば、同く童子も黄色なり、と答へしかば、国師、供奉に云、汝が見、童子にこえず。汝も黄色なりと云、童子も黄色也と云。是、同見なるべし。然ば、童子、国皇の師として、真色を答へし。汝が見所、常途にこえず。

SHŌBŌGENZŌ ZUIMONKI, BOOK 5

Compiled by the attendant Ejō

5-1

One day, on the occasion of a study meeting, [Dōgen] instructed:

Students of the Way! We should not cling to our personal views. Even when we have some understanding, we should still think that there might be something not right [with our views], or that there might be insights that are superior [to our opinions]. We should visit widely with a variety of teachers, and we should investigate our predecessors' words. Furthermore, we should not firmly adhere even to the sayings of our predecessors. [We should] consider that their words might be mistaken, or even if we believe them, if there is superior understanding, we should gradually develop our own understanding.

Long ago, a certain imperial attendant monk[247] visited the assembly of National Teacher Zhong.[248] The national teacher asked him, "What color are the grasses in the south?" The monk said, "Yellow." He also asked a boy who was there, and the boy replied the same way: "Yellow." Then the national teacher said to the attendant monk, "Your view is not superior to the boy's. You said yellow. The boy also said yellow. You and the boy have the same view. If so, the boy could be the emperor's teacher and answer with the true color. Your view is not beyond the ordinary."[249]

　後来、有人云、供奉が常途こへざる、何のとがか有ん。童子と同く、真色を説、是こそ真の知識たらめ、と云て、国師の義をもちゐず。

　故に知りぬ、古人の言をもちゐず、只、誠の道理を存ずべき也。疑心はあしき事なれども、又、信ずまじき事を、かたく執して、尋べき義をも、とぶらはざるは、あしき也。

5-2

又、示曰、

　学人、第一の用心は、先、可離我見。離我見者、不可執此身。縦、窮古人語話、雖常坐如鉄石、著此身、不離者、万劫千生、不可得仏祖道。何況、雖悟得権実教法・顕密聖教、不離執此身之心者、徒数他宝、自無半銭之分。只請、学人静坐して、以道理、可尋此身之始終。身躰髪膚者、父母之二滴、駐於一息、離散於山野而、終作泥土。何以故、執身耶。況、以法見之、十八界之聚散、何法定為我身。雖教内教外別、我身之始終不可得事、以之、為行道之用心事、是同。先、達此道理、実仏道顕然者也。

Years later someone commented, "What is wrong with the fact that the attendant monk's view is not beyond the ordinary? He said the true color just as the boy did. The attendant monk must be a true teacher." So saying, he did not accept the national teacher's opinion.

From this, we understand that, just as [this person] did not accept the ancient's opinion, we [too] should simply understand the true reality [rather than accepting the view of an authority]. Even though a doubtful mind is bad, it is also bad to cling to something we should not believe and to not investigate what should be investigated.

5-2

[*Dōgen*] *also instructed*:

The primary concern for students [of the Way] must be, first of all, to detach ourselves from personal views.[250] To detach from our personal views is to not cling to our bodies. Even if we penetrate the sayings and stories of the ancients and sit unceasingly like iron or a rock, if we attach to our bodies without letting go, we will not be able to attain the Way of the buddhas and ancestors [, even if we practice] for ten thousand eons or thousands of lifetimes. It goes without saying that even if we are able to understand the provisional or genuine teachings, or the sacred teachings of the exoteric or esoteric scriptures,[251] but we are not free from the mind that clings to our bodies, we vainly calculate others' wealth without owning even a halfpenny of our own.[252] I only ask you, students, to sit quietly and investigate the beginning and the end of this body from the basis of reality. Our body, hair, and skin originally comprised the two droplets from our father and mother. When our breath stops, they will disperse and finally turn into mud and soil on the mountains and fields. How can we cling to our bodies?[253] Furthermore, when we see from the basis of the Dharma, we are [nothing but] the gathering and dispersing of the eighteen elements.[254] Which one can we identify as ourselves? Although there are differences between the teaching schools[255] and the [Zen] school [that is] outside the teaching, they both show the

5-3

一日、示云、

　古人云、霧の中を行けば、不覚衣しめる。よき人に近づけば、不覚よき人となる也。昔、倶胝和尚に使へし、一人の童子のごときは、いつ学し、いつ修したりとも見へず、不覚ども、久参に近づいしに、悟道す。坐禅も、自然に、久しくせば、忽然として大事を発明して、坐禅の正門なる事を、知る時も有べし。

5-4

嘉禎二年、臘月除夜、始請懐弉於興聖寺首座。即小参次、請秉払。初任首座。即、興聖寺最初の首座也。

　小参に云、

　宗門の仏法伝来の事、初祖西来して、少林に居して、機をまち、時を期して、面壁して坐せしに、其年の窮臘に、神光、来参しき。初祖、最上乗の器なりと知て接得す。衣法ともに相承伝来して、児孫天下に流布し、正法今日に弘通す。

　初て首座を請じ、今日初て秉払をおこなはしむ。衆のすくなきに、はばかること莫れ。身、初心なるを顧ことなかれ。汾陽は纔に

ungraspability of the self from the beginning to the end and make this truth the [basic] attitude toward practicing the Way. On this point, both are the same. First of all, we must penetrate this truth. Then, the Buddha Way will become truly clear.

5-3

One day, [Dōgen] instructed:

An ancient said, "When we walk in the mist, without knowing it our clothing becomes moist."[256] If we keep company with good people, we will unwittingly become a good person. Long ago, the attendant boy who served Master Juzhi,[257] without knowing that he was studying and practicing, realized the Way because he had been closely attending the long-experienced practitioner. Zazen is the same. With zazen also, if you do it for a long time, naturally the time will come when you suddenly clarify the great matter, and you will know that zazen is the true gate [to the Buddhadharma].

5-4

In the second year of the Katei era (in 1236), on the last day of the twelfth month, Ejō was appointed the first head monk of Kōshō-ji.[258] After an informal gathering,[259] I [Ejō] was invited to take up the whisk[260] [and give a Dharma talk]. This was the first time I had been appointed as a head monk. I was [also] the first head monk of Kōshō-ji.

[Dōgen] said in his speech during the informal gathering:

[This is how] the Buddhadharma of our tradition was transmitted. The First Ancestor[261] came from the West and stayed at Shaolin temple, sitting facing the wall, waiting for a capable person and the time to transmit [the Dharma]. One December, Shenguang came to practice [with him].[262] The First Ancestor knew that he was the vessel of the supreme vehicle[263] and gave him guidance. He transmitted both

六七人、薬山は十衆に満ざる也。然れども仏祖の道を行じて是を
叢林のさかりなると云き。

　見ずや、竹の声に道を悟り、桃の花に心を明めし。竹、豈、利
鈍有り迷悟有んや。花、何ぞ浅深有り賢愚有ん。花は年々に開く
れども、皆、得悟するに非ず。竹は時々に響けども、聴物ことごと
く証道するに非ず。只、久参修持の功にこたへ、弁道勤労の縁を
得て、悟道明心する也。是、竹の声の、独り利なるに非ず。又、花
の色の、ことに深きに非ず。竹の響き妙なりと云へども、自の縁を
待て声を発す。花の色、美なりと云へども、独開るに非ず。春の時
を得て光を見る。

　学道の縁も又是の如し。人々皆な道を得ことは、衆縁による。
人々自利なれども、道を行ずる事は、衆力を以てするが故に。
今、心を一つにして、参究尋覚すべし。玉は琢磨によりて器とな
る。人は練磨によりて仁となる。何の玉か、はじめより光有。誰人
か、初心より利なる。必ずみがくべし。須練。自、卑下して、学道を
ゆるくする事なかれ。

　古人云、光陰虚くわたる事なかれ。今、問、時光は、をしむに
よりてとどまるか。をしめども、とどまらざるか。又、問、時光虚渡
らず。人虚く渡る。時光をいたづらに過す事なく、学道をせよと云
也。是如参同心にすべし。

　我独挙揚せんに、容易にするにあらざれども、仏祖行道の
儀、皆、是の如くなり。如来にしたがつて得道するもの多けれども
又、阿難によりて悟道する人もありき。新首座、非器也と卑下する

the robe and the Dharma [to the Second Ancestor]. Since then, their descendents spread throughout the country, and the true Dharma has pervaded down to this present day.

I have appointed the first head monk, and today, I allow him to take the whisk [to give a talk]. Do not be afraid of the small number of people [in this assembly]. Do not be concerned that you are a beginner. At Fenyang, they had only six or seven people; at Yaoshan, they had less than ten people.[264] However, they practiced the Way of the buddhas and ancestors. [They] were considered to be flourishing monasteries.

Do you not see that [Xiangyan Zhixian] realized the Way upon hearing the sound of [a piece of tile hitting] bamboo, and [Lingyun Zhiqin] clarified the mind upon seeing peach blossoms?[265] Are there any bamboos that are sharp or dull-witted, deluded or enlightened? Are there blossoms that are shallow or deep, wise or foolish? Blossoms bloom every year, but not everyone realizes the Way. Bamboos often make sounds, but not all of the hearers verify the Way. Only through the virtues of long-term study and continuous practice, with the condition of diligent effort in the wholehearted practice of the Way, do we realize the Way and clarify the mind. These things did not occur because the sound of the bamboo was especially sharp on its own, or because the color of the flowers was particularly profound. Although the sound of bamboo is wondrous, the sound occurs because of [the bamboo's] conditions.[266] Although the color of blossoms is beautiful, they do not bloom on their own. They see the light when the springtime has come.

The conditions of studying the Way are also like this. Each of us attains the Way because of the assistance from people in the sangha. Although everyone is sharp-witted, we can [only] practice the Way because of the power of the assembly. Therefore, we should now unify our minds to study and investigate [the Way] together. A jewel becomes a vessel by being polished. People become benevolent through cultivation. What jewel glitters from the outset? Who can be sharp-witted from the time they are beginners. We should polish

ことなく、洞山の麻三斤を挙揚して、同衆に示すべしと云て、座を
おりて、再、鼓を鳴して、首座秉払す。是、興聖最初の秉払也。芉
公、三十九の年也。

5-5

一日、示云、

　俗人の云、何人か厚衣を欲せざらん。誰人か重味を貪らざら
ん。然ども、みちを存ぜんと思ふ人は、山に入、水にあき、さむき
を忍び、餓をも忍ぶ。先人、くるしみ無きにあらず、是を忍で、みち
を守れば、後人、是を聞てみちをしたひ、徳をこふる也。

　俗の賢なる、猶、如是。仏道、豈、然ざらんや。古人も皆金骨に
非ず。在世もことごとく上器に非ず。大小律蔵によりて、諸比丘を
かんがふるに、不可思議の、不当の心を起すも有き。然ども、後に

and cultivate without fail. We should not underestimate ourselves nor slacken our practice of the Way.

An ancient said, "Do not spend your days and nights in vain."[267] Now I ask you: Does time stop passing if we hold it dear? Or does it continue to pass even if we lament [its passing]? I also ask you: Does time pass vainly? Or do people spend time in vain? This means that we should practice the Way without spending time wastefully. Practice in this way with unified minds.

It is not easy to uphold [the Dharma] by myself [, so I ask the new head monk to assist me]. The Way practiced by the buddhas and ancestors is always like this. There are many who attained the Way by following the teaching of the Tathāgata, but there were some who [instead] realized the Way from the instruction of Ānanda.[268] New head monk! Do not deprecate yourself, saying that you are not a vessel [of the Dharma]. Give a talk to your fellow practitioners on the story of Dongshan's "three pounds of hemp."[269] So saying, he descended from his seat. The drum was struck again, and the head monk [Ejō] took the whisk. That was the first "taking of the whisk" at Kōshō-ji. At that time, Ejō was thirty-nine years old.

5-5

One day, [Dōgen] instructed:

A layperson said [to me], "Who does not desire fine clothing? Who does not indulge in rich flavors? However, people who aspire to live in the Way enter the mountains, get water from the river, endure cold, and endure hunger.[270] It is not that ancient people did not suffer. Because they endured such hardships and protected the Way, later people who hear of such examples yearn for the Way and cherish their virtues."

Even in lay society, the wise have been like this. In the Buddha Way, we should not fail to be the same. Not all ancient people had golden bones;[271] not all people were superior vessels [of the Dharma]

は皆得道し、羅漢となれり。しかあれば、我等も、悪くつたなしと
云へども、発心修行せば、得道すべしと知て、即ち発心する也。古
へも皆な苦をしのび、寒をたへて、愁へながら修道せし也。今の
学者、くるしく愁るとも、只、強て学道すべき也。

5-6

学道の人、悟を得ざる事は、即ち、古見を存ずる故也。本より誰れ
教へたりとも、知らざれども、心と云へば、念慮知見なりと思ひ、
草木なりと云ば信ぜず。仏と云ば、相好光明あらんずると思て、
瓦礫と説けば、耳を驚かす。即、此見、父も相伝せず、母も教授
せず。只、無理に久く人の言につきて、信じ来れる也。然れば、今
も、仏祖、決定の説なれば、心を改めて、草木と云ば草木を心と
しり、瓦礫を仏と云ば、即ち、本執を、あらため去ば、真道を得べ
き也。

　古人云、日月明なれども、浮雲掩之、叢蘭茂せんとするとも、
秋風吹之破る。貞観政要に引之、賢王と悪臣とに喩ふ。今は云
く、浮雲掩へども久からず、秋風やぶるともひらくべし。臣わろくと
も、王の賢、久くは転ぜらるべからず。今、仏道を存ぜしも、是の
如くなるべし。何に悪を、しばらくをかすとも、堅く守り、久くたも
たば、浮雲もきえ、秋風も、とどまるべき也。

while [Shakyamuni] was alive. When we consider many monks mentioned in the Vinaya Piṭaka of either the Mahāyāna or Hīnayāna, some aroused unbelievably evil minds.[272] However, later they attained the Way and became arhats.[273] Therefore, even though we are bad and inferior, we arouse the mind of awakening because we know that if we arouse the mind of awakening and practice, we will eventually attain the Way. Even in ancient times, all people endured hardships, withstood the cold, and practiced the Way amid their troubles. Students of today! Even if we suffer [from physical pain] or mental anguish, we should force ourselves to practice the Way.

5-6

Students of the Way! You do not attain realization, because you hold on to your old fixed views. Without knowing who taught you, you think that "mind" is the functioning of your thoughts, knowledge, and views. You do not believe me if I say that [the mind] is grasses and trees.[274] You think that the Buddha must have various physical characteristics and a radiant halo. If I say that [the Buddha] is broken tiles and pebbles, your ears are astonished.[275] Such views were not transmitted from your father or taught by your mother. You have believed them without reason, simply being influenced for a long time by the people who have said [such things]. Therefore, because [what I have said] is a definite saying of the buddhas and ancestors, you should reform your mind; when it is said that "mind" is grasses and trees, you should understand that grasses and trees are "mind," and if you are told that "Buddha" is tiles and pebbles, you should believe that tiles and pebbles are "Buddha." Thus, if you continue to transform your original attachment [to your old views], you will be able to truly attain the Way.[276]

An ancient said, "Though the sun and the moon shine brightly, floating clouds cover them over. Though clusters of orchids are about to bloom, autumn winds blow, causing them to wither." This saying is

5-7

一日、示云、

　学人、初心の時、道心有ても無ても、経論・聖教等よくよく見る
べく、学ぶべし。

　我、初めてまさに無常によりて、聊か道心を発し、あまねく諸
方をとぶらひ、終に山門を辞して、学道を修せしに、建仁寺に寓
せしに、中間に正師にあはず、善友なきによりて、迷て邪念をお
こしき。教道の師も、先づ学問先達にひとしくよき人（と）なり、国
家に知れ、天下に名誉せん事を教訓す。よて教法等を学するに
も、先、此国の上古の賢者に、ひとしからん事を思ひ、大師等に
も同からんと思て、因、高僧伝、続高僧伝等を、披見せしに、大
国の高僧、仏法者の様を見しに、今の師の教への如には非ず。
又我がおこせる心は、皆経論・伝記等には、厭い悪み、きらへる
心にて、有りけりと思より、漸く心つきて思に、道理をかんがふれ
ば、名聞を思とも、当代下劣の人に、よしと思はれんよりも、上古
の賢者、向後の善人を可恥。ひとしからん事を思とも、此国の人

found in the *Essentials of Government of the Zhenguan Period*,[277] comparing a wise king with his evil ministers. Now I would say, even if floating clouds covered [the sun and the moon], they will not remain for a long time. Even if autumn winds wither the flowers, they will bloom again. Even if the ministers are evil, if the king is wise, he will not be deceived for long. Practicing the Buddha Way should be the same. No matter what evil we might commit for a while, if we remain steadfast and maintain [our practice] for a long time, the floating clouds will disappear and the autumn winds will cease.

5-7

One day, [Dōgen] instructed:

Students! When you have the mind of a beginner,[278] whether you have aroused the mind of awakening or not, you should thoroughly read and study the sacred scriptures: sutras, commentaries, and so on.

I first aroused the mind of awakening to some degree because of [seeing] impermanence.[279] I widely visited various districts and finally left [the monastery on] Mt. Hiei and practiced the Way, staying at Kennin-ji. During that time, I did not meet a true teacher and did not have good [spiritual] friends, and therefore I aroused mistaken thoughts within delusions. Even my instructors taught me that, first of all, I should become an eminent person who could be the equal of our predecessors in study, become known in the nation, and be an honorable person in the world. Because of such instructions, when I studied the Dharma teachings, I desired to become equal to the ancient wise people in this country, or I intended to become the same as those who received the title of great master,[280] and so on. When I read the *Biographies of Eminent Monks*, the *Continued Biographies of Eminent Monks*,[281] and so on to study how the eminent monks and practitioners of the Buddhadharma lived in the great country [of China], I found that those people were not as my teachers taught. I began to understand that these ambitions I had aroused were thoughts despised and hated

よりも、唐土天竺の先達、高僧を可恥、かれにひとしからんと思べし。乃至諸天冥衆、諸仏菩薩等を恥、かれにひとしからんとこそ、思べきに、道理を得て後には、此国の大師等は、土かはらの如く覚て、従来の身心皆改ぬ。

佛の一期の行儀を見れば、王位を捨てて入山林、学道を成じて後も、一期乞食すと見たり。律に云、知家非家、捨家出家。ふるく云く、誇て上賢に、ひとしからんと、思ふことなかれ、いやしうして、下賤にひとしからんと、思ふことなかれ、と云は、倶に慢心也。高しても、下らんことを、わするることなかれ、安んじても、あやうからんことを、忘すること莫れ。今日存すれども、明日と思ふことなかれ。死に至りあやうきこと、脚下に有り。

又、云、

愚癡なる人は、其の詮なき事を思ひ云也。此につかはるる老尼公、当時いやしげにして有るを、恥るかにて、ともすれば、人に向ては、昔し上郎にて、有し由をかたる。喩へば今の人に、さありけりと、思はれたりとも、何の用とも覚へず。甚無用也と覚る也。

皆、人のおもはくは、此心有るかと覚るなり。道心無き程も知らる。此らの心を改て、少し人には似べき也。

又、或は、入道の極て無道心なる、去難き知音にて有に、道心をこらんと、仏神に祈祷せよと云んと思ひ、定めて、彼れ腹立して中たがふこと有ん。然ども、道心を、をこさざらんには、得意にても、たがひに、詮なかるべし。

in all of the sutras, commentaries, and biographies. Then, considering the true principle, I gradually realized that instead of being thought of as a good person by inferior people in this age, if I think of fame I should instead humbly compare myself with ancient wise people or good people in later generations. If I wish to be equal [to someone], instead of [comparing myself with the inferior] people in this country, I should humbly compare myself with the predecessors and great monks in China and India. I should aspire to become equal to them. Also, I should humbly compare myself with various heavenly beings, unseen beings, all buddhas and bodhisattvas, and so on and intend to become equal to them. Once I had understood this truth, I began to think that those [who were honored with] the title of great master and so on in this country were like dirt or broken tiles. I completely reformed my body and mind from what they had been up to that point.

When we examine the Buddha's activities during his lifetime, [we see] he abandoned his claim to the throne and entered the mountain forests. I have read that even after he had completed the Way, he begged for food for [the rest of] his lifetime. In the Vinaya, it is said, "Knowing that home is not home, abandon home and leave home."[282] An ancient said, "Do not be arrogant and consider yourself equal to superior, wise people. Do not deprecate yourself and think you are equal to inferior people."[283] This means that both are a kind of arrogance. Though you may be in a high position, do not forget that you may fall down. Though you may be safe now, remember that you may have to face danger. Though you may be alive today, do not think that you will be alive tomorrow. The danger of death is right at your feet.

[*Dōgen*] *also said*:

Foolish people think and speak of senseless things. There is an old nun working for this temple. She seems to be ashamed of her current humble situation, and she tends to talk to others about how she used

5-8

示云、

　三覆して後に云へ、と云心は、おほよそ物を云んとする時も、事を行はんとする時も、必、三覆して後に、言行べし。先儒多くは、三たび思ひかへりみるに、三びながら善ならば、言ひおこなへ、と云也。宋土の賢人等の心は、三覆をば、いくたびも、覆せよと、云也。言ばよりさきに思ひ、行よりさきに思ひ、思ふ時に、必、たびごとに、善ならば、言行すべしと也。

　衲子も又かならず、しかあるべし。我ながら思ふことも、云ことも、主にも、知られずあしきことも、有るべき故に、先づ仏道にかなふや、いなや、とかへりみ、自他のために、益有りやいなやと、能々思ひかへりみて後に、善なるべければ、行ひもし、言ひもす

to be a lady of the upper class. Even if people here believe she used to be so, there is not any merit in it. I think it is quite useless.

It seems that most people tend to have this sort of sentiment. We can see that such people lack the mind of awakening. When we reform such a frame of mind, we will become a bit more like people [of the Way].

Also, there is a certain lay monk[284] who completely lacks the mind of awakening. Because he is a close friend, he is difficult for me to avoid. I would like to tell him to pray to buddhas and gods to allow him to arouse the mind of awakening.[285] He would certainly get angry, and he could fall out with me [if I did so]. And yet, unless he arouses the mind of awakening, it is pointless for both of us to be close friends.

5-8

[*Dōgen*] *instructed*:

There is a saying, "Speak after reflecting three times." This means that when we want to say something or do something, we should reflect three times before we say or do it. The ancient Confucians often said that they should consider everything three times, and if they thought it to be good each time, they should say or do it. When the wise people of China advise us to reflect on things three times, they meant many times. We should ponder before speaking and consider before acting, and if it is definitely good each time we think about it, we should say or do it.

We patch-robed monks should also be the same. Because, even if we do not realize it, there might be something wrong with what we think and what we say; we first of all need to reflect on whether or not it is in accordance with the Buddha Way and consider whether it is beneficial to both ourselves and others. After that, if it is good, we should do it or say it. Practitioners! If you keep this attitude, you will never go against the Buddha's will during your lifetime.

べき也。行者、若、此の心を守らば、一期、仏意に、そむかざるべ
し。

　昔年、建仁寺に、初めて入し時は、僧衆、随分に、三業を守
て、仏道の為、利他の為ならぬことをば、不言、せじと、各々心を
立てし也。僧正の余残有し程は如是。今年今月は、其儀無し。今
の学者可知。決定して自他の為、仏道の為に、可有詮事ならば、
身を忘ても、言ひもし行もすべき也。其詮なき事をば、言行すべか
らず。宿老耆年の言行する時は、若臘にては、言を交べからず。仏
制也、能々これを忍ぶべし。

　身を忘て、みちを思ふ事は、俗、猶、此の心なり。

　昔、趙の藺相如と云ひし者は、下賤の人なりしかども、賢によ
りて、趙王にめしつかはれて、天下を行ひき。趙王の使として趙
璧と云玉を、秦国へつかはされしに、かの璧を、十五城にかへん
と秦王云し故に、相如にもたしめてつかはすに、余の臣下議して
云、これ程の宝を、相如程のいやしき人に、もたせつかはす事、
国に人なきに似たり。余臣の恥也。後代のそしりなるべし。路にし
て此相如を殺して、玉を奪取れ、と議しけるを、時の人、相如に
かたりて、此使を辞して、命を守るべし、と云ければ、相如云、某
甲敢て辞すべからず。相如、王の使として、玉をもち、秦に向に、
倭臣のためにころさると、後代に聞ん為に、我悦也。我身は死す
とも、賢名はのこるべし、と云て、終に向ぬ。余臣、此の言を聞
て、我等この人を、うちえん事、有べからずとて、留まりぬ。

Years ago, when I first entered Kennin-ji,[286] all the monks in the
assembly guarded their three actions [of body, speech, and thought]
according to their capabilities, and each of them resolved not to say
or do anything that was not beneficial to the Buddha Way and for
other people. After the superintendent of monks[287] passed away, the
monks maintained the same attitude while his influence remained.
These days, there is no one who maintains such an attitude. Today's
students should understand this. If something is definitely meaningful for ourselves and others as well as for the Buddha Way, we must
forget our own [ego-centered] self and say or do it. We should not
say or do anything meaningless. When elders or seniors are saying
or doing something, younger monks should not interrupt them. This
is a regulation set down by the Buddha. Be careful and practice this
regulation well.

Even laypeople may have the determination to forget themselves
and think of the Way.

In ancient times, there was a person whose name was Lin Xiangru
of the State of Zhao.[288] Although he was from a lower class family,
because of his wisdom he was taken into service by the king of Zhao
to administer the affairs of the country. Once, as envoy of the king,
he was dispatched to deliver a piece of jade called the *bi*[289] of Zhao
to the country of Qin. Because the king of Qin had said he would
exchange fifteen cities for the *bi*, Xiangru was sent to carry it. At that
time, the rest of the ministers conspired against him saying, "If such
a precious treasure is entrusted to a man of low birth like Xiangru, it
will look like there is no one capable in this country [to whom it could
be entrusted]. It will be shameful for the rest of the ministers. We will
be looked down upon by people of later generations. We should kill
him while he is on his way and take the jade." At the time, someone
informed Xiangru of this and advised him to decline the mission in
order to save his life. Xiangru said, "I dare not decline. It would be my
pleasure for it to be known to later generations that Xiangru, envoy
of the king, was killed by evil ministers while on his way to Qin with

　相如、終に秦王にまみえて、璧を秦王に与へしに、秦王、十五
城を与へまじき気色を見て、はかり事を以て、秦王に語て云、其
玉、きず有り、我、是を示ん、と云て、玉を乞得て後、相如云く、
王の気色を見るに、十五城を惜しめる気色あり。然れば、我が
頭、此玉をもて、銅柱にあて、うちわりてん、と云て、怒れる眼を以
て、王をみて、銅柱のもとによる、気色、まことに、王をも犯しつべ
かりし時に、秦王云、汝、玉をわる事なかれ、十五城、与ふべし。
相はからはん程、汝璧をもつべし、と云しかば、相如、ひそかに人
をして、璧を本国にかへしぬ。

　又、澠池にして趙王と秦王と、共にあそびしに、趙王は琵琶
の上手也。秦王命じて弾ぜしむ。趙王、相如にも、云いあはせず
して、即、琵琶を弾ぜし時に、相如、命にしたがへる事をいかり
て、我行きて、秦王に簫をふかしめん、とて秦王に告て云、王は簫
の上手也。趙王、聞かんとねがふ。王、ふき給べし、と云しかば、
秦王、是を辞せしかば、相如云、若、辞せば、王をうつべし、と云
て、近づく時に、秦の将軍、剣を以て、ちかづきよる。相如、これを
にらむ。両目のほころび、さけにけり。将軍、剣をぬかずして、かへ
りしかば、秦王、終に簫を吹くと云へり。

　又、後に、大臣として、天下を行し時に、かたはらの大臣、
我にかさむ事を、そねみて打んとす。時に相如、所々ににげかく
れ、わざと参内の時は参会せず、おぢおそれたる気色也。時に相
如が家人、かの大臣を打ん事、やすき事也。何の故にか、おぢか
くれ給ふ。相如云、我れ、彼れをおづるに非ず。我れ、目をもて、

the jade. Even though I might be killed, my name as a wise man will remain." So saying, he left for Qin. When the other ministers heard what he had said, they gave up their plot, saying, "It is not possible for us to kill this person."

Finally, Xiangru met the king of Qin and gave him the *bi*. However, he realized that the king of Qin was not willing to give the fifteen cities for it. Xiangru thought up a plan and said, "There is a flaw in this jade. I will show it to you." So saying, he took the jade back, and continued, "From your demeanor, Your Majesty, you seem to deny us the fifteen cities. If that is the case, I will break this jade with my head, hitting it against the bronze pillar!" Glowering at the king with angry eyes, he moved toward the bronze pillar as if he were really going to break the jade. The king of Qin said, "Do not break the *bi*. I will hand over the fifteen cities. Keep the *bi* while I make the arrangements." Afterward, Xiangru had one of his men secretly take the jade back to his country.

Later, the kings of Zhao and Qin met at a place named Mianchi for a party. The king of Zhao was a skillful lute player. The king of Qin asked him to play. The king of Zhao played the lute without consulting Xiangru. Xiangru then became angry because his king had obeyed an order of the king of Qin. He said, "I will go and make the king of Qin play the flute." He approached the king of Qin and said, "Your Majesty, you are a skillful player of the flute. The king of Zhao would appreciate listening to you very much. Your Majesty, please play." The king of Qin refused. Xiangru said, "If you decline, I will kill you." A general of Qin reached for his sword and rushed toward Xiangru. Xiangru glared furiously at the general, who became frightened and retreated without drawing his sword. Then the king of Qin finally played the flute.

Later, Xiangru became the prime minister and administered the affairs of the country. One time, another minister, envious of Xiangru's higher status, tried to kill him. At that time, Xiangru fled and hid himself here and there. He appeared to be afraid of the minister; even when he was supposed to go to the court, he did not. One of

秦の（将）軍をも退け、秦の玉をも奪き。彼大臣打べき事、云に
もたらず。然れども、軍をおこし、つはものをあつむる事、敵国の
ため也。今、左右の大将として、国を守る。若、二人、中をたがひ
て、軍を興さば、一人死せば、隣国の、一方かけぬる事をよろこ
びて、軍を興すべし。故に二人ともに全くして、国を守んと思ふに
よ（つ）て、かれと軍を興さず。彼の大臣、此の言を、かへり聞て、
恥て来拝して、二人和、国を治む。

　相如、身を忘れ、道を存る事、如是、今、仏道を存ぜん事も、
かの相如が心の如くなるべし。若、みち有りては死すとも、み（
ち）なうしていくる事なかれ、と云也。

　又、云く、

　善悪と云事、難定。世間の綾羅錦繡をきたるを、よしと云い、
麁布糞掃を、わるしと云。仏法には、是をよしとし、清とす。金銀
錦綾をわるしとし、穢れたりとす。如是、一切の事にわたりて皆然
り。

　予がごときは、聊か韵声をととのへ、文字をかきまぐるを、俗
人等は、尋常なる事に云も有り。又、或人は、出家学道の身とし
て、如是事知れる、と、そしる人も有り。何れを定て善ととり、悪と
するべきぞ。

　文に云、ほめて白品の中に有るを、善と云ふ。そしりて黒品の
中におくを、悪と云。又、云、苦をうくべきを悪と云、楽を招くべき
を善と云。

Xiangru's retainers said, "It is easy to kill that minister. Why do you hide in fear?" Xiangru said, "I am not afraid of him. With my eyes I defeated the general of Qin. I also took back the jade from the king himself. Needless to say, it would be easy to kill the minister. However, the raising of an army and the gathering of troops should be for defending our country against our enemies. As its ministers, we are now in charge of protecting the country. If the two of us quarrel and fight with each other, one of us will die. One half will then be lost. If that happens, neighboring countries will take delight and attack us. Therefore, I hope the two of us together remain unharmed in order to protect our country. This is why I do not fight with him." Upon hearing of this, the [jealous] minister became ashamed of himself and visited Xiangru to express his regret. The two of them then cooperated on the task of governing the country.

Xiangru forgot himself and carried out the Way like this. Now in maintaining the Buddha Way, we should keep the same attitude as Xiangru. There is a saying, "We may die for the Way; do not live without it."[290]

[*Dōgen*] *also said*:

It is difficult to determine what is good or bad. In the mundane world, people say that it is good to wear garments made of fine cloth with golden embroidery and bad to wear robes made of coarse cloth and abandoned rags. In the Buddhadharma, the latter is good and pure, while luxurious garments embroidered with gold and silver are considered bad and defiled. In this way, the same is true for everything.

In my case, too, because I sometimes compose poetry, arranging rhyme and tone, or effortlessly write prose, some laypeople [praise me], saying it is extraordinary. And yet, there are others who criticize me for knowing such things despite being a monk who has left home and is studying the Way. What shall we take as good and abandon as bad?

It is said in a scripture, "That which is praised and pure is good; that which is despised and is impure is evil." It is also said, "Things

　如是、子細に分別して、真実の善をと(つ)て行じ、真実の悪を見てすつべき也。僧は清浄の中より来れば、物も、人の欲をおこすまじき物をもて、よしとし、きよしとする也。

　又、云、

　世間の人、多分云、学道の志あれども、世のするゐ也、人くだれり、我根、劣也。不可堪如法修行。只、随分に、やすきにつきて、結縁を思ひ、他生に開悟を期すべし、と。

　今云、此の言は全、非也。仏法に正像末を立事、しばらく一途の方便也。真実の教道は、しかあらず。依行せん、皆、うべき也。在世の比丘、必しも、皆な勝たるに非ず。不可思議に、希有に浅増しき心ろね、下根なるもあり。仏、種々の戒法等を、わけ給事、皆な、わるき衆生、下根の為也。人々、皆、仏法の機也。非器也と思ふ事なかれ。依行せば、必ず可得也。既に心あれば、善悪を分別しつべし。手足あり、合掌行歩に、かけたる事あるべからず。仏法を行ずるに、品をえらぶべきに非ず。人界の生は、皆、是、器量也。余の畜生等の、性にては不可叶。学道の人は、只、明日を期する事なかれ。今日今時ばかり、仏に随て行じゆくべき也。

that bring about suffering are called evil; things that invite joy are called good."

In this way, we should carefully figure out in detail what is really good, take it up, and practice it, and [likewise] see what is really evil and discard it. Because a sangha is born from the realm of purity, things that do not arouse human desires are considered good and pure.

[*Dōgen*] *also said*:

Many people of worldly society say, "Although I have the aspiration to study the Way, the world is in the age of the last Dharma.[291] People's quality has been declining, and I have only inferior capabilities. I cannot bear to practice in accordance with the Dharma. I would like to follow an easier path that is suitable to me, to merely make a connection [with the Buddha], and hope to attain realization in a future lifetime."

Now, I say that this utterance is totally wrong. In the Buddhadharma, distinguishing the three periods of time—the ages of the true Dharma, the semblance Dharma, and the last Dharma—is only a temporary expedient. The genuine teaching of the Way is not like this. When we practice, all of us should be able to attain [the Way]. Monks while [Shakyamuni] was alive were not necessarily superior. There were some monks who had incredibly despicable minds and who were inferior in capacity. The Buddha set forth various kinds of precepts for the sake of bad people and inferior people.[292] Each and every human being has the possibility [to clarify] the Dharma. Do not think that you are not a vessel [of the Buddhadharma]. When we practice in accordance [with the Dharma], all of us should be able to attain [the Way]. Because we already have a mind, we can distinguish between good and bad. Because we have hands and feet, we do not lack anything for doing *gasshō*[293] and walking. In practicing the Buddhadharma, we should not be concerned with the quality [of people]. All beings within the human realm are all vessels. It is not possible [to practice the Buddhadharma] if we are born as animals or something else. People who

5-9

示云、

　俗人の云、城を傾る事は、うちにささやきこと、出来るによる。
又、云、家に両言有る時は、針をもかふことなし、家に両言無時
は、金をもかふべし。

　俗人、猶、家をもち、城を守るに、同心ならでは、終に亡と云へ
り。況、出家人は、一師にして水乳の和合せるが如し、又、六和敬
の法あり。各々寮々を構へて、心身を隔て、心々に学道の用心す
る事なかれ。一船に乗て海を如渡。同心、威儀を同くし、互に非
をあげ、是をとりて、同く学道すべき也。是、仏世より行じ来れる
儀式也。

5-10

示云、

　楊岐山の会禅師住持の時、寺院旧損して、わづらい有し時
に、知事申して云、修理有るべし。

　会云、堂閣やぶれたりとも、露地樹下には、勝れたるべし、一
方やぶれてもらば、一方のもらぬ所に居して、坐禅すべし。堂宇造
作によりて、衆僧可得悟者、金玉をもても、つくるべし。悟は居所
の善悪によらず。只、坐禅の功の、多少に有るべし。

study the Way should not wait for tomorrow. Only today and in this moment, we must practice following the Buddha.

5-9

[*Dōgen*] *instructed*:

Laypeople say, "A castle falls when people begin to whisper words inside its walls." It is also said, "When there are two opinions in a house, not even a needle can be bought; when there is no conflict of opinions in a house, even gold can be bought."

Even laypeople say that to maintain a household or to protect a castle, unless there is unity of mind, it will be ruined. All the more should home-leavers who practice under a single teacher be harmonious, like a mixture of water and milk. There is also the Dharma of the six ways of harmony.²⁹⁴ Do not set up individual rooms that create separations among people's body and mind, and do not practice the Way with different mental attitudes. [Our life in this monastery is] like crossing the ocean in a single boat. We should have unity of mind, share the same dignified conduct, give advice to mutually reform each other's faults, follow the good points of others, and practice the Way uniformly. This is how people have been practicing since the time of the Buddha.

5-10

[*Dōgen*] *instructed*:

When Zen Master Fanghui²⁹⁵ of Mt. Yanqi was the abbot, the temple was dilapidated, and the monks were troubled. The temple administrators said, "It should be repaired." Fanghui said, "Even though the buildings are dilapidated, it is certainly a better place [to do zazen] than on the bare earth or under a tree. If one section is broken and leaks, we should [just] move to another spot and practice zazen where there are no leaks. If the monks of the assembly could attain realization depending on the condition of the temple buildings, [then] we ought to construct one with gold and jewels. Realization has

翌日の上堂に云、楊岐はじめて住するに、屋壁疎也。満床に
ことごとくちらす、雪の珍珠。くびを縮却して、そらに嗟噓す。かへ
りて思ふ、古人の樹下に居せし事を。ただ仏道のみに非ず、政道
も是の如し。太宗はいやをつくらず。龍牙云、学道は先づ須く、貧
を学べし。貧を学して、貧なる後に、道まさにしたし、と云へり。
昔、釈尊より、今に至まで、真実学道の人、一人も宝に饒なりと
は、聞ず見ざる処也。

5-11

一日、ある客僧の云、近代の遁世の法、各々時料等の事、かまへ
て後、わづらひなき様に支度す。これ小事なりと云へども、学道の
資縁なり、かけぬれば、事の違乱出来。今、此御様を承り及に、
一切、其の支度無く、只、天運にまかす。こと実ならば、後時の違
乱あらん、如何。

　示云、

　事、皆、先証あり、敢て私曲を存ずるに非ず。西天東地の仏
祖、皆、如是。私に活計を至ん、不可有尽期。又、いかにすべしと
も定相なし。この様は、仏祖、皆な、行じ来れるところ、私なし。
若し事闕如し、絶食せば、其時こそ、退しもし、方便をもめぐらさ
め。かねて思ふべきに非ず。

nothing to do with whether a dwelling place is good or bad; it depends only upon diligence in zazen."

The next day, in a formal Dharma discourse, he said, "I have now become the abbot of Yanqi; the roof and walls have many cracks and holes. The entire floor is covered with precious jewels of snow. The monks hunch their shoulders [from the cold] and sigh in the darkness.[296] It reminds me of ancient sages sitting under the trees."

Not only the Buddha Way but the way of politics is also like this. Emperor Taizong [of the Tang dynasty] did not build a new palace.[297] Longya[298] said, "To study the Way we should first of all learn poverty. After having learned poverty and having become poor, we will be intimate with the Way." From the ancient times of Shakyamuni Buddha up to the present day, I have never seen or heard of a person who genuinely practiced the Way and possessed great wealth.

5-11

One day, a visiting monk said, "In recent times, the method of renouncing the world has been to prepare food and other necessities for each person beforehand so as not to have to worry about them later. Although this is a trifling matter, it is a helpful foundation for the practice of the Way. If these [necessities] are lacking, our practice will be disturbed. According to what I have heard about [how you practice] here, you make no such preparations and entrust everything to fate. If this is really true, you will be troubled later on, will you not? What do you think?"

[*Dōgen*] *instructed*:

Everything [I do] has a precedent. I do not merely rely on my personal preference. All the buddhas and ancestors in India and China lived in this way. If we privately make a plan for our livelihood, there is no time [we can be free from the problems they cause]. Also, there is no definite way [to make such preparations]. This is the way all buddhas and ancestors have been practicing, not [just] me. If we run

5-12

示云、

　伝へ聞きき、実否を知らざれども、故持明院の中納言入道、
或時、秘蔵の太刀を、ぬすまれたりけるに、さぶらひの中に、犯人
有りけるを、余のさぶらひ、沙汰し出て、まゐらせたりしに、入道の
云、是は我がたちに非ず。ひが事なり、とて、かへしたり。決定、其
の太刀なれども、さぶらひの恥辱を思て、かへされたりと、人皆是
を知りけれども、其時は無為にて過し。故に、子孫も繁昌せり。

　俗、猶、心あるは是の如し。況や出家人、必ず此心有べし。
出家人は、財物なければ、智恵功徳をもて宝とす。他の無道心な
る、ひが事なんどを、直に面てにあらはし、非におと（す）べから
ず。方便を以て、かれ腹立つまじき様に云べき也。暴悪なるは、其
法久しからず、と云。たとひ法をもて、呵責すれども、あらき言ばな
るは、法も久しからざる也。小人と云は、いささか人のあらき言ば
に、即ち腹立して、恥辱を思也。大人はしかあらず。たとひ打たり
とも、報を思はず。国に小人多し。つつしまずは、あるべからず。

正法眼蔵随聞記　五　終

out of food and have nothing to eat, only then should we reevaluate and come up with skillful means [to fix the situation]. We should not think about such things in advance.

5-12

[*Dōgen*] *instructed*:

I indirectly heard [the following story], though I am not sure whether it is true. The late Middle Councilor Jimyōin, who was a lay monk, once had a treasured sword stolen.[299] The perpetrator was among his retainers. The other warriors arrested the man and brought [the sword] to the councilor. The lay monk said, "This is not my sword. There has been a mistake." He then gave the sword back [to the warrior]. Although it was certainly his sword, he gave it up because he thought of the shame of the warrior. Although everyone knew [the truth], the situation ended without trouble. As a result, the councilor's descendents flourished.

Even among the laity, those who are thoughtful [of others] are like this. All the more should monks have the same thoughtfulness. Because it is a matter of course that we monks have no wealth, we should consider our wisdom and virtue as our treasures. Even when someone does something contrary to the mind of awakening, we should not immediately express our criticism and judge the person to be evil. We should search for skillful means and speak in such a way that does not make the person angry. It is said that "the Dharma does not last long if expressed violently." Even if we should scold a person in accordance with the Dharma, if we use rough language the Dharma will not remain long. Narrow-minded people quickly become angry and think of their shame when they are criticized with harsh words. Magnanimous people are not like this. Even when hit, they would never think of revenge. In our country, there are many narrow-minded people. We must be careful.

The End of the Fifth Book of *Shōbōgenzō Zuimonki*

正法眼蔵随聞記　六

侍者　懐奘　編

6-1

一日、示云、

　仏法の為には、身命をおしむ事なかれ。俗、猶、みちを思へば、身命をすて、親族をかへりみず、忠節をつくす。是を忠臣とも、賢者とも云也。

　昔、漢の高祖、隣国と、軍を興す時、有る臣下の母、隣国に有き。官軍も二た心有んかと疑き。高祖も、若、母を思て、敵国へさる事もや、有らんずらん。若、さるならば、軍やぶるべし、とあやぶむ。

　ここに母も、我子、若、我故に二心もや、有ずらん、と思て、いましめて云、我れによりて、我国に来ことなかれ。我によりて、軍の忠をゆるくする事なかれ。我、若、いきたらば、汝ぢ、若、二心もこそ、有ん、と云て、剣に身をなげてうせしかば、其の子、もとより、二心なかりしかば、其の軍に忠節を至す志深かりけると云。

Shōbōgenzō Zuimonki, Book 6
Compiled by the attendant Ejō

6-1

One day, [Dōgen] instructed:

For the sake of the Buddhadharma, do not hold your bodily life dear. Even when laypeople think of the Way,[300] they cast away their lives and do not concern themselves with their families; they remain true and maintain their fidelity. Such people are called "faithful subjects" or "wise people."

In ancient times, Gaozu of Han[301] waged a war against a neighboring country. At that time, the mother of one of his ministers lived in that neighboring country. The imperial army suspected the minister of treachery. Gaozu was also afraid that this minister, thinking of his mother, might defect to the hostile country, which would result in the war being lost.

Separately, his mother [also] thought that her son might have divided loyalties on her account. She admonished him, saying, "Do not come to our country because of me. Do not neglect your loyalty to the army because of me. If I remain alive, you might be treacherous." So saying, she threw herself upon a sword and died. Because her son was never of two minds, it is said that he devoted himself to his duties in the war with loyalty and firm determination.

Needless to say, patch-robed monks practicing the Buddha Way, when completely without a divided heart, are truly in accordance with

　況や衲子の仏道を行ずる、必ず二た心なき時、真とに仏道にかなふべし。仏道には慈悲智恵、もとよりそなはれる人もあり。たとひ無けれども、学すればうる也。只だ身心を倶に放下して、三宝の海に廻向して、仏法の教へに任せて、私曲を存ずる事なかれ。

　漢の高祖の時、ある賢臣の云、政道の理乱は、縄の結ほれるを解が如し。急にすべからず。能々結び目をみて解べし。仏道も是の如し。能々道理を心得て、行ずべき也。法門をよく心得る人は、必ず道心ある人の、よく心得る也。いかに利智聡明なる人も、無道心にして、吾我をも不離、名利をも不捨得人は、道者ともならず、正理をも心得ぬ也。

6-2

示云、

　学道の人は、吾我の為に、仏法を学する事なかれ。只、仏法の為に、仏法を学すべき也。その故実は、我身心を、一物ものこさず放下して、仏法の大海に廻向すべき也。其後は一切の是非を、管ずる事無く、我心を存ずる事なく、難成ことなりとも、仏法につかはれて、強ひて是をなし、我心になしたきことなりとも、仏法の道理に、なすべからざることならば、放下すべき也。穴賢、仏道修行の功をもて、代りに善果を、得んと思ふ事無れ。只、一たび仏道に、廻向しつる上は、二たび自己をかへりみず、仏法のお

the Buddha Way. Regarding the Buddha Way, there may be some who inherently have compassion and wisdom from the outset. Even if we lack such qualities, we will be able to attain [the Way] if we study [it sincerely]. We need to simply cast away both body and mind, dedicate[302] ourselves to the ocean of the Three Treasures, entrust everything to the teachings of the Buddhadharma, and refrain from holding on to our biased personal views.

In the time of Gaozu of Han, a wise minister remarked, "Fixing the disorder of the way of politics is like untying a knotted rope. Do not be in a hurry. Loosen it only after the knot has been examined closely." The Buddha Way is the same. We should practice it [only] after having fully understood the principles of the Way. Those who carefully understand the Dharma gates will have the mind of awakening without fail.[303] No matter how intelligent or sharp we may be, if we lack the mind of awakening, if we do not detach ourselves from our [ego-centered] self, and if we are unable to abandon fame and profit, we will neither be able to become a person of the Way nor be able to understand true reality.

6-2

[*Dōgen*] *instructed*:

Students of the Way! We should not study the Buddhadharma for the sake of our own [ego-centered] self. We should study the Buddhadharma simply for the sake of the Buddhadharma. The genuine way to do so is to completely cast away body and mind, leaving nothing [behind] and dedicating [ourselves] to the great ocean of the Buddhadharma. After that, without being concerned about the right and wrong of each thing, without clinging to our own views, even if it is difficult to endure, we should allow ourselves to be used by the Buddhadharma when doing things.[304] Even if we want to do something, we should give it up if it is not in accordance with the principles of the Buddhadharma. We should never ever expect to obtain good results in exchange for our efforts in practicing the Buddha Way. Once we are

きてに任せて、行じゆきて、私曲を存ずること莫れ。先証、皆、如是。心にねがひて、もとむる事無ければ、即ち大安楽也。

世間の人にまじはらず、己が家ばかりにて、生長したる人は、心のままにふるまひ、おのれが心を先きとして、人目を知らず、人の心をかねざる人、必ず、あしき也。学道の用心も是の如し。衆にまじはり、師に随ひて、我見を立せず、心をあらため行けば、たやすく道者となる也。

学道は先づ須く、貧を学すべし。猶を利を捨てて、一切へつらふ事なく、万事なげすつれば、必ずよき僧となる也。大宋によき僧と、人にも知られたる人は、皆な貧道也。衣服もやつれ、諸縁ともしき也。

往日、天童山の書記、道如上座と云し人は、官人宰相の子なり（し）かども、親族にもむつびず、世利をも、むさぼらざりしかば、衣服のやつれ、破壊したる、目もあてられざりしかども、道徳、人に知れて、大寺の書記ともなりしなり。予、かの人に問云、和尚は官人の子息、富貴の孫也。何ぞ身に近づくるもの、皆、下品にして貧道なる。これ答云、僧となれれば也。

dedicated to the Buddha Way, we should never look back at ourselves. We should just continue practicing in accordance with the regulations of the Buddhadharma without considering twisted personal views. The examples of past practitioners have all been like this. When we no longer seek anything on the basis of our [ego-centered] mind, this itself is great peace and joy.[305]

Those who have never kept company with others in the world and have grown up only within their own families behave as they wish and put priority on fulfilling their own hearts' desires. They never think of how others see them and do not care how others feel. Without fail, such people are bad. The points to watch in practicing the Way[306] are also like this. We should keep company with others [in the sangha] and follow our teacher without setting up personal views. If we continue reforming our minds [in this way], we will easily become people of the Way.

In studying the Way, we should first of all study poverty. We should abandon profit, not ingratiate ourselves [to those with power] at all, and cast everything away. We will then become good monks without fail. In great Song China, those who were known as eminent monks all lived in poverty for the sake of the Way. Their robes were tattered, and they were short of other provisions.

A while ago, there was a senior monk named Daoru who was appointed as the secretary[307] of Tiantong monastery. Although he was the son of a minister of the government, because he had completely left his family and relatives and never coveted worldly profit, his robes were so tattered that he was too terrible to look at. And yet his virtue in the Way was known among people, and he became the secretary of a great monastery. I asked this man, "Master, you are the son of a high government official and the grandson of a wealthy man. Why are your belongings so shabby? Why do you live in such poverty?" He answered, "Because I have become a monk."

6-3

一日、示云、

　俗人の云、財はよく身を害す、昔も有之、今も有之、と。言は、昔、一人の俗人あり、一人の美女をもてり。威勢ある人、これをこふ。かの夫、是を惜む。終に軍を興して、かこめり。彼いへ、既に、うばいとられんとする時き、かの夫、（云）、なんぢが為めに命をうしなふべし。かの女云、我れ、汝が為に命をうしなはん、と云て、高楼よりおちて死ぬ。其後かの夫、うちもらされて、命遁れし時、いひし言ば也。

　昔、賢人、州吏として、国を行なふ時に、息男あり。父を拝してさる時、一疋の縑をあたふ。息の云、君、高亮也。此縑、いづくよりか得たる。父云、俸禄のあまり有り。息、かへり皇帝に参ず。（帝）はなはだ其の賢を感ず。かの息男申さく、父、猶、名をかくす。我は猶、名をあらはす。父の賢すぐれたり。

　此心は、一疋の縑は、是、少分なれど、賢人は、私用せざる事、聞へたり。又、まことの賢人は、猶、賢の名をかくして、俸禄なれば、使用するよしを云。俗人、猶、然り。学道の衲子、私を存ずる事なかれ。又、まことの道を好まば、道者の名をかくすべき也。

　又、云、

　仙人ありき。有る人問云く、何がして仙をえん。仙の云、仙を得んと思はば、道をこのむべし。然あれば、学人仏祖を得んと思はば、すべからく、祖道を好むべし。

6-3

One day, [Dōgen] instructed:

A layman said, "Wealth can damage one's life. This is [true] in the past and in the present as well." This refers to a story in ancient times about a layman who married a beautiful woman. A powerful man told the layman to give the woman to him. The husband was unwilling to do so. In the end, an army surrounded [the layman's house]. When his house was about to be taken away, the husband said [to his wife], "I will give up my life for you." The woman said, "[No,] I will give up my life for you," and so saying, she jumped from a lofty building, killing herself. Later, the husband—who had failed to be killed, and escaped with his life—told this story.[308]

Long ago, a wise man governed a province as a government official. He had a son. When the son visited his father, he bowed and said farewell, and the father gave him a bolt of fine silk. The son said, "You are a person of high integrity. Where did you get this silk?" The father said, "This is left over from my official pay." The son returned [to the capital] and met with the emperor [to whom he related what his father had done]. The emperor admired the father's wisdom. The son said, "My father hid his reputation. I reveal his reputation. My father's wisdom is superior to mine."[309]

This story teaches us that even though the bolt of silk was trivial, the wise man did not take it for his private use. It also tells us that this truly wise man concealed his reputation for wisdom. He said he would use it [only] because the silk was a part of his own official pay. Even a layman was like this. A patch-robed monk studying the Way should not seek any personal [benefit]. Moreover, if we care for the true Way, we should hide our reputation as a person of the Way.

[Dōgen] also said:

There was once a mountain immortal.[310] Someone asked him, "How does one become an immortal?" The immortal said, "If you want to become an immortal, you should be fond of the Way."[311]

6-4

示云、

　昔、国皇有り、国をさめて後、諸臣に告、我よく国を治む、賢
也。諸臣皆云、帝は甚よくをさむ。一臣ありて云、帝、賢ならず。
帝云、故へ如何。臣云、国を打取りし時、帝の弟にあたへずして、
息にあたふ。帝の心にかなはずして、おひたてられて後、又、一臣
に問、朕よく仁帝なりや。臣云、甚よく仁なり。帝云、其故如何。臣
云、仁君には忠臣有り。忠臣は直言ある也。前臣、はなはだ直言
也。是れ忠臣也。仁君にあらずはえじ。即ち、帝、是を感じて、前臣
をめしかへされぬ。

　又云、

　秦の始皇の時、太子、花園をひろげんとす。臣の云、尤、もし花
園ひろうして、鳥類多くは、鳥類をもち、隣国の軍をふせいつべ
し。よて其事とどまりぬ。

　又、宮殿をつくり、はしをぬらんとす。臣の云、もとも然るべ
し。はしをぬりたらば、敵はとどまらん。よて其事も、とどまりぬ。

　云心は、儒教の心、如是。たくみに言を以て、悪事をとどめ、
善事をすすめし也。衲子の人を化する、善巧として、其の心あるべ
し。

Therefore, students, if you wish to become buddha-ancestors, you should be fond of the Way of the ancestors.

6-4

[*Dōgen*] *instructed*:

Long ago there was an emperor. After having established his rule, he inquired of his ministers, saying, "I have governed this country well. Am I wise?" All the ministers said, "Emperor! You have ruled very well." One minister said, "Your Majesty! You are not wise." The emperor asked, "What is the reason?" The minister said, "When you conquered a country, you did not give it to your younger brother but to your son." The emperor was offended and expelled the minister. Later, he asked another minister, "Am I a benevolent emperor?"[312] The minister said, "You are exceedingly benevolent." The emperor asked, "What is the reason?" The minister said, "A benevolent ruler has loyal ministers. Loyal ministers make straightforward remarks. That minister's opinion was very straightforward. He is a loyal minister. If you were not a benevolent emperor, you would not have [such a minister]." The emperor was impressed by this and immediately summoned the previously mentioned minister.[313]

[*Dōgen*] *also said*:

During the time of the [Emperor] Shihuang of Qin,[314] the crown prince wanted to enlarge his flower garden. A minister said, "That makes sense. If you enlarge the flower garden and you have many birds, you will be able to use the birds to defend your country from the attacks of neighboring enemies." Because of this [remonstrance], the project was given up.

[The crown prince] also wanted to build a palace with lacquered stairs. A minister said, "That is an excellent idea. If the stairs are lacquered, enemies will stop invading." Because of this [remark], that project was also given up.[315]

6-5

一日、僧問云、智者の無道心なると、無智の有道心なると、始終如何。

示云、

無智の道心、始終、退する事多し。智恵有る人、無道心なれども、ついに道心をおこす也。当世、現証、是多し。しかあれば、先ず道心の有無をいわず、学道勤労すべき也。

又云、

内外の書籍に、まづしうして、居所なく、或は滄浪の水にうかび、或は首陽の山にかくれ、或は樹下露地に端坐し、或は塚間深山に、草庵する人あり。又、富貴にして財多、朱漆をぬり、金玉をみがき、宮殿等をつくるもあり。倶に書籍にのせたりと云へども、褒めて後代をすすむるには、皆、貧にして、無財なるを以て本とす。そしりて、来業をいましむるには、財多をば、驕奢のものと云てそしる也。

6-6

示云、

This story tells us that the mind of Confucianism is like this. Using skillful sayings, they prevent wrongdoing and encourage good actions. Patch-robed monks should also have this kind of skillfulness when teaching others.

6-5

One day, a monk asked, "In the long run, what is the difference between a wise person without the mind of awakening and an unwise person with the mind of awakening?"

[*Dōgen*] *instructed*:

In many cases, [those with] the mind of awakening [but] without wisdom will eventually regress. People with wisdom, though lacking the mind of awakening, will eventually arouse the aspiration for the Way. In the present day there are many actual examples of this. Therefore, without discussing whether we have aroused the mind of awakening or not, we should, first of all, make diligent effort in studying the Way.

[*Dōgen*] *also said*:

In both Buddhist and non-Buddhist texts, [we find] people who were so poor that they did not have a fixed abode: some wandered floating on the water of the Canglang River,[316] some hid themselves on Shouyang Mountain,[317] some sat upright on the bare ground under a tree, and some built their hermitages in graveyards or in the deep mountains. On the other hand, some were wealthy and prominent, who built palaces coated with vermilion lacquer and adorned with gold and jewels. We find both kinds of people in various texts, but those who were poor and without possessions are praised as paragons for later generations. When admonishing deeds [that create bad] karma in the future, [these texts] criticized those who were wealthy as being people of extravagance and arrogance.

6-6

[*Dōgen*] *instructed*:

学人、人の施をうけて、悦ぶ事なかれ。又、うけざる事なかれ。故僧正云、人の供養を得て悦ぶは、制にたがふ。悦ばざるは、檀那の心にたがふ。是の故実は、我に供養ずるに非ず、三宝に供ずる也。故に彼の返事に云べし。此供養、三宝定て、納受あるらん。申けがす、と云べき也。

6-7

示云、

ふるく云、君子の力ら、牛に勝れたり。しかあれども、牛とあらそはず。今の学人、我智恵を学人にすぐれて存ずとも、人と諍論を好む事なかれ。又、悪口をもて、人を云い、怒目をもて、人を見る事なかれ。今の世の人、多く財をあたへ、恩をほどこせども、瞋恚を現じ、悪口を以て謗言すれば、必ず逆心を起す也。

6-8

示云、

真浄の文和尚、衆に示云、我れ昔雪峰と、ちぎりを結びて、学道せし時、雪峰、同学と法門を論じて、衆寮に高声に諍談す。つひにたがひに、悪口に及ぶ。よて喧嘩す。事、散じて、峰、真浄にかたりて云、我れ、汝ぢと同心同学也。契約あさからず。何が故に、我れ人とあらそふに、不口入。浄、揖して恐惶せるのみ也。

Students! We should not take delight when receiving offerings from people. Still, we should not reject them either. The late superintendent of monks[318] said, "It goes against the precepts to rejoice upon receiving offerings. But if we do not rejoice, we go against the good hearts of donors." The ancient practice regarding this point is [understanding] that the offerings are not made for our personal benefit but offered to the Three Treasures. Therefore, in reply [to the donors], we should say, "This offering will certainly be accepted by the Three Treasures. I humbly transmit [it on your behalf]."

6-7

[*Dōgen*] *instructed*:

It was said in ancient times, "The power of a virtuous person is superior to [that of] an ox. However, [such a person] does not compete with an ox." Students of today! Even if you think that your wisdom and knowledge are superior to those of others, you should not be fond of arguing with them. Moreover, we should not abuse others with bad mouths or glare at others with angry eyes. As for today's worldly people, even if someone has given them abundant wealth and done them favors, they would [still] definitely arouse negative feelings if [their benefactors were to] display anger and slander them with insults.

6-8

[*Dōgen*] *instructed*:

Master Wen of Zhenjing[319] instructed his assembly saying, "Long ago when I had vowed to keep friendship and study the Way together with Yunfeng,[320] Yunfeng once argued about the Dharma teachings with a fellow student in the assembly dormitory, where they quarreled in loud voices. Eventually they began to argue, trading insults with each other. In the end they got into a fight. After the matter ended, Yunfeng said to me, 'You and I are close friends practicing together with one mind. Our friendship is not shallow. Why did you not support

其後、かれも、一方善知識たり。我も今住持たり。そのかみお
もへらく、法門論談すら、畢竟じて無用也。況や諍論は、定、僻事
なるべし。我れ争て、何にの用ぞと思ひしかば、無言にして止り
ぬ。

今の学人も門徒も、其の跡を思ふべし。学道勤労の志有ば、
時光を惜で学すべし。何の暇まにか、人と諍論すべき。畢竟じて自
他ともに無益也。何況や世間の事においては、無益の論をすべ
からず。君子の力らは、牛にもすぐれたり。しかれども牛と相ひ争
はず。我れ法を知れり。彼れにすぐれたりと思ふとも、論じて彼を
難じ負かすべからず。若、真実に、学道の人有りて、法を問はば、
惜むべからず。為に開示すべし。然れども、猶を其れも、三度問は
れて、一度答ふべし。多言閑語する事なかるべし。此の咎は身に
有り。是、我を諫らるると思しかば、其後、人と法門を諍論せず。

6-9

示云、

古人、多は云、光陰虚度る事なかれ。或云く、時光徒に過こと
なかれ、と。学道の人、すべからく、寸陰を惜むべし。露命消へや
すし。時光すみやかに移る。暫く存ずる間に、余事を管ずる事無
く、只、須学道。

me when I was arguing with that person?' I could do nothing but feel small, folding my hands [and lowering my head].

Later Yunfeng became an eminent master, and I, too, am now an abbot. At the time I thought that even arguing about the Dharma teachings was ultimately useless, not to mention fighting, which was definitely mistaken. Because I thought it was useless to fight, I kept silent."

Today's students and [lay] disciples alike should consider this preceding example. If we aspire to make diligent efforts in studying the Way, we must cherish the time we have to study. When do we have spare time to quarrel with others? Ultimately speaking, [arguing] brings no benefit either to us or to others. Needless to say, we should not engage in any futile disputes over mundane affairs. The power of a virtuous person is superior to [that of] an ox. However, the person does not compete with an ox. Even if we think we understand the Dharma teachings and that we are superior to others, we should not argue, criticize, and defeat them. If there is a sincere student who asks us about the Dharma, we should not withhold [our knowledge]. We should explain and share. However, even in such cases, only after we have been asked three times should we answer one time.[321] We should neither speak too much nor engage in idle talk. I myself had this fault. Because I thought [Zhenjing's] admonishment applied to me, I have subsequently never quarreled about Dharma teachings with others.

6-9

[Dōgen] instructed:

Many ancients said, "Do not spend your days and nights in vain."[322] Or they said, "Do not pass time wastefully." Students of the Way! We should cherish every moment [we have]. Our dew-like life disappears easily; time passes swiftly. For the brief time that we exist, we should not care for other affairs; we should devote ourselves to just studying the Way.

　今の時の人、或は父母の恩すてがたしと云、或は主君の命そむきがたしと云、或は妻子の情愛、離れがたしと云、或は眷属等の活命、我れを存じがたしと云、或世人謗つべしと云、或貧して道具調へがたしと云、或非器にして、学道にたへじと云。如是等の、世情をめぐらして、主君父母をもはなれず、妻子眷属をもすてず、世情にしたがひ、財色を貪るほどに、一生虚く過て、まさしく命の尽くる時にあたりて後悔すべし。

　須く閑に坐して、道理を案じて、終にうち立ん道を、思ひ定むべし。主君父母も、我に悟りを与ふべきに非ず。恩愛妻子も、我がくるしみを、すくふべからず。財宝も死をすくはず。世人終に我をたすくる事なし。非器なりと云て、修せずは、何の劫にか得道せん。只、須、万事を放下して、一向に学道すべし。後時を存ずること莫るべし。

6-10

一日、示云、

　学道は、須く吾我をはなるべし。たとひ千経万論を、学し得たりとも、我執をはなれずは、つひに魔坑におつ。古人云、仏法の身心なくは、焉、仏となり祖とならん。我をはなると云は、我が身心をすてて、我が為に仏法を、学すること無き也。只、道のために学すべし。身心を仏法に放下しつれば、くるしく愁ふれども、仏法にしたがつて行じゆく也。乞食をせば、人、是をわるしと、思はん

These days, some people say that they cannot abandon their debts of gratitude to their parents; some say they cannot disregard the orders of their lords; some say they cannot part from the affection of their wives and children; some say when they consider their families' and relatives' survival, they cannot [pursue] their own wishes; some say worldly people would slander them; some say they are poor and cannot afford monks' supplies; and some say because they are not vessels [of the Dharma], they are not capable of enduring the practice of the Way. Because they consider matters with worldly sentiments such as these, they cannot leave their lords, fathers, and mothers, or abandon their wives, children, or relatives. They go on following worldly sentiments and clinging to their desires for wealth and sexual greed. Consequently, they spend their whole lifetimes in vain and cannot help feeling regret when their lives are exhausted.

We should sit calmly, ponder reality, and determine the path we will finally take after departing [from this life in preparation for the next life]. Neither our lords nor our fathers or mothers are able to give us realization. Nor can our wives or children save us from suffering. Nor can our wealth save us when we die. Worldly people can never help us [with such matters]. If we avoid practicing on the grounds that we are not vessels [of the Dharma], in which eon will we be able to attain the Way? We should simply cast everything aside and wholeheartedly devote ourselves to the practice of the Way. Do not think that there is any later time [to practice].

6-10

One day, [Dōgen] instructed:

In studying the Way, we should by all means depart from our [ego-centered] self. Even if we are able to study a thousand scriptures or ten thousand commentaries, if we do not free ourselves from self-attachment, we will eventually fall into the pit of demons. An ancient said, "If we lack the body and mind of the Buddhadharma, how is it possible to become a buddha-ancestor?" To depart from ego-attachment

ずるなんど、是如く思ふ程に、何にも仏法に入り得ざる也。世情の
見をすべて忘て、只、道理に任て、学道すべき也。我が身の器量
をかへりみ、仏法にもかなふまじき、なんど思も、我執をもてる故
也。人目をかへりみ、人情をはばかる、即、我執の本也。只すべか
らく、仏法を学すべし。世情に随ふこと無れ。

6-11

一日、弉問云、叢林の勤学の行履と云は如何。

　示云、

　只管打坐也。或は閣上、或は楼下にして、常坐をいとなむ。人
に交り物語をせず、聾者の如く、唖者の如くにして、常に独坐を
好む也。

6-12

一日、参次に、示云、

　泉大道の云、風に向て坐し、日に向て眠る。時の人の錦被た
るにまされり。此のことば、古人の語ばなれども、すこし疑ひ有
り。時の人と云は、世間貪利の人を云か。若然ば、敵対尤もくだ

means to cast aside body and mind and never study the Buddhadharma for our own benefit. We should simply study [the Way] for the sake of the Way. Having cast our body and mind into the Buddhadharma, no matter how painful it might be or even if we might be distressed, we should continue to practice following the Buddhadharma. We might think that if we beg for food, people will think ill of us. As long as we think in this way, we will never be able to enter the Buddhadharma. We should forget all views based on worldly sentiments and just practice the Way, entrusting ourselves to its principles. Reflecting on our capability and thinking that we are not able to practice in accordance with the Buddhadharma is also due to our ego-attachment. Being concerned with the public gaze and worrying about opinions based on human sentiments is the root of ego-attachment. We should simply study the Buddhadharma. Do not follow worldly sentiments.

6-11

One day, Ejō asked, "How would you say we should conduct ourselves when studying diligently within a monastery?"

[Dōgen] *instructed*:

Just sit [*shikantaza*].[323] Wherever you are, either upstairs or downstairs, always devote yourself to sitting. Without engaging in idle talk with people, being like one who is deaf and dumb, always be fond of sitting alone.

6-12

One day during a meeting, [Dōgen] instructed:

Dadao Guquan[324] said, "Sitting in the wind and sleeping in the sun: this is superior to the people of today who wear brocade." Although these are the words of an ancient, I have a small question. Does the phrase "people of today" refer to people in the mundane world who covet profit? If so, such a comparison is most ridiculous. Why did he

れり。何ぞ云にたらん。若学道の人を云か。然ば何ぞ、錦被と云
ん。

　此の心をさぐるに、猶、錦を重くする心有やと聞ゆ。聖人はし
からず。金玉と瓦礫と、ひとしくす。執する事なし。故に釈迦如来、
牧牛女が乳の粥を得ても食し、馬麦を得ても食す。何もひとしく
す。法に軽重なし、情愛浅深あり。

　今の世に金玉を重しとて、人の与れども、取ず、木石をば軽し
とて、是を愛するも有り。思べし、金玉も本来、土中より得たり、木
石も大地より得たり。何ぞ一つをば重しとて取ず、一をば軽しとて
愛せん。此心を案ずるに、重を得て執すべき心ろ有らんか。軽を
得て愛する心有らば、とが、ひとしかるべし。是れ学人の用心すべ
き事也。

6-13

示云、

　先師全和尚入宋せんとせし時、本師叡山の明融阿闍梨、重病
に沈み、すでに死なんとす。

　其時、この師云、我、既に老病に沈み、死去せんとする事、近
にあり、汝ぢ一人老病をたすけて、冥路をとぶらふべし。今度の入
唐、暫く止て、死去の後、其本意をとげらるべし。

have to mention such a thing? Does it refer to people studying the Way? If so, why did he say they are wearing brocade?

As I investigate his frame of mind, it sounds as if he still values brocade. Holy people are not like this. They see gold or jewels and tiles or pebbles as equal. They are not attached [to either]. This is the reason why the Tathāgata Shakyamuni accepted and ate the milk porridge offered by the milkmaid, and he also ate grain used to feed horses.[325] He accepted both equally. In the Dharma, there is no valuable or worthless. [However,] in human affection there is shallowness or depth.

In the present age, there are some people who value gold and jewels and yet do not accept them when people offer them, but they consider trees and stones valueless yet love such things. We should consider that we get gold and jewels from the soil, while trees and stones are also from the great earth. For what reason should we consider one thing valuable and not accept it yet consider another thing valueless and love it? When I examine such people's frame of mind, it seems that they worry about attachment if they obtain something valuable. Even if they acquire something valueless yet love it, they will have the same fault. This is what students should keep in mind.

6-13

[*Dōgen*] *instructed*:

When my late master Preceptor Myōzen[326] was about to go to Song China, his original master, Ācārya Myōyu[327] on Mt. Hiei, became seriously ill and was close to death. At the time, the master [Myōyu] said, "I am descending into old age and sickness; my death must be near at hand. You alone [must] take care of me in my aging and sickness, and see me off when I depart on the dark road.[328] For now, put off going to China for a while, and after my death carry out your true intention."

At that time, my late master [Myōzen] called his disciples and fellow practitioners together to discuss this matter. He said, "Since I

　時に先師、弟子及同朋等をあつめて、商議して云、我、幼少の時、双親の家を出でて後、此師の覆育を蒙て、今、成長せり。世間養育の恩、尤も重し。又出世法門の事、大小権実教文、因果をわきまへ、是非を知て、等輩にもこえ、名誉を得たる事も、又仏法の道理を知て、今入宋求法の志を、おこすまでも、彼の恩に非ずと云こと無し。然るに、今年、すでに窮老して、重病の床に臥し給へり。余命存じがたし。後会、期すべきに非ず。よてあながちに是をとどむ。彼の命もそむき難し。今、不顧身命、入宋求法するも、菩薩の大悲、利生の為也。彼の命をそむき、宋土にゆかん道理如何。各々、存知を、のべらるべし。

　時に人々、皆云、今年の入宋止るべし。老病、已に窮れり。死去、定なり。今年ばかり止て、明年の入唐、尤然る可し。彼の命をもそむかず、重恩をも忘れず。今一年半年の、入唐の遅々、何のさまたげか有ん。師弟の本意も、相違せず、入宋の本意も、如意なるべし。

　時に我れ末臘にて云、仏法の悟り、今はさて有りなんと、おぼしめさるる義ならば、御とどまり然るべし。

　先師の云、然か也。仏法修行のみち、是程にて、さても有りなんと存ず。始終是の如くならば、さりとも出離、などかと存ず。

　我、云、其の義ならば、御とどまり有るべし。

　時に先師、皆の議をはりて云、各々の議定、皆とどまるべき、道理なり。我が所存は然らず。今度止りたりとも、決定死ぬべき人ならば、其によりて、命のぶべからず。又、我とどまりて、看病外護

left my parents' home in my childhood, I have been brought up under this master's protection and educated by him until reaching my present maturity. In worldly terms, I have a most heavy debt of gratitude. Also, I have studied the Dharma gates that are beyond the worldly realm, such as the verbal teachings of Mahāyāna and Hīnayāna, and the provisional as well as the genuine teachings. I have come to understand the principle of causes and results, and learned right from wrong. I have surpassed my fellow students and gained honor. Now I understand the truth of the Buddhadharma and aspire to go to China to seek the Dharma. This has all been enabled solely by my master's kind nurturing. However, this year he has become seriously ill due to old age, and he is lying on his deathbed. We do not know how much longer he can live. [If I leave now] I cannot expect to meet him again. Therefore, he strongly urges me to postpone [my plan]. It is difficult to disobey my master's request. Now I am about to go to China to seek the Dharma without holding my life dear. This derives from great bodhisattva compassion for the sake of benefiting living beings. Is there any reason to disobey [my master] and go to the land of Song [China]? Each of you, please tell me what you think."

At the time, each and every one of them said, "Give up journeying to China this year. His aging and sickness are already critical, and he will surely die. Giving up [your plan] this year and going to China next year would be the most appropriate [course of action]. You would neither go against your master's request nor disregard your great debt of gratitude to him. There is nothing wrong with postponing your trip to China for one or half a year. It would not go against the true intention of the master-disciple [relationship], and still you would be able to realize your true intention to go to China."

At that time, as the least senior monk, I said, "If you think that your realization of the Buddhadharma is what it should be, you should put off [your trip to China]." My late master said, "That is so. I think that the practice of the Buddhadharma should be like this. If I continuously [practice] in this way, I think I will be released [from saṃsāra]."[329]

せんによりて、苦痛も、やむべからず。又最後に我があつかひ、勧めんによりて、決定、生死を可離道理にもなし。只、一旦、命に随ひたる、うれしさばかりか。是によりて、出離得道の為に、一切無用也。誤て求法の志をさへて、罪業の因縁となるべし。然に、若、入唐求法の志を遂て、一分の悟をも、ひらきたらば、一人有漏の迷情にこそ、たがふとも、多人得道の縁となるべし。功徳若勝れば、又師の恩報じつべし。たとひ又渡海の間に死て本意をとげずとも、求法の志をもて死せば、玄奘三蔵のあとをも思ふべし。一人の為に、うしなひやすき時を、空くすぐさん事、仏意にかなふべからず。よて今度の入唐、一向に思ひきりをはりぬ、とて、終に入宋しき。

　先師にとりて、真実の道心と、存ぜし事、是等の心也。然れば、今の学人も、或は父母の為、或は師匠の為に、無益の事を行じて、徒に時を失ひ、勝れたる道を指おきて、光陰をすぐす事無れ。

　時に弉公云、真実求法の為には、有漏の父母、師僧の障縁を、すつべき道理、然るべし。但し、父母恩愛等のかたをば、一向に捨離すとも、又菩薩の行を存ぜん時、自利をさしおきて、利他をさきとすべきか。然に、老病にして、又他人のたすくべきもなく、我一人其の人にあたりたるを、自の修行を思て、彼をたすけずは、菩薩の行にそむくか。又大士の善行を不可嫌。縁に対し事に随て、仏法を存べきか。若、是らの道理によらば、又ゆいてたすくべきか如何。

I said, "If you think so, you should stay." After all of us expressed our opinions, my late master said, "All of you agree that I should stay. My intention differs. Even if I put off my trip this time, one who is certain to die will not prolong his life. Also, by my remaining here, taking care of him in his sickness and looking after him, his pain and suffering will not cease. Also, simply because I took care of him before his death would not mean that he would definitely be able to depart from life-and-death. There would be only short-lived happiness from following his request. This would be entirely useless for gaining emancipation and attaining the Way. To mistakenly hinder my aspiration to seek the Dharma would be a cause and condition of unwholesome karma. On the other hand, if I carry out my aspiration to go to China to seek the Dharma and gain a bit of realization, even though it goes against one person's defiled feelings, it will become a cause for attaining the Way for many people. If this merit is greater, it will help to repay the debt of gratitude to my master. Even if I die while crossing the ocean and fail to accomplish my original intention, because I will have died with the aspiration of seeking the Dharma [, my vow will not cease in a future life]. We should remember the Tripiṭaka Master Xuanzang's traces.[330] Vainly spending time, which is easily lost, for the sake of one person would not be in accordance with the Buddha's will. Therefore, I have firmly resolved to go to China now." Having said this, in the end he went to China.

For my late master, the true mind of awakening is this kind of mental attitude. This being the case, today's students should also not spend their time in vain involved in useless things for the sake of their parents or masters. We should not spend our time setting aside the superior Buddha Way.

At that time, Ejō asked, "For the sake of truly seeking the Dharma, we must eliminate the contaminants that exist caused by our obligations to our parents or masters. It is just as you say. However, although we completely renounce our obligations and affection for our parents and others, when we aspire to bodhisattva practice, we should still put aside personal benefit and put primary importance on benefiting

示云、

　利他の行も自行の道も、劣なるをすてて、すぐれたるを取る
は、大士の善行也。老病をたすけんとて、水菽の孝を至すは、今
生暫時の妄愛、迷情の悦びばかり也。背きて無為の道を学せん
は、たとひ遺恨はありとも、出世の縁となるべし。是を思へ、是を
思へ。

6-14

一日、示云、

　世間の人、自云、某甲し、師の言を聞に、我が心にかなはず。
我思に、此言非也。其心如何。若、聖教等の道理を心得をし、す
べて、其の心に違する、非也と思か。若、然らば何ぞ師に問ふ。又
ひごろの情見をもて云か。若、然らば、無始より以来の妄念也。学
道の用心と云は、我心にたがへども、師の言ば、聖教のことばな
らば、暫く其に随て、本の我見をすてて、改めゆく、此の心、学道
の故実也。

　我れ当年、傍輩の中に、我見を執て、知識をとぶらひし、我心
に違をば心得ずと云て、我見に相叶を執て、一生虚く、仏法を会

others. If so, if an aged person were seriously ill, and no one but I could nurse them, if I only thought of my own practice without helping them, it would seem to go against bodhisattva practice, would it not? Also, a *mahāsattva*[331] should not avoid carrying out wholesome actions. Should we not consider the Buddhadharma according to circumstances and the particular situation? For these reasons, should we not go and help such a person? What do you think?"[332]

[*Dōgen*] *instructed*:

Whether acting for the benefit of others or practicing for ourselves, the good practice of a *mahāsattva* is to abandon what is inferior and to take what is superior. To care for sick and aged parents in poverty[333] is only a temporary pleasure arising from illusory love and deluded sentiment in this brief life. If we go against [our defiled sentiments] and study the Way of non-action, even though we may be resented [by others], it will bring about a positive connection beyond the mundane world. Consider this well! Consider this well!

6-14

One day, [*Dōgen*] *instructed*:

People of the world say of themselves, "Although I listen to my master's sayings, they do not satisfy my mind." I think such a statement is mistaken. How are such thoughts possible? Do they have [their own] understanding of the principles of the sacred teachings and so on and consider everything that does not coincide with their opinions to be wrong? If so, why do they consult their masters? Or do they say such things because their views are rooted in habitual [deluded] sentiment? If this is the case, these are delusory thoughts from the beginningless beginning. An essential point we should keep in mind in our study of the Way is that we should give up and reform our egotistical views. Even if [some teachings] go against our own preferences, if those are our master's sayings, or statements from the sacred scriptures, we must follow them for the time being. This is the genuine mental attitude in the study of the Way.

せざりしを見て、知、発して、学道は不可然と思て、師の言に随
て、暫く道理を得て、其後、看経の次に、或経に云、仏法を学せん
とおもはば、三世の心を相続する事なかれ、と。知りぬ、先の念
を記持せずして、次第に改めゆくべきり。書に云、忠言は耳にさ
かふ、と、我が為に忠なるべき言ば、耳に違する也。違すれども強
て随はば、畢竟じて益あるべき也。

6-15

一日、雑話の次に云、

　人の心、元より善悪なし。善悪、縁に随ておこる。仮令、人、
発心して、山林に入る時は、林家はよし、人間はわるしと覚。又、
退心して山林を出る時は、山林はわるしと覚ゆ。是、即ち、決定し
て、心に定相なくして、縁にひかれてともかくもなる也。故に善縁
にあへばよくなり、悪縁に近づけば、わるくなる也。我が心、本よ
りわるしと思ふことなかれ。只、ただ善縁に随ふべき也。

　又、云、

　人心は、決定、人の言に随ふと存ず。大論に云、喩へば愚人
の手に、摩尼を以てるが如し。人、是を見て、汝ぢ下劣なり。自、

Early on, among my fellow practitioners there was one who visited masters while clinging strongly to his own views. He [refused to accept] whatever differed from his opinions, saying that it did not make sense to him, and held on to only what accorded with his own views. He spent his whole life in vain without understanding the Buddhadharma. Observing [his attitude,] I realized that studying the Way should not be like that. I followed my master's sayings and, to a degree, attained the truth of the Way. Later, I found the following passage while reading a scripture: "If you wish to study the Buddhadharma, do not continue to hold on to the [conditioned] mind of the past, present, and future."[334] I understood that we must gradually reform previous thoughts without holding firmly to them. In a text it is said, "Good advice sounds harsh to the ear."[335] Words [that are said] faithfully on our behalf are offensive to our ears. Even though it may be contrary [to our preferences], if we force ourselves to follow this advice and carry it out, there will be benefits in the end.

6-15

One day, during a miscellaneous talk, [Dōgen] said:

Originally, the human mind is neither good nor evil. Good and evil arise depending on conditions. For example, when people arouse the mind of awakening and enter a mountain forest, they think that a dwelling in the woods is good and the human world is bad. And when their aspiration has waned and they leave the mountain forest, they think the mountain forest is bad. This is because the human mind has no fixed characteristics; it changes in this way or that, influenced by circumstances. Consequently, if we encounter good conditions, the mind becomes good. If bad conditions draw near, the mind becomes bad. Do not think that the mind is fundamentally evil. We should simply follow good circumstances.

[Dōgen] also said:

I think the human mind definitely changes depending upon the words of others. The *Great Treatise*[336] states, "For example, it is like a

手に物をもてり、と云を聞て思はく、珠は惜しし、名聞は有り、我
は下劣ならじ、と思ふ。思ひわづらひて、猶、名聞に引れて、人の
言について、珠をおいて、後に、下人に取らしめんと思ふ程に、
珠を失、と云。

　人の心は如是。一定、此言、我が為によしと思へども、人の語
につく事あり。されば、何に本とよりあしき心なりとも、善知識にし
たがひ、良人久語を聞ば、自然に心もよくなる也。悪人にちかづ
けば、我が心にわるしと思へども、人の心に暫く随ふほどに、や
がて真実にわるくなる也。

　又、人の心、決定して、ものを此の人に、とらせじと思へども、
あながちにしひて、切に重ねて云へば、にくしと思ひながら与
也。決定して与んと思へども、便宜あしくて、時すぎぬれば、さて
やむ事も有り。

　然らば、学人、道心なくとも、良人に近づき、善縁にあふて、
同じ事をいくたびも、聞き見べき也。此言、一度聞き見れば、今は
見聞かずともと思ことなかれ。道心一度発したる人も、同じ事な
れども、聞くたびにみがかれて、いよいよ、よき也。況や、無道心の
人も、一度二度こそ、つれなくとも、度々重なれば、霧の中を行く
人の、いつぬるるとおぼえざれども、自然に恥る心もおこり、真と
の道心も起る也。

　故に、知りたる上にも、聖教を又々見るべし、聞くべし。師の言
も、聞たる上にも、聞きたる上にも、重々聞くべし、弥よ深き心有
る也。道の為にさはりと、なりぬべき事をば、かねて是に近づく

foolish person who has a precious jewel in his hand. Someone sees him and says, 'You are so vulgar, holding things in your own hands.' Hearing this, he thinks, 'This jewel is precious, yet my reputation is also important. I do not want to be thought of as vulgar.' Worried about this and pulled around by [the idea of his] reputation, he finally follows the person's words. He decides to put down his jewel and later has his servant take it. In the end, he loses the jewel."

The human mind works in this way. Even though we may think a certain thing is undoubtedly good for us, sometimes we [instead] go along with what other people say. Therefore, no matter how evil the mind seems to be originally, when we follow a good master and listen continuously to what good people say, the mind naturally becomes good. If we associate with evil people, even though we may think they are bad, eventually we will fall under such people's influence, and finally our mind truly becomes evil.

Also, although we may have determined in our mind not to give a certain thing to a certain person, if they strongly and repeatedly press us, we may give it to them unwillingly even though we dislike them. What is more, even if we decide to give the thing to a person [whom we do like], we might not [do so] if we do not have a good opportunity.

Therefore, even if we have not yet aroused the mind of awakening, we should become close with good people, meet with good conditions, and listen to and look at the same things again and again. Do not think that we do not need to listen anymore because we have already heard something once. Even if we have aroused the mind of awakening once, when we hear the same things over and over, [our mind] will become more polished, and we will improve more and more. Moreover, even if we still lack the mind of awakening and do not find it interesting the first and second time, [when we listen] again and again repeatedly, it is like walking through mist.[337] Just as we become wet without noticing it, we will naturally feel ashamed [of our previous lack of understanding,] and the true mind of awakening will arise.

べからず。善友には、くるしく、わびしくとも、近づきて行道すべき
也。

6-16

示云、

　大恵禅師、或時、尻に腫物を出す。医師、是を見て、大事の物
也、と云。恵云、大事の物ならば、死すべしや。医云、ほとんどあ
やふかるべし。恵云、若、死ぬべくは、弥、坐禅すべし、と云て、
猶、強盛に坐したりしかば、かの腫物、うみつぶれて、別の事なか
りき。

　古人の心、如是。病を受ては、弥、坐禅せし也。今の人の、病
なからん、坐禅ゆるくすべからず。

　病は心に随て、転ずるかと覚。世間にしやくりする人、虚言を
もし、わびつべき事をも、云ひつげつれば、其れをわびしき事に
思ひ、心に入て陳ぜんとするほどに、忘て、その病止る也。

　我も当時み、入宋の時き、船中にして痢病をせしに、悪風出来
て、船中さわぎし時、病忘て止まりぬ。

　是を以つて思ふに、学道勤学して、他事を忘れば、病もおこる
まじきか、と覚る也。

For this reason, even if we have understood the sacred scriptures, we must read and listen to them again and again. We must listen to what our master says over and over, even if we have heard it many times before. The meaning will be increasingly profound. For the sake of the Way, we should not get close to or be involved in matters that might obstruct it. Even if it is difficult and dull, we should become close with good friends and practice the Way [with them].

6-16

[*Dōgen*] *instructed*:

Zen Master Dahui once had a tumor on his buttocks.[338] A doctor examined it and said, "This is serious." Dahui asked, "Is it serious enough that I might die?" The doctor replied, "It is likely fatal." Dahui said, "If I am going to die, I ought to do zazen even more." He sat with strong determination, eventually the tumor broke open, pus oozed out, and he recovered.

This ancient's mind was like this. When he became sick, he did zazen all the more. We people today, being healthy, should not slacken in our zazen.

I think that sicknesses change in accordance with our minds. In the mundane world, when someone has the hiccups, if someone else tells a lie that shocks them and captures their attention, the person will be taken by surprise and try to say something and, in the process, forget about the hiccups, and they will stop [having the hiccups].

On my journey to Song China I was suffering from diarrhea while on board the ship, yet when a storm came and there was an uproar on board, I forgot about the sickness, and it went away.

Considering this, I think that when we diligently study and practice the Way and forget everything else, no illnesses will arise.

6-17

示云、

　俗の野諺に云、唾せず聾せざれば、家公とならず。云心は、人の毀謗をきかず、人の不可を云はざれば、よく、我が事を成ずる也。如是なる人を、家の大人とす。是、即、俗の野諺也と云へども、取つて衲僧の行履としつべし。他のそしりにあはず、他のうらみにあはず、いかでか我が道を行ぜん。徹得困の者、是を得べし。

6-18

示云、

　大恵禅師の云、学道は須く、人の千万貫銭を、おえらんが、一文をも、もたざらん時き、せめられん時の心の如くすべし。若し、此の心ろ有らば、道を得こと易し、と云へり。

　信心銘云、至道かたき事なし。但、揀択を嫌ふ。揀択の心を放下しつれば、直下に承当する也。揀択心放下すと云は、我を離るる也。所謂、我身仏道をならん為に、仏法を学すること莫れ。只、仏法の為に、仏法を行じゆく也。たとひ千経万論を学し得、坐禅、とこをやぶるとも、此心無くは、仏祖の道を不可学得。只、須く身心を仏法の中に放下して、他に随ふて、旧見なければ、即ち直下に承当する也。

6-17

[*Dōgen*] *instructed*:

There is a proverb in the lay realm that says, "Unless you become deaf and dumb, you cannot become the head of an [extended] family." This means that if we do not hear criticism from others and do not speak of the faults of others, we will be able to be successful in our work. A person like this can be the great head of a family. Although this is a proverb in the lay realm, we must apply it to our conduct as patch-robed monks. Without being disturbed by slanderous remarks from others, and without reacting to the resentment of others, how can we practice our own Way? Thoroughly devoted[339] people can attain this.

6-18

[*Dōgen*] *instructed*:

Zen Master Dahui said, "You should practice the Way with the mental attitude of a person who owes ten million strings of coins[340] and is being forced to repay them when penniless. If you have this frame of mind, attainment of the Way is easy."[341]

It is said in the "Faith in Mind Inscription,"[342] "The ultimate Way is not difficult; it only dislikes picking and choosing." When we cast away the mind of preference, we will immediately be able to accept [the Way] just as it is. To cast away the mind that picks and chooses is to separate from the [ego-centered] self. This is to say that we must not study the Buddhadharma to accomplish the Buddha Way for our own sake. We continue to practice the Buddhadharma only for the sake of the Buddhadharma. Even if we were able to study a thousand scriptures and ten thousand commentaries and do zazen hard enough to destroy the floor beneath us, without this frame of mind it would not be possible to study and attain the Way of the buddhas and ancestors. We must simply cast body and mind into the midst of Buddhadharma. If we follow [our teachers]

6-19

示云、

　春秋に云、石の堅き、是をわれども、其の堅きこと奪べからず。丹のあかき、是をわれども、其あかき事を奪べからず。玄沙、因に、僧、問、如何是堅固法身。沙云、膿滴々地。けだし、同じ心なるべきか。

6-20

示云、

　古人云、知因識果の知事に属して、院門の事すべて管せず。言心は、寺院の大小事、須、管せず、只、工夫打坐すべしと也。

　又、云、

　良田万頃よりも、薄芸、身にしたがふるには如かず。

　施恩は報をのぞまず、人に与て、おうて悔ること無れ。

　口を守こと、如鼻すれば、万禍不及、と云へり。

　行、堅き人は、自ら重ぜらる。才、高き人は、自伏せらる。

　深く耕して浅く種る。猶、天災あり。自利して人を損ずる、豈、果報なからんや。

　学道の人、話頭を見る時、目を近け、力をつくして、能々是を可看。

without [attachment to] our former views, we will immediately be in accordance with [the Way].

6-19³⁴³

[*Dōgen*] *instructed*:

In *The Spring and Autumn Annals*³⁴⁴ it is said, "Stones are hard; even if we break one, we cannot eliminate its hardness. Cinnabar is red; even if we break a piece of it, we cannot eliminate its redness." Related to this, a monk once asked Xuansha,³⁴⁵ "What is the indestructible Dharma body?" Xuansha said, "Pus is dripping."³⁴⁶ I think this has the same meaning [as what is said in *The Spring and Autumn Annals*].

6-20

[*Dōgen*] *instructed*:

An ancient said, "Entrusting everything to the temple administrators who know causes and understand results, one is not involved in any administrative matters of the monastery." The meaning of this saying is that one should not be concerned with either large or small matters of temple business; rather one should dedicate oneself solely to sitting.³⁴⁷

[*Dōgen*] *also said*:

Owning thousands of acres of productive rice fields is not as good as mastering even a minor skill [we can use ourselves].

We should do favors for others without expecting any return. After having given something to someone, we should not harbor regret.

It is said, "Keep your mouth [as silent as] your nose, then ten thousand troubles will not reach you."

Those who practice solidly will naturally be respected. Those who are highly talented will eventually be humbled.

Even if we plow deep and plant shallow, we may still suffer some natural disaster. If we benefit ourselves while harming others, how can we avoid receiving [negative karmic] results?

6-21

示云、

　古人云、百尺の竿頭に、更、一歩を進むべし。此の心は、十丈の、さをのさきにのぼりて、猶手足をはなちて、即ち身心を、放下せんがごとし。是について、重々の事あり。

　今の世の人、世を遁れ、家を出たるに似れども、行履をかんがふれば、猶を真の出家にては、無きも有り。所謂出家と云は、先づ吾我名利を、はなるべき也。是をはなれずしては、行道、頭燃をはらひ、精進、手足をきれども、只、無理勤苦のみにて、出離にあらざるも有り。

　大宋国にも、難離、恩愛をはなれ、難捨世財をすてて、叢林に交り、祖席をふれども、審細に此の故実を知らずして、行じゆくによりて、道をもさとらず、心をも明らめずして、いたづらに一期をすぐすも有り。

　其故は、人の心のありさま、初めは道心をおこして、僧にもなり、知識に随へども、仏とならん事をば、思ずして、身の貴く、我が寺の貴き由を、施主檀那にも知られ、親類境界にも云ひ聞かせ、何にもして人に貴とがられ、供養せられんと思ひ、あまつさへ、僧ども不当不善なれども、我れ独り道心も有り、善人なるやうを、方便して云ひ聞せ、思い知らせんとする様もあり。是は、不足言の人、五闡提等の、在世の悪比丘の如く、決定、地獄の心ば

Students of the Way! When you see the fundamental point,[348] you must draw your eyes close and make exhaustive efforts to examine it.

6-21

[*Dōgen*] *instructed*:

An ancient said, "At the top of a hundred-foot pole, you must advance one step further."[349] This means that we should climb up to the top of a hundred-foot pole and, further, release both our hands and our feet; in other words, this is like casting aside body and mind. There are various degrees in this regard.

Even though it seems that some people of the world today have renounced the world and left their homes, if we examine their conduct, there are also those who are not yet true home-leavers. Those who are called home-leavers must first of all give up the [ego-centered] self as well as fame and profit. Unless we become free from these, even if we practice the Way as if extinguishing a fire enveloping our heads,[350] or zealously cut off our hands or legs,[351] it would only be a meaningless hardship that has nothing to do with renunciation.

Even in great Song China, there are those who have separated themselves from [familial] affection from which it is hard to separate; have abandoned worldly wealth, which is difficult to abandon; have joined communities of practitioners; and have visited various monasteries. Some of them, however, have been spending their lives in vain, because they practice without clearly understanding this essential point [about abandoning affection and wealth]. They neither realize the Way nor clarify the mind. There are some people whose mental attitudes are as follows.

Although in the beginning they arouse the mind of awakening, become monks, and follow their teachers, instead of aspiring to become buddhas, they only concern themselves with making it known to their patrons, supporters, and relatives how respectable they are or how high the status of their temple is. They try to make people revere them and make offerings to them. Furthermore, they claim that other

え也。是を、物もしらぬ在家人は、道心者、貴き人、何んど思もあり。

　此のきはを、すこしたち出でて、施主檀那を貪ず、親類恩愛をもすてはてて、叢林に交り行道するも有れども、本性懶惰懈怠なる者は、ありのままに、懈怠ならんことも、はづかしきかして、長老首座等の見る時は、相構て行道する由をして、見ざる時は、事にふれて、やすみ、いたづらならんとするも有り。是は在家にして、さのみ不当ならんよりは、よけれども、猶、吾我名利の、すてられぬ心ばへ也。

　又、すべて師の心をもかねず、首座兄弟の見不見をも思はず、つねに思はく、仏道は人の為めならず、身の為也と云て、我身心にて仏になさんと、真実にいとなむ人も有り。是は、以前の人々よりは、真の道者かと覚れども、是も猶を、吾我を思て、我身よくなさんと思へる故に、猶を、吾我を離ず。又、諸仏菩薩に、随喜せられんと思ひ、仏果菩提を、成就せんと思へる故に、名利の心、猶、捨てられざる也。

　是までは、いまだ百尺の竿頭をはなれず、とりつきたる如し。只、身心を仏法になげすてて、更に悟道得法までも、のぞむ事なく、修行しゆく、是を不染汚の行人と云也。有仏の処にもとどまらず、無仏の処をもすみやかにはしりすぐ、と云、この心なるべし。

monks are all misguided and immoral, that only they are good monks with the mind of awakening. They try to persuade people to believe their words. People like this are not even worth criticizing; they are like the five evil monks who were *icchantika*[352] during the time when [the Buddha] was in this world. Their mental attitude will definitely make them fall into hell. There are also laypeople who do not know these things and think that [such monks] are possessors of the mind of awakening, respectable people, and so forth.

There are some who are slightly better than these people. They do not covet offerings from donors or patrons, have abandoned their affection toward family and relatives, have joined the monastic community, and practice the Way together with the assembly. However, though they feel ashamed of being idle, because they are lazy by nature, they pretend to be practicing when the abbot or the head monk is watching, yet when no one sees them, they rest whenever possible, neglecting to do what they are supposed to do. These people are better than similarly irresponsible laypeople, but they still cannot cast away their [ego-centered] selves or [desires for] fame and profit.

There are also those who are not concerned with what their teacher thinks or whether the head monk or other fellow practitioners are watching or not. They always think that practicing the Buddha Way is not for the sake of others but only for their own sake; such people desire to become buddhas with their own minds. They truly practice diligently. Even though they genuinely seem to be people of the Way compared with the aforementioned people, because they still think of themselves and think they can improve themselves, they have still not become free from their [ego-centered] selves. They also want to be admired by buddhas and bodhisattvas; they desire to attain Buddhahood and awakening; consequently, they still cannot cast away their minds [aimed at] fame and profit.

Up to this point, none of these people have yet left the hundred-foot pole; they remain clinging to it. Those who simply cast body and mind into the Buddhadharma and continue to practice without

6-22

示云、

　衣食の事、兼ねてより、思ひあてがふ事なかれ。たとひ、乞食
の処なりとも、失食絶煙の時、其処にして乞食せん、其人に用事
云はん、なんど思ひたるも、即ち、物をたくわへ、邪食にて有る
也。衲子は、雲の如く定れる住処もなく、水の如くに流れゆきて、
よる所もなきを、僧とは云也。直饒、衣食の外に、一物ももたずと
も、一人の檀那をも、たのみ、一類の親族をも思ひたらんは、即
ち自他ともに、結縛の事にて、不浄食にてある也。如是不浄食等
をもて、やしなひ、もちたる身心にて、諸仏の清浄の大法を、悟ら
ん、心得んと、思とも、何にもかなふまじき也。たとへば、藍にそめ
たる物はあおく、蘗にそめたるものは、きなるが如に、邪命食をも
て、そめたる身心は、即ち邪命身也。此身心をもて、仏法をのぞ
まば、沙をおして、油をもとむるが如し。只、時にのぞみて、ともか
くも、道理にかなふやうに、はからふべき也。兼て思ひたくわふる
は、皆たがふ事也。能々思量すべき也。

6-23

示云、

the desire either to realize the Way or attain the Dharma can be called "undefiled practitioners." This is what is meant by the saying, "Not staying where a buddha exists, and running quickly from where no-buddha exists."[353]

6-22

[*Dōgen*] *instructed*:

When it comes to obtaining food and clothing, we must not make arrangements in advance. Even regarding the place for begging for food, if we think that when we run out of food and have nothing to cook, we should beg for food at a particular place, or we should ask a particular person for what we need, then this is the same as storing food.[354] This is food [gained by] improper [means]. A patch-robed monk should be like a cloud with no fixed abode, like flowing water with nothing to rely on. Such a person is called a monk. Even if one possesses nothing but robes and a bowl, if one relies on some patron or close relative, they are both bound to each other [by affection] and the food becomes impure. It is impossible to realize or understand the pure great Dharma of all buddhas with a body and mind fed and maintained by impure food. Just as cloth dyed with indigo becomes blue and cloth dyed with the Amur cork tree becomes yellow, a body and mind dyed with food [obtained through] wrong livelihood[355] becomes a body of wrong livelihood. Desiring to attain the Buddhadharma with such a body and mind is like pressing sand to get oil. In each situation, we must simply handle everything in accordance with the Way. All the things we plan in advance [to make our lives secure] go against [the Way]. We must consider this very carefully.

6-23

[*Dōgen*] *instructed*:

　学人、各々知るべし。人々、一の非あり。憍奢、是、第一の非
也。内外の典籍に、同く是れをいましむ。

　外典に云、貧くしてへつらはざるは有れども、富ておごらざる
は無し、と云て、猶、とみを制して、おごらざる事を思ふ也。此事、
大事也。能々是を思ふべし。

　我身、下賤にして、人におとらじと思ひ、人にすぐれんと思は
ば、憍慢のはなはだしきもの也。是はいましめやすし。仮令、世間
に、財宝にゆたかに、福力もある人、眷属も囲遶し、人もゆるす。
かたはらの人の、いやしきが此を見て、卑下する。此のかたはら
の人の、卑下をつつしみて、自躰福力の人、いかやうにかすべ
き。憍心なけれども、ありのままにふるまへば、傍らの賤き、此を
いたむ。すべての大事也。是をよくつつしむを、憍奢をつつしむと
云也。我身とめれば、果報にまかせて、貧賤の見、うらやむを、は
ばからざるを、憍人と云也。

　古人の云、貧家の前を、車に乗て、過る事なかれ、と云へり。
然ば、我身、車にのるべくとも、貧人の前をば可憚と云へり。外典
に如是。内典も又如是。

　然るに、今の学人僧侶は、知恵法文をもて、宝とす。是を以
て、おごる事なかれ。我れよりおとれる人、先人傍輩の非義をそ
しり非するは、是れ憍奢のはなはだしき也。

　古人云、智者の辺にしては、まくるとも、愚人の辺にして、かつ
べからず。我身よく知りたる事を、人のあしく知りたりとも、他の非
を云は、又是、我が非也。法文を云とも、先人の愚をそしらず。

Each and every student must know that everyone has one fault. Arrogance is the greatest fault. Both Buddhist and non-Buddhist texts admonish against this.

In a non-Buddhist text, it is said, "Although there are some who are poor but do not curry favor, there are none who are rich but not arrogant."[356] This text admonishes us not to become arrogant even if we are wealthy. This matter is an important one. We must consider it very carefully.

If we are of humble birth and desire not to be inferior to the next person, or hope to surpass them, this is a typical example of arrogance. This is easy to admonish. Even in the mundane world, relatives gather around a person who is wealthy, fortunate, and powerful, and they allow that person [to do anything]. In such a case, humble people around such a person disparage themselves [due to feeling inferior]. How can such a person with fortune and power avoid causing people around him to deprecate themselves? Even if the person does not have an arrogant mind, if he behaves naturally, the lowly people around him are pained. This is an important consideration in every situation. To restrain oneself in this kind of situation is to restrain arrogance. A person who enjoys his wealth, relying on his karmic rewards while paying no attention to the poor and lowly who envy him, is called an arrogant person.

An ancient said, "Do not pass in front of a poor man's house riding a chariot." This therefore says that even if we are able to ride a chariot, we must have scruples in front of poor people. Non-Buddhist texts [have admonitions] like this. Buddhist scriptures also [have admonitions] like this.

However, students and monks nowadays consider wisdom and [knowledge of] the Dharma teachings to be their wealth. Do not be haughty with these. To speak of the faults of people inferior to oneself or to criticize one's senior or fellow practitioners' mistakes, these are exceedingly arrogant.

An ancient said, "Even if you are defeated in front of a sage, do not win in front of a fool." When someone misunderstands things we

又、愚癡、未発心の人の、うらやみ、卑下しつべき所にては、能々
是を思べし。

　建仁寺に寓せしとき、人々多く法文を問き。非も咎がも有りし
かども、此の儀を深く存じて、只、ありのままに、法の徳をかたり
て、他の非を不云。無為にてやみき。愚者の執見深きは、我が先
徳の非を云へば、瞋恚をおこす也。智恵ある人の、真実なるは、
法のまことの義をだにも、心得つれば、不云とも、我非及我が先
徳の非を、思ひ知りあらたむる也。是くの如きの事、能々思ひ知る
べし。

6-24

示云、

　学道の最要は、坐禅、是、第一也。大宋の人、多く得道する
事、皆、坐禅の力也。一文不通にて、無才愚鈍の人も、坐禅を専
らにすれば、多年の久学、聡明の人にも勝れて出来する。然ば、
学人、祇管打坐して、他を管ずる事なかれ。仏祖の道は、只、坐
禅也。他事に順ずべからず。

　芉問て云、打坐と看語と、ならべて、是を学するに、語録公案
等を見には、百千に一つ、いささか心得られざるかと、覚る事も
出来る。坐禅は、其程の事もなし。然ども、猶、坐禅を好むべき
か。

know well, speaking of the other's faults is still our fault. When talking about the Dharma writings, do not criticize the foolishness of the predecessor [of the person with whom you are talking]. Also, when ignorant people who have not yet aroused the mind of awakening become envious or abase themselves, we must carefully consider this point.

While I was staying at Kennin-ji, many people asked me about the Dharma teachings.[357] Even though there were faults and errors [in their views], I kept this point deep in my heart and only talked about the virtue of the Dharma as it is, instead of speaking of the faults of others. I avoided trouble in this way. If we speak of the faults of the respected elders of fools who are deeply attached to their own opinions, it will arouse their anger. If people with wisdom and sincerity understand the true meaning of the Dharma, even if we do not say [anything regarding their faults], they will realize their own mistakes and the mistakes of their respected elders and reform them. We must consider this thoroughly.

6-24

[*Dōgen*] *instructed*:

The most essential matter in studying the Way is zazen. In great Song China many people attained the Way, and all did so through the power of zazen. If even an untalented, dull-witted person who cannot penetrate a single sentence devotes himself to zazen practice, he can exceed an intelligent person who has been studying for many years. Therefore, students must just sit [*shikantaza*] without being involved in other things. The Way of the buddhas and ancestors is simply zazen. Do not follow other things.

Ejō asked, "In learning both sitting and the reading of sayings, when I read the recorded sayings or kōans, I feel I am only able to understand one thing out of a hundred or a thousand. In zazen there is nothing like that. Should we nonetheless still be fond of zazen?"

[*Dōgen*] *instructed*:

示云、

　公案話頭を見て、聊か知覚ある様なりとも、其は仏祖の道に、とほざかる因縁也。無所得、無所悟にて、端坐して、時を移さば、即祖道なるべし。古人も、看話、祇管打坐ともに進めたれども、猶、坐をば、専ら進めし也。又、話頭を以て、悟をひらきたる人、有とも、其も坐の功によりて、悟の開くる因縁也。まさしき功は、坐にあるべし。

Even if you may seem to have some understanding when examining kōans or their fundamental points,[358] [such studies] keep you distant from the Way of the buddhas and ancestors. To spend your time sitting upright with nothing to gain and nothing to realize is the Way of the ancestors. Although the ancients recommended both reading [kōan] stories and just sitting [*shikantaza*], they still principally promoted sitting. Although there are some who have gained realization through the fundamental points [of kōans], this is also due to the merit of sitting. It is the cause and condition of the unfolding of realization. True merit can only be from sitting.

先師永平弉和尚、在学地日、学道至要、随聞記録、所以謂随聞。如雲門室中玄記、如永平宝慶記。今録集六冊、記巻、入仮名正法眼蔵拾遺分内。六冊倶嘉禎年中記録也。

正法眼蔵随聞記　　六　　終

康暦二年五月初三日於宝慶寺浴主寮書焉。

三州簱頭郡中島山長円二世暉堂写也。
寛永二十一甲申歳八月吉祥日

[FIRST COLOPHON]

My late teacher Preceptor Ejō of Eihei-ji while he was studying in days past, recorded the most essential points in practicing the Way following [the order] in which he heard [them], which is why [this text] is called "*The Following and Heard [Record]*."[359] This is like *The Record of Profundity*,[360] from the abbot's chamber of Yunmen, and like *The Record of the Hōkyō Era*[361] of Eihei [Dōgen]. I have now compiled them into six volumes and put them into the appendix of the *Kana shōbōgenzō*.[362] All six volumes were recorded within the Katei era (1235–1238 CE).

THE END OF THE SIXTH BOOK OF *SHŌBŌGENZŌ ZUIMONKI*

[SECOND COLOPHON]

Copied on the third day of the fifth month in the second year of Koreki (1380 CE) at the dormitory for the bath manager[363] of Hōkyō-ji.[364]

[THIRD COLOPHON]

This was copied by Kidō, the second abbot of Mt. Nakajima's Chōen[-ji] in Hazu district, Sanshu.[365]

On the auspicious day in the eighth month of the twenty-first year of Kanei (1644 CE).

Part Two

White Snow on Bright Leaves

A Collection of Dōgen Zenji's Waka

Translation and comments by Shōhaku Okumura
Edited by Shōryū Bradley, Jōkei Molly Delight
Whitehead, and Dōju Layton

INTRODUCTION

Dōgen and Poetry

Eihei Dōgen is considered one of the great masters in the history of Japanese Buddhism. He was a reformer of Buddhist monastic practice and the founder of the first independent Sōtō Zen monastery in Japan based on the zazen practice of *shikantaza* (只管打坐; "just sitting"). He was not only the leader of a Zen community but also a wonderful writer. His collection of writings in Japanese entitled *The True Dharma-Eye Treasury* (正法眼藏; Jp. *Shōbōgenzō*) is cherished by Buddhists, religious scholars, philosophers, and lovers of literature around the world. He also wrote extensively in Chinese, including *The Record of the Hōkyō Era* (宝慶記; Jp. *Hōkyō ki*), *Points to Watch in Practicing the Way* (学道用心集; Jp. *Gakudō yōjinshū*), and the works that were later compiled into *Pure Standards of Eihei-ji* (永平清規; Jp. *Eihei shingi*). Finally, he was a poet, composing more than four hundred Chinese poems included in *Dōgen's Extensive Record* (永平広録; Jp. *Eihei kōroku*), as well as some Japanese waka poems. *Waka* (和歌) literally means "Japanese poetry," as opposed to *kanshi* (漢詩), which are Chinese poems. The most popular form of waka, called *tanka* (短歌), usually has five lines totaling thirty-one syllables (5-7-5-7-7).[366] Part 2 is a translation of a Japanese collection of Dōgen's waka with my commentary on each poem.

It is well known among Dōgen scholars and practitioners that in *Shōbōgenzō Zuimonki* (正法眼藏隨聞記) Dōgen disparaged the value of literature:

Zen monks these days are fond of studying literature as a grounding to compose verses or write Dharma words. This is wrong. Even if you cannot compose verses, just write what you think in your mind. Even if your style is not sophisticated, write down the Dharma gates. People without the mind of awakening will not read it if your writing style is not well polished, but even if the style is embellished and there are excellent phrases in it, such people would only play with the words without grasping the principle [behind them]. I have been fond of studying [literature] since my childhood, and even now I have a tendency to contemplate the beauty in the words of non-Buddhist texts. Sometimes I even refer to the *Selections of Refined Literature* or other classic texts. Still, I think it is meaningless, and it should cease immediately.[367]

In my case, too, since I sometimes compose poetry, arranging rhyme and tone, or effortlessly write prose, some laypeople praise me, saying this is extraordinary. And yet, there are others who criticize me for knowing such things despite being a monk who has left home and is studying the Way. What shall we take as good and abandon as bad? [368]

In these talks, Dōgen is saying two things. He tells us that since childhood, he thoroughly studied and enjoyed literature, both Chinese and Japanese prose and poetry. He was very knowledgeable, and he wrote his own poems even after he became a Buddhist monk. But he is also saying that he believes such knowledge and writing skills are not only valueless experiences but even obstacles for studying the Buddha Way.

Some think, based on these sayings, that Dōgen contradicted himself by writing so many poems. But Dōgen was a complex person. Despite these comments, he hosted a gathering of monks to compose poems on the harvest-moon night each year, and many Chinese poems are included in *Dōgen's Extensive Record*.

In his poems, Dōgen expressed his understanding without much consideration of sophisticated wording or rhetorical techniques. If he had wanted to, he presumably could have written highly embellished poems, as people did at the emperor's court from where he originally came, but the waka poems attributed to Dōgen are simple and without much ornamentation. I think Dōgen's comments in *Zuimonki* resemble what the famous Sōtō monk-poet Ryōkan (良寛; 1758–1831 CE) said about his own poetry:

> Who says that my poems are poems?
> My poems aren't poems at all.
> When you understand
> That my poems really aren't poems
> Then we can talk poetry together.[369]

Another poem by Ryōkan elaborates this point:

> How pitiful, those virtuous fellows!
> Moving into the recesses, they immerse
> themselves in composing poetry
> For Ancient Style, their models
> are the poems of Han and Wei
> For Recent Form,
> the T'ang poets are their guide
> With gaudy words their lines are formed
> And further adorned by
> novel and curious phrases
> Yet if they fail to express
> what's in their own minds
> What's the use, no matter
> how many poems they compose![370]

Dōgen and Ryōkan do not say they should not write poems—but rather their poems should not be evaluated by worldly standards such as literary devices and flowery styles.

FAMILY AS THE SOURCE OF DŌGEN'S LITERARY SENSIBILITY

Dōgen was born into the Minamoto (源) family descended from Emperor Murakami (村上天皇; 926–967 CE). His family was also called Koga (久我) or Murakami Genji (村上源氏).[371] His father was Minamoto no Michitomo (源通具; 1171–1227 CE) who held the position of major councilor (大納言; Jp. *dainagon*) in the emperor's court.[372] We do not know much about Dōgen's mother, but according to the biography of Dōgen in the *Record of Kenzei* (建撕記; Jp. *Kenzei ki*), it seems she was a daughter of Fujiwara no Motofusa (藤原基房; 1144–1230 CE), the former chief advisor to the emperor (関白; Jp. *kanpaku*).

Dōgen is said to have read a collection of Chinese poems when he was four years old. He received the best education available, intended to train an aristocrat to become a high-ranking court officer of the imperial government. For such a position, one needed to be not only a capable politician but also a scholar and poet. Dōgen's father was an excellent waka poet and one of the editorial board members responsible for creating the *New Collection of Poems Ancient and Modern* (新古今和歌集; Jp. *Shin kokin wakashū*). This is one of the eight anthologies of waka created at the imperial court, and it is considered to be one of the three most influential, together with *Man'yōshū* (万葉集, literally "*Collection of Ten Thousand Leaves*") and the *Collection of Poems Ancient and Modern* (古今和歌集; Jp. *Kokin wakashū*). Dōgen's grandfather Michichika (通親; 1149–1202 CE) was also an eminent politician and waka poet.

In fact, Dōgen's ancestry included numerous great waka poets, both men and women. Many of their works are collected in the *New Collection of Poems Ancient and Modern*. Although, as he mentioned in *Zuimonki*, Dōgen was fond of studying the Chinese classics and the poetry of both China and Japan as a child, it seems when he renounced his aristocratic family and became a Buddhist monk at thirteen, he gave up his interest in the rhetorical techniques he had been taught.

Although he quit composing waka with the sophisticated literary devices used, for example, in the *New Collection of Poems Ancient and Modern*, Dōgen occasionally included his own waka in his letters. When asked, he also composed and used them as aids in teaching the Dharma. Because waka were considered a less important method of expressing insight than Chinese poems, Dōgen probably had no intention of creating a waka anthology. In Japanese Buddhist communities Chinese was the primary language for formal writing, just as Latin was for Western Christians. Following the custom of Chinese Zen monasteries, when he gave formal Dharma hall discourses (上堂; Ch. *shàngtáng*; Jp. *jōdō*), Dōgen usually included Chinese poems. There are more than four hundred Chinese poems in *Dōgen's Extensive Record*. Yet it is possible people who received Dōgen's waka also kept them as personal treasures, and some may have memorized them. Such poems were probably gathered later into a collection.

COLLECTIONS OF DŌGEN'S WAKA

Part 2 includes my translations of Dōgen's waka included in the Japanese text *Dōgen Zenji waka shū* (道元禅師和歌集), which is found in volume seventeen of *Dōgen Zenji zenshū* (道元禅師全集), a complete collection of all of Dōgen's writings published by Shunjusha (春秋社) in 2010. I have written a short commentary on each poem. In the Shunjusha text, Bunji Takahashi (高橋文二), a professor emeritus at the Sōtō Zen–affiliated Komazawa University and scholar of Japanese literature, rendered the waka into modern Japanese and added notes on each, as well as a bibliographical essay. Although I did not translate his notes, they were enormously helpful to me.

The Shunjusha text is based on the collection of Dōgen's waka included in *Kenzei's Record of the Life of Dōgen Zenji, Founder of Eihei-ji* (永平開山道元禅師行状建撕記; Jp. *Eihei kaisan Dōgen Zenji gyōjō Kenzei ki*) written by Kenzei (建撕; 1415–1474 CE), the fourteenth abbot of Eihei-ji. This text is usually known by its abbreviated title, the *Record of Kenzei* (建撕記; Jp. *Kenzei ki*). It is not clear exactly when this biography was written.

According to the great Dōgen scholar Dōshū Ōkubo (大久保道舟; 1896–1994 CE), Kenzei was abbot of Eihei-ji from 1468 to 1474. The *Record of Kenzei* was probably written before 1472, when there was a big fire at Eihei-ji.[373] Beginning in the second half of the twentieth century, several old, hand-copied versions of the *Record of Kenzei* came to light. Professor Kōdō Kawamura (河村孝道) produced a side-by-side comparison of most of them in *Shohon taikō: Eihei kaisan Dōgen zenji gyōjō Kenzei ki* (諸本対校：永平開山道元禅師行状建撕記) published by Daishūkan Shoten (大修館書店) in 1975. The source text for Shunjusha's text is the oldest hand-copied version, made by a monk named Zuichō (瑞長) in 1589.

In the *Record of Kenzei*, a collection of Dōgen's waka follows the description of his death and funeral. In Zuichō's manuscript, there are fifty-one waka included in this collection. In addition, there are two more waka that are included within the biographical portion of the text in the *Record of Kenzei* (numbers 52 and 53 in this book), for a total of fifty-three poems. In the other versions of the *Record of Kenzei*, the number of poems is slightly different.

Around 1420, Kishun (喜舜; n.d.), the eighth abbot of Hōkyō-ji (宝慶寺) and resident monk of Tōun-ji (洞雲寺), copied some of Dōgen's waka and supposedly offered them to Kenkō (建綱; 1413–1469 CE), the thirteenth abbot of Eihei-ji.[374] It is not clear whether Kishun copied a manuscript that already contained a collection of waka, or if he himself collected the poems from various places.

After being asked by a patron of Eihei-ji to write a biography of Dōgen Zenji, Kenkō delegated this project to his Dharma heir, Kenzei, asking him to include the waka Kishun had given him. This is how a collection of Dōgen Zenji's waka appeared in the *Record of Kenzei*, in which they were passed down for several centuries. We do not have information regarding Dōgen's waka poems before Kishun's collection, with one exception: Dōgen's fourth-generation descendent, Keizan Jōkin (瑩山紹瑾; 1268–1325 CE), referred to one of Dōgen's waka in the Dharma words (法語; Jp. *hōgo*) he wrote to a patron, discussed in my commentary on waka 45 in this book.

In 1754 the great monk-scholar Menzan Zuihō (面山瑞方; 1683–1769 CE) revised, annotated, and published the aptly named *Revised and Annotated Record of Kenzei* (訂補建撕記; Jp. *Teiho kenzei ki*) as a woodblock-printed book, which added his own interpretations regarding Dōgen's life. However, Menzan did not inlcude the collection of Dōgen's waka. Instead, several years before in 1747, Menzan extracted the waka from the *Record of Kenzei* and published them as an independent book titled *Verses on the Way from Sanshō Peak* (傘松道詠; Jp. *Sanshō dōei*). According to Menzan's *Revised and Annotated Record of Kenzei*, Sanshō was the original mountain name of Daibutsu-ji (大仏寺), the temple Dōgen founded that was later renamed Eihei-ji.

Hand-copied manuscripts remained stored in the treasuries of old temples while Menzan's woodblock-printed books of both the *Record of Kenzei* and *Verses on the Way from Sanshō Peak* circulated widely within the Sōtō Zen community. They came to be considered the only authentic sources of Dōgen's biography and his collection of waka. Until the middle of the twentieth century, all traditional commentaries on Dōgen's waka were based on Menzan's *Verses on the Way from Sanshō Peak* rather than earlier manuscripts.

After World War II, Sōtō Zen scholars tried to find the older, hand-copied versions of Dōgen's writings, his waka, and the *Record of Kenzei*. They discovered various versions of the *Record of Kenzei*, each of which included a waka collection, as mentioned previously. These collections were quite different from Menzan's *Verses on the Way from Sanshō Peak*. Menzan had changed the titles and order of the poems, added some poems he found elsewhere, and even changed the wording of some waka. Because Menzan was a great scholar, he likely thought that whatever did not make sense to him was a mistake made in the process of hand copying. He likely wanted to create the most reliable and authoritative collection of Dōgen's waka according to the knowledge he had at the time. Today's scholars no longer use the title *Verses on the Way from Sanshō Peak* to refer to Dōgen's collection of waka but instead simply call it the *Collection of Dōgen Zenji's Waka* (道元禅師和歌集; Jp. *Dōgen Zenji waka shū*)

Nanboku Oba (大場南北) was the first person who criticized Menzan's *Verses on the Way from Sanshō Peak* in his articles "Dōgen Zenji Sanshō dōei no kenkyū" (道元禅師傘松道詠研究) and "Dōgen Zenji wakashū shinshaku" (道元禅師和歌集新釈). Yōko Funatsu (船津洋子), a scholar of Japanese literature, also studied the waka in *Verses on the Way from Sanshō Peak* and wrote, "In my view, among the waka considered to have been written by Dōgen, there is no way we can prove that they were really composed by Dōgen himself."[375] Kōgai Maruyama (丸山劫外) pointed out a few mistakes in Funatsu's discussion and concluded that the fifty-three waka collected by Kishun were truly composed by Dōgen.[376] Various scholars have different opinions about whether some or all of the waka are really Dōgen's or not.

In the Shunjusha text, another thirteen waka are included as addenda. These were added much later by people who created independent editions of Dōgen's waka in the Tokugawa period (1603–1868 CE). Because even the *Record of Kenzei* was written about two hundred years after Dōgen's death, it is difficult to know the true relationship between Dōgen and the waka attributed to him.

Although modern scholars are skeptical about whether these waka were composed by Dōgen, there is no information available to prove they were *not* written by him. In any case, for the e-newsletters of Sanshin Zen community, I have been translating and commenting on these waka assuming they are Dōgen's. If any evidence to the contrary is found, I do not mind removing them from the collection. Since I am not a formal scholar, I cannot determine which poems are definitely Dōgen's and which are not.

The question that interests me is this: if these *are* Dōgen's poems, what did he want them to teach us? To make connections between the waka and what Dōgen wrote elsewhere, I quote passages from his other works that relate to the topics in the poems. I have occasionally given Dharma talks on these waka, and I have found that talking about the poems and the teachings underlying them is a useful and focused way to study Dōgen.

DŌGEN'S WAKA IN MODERN TIMES

Dōgen became well known among Japanese intellectuals outside the Sōtō Zen community after the famous philosopher Tetsurō Watsuji (和辻哲郎; 1889–1960 CE) wrote his essay "The Śramaṇa Dōgen" (沙門道元; Jp. "Shamon Dōgen") in 1926. Watsuji wrote about Dōgen and his ideas, mainly based on *Shōbōgenzō Zuimonki*. He quoted Dōgen's thoughts on literature and concluded, "Dōgen did not merely oppose Buddhist art; he also said people should 'ignore any discussions' of literary arts, poetry, and the like. What purpose do honeyed words and beautiful passages of literature serve in attaining enlightenment?"[377]

After Watsuji, many Japanese writers became interested in Dōgen and wrote about him, primarily drawing on *Zuimonki* and the *Shōbōgenzō*. At that time Dōgen's poetry was less valued than his philosophical writings. However, in 1968 when Yasunari Kawabata (川端康成; 1899–1972 CE) became the first Japanese novelist to receive the Nobel Prize in Literature, he gave an acceptance speech entitled, "Japan, the Beautiful, and Myself" (美しい日本の私; "Utsukushii Nihon no watakushi") in Stockholm. At the beginning of this speech, he introduced Dōgen's waka number twelve of this book. Since then, Dōgen's waka have become well known among many Japanese intellectuals. Some of them have said, among other things, that Dōgen's literature, which negated literature, opened a new horizon in the world of Japanese literature.

From my perspective as a Buddhist practitioner, these discussions of modern writers regarding the value of literature sound like idle talk. From the time of Shakyamuni, Buddhist masters have questioned the ability of language to express reality beyond discrimination and conceptualization, and yet these masters all tried to express this reality using language, including Dōgen. As he discussed in the *Shōbōgenzō* fascicle "Being Able to Speak" (道得; Jp. "Dōtoku"), Dōgen never dismissed the importance of expressing reality, with or without language.

I hope this collection helps the reader become familiar with various aspects of Dōgen's teaching. Unless otherwise noted, quotations from Dōgen Zenji's writings are my own unpublished translations.

ACKNOWLEDGMENTS

As mentioned above, I translated and wrote comments on each waka poem from *Dōgen Zenji Wakashū* for the Sanshin Zen Community's newsletter over the course of several years. During that period, Musō Jim Biggs, who was responsible for preparing the newsletter, edited my English each month. After I had worked through all of the waka, Jōkei Molly Whitehead compiled the translations and edited the rough draft. We initially thought the waka and commentary would be published as a standalone book, but when the decision was made to combine it with the new translation of *Shōbōgenzō Zuimonki*, Shōryū Bradley and Dōju Layton worked to further edit the text in order make it more consistent with the style we used in the translation of *Zuimonki*. They worked with Ben Gleason, the editor from Wisdom Publications, in order to complete this process. I would like to express my heartfelt gratitude to all of them as well as to the many others who helped and supported this translation project. Thirteen of the waka poems were included in *Zen of Four Seasons: Dogen Zenji's Waka*, published by Dōgen Institute on the occasion of the fifteenth anniversary of Sanshin-ji, so I would also like to thank everyone who was involved in the production of the book as well.

Gassho,
Shōhaku Okumura

TRANSLATION AND COMMENTARY

道元禅師和歌集

Dōgen Zenji waka shū
Dōgen Zenji's Collection of Waka

題法華経　五首
DAI HOKKE KYŌ GOSHU
FIVE POEMS ON THE *DHARMA FLOWER SUTRA*

1
夜もすがら　　　*yomo sugara*
終日になす　　　*hinemosu ni nasu*
法の道　　　　　*nori no michi*
皆この経の　　　*mina kono kyō no*
声と心と　　　　*koe to kokoro to*

Through the night
and the day
everything we do in the Way
is the sound and heart of this sutra

The *Dharma Flower Sutra* (法華経; Jp. *Hokke kyō*) is a translation of the Sino-Japanese abbreviation for the full title of the *Lotus Sutra*; the full title in English would be *Sutra of the Wondrous Dharma of the Lotus Flower* (妙法蓮華經; Ch. *Miàofǎ liánhuá jīng*; Jp. *Myōhō renge kyō*; Skt. *Saddharma puṇḍarīka sūtra*). This is the most important sutra in Tendai, the school of Buddhism in which Dōgen Zenji was originally ordained and the tradition in which he studied for several years before practicing Zen. Even later in his life, he quotes this sutra in the *Shōbōgenzō* and other writings, and he refers to the *Lotus Sutra* as the "king of sutras." Just before dying, he is even said to have recited one of its chapters. For Dōgen, the *Lotus Sutra* was not merely a written text; to him, everything we experience is the sound and heart of the sutra.

In the "Model for Practicing the Way" (辨道法; Jp. "Bendōhō"), one of the six independent writings later compiled into the *Pure Standards of Eihei-ji* (永平清規; Jp. *Eihei shingi*), Dōgen describes the daily routine of practice in the monks' hall (僧堂; Jp. *sōdō*). The day begins with evening zazen and ends with afternoon zazen. This means practice does not begin when monks wake up in the morning and end when they go to bed, as we usually think. Even sleeping at night is part of daily practice. Everything done for the Dharma is practice of the Way and the sound and heart of this sutra.

2

谷に響き	*tani ni hibiki*
峯に鳴く猿	*mine ni naku saru*
妙妙に	*taedae ni*
ただこの経を	*tada kono kyō o*
説くとこそ聞け	*toku to koso kike*

In the valley
echoes
on the peak
monkeys chattering
I hear them exquisitely expounding this sutra

This is the second of Dōgen's five waka on the *Lotus Sutra*. In the valley there is continuous music, presumably from a stream, and on the peak monkeys are gibbering intermittently. *Taedae ni* (妙妙に) is a play on words, meaning both "intermittently," and "wondrously" or "exquisitely."

Dōgen hears the valley stream and monkeys' chattering as wondrous Dharma or true Dharma. Some commentaries on Dōgen's waka have suggested this poem may have been composed while Dōgen was a teenaged novice monk at the Tendai monastery on Mt. Hiei, studying the *Lotus Sutra*.

When I lived in Kyoto, I often walked up Mt. Hiei and sometimes saw troops of monkeys. Since ancient times, these monkeys have been considered messengers of the guardian god of the mountain. As we do not know the date of this poem, the scholars' assumption about its composition could be correct.

However, when I read the five waka about the *Lotus Sutra*, I hear echoes of what Dōgen wrote in the *Shōbōgenzō* fascicles "Mountains and Waters Sutra" (山水經; Jp. "Sansui kyō") and "Sounds of Valley Streams, Colors of Mountains" (谿聲山色; Jp. "Keisei sanshoku"). Even though he uses the title of the *Lotus Sutra*, he is not necessarily referring to the actual written text. In the fascicle of the *Shōbōgenzō* titled "Buddha's Teachings" (仏教; Jp. "Bukkyō"), he wrote:

> The sutra I am talking about is none other than the entire ten-direction world. There is no time and place that is not the sutra. The sutra is written in the words of ultimate truth and conventional truth; the words of the heavenly realm, the human realm, the animal realm, and the fighting-spirit realm; the words of the hundred grasses and the ten thousand trees. For this reason, all things long, short, square, or round, blue, yellow, red, or white, which are stately arrayed throughout the entire ten-direction world, without exception are the words of the sutra and the surface of the sutra. We consider them the furnishings of the great Way and regard them as the sutra of Buddha's family.

When we consider this waka as an expression of this insight, it is also possible to assume the poem was written much later, at Kōshō-ji (興聖寺) or Eihei-ji (永平寺).

3

この経の	*kono kyō no*
心を得れば	*kokoro o ureba*
世の中に	*yononaka ni*
売り買う声も	*uri kau koe mo*
法を説くかな	*nori o toku kana*

Grasping the heart
of this sutra
even the voices of buying and selling
in the world
expound the Dharma

This waka explains that not only nature's sounds, but also merchants' voices in the marketplace expound the Dharma. Commenting on the *Lotus Sutra*, Tiantai Zhiyi said, "All means of livelihood and industries in the world, without exception, do not differ from true reality."[378] In the *Shōbōgenzō* fascicle "The Bodhisattva's Four Embracing Actions" (菩提薩埵四摂法; Jp. "Bodaisatta shishōbō"), Dōgen writes, "To launch a boat or build a bridge is the practice of *dana-paramita*. When we carefully study the meaning of giving, receiving our body and giving up our body are offerings. Earning a livelihood and managing a business are, from the outset, nothing other than giving."[379]

According to some commentaries, this poem expresses the meaning of a kōan in which the Chinese Zen master Panshan Baoji (盤山寶積; Jp. Banzan Hōshaku; 720–814 CE) was awakened upon hearing a comment made by a merchant in a marketplace. Dōgen Zenji quotes the kōan in *Dōgen's Extensive Record* (永平広録; Jp. *Eihei kōroku*):

Once Panshan was walking through the marketplace and saw a customer buying pork. [Panshan heard the customer] say to the butcher, "Cut me one good piece." The butcher put the knife down, stood with hands folded in *shashu*, and said, "Sir, which is not a good piece?" Upon hearing these words, Panshan had insight.[380]

I wonder whether or not we in modern times would agree that all the advertising in various media that stimulates our desire and greed is still expounding the Dharma.

4

峯の色	*mine no iro*
谷の響も	*tani no hibiki mo*
皆ながら	*mina nagara*
わが釈迦牟尼の	*waga shakamuni no*
声と姿と	*koe to sugata to*

Colors of mountain peaks
and echoes of valley streams:
all as they are
nothing other
than my Shakyamuni's voice and image

"My Shakyamuni" sounds strange. "Our Shakyamuni" might sound better. However, this is a literal translation of Dōgen's expression *waga shakamuni*. *Waga* is the possessive form of *ware*, or "I." Dōgen is expressing the unity of the self (Jp. *ware*) and Shakyamuni, in this case Shakyamuni's Dharma body (法身; Ch. *fǎshēn*; Jp. *hōshin*; Skt. *dharmakāya*), which is the entire network of interdependent origination. An equivalent expression might be Dōgen's use of "total function" (全機; Jp. *zenki*).

Once when I was in high school during final exams, my seat was by a window. There was a tennis court outside, and the window was covered with wire netting. I felt imprisoned.

Beyond the tennis court, there was another building. I saw a few birds on the roof enjoying their lives in the morning sun. They looked completely free. I erased all the answers I had written on my exam paper. I wanted to quit school.

After the exam, I walked to the mountainside. It was the end of the rainy season, and there was a valley stream flowing rapidly. Like many teenagers, I thought I was a poet. I wanted to hear exactly what the stream sounded like—not the meaning of the sound but the sound itself. We have many onomatopoeias in Japanese for the sounds of flowing water, such as *sarasara*, *chorochoro*, and *gougou*. I wanted to hear the *real* sound. I listened carefully to the stream for about an hour. I found there was no way to copy the sound with letters.

That was my first meditative experience. I discovered that my emotions calmed; I was no longer upset. I was fifteen and knew nothing about Buddhism or Zen. But after that moment, my way of viewing the world changed forever. I felt that whatever we thought, using words and concepts was simply an incomplete copy of the sounds of nature, like the onomatopoeias of flowing water. Since then, when I have had some problem to consider, and particularly when I fall into negative thinking, I try to walk in nature and listen to the sounds of flowing water, ocean waves, wind, or birdsong.

Dōgen Zenji wrote the following in the *Shōbōgenzō* fascicle "Sounds of Valley Streams, Colors of Mountains" (谿聲山色; Jp. "Keisei sanshoku"):

When we are truly practicing, sounds and colors of the valley, colors and sounds of the mountains never begrudge the eighty-four thousand verses. When we do not begrudge our fame, profit, body, and mind, neither do the valleys and mountains begrudge expounding the Dharma.

The nineteenth chapter of the *Lotus Sutra*, "The Blessing of the Dharma Teacher," (法師功德; Jp. "Hōsshi kudoku") says that when practitioners accept, embrace, and explain the *Lotus Sutra*, they receive numberless blessings and their six sense organs are purified. When our eyes and ears are free of the three poisonous minds of greed, anger, and ignorance, the sounds and colors of mountains and valley streams are revealed as they are. Although I did not know this when I was fifteen, I may have heard one of those verses of the valley stream.

5

誰とても	dare totemo
日影の駒は	hikage no koma wa
嫌はぬを	kirawanu o
法の道得る	nori no michi uru
人ぞ少なき	hito zo sukunaki

Although no one outruns
the horse of sunlight
those who attain the way
are rare

This is the last of Dōgen's waka relating to the *Lotus Sutra*. "The horse of sunlight" is a translation of *hikage no koma*. *Koma* means "horse," the fastest runner in ancient times. *Hikage* means "sunlight," or the passing of time, as in the similar expression *kōin* (光陰; literally "light and shadow"). Time is galloping like a horse. This expression conveys the swiftness of impermanence. In chapter twenty-two of the *Zhuangzi*, "Knowledge Travels North," it is said, "Human life between heaven and earth is like the passing of a white horse seen through a crevice in the wall."[381]

We cannot avoid impermanence, but this need not be a negative in our lives. Dōgen Zenji wrote in the *Shōbōgenzō* fascicle "Thusness" (恁麼; Jp. "Inmo"):

Even the body is not our personal possession; our life is moving through the passage of time, and we cannot stop it even for an instant. Where have our rosy cheeks gone? Even if we wish to find them, there is no trace. When we carefully contemplate, we understand that there are many things in the past that we can never see again. The sincere red heart does not stay either—bit by bit, it comes and goes. Although there is sincerity, it does not stagnate within the boundaries of the individual, ego-centered self. Although it is thus, there are some who arouse awakening mind without any particular reason. From the time this mind is aroused, we throw away everything we have been toying with. We wish to listen to what we have never heard, and we wish to verify what we have never verified. All these are not simply our personal activities.

Realizing and experiencing impermanence can be a precious opportunity to arouse the mind of awakening, which allows us to study and practice the Buddha Way. As Dōgen wrote in the previous four waka on the *Lotus Sutra*, the Dharma is always expounded by all things, and yet not many people arouse the mind of awakening and attain the Way. In this poem, Dōgen expresses his sadness about this fact.

6

寛元二年九月廿五日、初雪一尺あまりふるに御詠
kangen ninen kugatsu nijūgonichi hatsuyuki isshaku amari furuni goei
Poem on the Occasion of Over a Foot of Snow Falling on the Twenty-Fifth Day of the Ninth Month of the Second Year of the Kangen Era (1244)

長月の	*naga-tsuki no*
紅葉の上に	*momiji no ue ni*
雪ふりぬ	*yuki furinu*
見ん人誰か	*min hito dareka*
歌をよまざらん	*uta o yoma zaran*

In the month of long nights
it snowed on the bright leaves
Why don't those who see this
compose a poem?

Dōgen and his sangha moved from Kyoto to Echizen province in 1243. The new monastery, Daibutsu-ji (大仏寺)—later called Eihei-ji (永平寺)—was built in 1244. The opening ceremony for the Dharma hall (法堂; Jp. *hattō*) took place on the first day of the ninth month. This poem was composed at the end of that month. The monks' hall was completed shortly thereafter, and the sangha moved into the new temple.

Naga-tsuki is the shortened form of *yonaga-tsuki* (夜長月), which means the month of lengthening nights, the ninth lunar month (which can begin anywhere from the end of September to the first weeks of October). This is normally the season of changing leaves; snow is rare. However, that year's first snow fell while yellow and red leaves were still on the trees. It seems the wind's direction changed, and due to the incoming cold air from Siberia, the temperature suddenly dropped. This is possible in the Hokuriku region (北陸地方; *Hokuriku chihō*) where Eihei-ji is located, which faces the Sea of Japan. Because such a thing never happens in Kyoto, it must have surprised Dōgen. He uses this rare phenomenon as an expression of the Dharma.

The whiteness of snow represents oneness, while the bright colors of the leaves manifest multiplicity. Each tree has its unique nature, shape, height, flower, fruit, and leaf color. Oneness and multiplicity live together. How can we express this interpenetration of absolute reality (oneness and equality) with conventional reality (multiplicity and diversity)? This is one of the essential points of our Dharma study and practice. How can we perceive and express the oneness of everything within the myriad things we encounter?

7

宝治元丁未年、在鎌倉西明寺殿自北御方道歌を御所望の時、
詠教外別伝

hōji ganchōmitoshi, zai kamakura saimyōji dono ji kitaonkata dōka wo goshomō no toki ei kyōge betsuden

A Poem on the Separate Transmission Outside the Teachings,
Written on the Occasion of Lord Saimyōji's Wife Requesting
a Dharma Verse While Staying on the Outskirts of Kamakura in the Year of the Fire Sheep in the Hōji Era (1247)

荒磯の	*araiso no*
浪もえよせぬ	*nami mo e yosenu*
高岩に	*takaiwa ni*
かきもつくべき	*kaki mo tsuku beki*
法ならばこそ	*nori naraba koso*

Precisely because the Dharma
can be inscribed
only at the top of tall rocks
even waves cannot reach
along the rugged shore

Dōgen visited Kamakura for about six months, from the eighth
month of 1247 to the third month of the following year. Lord Saimyōji
(西明寺殿) was Hōjō Tokiyori (北条時頼;1227–1263 CE), the regent
of the Kamakura shogunate government at the time.

Kaki means "to write," but also "oyster." *Nori*, translated here as
"Dharma," can also mean the seaweed used in making sushi rolls.
Dōgen uses *kaki* and *nori* here as puns to create a double image of
Kamakura's coast and the nature of Dharma: a rugged shore where
oysters cling to tall rocks, and the Dharma can be inscribed only
beyond reach of the waves of habitual discriminating thought.

"Separate transmission outside the teachings" is a famous phrase
used for distinguishing the Zen tradition from the so-called teaching
schools. Zen practitioners insisted that the Buddha's heart, or the
absolute Dharma that cannot be described in words, had been transmitted to them. However, Dōgen criticized this idea in his 1242 fascicle of the *Shōbōgenzō* titled "Buddha's Teachings" (仏教; Jp. "Bukkyō").
There he wrote, "Therefore, do not believe the mistaken theory of 'a

separate transmission outside the teachings,' and do not misunderstand what the Buddha's teachings are."

In this waka he says the Dharma can be inscribed, but only on top of tall rocks beyond the reach of discriminating thought. This observation is different from the common usage of the phrase "separate transmission outside the teachings" to declare Zen superior to the written teachings on which other schools are based. It seems this waka expresses only the first half of a statement; we might add something like, "We should study the written teachings and practice them in our actual lives, which are beyond thinking."

8
詠尽十方界真実人体

ei jin-juppō-kai shinjitsu nintai

A Poem on How the Entire Ten-Direction World Is the True Human Body

世の中に	*yononaka ni*
真の人や	*makoto no hito ya*
なかるらん	*nakaru ran*
限りも見えぬ	*kagiri mo mienu*
大空の色	*ōzora no iro*

In this world
isn't there one true person?
Of course there is:
the color of the great sky
without any visible limit

"The entire ten-direction world is the true human body" is an expression often used by Dōgen Zenji. One of the origins of this idea is a saying of Changsha Jingcen (長沙景岑; Jp. Chōsa Keishin; 788–868 CE) that Dōgen quotes in the *Shōbōgenzō* fascicle "Radiant Light" (光明; Jp. "Kōmyō"):

The entire ten-direction world is the eye of the śramaṇa. The entire ten-direction world is the everyday speech of the śramaṇa. The entire ten-direction world is the entire body of the śramaṇa. The entire ten-direction world is the radiant light of the self. The entire ten-direction world exists within the radiant light of the self. Within the entire ten-direction world, there is no one who is not the self.

Śramaṇa (沙門; Jp. *shamon*) is a Sanskrit word for a religious home-leaver, that is, a monk. Shakyamuni Buddha taught that only the five aggregates (Skt. *skandha*) exist, and there is no fixed entity such as the ātman, soul, or ego that exists as the owner or operator of these aggregates. The Buddha maintained that the five aggregates of attachment (Skt. *pañca-upādāna-skandha*) are the root of suffering (Skt. *duhkha*). The aggregates are impermanent and without any fixed nature, and yet somehow they attach to a view of themselves as permanent and unchanging and think, "That is me." This causes the five aggregates to suffer, although there is not actually any fixed subject we can identify as "the sufferer." This collection of the five aggregates that attach to themselves is also called Māra, the embodiment of evil.

In the *Heart Sutra* we read, "Avalokiteśvara Bodhisattva, when deeply practicing *prajñā pāramitā*, clearly saw that all five aggregates are empty and thus relieved all suffering." This means when the bodhisattva sees that the five aggregates are empty and it is therefore impossible to attach to oneself, all suffering is relieved; the bodhisattva is nothing other than the five aggregates. When the five aggregates see their own emptiness and are released from attachment to themselves, these aggregates are then known as "Avalokiteśvara" rather than "Māra." Dōgen wrote in the fascicle of the *Shōbōgenzō* titled "Great Perfection of Wisdom" (摩訶般若波羅蜜; Jp. "Maka hannya haramitsu") that the five aggregates are five instances of *prajñā*, or wisdom.

On this issue, there is no discrepancy between the Buddha's teaching, the *Heart Sutra*, and Dōgen's expression. All point to the transformation of the five aggregates of attachment and suffering to the five aggregates of emptiness and freedom. In Dōgen's phrasing in "Great Perfection of Wisdom," this transformation is called "dropping off body and mind" (身心脱落; Jp. *shinjin datsuraku*). The five aggregates are nothing other than body (form, the first aggregate) and mind (the other four: sensations, perception, formations, and consciousness). The body and mind liberated from attachment to themselves are here called the "true human body." This true human body is never separated from the entire ten-direction world. Precisely because there is no fixed, independent self that can exist without relation to all other beings, we say the network of the entire world is the self. The "true person" (Jp. *makoto no hito*) refers to the selfless self that is connected with all things.

To understand this waka, it is helpful to know that the Chinese character for "sky" (空; Jp. *sora*; found here in *ōzora*) also means emptiness, and the Chinese character for "color" (色; Jp. *iro*) also means form (the first aggregate). The hidden message in the second half of this waka is "form is emptiness and emptiness is form" (色即是空、空即是色; Jp. *shiki sokuze kū, kū sokuze shiki*)—that is, form (the human body) and emptiness (the great sky; 大空; Jp. *ōzora*) are completely interdependent.

9
詠見桃花悟道
ei ken tōka godō
Poem on Realizing the Way upon Seeing Peach Blossoms

春風に	*harukaze ni*
綻びにけり	*hokorobi ni keri*
桃の花	*momo no hana*
枝葉にわたる	*eda ha ni wataru*
疑ひもなし	*utagai mo nasi*

Blown by the spring wind
peach trees in full blossom
without any doubts
extending branches and leaves

"Realizing the Way upon seeing peach blossoms" comes from the famous story of Lingyun Zhiqin (靈雲志勤; Jp. Reiun Shigon; n.d.), one of the Dharma heirs of Guishan Lingyou (Ch. 潙山靈佑; Jp. 潙山靈祐, Isan Reiyū). Dōgen introduces this story in the *Shōbōgenzō* fascicle "Sounds of Valley Streams, Colors of Mountains" (谿聲山色; Jp. "Keisei sanshoku") as one of the examples of insentient beings expounding the Dharma.

Lingyun had been practicing the Way for thirty years. Once while he was walking, he sat down to rest at the foot of a mountain and saw a distant village. It was spring, so he saw peach trees in full bloom. Suddenly he realized the Way. He composed a verse and offered it to Guishan:

> For thirty years, I have been looking for the sword.
> How many times have the leaves fallen, and the branches
>   grown anew?
> Since seeing the peach blossoms,
> I've had no more doubts.[382]

"Looking for the sword" refers to the story of a person whose sword fell into the water while riding in a boat. He marked the side of the boat where he had lost the sword, and another person asked, "What are you doing?" He answered, "I will look for the sword when the boat reaches the shore."

Lingyun compares his thirty years of practice seeking the Way to someone who loses his sword overboard and yet searches for it on the shore. The sword is already far away. During Lingyun's searching, the leaves fell each autumn and the branches grew each spring. He had not realized that the Way was right where he walked, where flowers bloom, leaves fall, and new shoots appear.

In the *Shōbōgenzō* fascicle "Buddha-Nature" (佛性; Jp. "Busshō"), Dōgen says, "The roots, stem, branches, twigs, and leaves are each equally the Buddha-nature—living the same life and dying the same death as the same *entire being*."[383]

10

詠十二時中不空過

ei jūniji chū fukūka

Poem on Not Vainly Spending One Moment in Twelve Hours

過にける	*sugi ni keru*
四十余りは	*yosoji amari wa*
大空の	*oozora no*
兎烏の	*usagi karasu no*
道にこそありける	*michi ni koso arikeru*

Forty-some years
have already passed!
I have been walking
the path of rabbit and crow
in the boundless firmament

Dōgen turned forty in 1240. This waka might have been written a few years later, around the time he moved from Kōshō-ji in Kyoto to Echizen province to found his new monastery Eihei-ji. In ancient Japan, a day and night were divided into twelve periods ("hours") named after twelve animals. Daichi Sokei (大智祖継; 1290–1366 CE)—a sixth-generation descendent of Dōgen, who was known as a great poet—wrote instructions to lay practitioners for these twelve periods called *Dharma Words for the Twelve Hours* (十二時法語; Jp. *Jūniji hōgo*). In that text Daichi wrote:

> From the hour of the tiger (3 to 5 a.m.) to the end of the hour of the cow (1 to 3 a.m.), throughout one day and night, there is no time to deviate from the continuous practice of the buddha ancestors. If you spend day and night practicing in accordance with the continuous practice of the buddha ancestors, then twenty or thirty years, or your entire lifetime, will be nothing but this one day and night.[384]

In Dōgen's waka, the rabbit refers to the moon and the crow to the sun. Japanese tradition says you can see a rabbit living in the full moon and a crow with three legs in the sun.[385] The path of the rabbit and crow means night and day, and it also signifies boundless space.

Dōgen Zenji is saying he has been walking the path of the moon and sun, time and space, and the network of interdependence of all things, following the Buddha's teachings.

In *Shōbōgenzō zuimonki*, Dōgen wrote:

An ancient said, "Do not spend your days and nights in vain." Now I ask you: Does time stop passing if we hold it dear? Or does it continue to pass even if we lament [its passing]? I also ask you: Does time pass vainly? Or do people spend time in vain? This means that we should practice the Way without spending time wastefully.[386]

This passage is part of Dōgen's speech on the occasion of his Dharma heir, Ejō, expounding the Dharma as the first head monk (首座; Jp. *shuso*) of Kōshō-ji (興聖寺). He says time never passes vainly, but we can spend time wastefully. Being mindful here and now, in each moment, is how we use time and space without wasting them.

11

詠父母初生眼

ei fubo shoshōgen[387]

Poem on the Eyes Received at Birth

尋ね入る　　　　　*tazune iru*
みやまの奥の　　　*miyama no oku no*
里なれば　　　　　*sato nareba*
もとすみなれし　　*moto sumi nareshi*
京なりけり　　　　*miyako narikeri*

The village in deep mountains
I entered seeking the Way
is nowhere but the capital city
I've always lived in

The title of this poem is taken from the nineteenth chapter of the
Lotus Sutra, "The Blessing of the Dharma Teacher" (法師功德; Jp.
"Hōsshi kudoku"). In this chapter the Buddha says Dharma teachers
who study, uphold, and explain the *Lotus Sutra* will earn uncountable
blessings upon their six sense organs. These senses will thus become
pure.

This means when we thoroughly study and understand the truth
of the *Lotus Sutra*, we can see the true reality of all beings with our
own eyes, the eyes received from our parents. We do not need to attain
divine eyes, one of the six supernatural powers (神通; Jp. *jinzū*; Skt.
abhijñā). With our ordinary eyes we can see the colors of mountains as
the Buddha's body and hear the sounds of streams as the Buddha's
voice. This is when all dharmas are the Buddhadharma, as Dōgen
wrote at the beginning of "Genjōkōan."

The *Lotus Sutra* elaborates:

Such good sons or daughters, with the pure physical eyes
received from their parents at birth, will see whatever exists,
whether exposed or hidden, in the three-thousand great
thousand-fold world—the mountains, forests, rivers, and seas
down to the deepest purgatory and up to the highest heaven.
They will see all the living beings in it and recognize all of the
causes and conditions and all of the effects and consequences
resulting from their past actions.[388]

This waka's "village in deep mountains" probably refers to the
place in Echizen province where Dōgen and his sangha moved from
Kyoto. The name Kyoto literally means "capital city." Dōgen moved
from the capital to the remote mountains to found his new monastery

for the genuine study and practice of the Dharma. Even though geographically it was a remote corner of the country, for him, seeing with the pure eyes of the Dharma, that location in the country was the true capital, where he had always lived.

Some scholars speculate that Dōgen abandoned Kyoto after failing in competition with other Zen masters to establish a prominent monastery like Tōfuku-ji (東福寺), founded by Rinzai Master Enni Benn'en (円爾弁円; 1202–1280 CE). However, at least in Dōgen's mind, he was not fleeing the city because he lost a competition; rather, I believe his motivation was his wish to escape competition itself. Kyoto was true saṃsāra, a world of conflict based on the three poisonous minds of greed, anger, and ignorance. When he moved to the mountains, he discovered that those mountains were the true capital city of the Dharma, or nirvana, where he could focus on studying and practicing with his disciples.

In traditional Zen literature, "capital city" refers to the capital of the Tang dynasty, Chang'an (長安; in English literally "eternal peace"). For example, there is this dialogue between Zhaozhou Congshen (趙州從諗; Jp. Jōshū Jūshin; 778–897 CE) and a monk:

> A monk asked, "Does a dog have Buddha-nature or not?"
> The Master said, "The door of every house leads to the capital (Chang-an)."[389]

In this dialogue, Zhaozhou says just as the door of every house is connected to the "capital" (eternal peace, Buddhahood, or nirvana), so too a dog definitely has Buddha-nature. In the *Shōbōgenzō* fascicle "Buddha-Nature" (佛性; Jp. "Busshō"), Dōgen's says the "entire being" of the dog is Buddha-nature.

12
詠本来面目
ei honrai no menmoku
Poem Expressing the Original Face

春は花   haru wa hana
夏ほととぎす   natsu hototogisu
秋は月   aki wa tsuki
冬雪きえで   fuyu yuki kiede
すずしかりけり   suzushi kari keri

Spring flowers
summer cuckoos
autumn moon
winter snow doesn't melt
all seasons pure and upright

The "original face" here refers to the true reality of all beings before it is processed by our discriminating, self-centered minds. This reality beyond thinking is not something metaphysical but simply concrete, phenomenal reality as it is. We are included in it. Yet because we are inside it, we cannot perceive it as the object of our sense organs. Reality lies beyond the separation between subject and object in which a subject conceives of things outside itself as objects. Flowers, cuckoos, moon, snow, and we ourselves are the elements of spring, summer, autumn, and winter, and each of these particulars fully expresses the entire season.

We can find an example of the scenery of each season as the true reality of all things in the lines composed by the Chinese Sōtō Zen Master Hongzhi Zhengjue (宏智正覚; Jp. Wanshi Shōgaku; 1091– 1157 CE) that appear as the verse commentary of case 1 in the *Book of Serenity* (Ch. 從容錄, *Cóngróng lù*; Jp. 従容錄, *Shōyō roku*).

The unique breeze of reality—do you see?
Continuously creation runs her loom and shuttle,
Weaving the ancient brocade, incorporating the forms of
    spring,
But nothing can be done about Mañjuśrī's leaking.[390]

The case is titled "The World-Honored One Ascends the Seat." This comes from a story in which the Buddha one day ascended his seat, and before he said anything, Mañjuśrī—the bodhisattva of wisdom—struck the gavel and said, "Clearly observe the Dharma of the King of Dharma; the Dharma of the King of Dharma is thus." Then the Buddha got down from his seat without saying anything. This kōan is about the true reality beyond language—the original face.

In Hongzhi's verse, the word used for "creation" is *kebo* (化母), which literally means "the mother who is the creator of all things." The mother continuously runs her loom and shuttle, weaving. The horizontal thread (the weft) represents space, while the vertical thread (the warp) symbolizes time. Using time and space as her loom, the mother weaves the scenery of each season, as beautiful as golden brocade. I think Dōgen is expressing the same idea as Hongzhi: the pure and upright scenery of each season is the true reality.

"Mañjuśrī's leaking" in the last line of Hongzhi's verse means that, in contrast to the Buddha's actual silence, Mañjuśrī verbally leaks the secret by explaining that the silence is the reality beyond dualistic language. This explanation is really something extra, but without his leaking it, we would not understand the meaning of the Buddha's silence. Dōgen's waka is itself another example of this "leaking."

In the Japanese lunar calendar, the first, second, and third months are spring; the fourth, fifth, and sixth months, summer; the seventh, eighth, and ninth months, autumn; and the tenth, eleventh, and twelfth months, winter. New Year's Day in the lunar calendar corresponds to about February 10 in the Gregorian calendar, so spring is from February to May; summer, May to August; autumn, August to November; and winter, November to February.

In the Kyoto region of central Japan, this division into four seasons of equal length makes sense. However, Japan consists of five main islands, ranging from Hokkaido in the north to Okinawa in the south. Hokkaido is at the same latitude as Minnesota, and Okinawa is at that of Florida. The actual climate in each area differs from the calendar seasons. These differences are important elements of the

Japanese seasonal sensitivity. For example, in waka number six, Echizen province—where Dōgen lived at the time of writing—had snow at the end of the ninth month, which would be very unlikely in Kyoto where he used to live. That is the basis of his surprise and the motif of the poem. Similarly, in waka number fifty, Dōgen says that although everything is still covered with snow, it is spring. And he finds a sign of spring in the first call of a warbler.

13

詠応無所住而生其心

ei ōmushojū nishō go-shin

Poem on Activating the Mind without Dwelling

水鳥の	*mizudori no*
行くも帰るも	*yuku mo kaeru mo*
跡たえて	*ato taete*
されども路は	*saredomo michi wa*
わすれざりけり	*wasure zari keri*

Waterbirds

fly away and return

leaving no trace

even so, they do not forget

the path

The expression "activating the mind without dwelling" in the title appears in the Chinese translation of the *Diamond Sutra* by Kumārajīva (鳩摩羅什; Ch. Jiūmóluóshí; Jp. Kumarajū; 344–413 CE). It means we should keep our minds functioning without attachment to any objects. Bodhisattvas are free from attachment to objects, and yet their minds do not become lifeless. Bodhisattva practice is not bringing our minds to a halt.

This expression has been important in Zen tradition because it was used in the enlightenment story of the Sixth Ancestor, Dajian

Huineng (大鑒惠能; Jp. Daikan Enō; 638–713 CE). One version says Huineng became awakened when he heard someone chanting the *Diamond Sutra* while he was selling firewood. Another version says he was awakened when the Fifth Ancestor Daman Hongren (大満弘忍; Jp. Daiman Kōnin; 601–674 CE) taught him this expression during the midnight Dharma transmission between the two ancestors.

In this poem, Dōgen Zenji expresses a fundamental characteristic of bodhisattva practice using the analogy of migratory birds. These birds fly amazingly long distances each year without leaving any trace, yet they never forget the path that leads to their precise destination. They transmit this path from generation to generation without a trace.

In the fascicle of the *Shōbōgenzō* "Only Buddha Together with Buddha" (唯佛與佛; Jp. "Yuibutsu yobutsu"), Dōgen wrote:

> Also, concerning birds flying in the sky, there is no way for animals walking on the earth to know the birds' tracks. They cannot follow the birds' path by seeing their traces even in their dreams. Because they do not know that there is such a path, they cannot even imagine it. And yet a bird can see the traces of hundreds or thousands of small birds having passed in flocks, or the tracks of so many lines of large birds having flown to the south or migrated to the north.

Dongshan Liangjie's (洞山良价; Jp. Tōzan Ryōkai; 807–869 CE) kōan, "The Path of Birds" (鳥道; Jp. "Chō dō") in *The Record of Dongshan* (洞山語錄; Jp. *Tōzan goroku*) and Hongzhi Zhengjue's verse "The sky is infinitely vast, a bird is flying far away" from his poem "Acupuncture Needle of Zazen" (坐禪箴; Jp. "Zazenshin") are the sources of Dōgen's inspiration for this waka.

14
詠不立文字
ei furyū monji
Poem on Not Depending on Words and Letters

言ひすてし   *ii suteshi*
その言葉の   *sono koto no ha no*
外なれば   *hoka nareba*
筆にも跡を   *fude ni mo ato o*
留めざりけり   *todome zari keri*

Because the Dharma is
beyond the words I spoke
it leaves no trace
in my brushstrokes

"Not depending on words and letters" (不立文字; Jp. *furyū monji*) is a famous motto of Zen. This expression is often used together with the phrase "mind-to-mind transmission" (以心伝心; Jp. *i shin den shin*). According to scholars, these expressions were coined between 750 and 850 CE in China, around the time of Mazu Daoyi (馬祖道一; Jp. Baso Dōitsu; 709–788 CE) and Shitou Xiqian (石頭希遷; Jp. Sekitō Kisen; 700–790). The scholar Jeffrey Broughton suggests it may have originated with the prominent monk Guifeng Zongmi (圭峰宗密; Jp. Keihō Shūmitsu 780–841 CE), citing the following passage from Zongmi:

Bodhidharma received dharma in India and personally brought it to China. He saw that most of the scholars of this land had not yet obtained dharma, that their understanding was based merely on scholastic nomenclature and numerical lists and that their practice was concerned only with phenomenal characteristics. Because his desire was to inform them that the moon does not lie in the finger [pointing at the moon] and that dharma *is* our mind, he just [raised the slogan] "a mind-to-mind transmission (*i shin den shin*); no involvement with the written word (*furyū monji*)."[391]

Since then, together with "separate transmission outside the teaching" (教外別伝; Jp. *kyōge betsuden*), these expressions have been used as

Zen catchphrases to declare Zen's superiority over Buddhist schools based on scriptures.

However, it is interesting to note that Dōgen did not use the phrase "not depending on words and letters" in either the *Shōbōgenzō* or *Dōgen's Extensive Record* (永平広録; Jp. *Eihei kōroku*). He did use "mind-to-mind transmission" in two fascicles of the *Shōbōgenzō*: "Entanglement" (葛藤; Jp." Kattō") and "Insentient Beings Expounding Dharma" (無情説法; Jp. "Mujō seppō"). In the latter, Dōgen used the expression in a negative way.

We must be careful when we read this waka and consider what Dōgen is expressing here about this cliché. Dōgen never negated the significance of language. In *Shōbōgenzō* "Being Able to Speak" (道得; Jp. "Dōtoku"), Dōgen wrote:

> When we are able to speak of the speakable, we do not-speak of the unspeakable. Even if we recognize that we are able to speak of the speakable, unless we penetrate the fact that the unspeakable is what we are not-able-to-speak, we have not yet attained the face of the buddha-ancestors or the marrow of the buddha-ancestors.

In this passage, Dōgen treats "not-speak" as an active verb instead of a simple negation of speaking. In this waka, Dōgen does not say that we should stop using a brush to write words. We should understand and express what we can to the limits of language, but we should also pay attention to the unspeakable. Dōgen's style is to go beyond thinking by thinking thoroughly. This resembles his saying from *Shōbō-genzō* "Seeing the Buddha" (見佛; Jp. "Ken butsu"): "Seeing form and seeing no-form is seeing the Tathāgata."

15

詠即心是仏

ei sokushin ze butsu

Poem on Mind Itself Is Buddha

鴛鴦か   *oshidori ka*
白鴎ともまた   *kamome tomo mata*
見へわかず   *miewakazu*
立つ浪あひの   *tatsu namiai no*
うきしづみかな   *uki shizumi kana*[392]

Mandarin ducks
or seagulls?
Impossible to distinguish
floating and sinking
among the rising waves

The title of this poem, "Mind itself is Buddha," is a famous saying of Mazu Daoyi (馬祖道一; Jp. Baso Dōitsu; 709–788 CE). Dōgen Zenji quotes this expression from the story of Damei Fachang (大梅法常; Jp. Daibai Hōjō; 752–839 CE) in several places in the *Shōbōgenzō* and *Dōgen's Extensive Record* (永平広録; Jp. *Eihei kōroku*). In *Shōbōgenzō* "The Mind Is Itself Buddha" (即心是仏; Jp. "Sokushin ze butsu"), Dōgen cautions us not to interpret the mind as our psychology prior to arousing the mind of awakening, or as our original nature as something permanent. He writes:

> The mind that has been authentically transmitted is "one mind is all Dharmas; all Dharmas are one mind. . . ." We clearly understand that the mind refers to the mountains, rivers, and the great earth; the sun, the moon, and the stars. . . . Therefore, "mind itself is Buddha" refers to all the buddhas who carry out arousing the mind of awakening, practice, awakening, and nirvana. Those who have not yet been carrying out [these things] are not "mind itself is buddha."

In "Dharma Discourse 319" in *Dōgen's Extensive Record*, Dōgen quotes the story of Damei's sitting in the mountains for thirty years after hearing Mazu's "mind itself is Buddha," and comments:

We should know that zazen is the decorous activity of practice after realization. Realization is simply just sitting. At this monastery we have the first monks' hall, so in this country of Japan this is the first we have heard of this, the first time we have seen it, the first time we have entered it, and the first time sitting in a monks' hall. This is fortunate for people studying the Buddha way. . . .

This "mind itself is Buddha" is very difficult to understand. Mind is fences, walls, tiles, and pebbles, and Buddha is a glob of mud or a clump of soil; Kiangsi [Mazu] expressed trailing mud and dripping water, Damei realized lurking in the grass and sticking to trees. Where can we find this mind itself is Buddha?[393]

In zazen practice we sit right within the reality beyond separation, where "the mind itself is Buddha" manifests. Dōgen is saying this mind is not within the dichotomy of mind and body or subject and objects. This mind includes body and mind, self, and all things in the universe. This mind is the entire network of interconnected origination. The dichotomies exist, but it is impossible to make ultimate distinctions between them.

In this waka, he expresses "mind itself is Buddha" using the scenery of a lake or seashore. The mandarin duck is a common bird in East Asia. A male mandarin is very colorful, and a seagull is white. Since they differ in appearance, it is easy to distinguish them under normal conditions unless they are far away. Possibly this is a scene at dawn or twilight when the birds are silhouetted, or in a fog or mist. The mandarin duck prefers freshwater but may also winter in coastal lagoons and estuaries, so the two can be found together. In this waka I think Dōgen portrays the scenery of our zazen.

16

詠行住坐臥

ei gyō jū za ga

Poem on Walking, Standing, Sitting, and Lying Down

守るとも   *mamoru tomo*

覚えずながら   *oboezu nagara*

小山田の   *oyamada no*

いたづらならぬ   *itazura naranu*

かがしなりけり   *kagashi narikeri*

Even without knowing he protects rice

the scarecrow

in the mountain's small paddy

doesn't exist in vain

In the fall when rice ripens, many birds come to eat it, and the farmers put scarecrows in their mountain paddies to protect the rice. Scarecrows in Japan often look like monks wearing black robes and bamboo hats. Because this waka refers to a small paddy on a hidden mountain, it is clear that no one sees or appreciates the scarecrow. Even the scarecrow himself does not know he is guarding rice; he is simply standing in a field. However, he is actually protecting the rice.

In Menzan's version of this waka collection, the title of this poem is "zazen." Zazen is not for our personal benefit. My teacher's teacher, Kōdō Sawaki Rōshi (沢木興道; 1880–1965 CE), said satori in zazen practice is like a burglar sneaking into an empty house. Although the burglar finally enters after strenuous effort, there is nothing to gain once he is there. According to a worldly view, that kind of an effort would be a waste of time, yet zazen has benefits beyond calculation. This is what Dōgen Zenji meant when he wrote in "Genjōkōan": "When buddhas are truly buddhas they do not need to perceive they are buddhas; however, they are enlightened buddhas and they continue actualizing Buddha."

A nearly identical waka is included in the *Recorded Sayings of Zen Master Bukkoku* (佛國禪師語錄; Jp. *Bukkoku zenji goroku*) which is a collection of the words of the Rinzai Zen master Kōhō Kennichi (高峰顕日; 1241–1316 CE), the abbot of the temple Kenchō-ji (建長寺) in Kamakura. Because of the similarity, scholars question whether this waka is really Dōgen's.

17

詠正法眼蔵

ei shōbōgenzō

Poem on the True Dharma-Eye Treasury

波も引き   *nami mo hiki*

風もつながぬ   *kaze mo tsunaganu*

捨小舟   *sute obune*

月こそ夜半の   *tsuki koso yowa no*

さかひなりけり   *sakai narikeri*

Waves settle

and wind calms

a tiny discarded boat drifts unmoored

the middle of the night

is completely the world of the moon

The title of this poem uses the term *shōbōgenzō*, which translates to "true Dharma-eye treasury." It is the term for the Dharma that has been transmitted from Shakyamuni through the succession of ancestors. Dōgen used this expression as the title of the essay collection that is his masterpiece.

In this poem, he describes the scenery of the ocean during a beautiful night. The wind and waves have died down, so it is very peaceful. A small, untied boat floats freely. The moon shines over this entire world, embracing everything within itself.

This waka reminds me of a verse composed by Xuedou Chongxian (雪竇重顯; Jp. Seccho Jūken; 982–1052 CE). Dōgen quoted this verse in *Instructions for the Cook* (典座教訓; Jp. *Tenzo kyōkun*):

One character, three characters, five, and seven characters.

Having thoroughly investigated the ten thousand things,

None has any foundation.

At midnight the white moon sets into the dark ocean.

When searching for the black dragon's pearl,
You will find they are numerous.[394]

Dōgen also quotes a saying by Panshan Baoji (盤山寶積; Jp. Banzan Hōshaku; 720–814 CE) in the *Shōbōgenzō* fascicle "Moon" (都機;
Jp. "Tsuki"): "The mind-moon is alone and completely round. Its light
swallows the myriad phenomenal things. The light does not illuminate
objects. Nor do any objects exist. Light and objects simultaneously
vanish. Then what is this?" In this fascicle, the moon, which normally
is a symbol for the absolute, is said to be present everywhere without
any separation.

When we read Xuedou's verse and Panshan's saying, I do not think
we need much explanation to appreciate this waka. One important
detail is the loose and discarded boat. I think this represents the five
aggregates (body and mind) dropped off (身心脱落; Jp. *shinjin datsuraku*), releasing us from self-clinging. To me this waka, like waka 15,
depicts our zazen.

18
詠涅槃妙心
ei nehan myōshin
Wondrous Mind in Nirvana

いつもただ	*itsumo tada*
我が古里の	*waga furusato no*
花なれば	*hana nareba*
色もかはらぬ	*iromo kawaranu*
過ぎし春かな	*sugishi haru kana*

Always
since these flowers invariably bloom
in my home village
the colors do not change
although spring passes

Nehan myōshin, meaning "wondrous mind in nirvana," is often used with the expression *shōbōgenzō,* or "true Dharma-eye treasury." *Shōbō-genzō nehan myōshin* refers to the life of bodhisattvas based on the true reality of all things, which is both form and emptiness. In the *Shōbō-genzō* fascicle "Total Function" (全機; Jp. "Zenki"), Dōgen wrote, "The great Way of all buddhas, when it is completely penetrated, is liberation and manifestation." Things are manifested completely as they are, and yet at the same time, they are liberated from what they are due to impermanence and no-self.

Bodhisattvas live in non-abiding; because of their wisdom they do not abide in saṃsāra, and yet because of their compassion they do not abide in nirvana. In saṃsāra they live conditioned lives, walking with all beings, and yet in each of their steps eternal nirvana is revealed.

In this waka, "these flowers" blooming in the original place ("home village") of bodhisattvas are what Dōgen called "flowers of emptiness." Dōgen wrote a fascicle of the *Shōbōgenzō* titled "Flower of Emptiness" (空華; Jp. "Kūge") in which he commented on Bodhidharma's expression "A flower opens with five petals":

> The true Dharma-eye treasury, the wondrous mind in nirvana
> that has been authentically transmitted without interruption
> until today, is called cataract-eyes and flowers of emptiness.
> Awakening, nirvana, Dharma-body, self-nature, and so on are
> two or three of the five petals that flowers of emptiness open.

In this passage, "two or three petals" represents the phenomena of our day-to-day conventional reality, while "five petals" is the absolute reality beyond discrimination. Dōgen sees each and every flower that blooms and falls (phenomena) as a flower of emptiness (the absolute). Flowers arise and perish, yet never arise or perish. Not only flowers, but also every phenomenal being and our practice activity are examples of the five petals of the flower of emptiness. They are always simply expressing the colors of emptiness. Spring passes, and yet the colors of emptiness never change.

草庵之偶詠　三十首

sōan no gūei sanjū shu

Thirty Miscellaneous Poems Written at the Grass Hut[395]

19

草庵に	*kusa no io ni*
ねてもさめても	*nete mo samete mo*
申すこと	*mōsu koto*
南無釈迦牟尼仏	*namu shakamuni butsu*
憐み給へ	*awaremi tamae*

In my grass hut
sleeping or waking
I always recite
"I take refuge in Shakyamuni Buddha;
bestow your compassion upon us!"

If we have read only Dōgen Zenji's philosophical writings, the feeling this waka expresses might seem out of character for him. However, in the *Shōbōgenzō* fascicle "Mind of the Way" (道心; Jp. "Dōshin") he wrote, "Asleep and awake, we should consider the merit of the Three Treasures. Asleep and awake, we should chant the Three Treasures."[396]

For Dōgen, Shakyamuni Buddha was not one particular Buddha among many Buddhas in Mahāyāna Buddhism. In the *Shōbōgenzō* fascicle "The Mind Is Itself Buddha" (即心是仏; Jp. "Sokushin ze butsu"), he wrote:

The term "all buddhas" refers to Shakyamuni Buddha. Shakyamuni is nothing other than "mind itself is Buddha." All buddhas in the past, present, and future, when they become buddha, unfailingly become Shakyamuni Buddha. This is "mind itself is Buddha."

My teacher Kōshō Uchiyama Rōshi had ill health throughout his life. From his early twenties, he lived with tuberculosis. When he could not practice zazen because of his physical condition, he silently chanted the name of the bodhisattva Avalokiteśvara, repeating the phrase *namu Kanzeon bosatsu* (南無觀世音菩薩; literally "homage to Avalokiteśvara bodhisattva"). He often said that zazen and chanting a buddha's or bodhisattva's name, whether Shakyamuni, Amitābha, or Avalokiteśvara, are basically the same; these are merely different names for the total functioning of the network of interdependent origination through which we are enabled to live.

In *Opening the Hand of Thought*, Uchiyama Rōshi wrote:

This small *I* is embraced by the immeasurable and boundless Amitabha Buddha. . . . It does not depend on whether I believe it or not. I am, in fact, embraced and saved by the immeasurable and boundless Amitabha. Being thankful for this, I chant *Namu amida butsu*. When we say this with our mouths, we are expressing our deep sense of gratitude. When we perform it with our whole body, it is zazen as the activity of the reality of life, the zazen of believing and sitting. When people of the Pure Land School chant *Namu amida butsu*, they are doing zazen with their mouths, and when we do zazen, we are performing *Namu amida butsu* with our whole body.[397]

20
おろかなる   *oroka naru*
われは仏に   *ware wa hotoke ni*
ならずとも   *narazu tomo*
衆生を渡す   *shujō o watasu*
僧の身ならん   *sō no mi naran*

Even though because I'm dull-witted
I won't become a buddha

I wish to be a monk
helping all living beings
cross over

This waka is about the first of the four bodhisattva vows, "Beings are numberless; I vow to free them" (衆生無邊誓願度; Jp. *shujō muhen sei gan do*). To "free" or "save" is a translation of *do* (度), which means to "cross over." According to Buddhist teachings, between this shore of saṃsāra and the other shore of nirvana lies a big river. A bodhisattva is like a ferryman who helps people across the river. This vow actually means the following: "I will not cross over and enter nirvana until I finish helping all living beings cross." This is an endless vow with an unreachable goal.

In the fascicle of the *Shōbōgenzō* "Arousing the Mind of Awakening" (發菩提心; Jp. "Hotsu bodai shin"), Dōgen Zenji said, "To arouse the mind of awakening means to take the vow, 'Before I myself cross over, I will help all living beings cross over,' and strive to fulfill this vow. Even if their outside appearance is humble, those who have aroused this mind are already the guiding teachers of all living beings."

In *Shōbōgenzō zuimonki*, Dōgen wrote:

All the buddhas and ancestors were originally ordinary people. While they were ordinary people they certainly did bad deeds and had evil minds. Some of them might have been dull-witted or even fools. However, since they followed their teachers, relied on [the Buddha's] teaching and practice, and transformed themselves, they all became buddhas and ancestors.

Today's people should also do the same. We should not disparage ourselves, thinking we are foolish or dull-witted. If we do not arouse the mind [of awakening] in this present lifetime, when can we expect to? If we are fond of [the Way], we will surely attain it.[398]

Even if we have aroused the mind of awakening, received the bodhisattva precepts, and taken the bodhisattva vows, we cannot be like the great bodhisattvas such as Avalokiteśvara, Mañjuśrī, Samant-abhadra, and Kṣitigarbha. We are still ordinary deluded beings. We may make many mistakes, but we still must help ourselves and others to find nirvana within saṃsāra. Actually, there is no boundary between saṃsāra and nirvana. Each time we do even a small thing to help others, free of self-centeredness, we experience nirvana here and now.

21

嬉しくも	*ureshiku mo*
釈迦の御法の	*shaka no mi-nori no*
あふみ草	*afumi-gusa*
かけても外の	*kaketemo hoka no*
道をふまばや	*michi o fumabaya*

How delightful!
I was able to meet
Shakyamuni's Dharma
I will never, ever walk
another path

This waka contains a double image that does not come through in the translation. In another possible interpretation, *afumi-gusa* is what is now called *aoi-gusa* (葵草), or *futaba-aoi* (二葉葵), in modern Japanese. This is a plant known as hazelwort or wild ginger in English, a low-growing herb found in forests with the scientific name *Asarum caulescens*. *Futaba-aoi* has long been the emblem of the Kamo shrines (賀茂神社; Jp. Kamo jinja), which are two of the oldest Shinto shrines in Kyoto, dating to the sixth and seventh centuries. The annual festival held at these shrines, the Aoi Matsuri (葵祭) on May 15, is named for this plant and is one of the three main yearly festivals in Kyoto even today. *Futaba-aoi* was also used in the crest of the Tokugawa shogunate family that ruled during the Edo period (1600–1868 CE).

In this waka, *afumi* is a pun on the verb that means "to meet" or "to encounter." *Kake* in *kaketemo*, which means "not at all" in the context of this waka, can also mean "to hang." During the festival, *futaba-aoi* is hung everywhere. So, the hidden image in this waka is the scenery of early summer. I am not sure why the joy of meeting the Buddhadharma and the Aoi Matsuri are connected here. Possibly, Dōgen Zenji wrote this waka to someone on the day of the festival, or the plant was blooming then.

In the *Shōbōgenzō* fascicle "Virtue of Leaving Home" (出家功徳; Jp. "Shukke kudoku"), Dōgen wrote about how rare and precious it is to encounter the Buddhadharma:

Not only have we already received a human body, which is difficult to receive, but we have also encountered Buddhadharma, which is rare to encounter. We should immediately discard all mundane associations, leave home, and study the Way. Kings, ministers, wives, children, and relatives can be encountered wherever we go. Buddhadharma is as difficult to encounter as an uḍumbara flower [which blooms only once every three thousand years].

And in the fascicle of the *Shōbōgenzō* called "Taking Refuge in the Three Treasures" (歸依三寶; Jp. "Kie sanbō), Dōgen quoted Shakyamuni's teaching about the reasons we should take refuge in the Buddha, Dharma, and sangha:

Being fearful of oppressive suffering, many people take refuge in gods in mountains, parks, forests, solitary trees, shrines, and so on. Taking refuge in such gods is neither excellent nor precious. By taking refuge in such gods, it is not possible to be liberated from the many kinds of suffering.

If all beings take refuge in Buddha, Dharma, and sangha, and in the four noble truths, they clearly observe [reality] with wisdom, they will understand their suffering, the cause of suffering, the eternal transcendence of suffering, and the eightfold noble path that leads to the peace of nirvana. Taking refuge in these is most excellent and precious. By taking refuge in the Three Treasures, it is possible to be liberated from the many kinds of suffering.

22

馳の馬	*yotsu no uma*
四の車に	*yotsu no kuruma ni*
乗らぬ人	*noranu hito*
真の道を	*makoto no michi o*
いかで知らまし	*ikade shiramashi*

Those who do not ride
on the four horses
and in the four carriages,
how could they know the true Way?

In the *Shōbōgenzō* fascicle "Four Horses" (四馬; Jp. "Shime"), Dōgen Zenji quotes teachings about four kinds of horses from a sutra in the *Connected Discourses* (雜阿含經; Jp. *Zō agon kyō*; Skt. *Saṃyukta āgama*) and the *Mahāyāna Mahāparinirvāṇa Sūtra* (大般涅槃經; Jp. *Dai hatsunehan gyō*).

In the *Connected Discourses*, the Buddha taught there are four kinds of horses. The first is most sharp-witted. It starts when it sees only the shadow of the whip and understands what the rider wants. The second pays attention when the whip touches its hair. The third notices when the whip strikes its flesh. The fourth wakes up only after the whip has penetrated to the bone.[399]

The Buddha explained the first horse is like people who realize impermanence after someone in another village dies; the second, when someone in their own village dies; the third represents those who realize impermanence when their parent dies; and the fourth, those who do not accept impermanence until they are facing their own death.

According to the *Mahāyāna Mahāparinirvāna Sūtra*, the first horse resembles people who accept the Buddha's teaching when they hear of the suffering of birth; the second, when they learn of birth and aging; the third, after seeing birth, aging, and sickness; and the fourth, only after perceiving birth, aging, sickness, and death.

In this waka, riding on the four horses signifies realizing impermanence and the suffering of life, accepting the Buddha's teachings, and arousing the mind of awakening. The four carriages refer to the sheep cart (representing the path of the *śrāvaka*), deer cart (the path of the *pratyekabuddha*), ox cart (the path of the bodhisattva), and great white ox cart ("the one vehicle," which includes all of the previous three) that appear in the third chapter of the *Lotus Sutra*. Riding in the four carriages means studying and practicing any Buddhist teachings or traditions. The *Lotus Sutra* claims only the last of the four represents the Buddha's true teaching, but Dōgen does not make such a discrimination.

We all see the reality of impermanence and various kinds of suffering in human life, but we do not often arouse the mind of awakening and ride the carriages of the Dharma. So how can we know the true Buddha way?

An example of seeing impermanence and consequently arousing the mind of awakening can be seen in the story of Paṭacārā, considered the foremost "Keeper of the Vinaya" among nuns and one of the leading female disciples of Shakyamuni Buddha. Impermanence was engraved in her heart through extremely difficult experiences.

Paṭacārā was a beautiful and self-motivated daughter of a rich merchant in Kosala. When she was young, she fell in love with a servant of her parents. She fled her parents' home to marry him, and they lived as farmers in a distant village for several years. When she was pregnant with her second child, she decided to return to her parents' home to give birth, but on their way a storm with heavy rain and thunder overtook them. Her husband went into a forest to get some trees to make a temporary shelter, but he was bitten by a poisonous snake and died. Paṭacārā continued to walk with their first child and the baby she had given birth to that night.

When she came to a river, it was swollen due to the heavy rain, so she decided to take her children one by one across the river. She left her older son on the shore and carried the newborn baby across. While she was returning to her older son, she screamed as she saw a vulture take her baby in its talons and fly away. Then, hearing his mother's voice, the older boy thought she was calling him and entered the river, which swept him away in its strong current. Having lost her husband and two children, Paṭacārā continued to walk toward her hometown. When she arrived, she heard that her parents' house had collapsed during the storm, killing her parents and brother. Paṭacārā had lost her entire family in one day.

Paṭacārā went insane—howling, tearing her clothes, and wandering here and there, weeping and wailing. After a while, she came to Jetavana monastery, where Shakyamuni was staying. He instructed his disciples not to obstruct her but to let her enter and come near him. She asked the Buddha to help her. The Buddha taught her about impermanence and said, "Paṭacārā, do not think you have come to someone who can help you. In your many lives, you have shed more tears for the dead than there is water in the four oceans." After he had given more teachings, Paṭacārā asked the Buddha to accept her as his disciple.[400]

Still today, many people have experiences of suffering similar to Paṭacārā's because of natural disasters and human-made events such as war and other kinds of violence. The question is whether we can use such experiences to awaken. And as with the four horses, how much suffering is necessary for us to do so?

23
山深み　　　　　*yama fukami*
峯にも谷も　　　*mine nimo tani mo*
声たてて　　　　*koe tatete*
今日もくれぬと　*kyō mo kurenu to*
日暮ぞなく　　　*higurashi zo naku*

Deep in mountains
on peaks and in valleys
raising loud voices
cicadas sing:
This day is already ending

Higurashi (日暮 or 蜩) is the Japanese name for the evening cicada (*Tanna japonensis*). It can be found all over Japan where it calls in the evening and early morning. In haiku, *higurashi* is a seasonal word denoting early autumn, but actually these insects chirp beginning in early summer. *Higurashi* literally means "closer of the day." A summer day is long, but if we spend it carelessly and wastefully, there is no way to retrieve it.

Cicadas represent the brevity of life. They stay underground for some years as larvae, but once they mature and appear above ground, they live a matter of weeks at most. They chirp wholeheartedly while they can, without wasting time. Their song expounds the Dharma of impermanence, urging us to live mindfully and attentively each moment.

Dōgen Zenji discussed the preciousness of every day in the fascicle of *Shōbōgenzō* titled "Continuous Practice" (行持; Jp. "Gyōji"):

Thus, a single day must be of great importance. If we live vainly for a hundred years, we will regret the days and months we wasted, and be sad for our bodies. Although we run around as slaves to sounds and sights for a hundred years, if we are able to practice even for one single day within that time, not only will we put our whole lives of a hundred years into this practice, we will also save those hundred years. We should cherish this body and life of one day through practice; we should respect this body through practice.

24
春風に   *haru kaze ni*
わが言葉の   *waga koto no ha no*

散りぬるを   *chirinuru o*
花の歌とや   *hana no uta to ya*
人のながめん   *hito no nagamen*

By the spring wind
my words
are blown and scattered
people may see them
the song of flowers

Koto no ha (言の葉) literally means "leaves of words," referring both to words in general and to a waka poem. On a spring day, flowers, probably cherry blossoms, are blown by the wind and fall to the ground. Dōgen's mind was also blown about by the spring wind, and a waka poem formed from the leaves of words. This is what "my words are blown and scattered" means. It also means Dōgen does not cling to his scattered words.

In the *Shōbōgenzō* fascicle "Sounds of Valley Streams, Colors of Mountains" (谿聲山色; Jp. "Keisei sanshoku"), Dōgen comments on a poem by the famous Chinese poet Su Shi (蘇軾; Jp. Soshoku; 1036–1101 CE) that says the sounds of valley streams are the voice of Shakyamuni expounding the Dharma and the colors of the mountains are the pure body of Buddha. When we are liberated from the five aggregates of attachment (Skt. *pañca-upādāna-skandha*), the objects of our sense organs cease to be the objects of our thoughts and desires (*nāma-rūpa*). Then, as Dōgen says at the beginning of "Genjōkōan," we see the myriad things as Buddhadharma.

When Dōgen writes this poem about falling flowers, he is expounding this truth. And yet, people probably think his poem is about admiring the beauty of the falling flowers as *nāma-rūpa*. Snow, moon, and flowers are such common motifs in poetry that people might consider any poem about flowers to be hackneyed.

In *The Zen Poetry of Dōgen*, the scholar Steven Heine offers another possible interpretation. He suggests that "the song of flowers" means the song sung *by* the flowers.[401] In this unusual interpretation, the poem is not a thing written by someone observing the flowers' beauty from a human perspective. Instead, the poem itself is the singing of the flowers.

25

あづさ弓	*azusayumi*
春の山風	*haru no yamakaze*
吹きぬらん	*fukinuran*
峯にも谷も	*mine nimo tani mo*
花匂ひけり	*hana nioi keri*

It seems the mountain spring wind
has begun to blow
on peaks and in valleys
myriad flowers are shining

Azusayumi literally means a "catalpa bow," but here it is used as a *pillow word* (枕詞; Jp. *makura kotoba*), a traditional poetic epithet, in this case to indicate the season of spring. Steven Heine translates *nioi* as "fragrance," but the word originally referred to color.[402] It can be translated as "shining," "luminous," or "bright."

This poem expresses the beauty of midspring, with its countless flowers. This is one of the most striking times of year. After a long and cold winter, the world becomes lovely and vigorous again. We, too, become joyful, and in Japan people host parties underneath the cherry blossoms. It is fine to enjoy the beautiful spring, but we need to remember that, particularly for farmers, this is also the time to prepare for working in the fields. The time of flowers is brief. Another long, hot, and humid summer is coming.

Near the end of *Instructions for the Cook* (典座教訓; Jp. *Tenzo kyōkun*), where Dōgen discusses the significance of magnanimous mind (大心; Jp. *daishin*) beyond discrimination, he says: "Carrying half a pound, do not take it lightly; lifting forty pounds should not seem heavy." We need to live with steadiness through both favorable and adverse circumstances, without being overwhelmed by whatever conditions that may arise.

26
頼みこし   *tanomi koshi*
昔の主や   *mukashi no shū ya*
木綿襷   *yuudasuki*
あはれをかけよ   *aware o kakeyo*
麻の袖にも   *asa no sode ni mo*

Ancient gods
whom Shinto priests in cotton sashes
worship and rely on
please bestow mercy
on this Buddhist monk too
in his robe with hemp sleeves

In his book, *Dōgen no waka* (Dōgen's waka), Akio Matsumoto (松本章男) assumes this waka is about the annual Shinto event at the end of summer, on the thirtieth day of the sixth month at the Kamo shrines in Kyoto.[403] Matsumoto suggests Dōgen composed the poem while he was in Kyoto at this festival. Although he was a Buddhist monk, Dōgen asks for mercy from the Shinto gods.

Buddhism was officially introduced to Japan in the sixth century CE. Initially there were some conflicts between people who supported Buddhism and others who thought they should not worship what they perceived to be a foreign god (the Buddha). However, Buddhism and Shintoism quickly became syncretized. By the time of Dōgen, this blending of the two religions had become part of Japanese culture. As in other Asian Buddhist countries, Japanese Buddhism did not fight against the country's native folk beliefs, in this case what we now call Shinto. Some people thought of Shinto gods as living beings who were still transmigrating in saṃsāra and wanted to take refuge in Buddhism to be released into nirvana. Others saw Shinto gods as manifestations of buddhas, bodhisattvas, or Buddhist guardian deities, an idea called *honji suijaku* (本地垂迹; literally "manifestations of the original ground"). Many Shinto shrines included Buddhist temples, and many temples had shrines. This mingling continued until the second half of the nineteenth century, when the Meiji government intervened to separate Shintoism and Buddhism under a policy called *shinbutsu bunri* (神仏分離). Because Buddhism originated outside Japan, the government concluded it was not useful in promoting nationalism.

As this poem shows, Dōgen was not opposed to Shinto. Instead, it seems that for him and many other Japanese people, Shinto was not seen as a distinct religion but simply a Japanese way of life.

27
おろかなる	*oroka naru*
心一つの	*kokoro hitotsu no*
行く末を	*yukusue o*
六つの道とや	*mutsu no michi toya*
人の踏むらん	*hito no fumu ran*

As destinies driven only
by their ignorant minds
people seem to walk
the path of the six realms

One of Buddhism's best-known teachings is transmigration within the six realms of saṃsāra's cycle of rebirth (heavenly beings, human beings, fighting spirits, animals, hungry ghosts, and hell dwellers). "Destinies" here does not mean a kind of specific, predetermined fate, but rather that depending on the karma we create in this lifetime, we will be reborn in a particular realm in the next lifetime; this process will continue without release. This ceaseless movement is caused by the three poisonous minds of greed, anger, and ignorance. The Buddha taught the way of liberation from this cycle through the practice of the eightfold path.

The final word of the last line, *ran*, expresses a conjecture. In this waka, Dōgen says people "seem to walk" instead of concluding that they are actually walking the path of the six realms. Most likely he means that at least some of these people are intentionally walking the path of samsāra to carry out their bodhisattva practice based on their vows.

In "Sounds of Valley Streams, Colors of Mountains" (谿聲山色; Jp. "Keisei sanshoku"), Dōgen comments, "After having aroused the mind of awakening, even if they transmigrate within the six realms through the four kinds of birth, the causes and conditions of transmigration will become practices and vows for awakening."

Here, Dōgen points to one of the most important teachings of Mahāyāna Buddhism: the oneness of samsāra and nirvana. In his *Talk on the Wholehearted Practice of the Way* (辨道話; Jp. *Bendōwa*) Dōgen urges, "You should completely awaken to life-and-death as exactly nirvana. You can never speak of nirvana as outside life-and-death."[404] "Life-and-death" (生死; Jp. *shōji*) as a Buddhist term refers to samsāra: repeatedly being born, living, and dying.

In the *Shōbōgenzō* fascicle "Life-and-Death" (生死; Jp. "Shōji"), Dōgen explains:

Seeking after buddha outside life-and-death is like trying to go to Yue in the south with the front of our cart heading north or trying to see the northern stars [the Big Dipper] while facing south. If we seek buddha outside life-and-death, we accumulate the causes of life-and-death even more and lose the path of liberation. Just understand that life-and-death is itself nirvana and neither dislike life-and-death nor seek after nirvana. Only then can we be released from life-and-death.

28

足びきの	*ashibiki no*
山鳥の尾の	*yamadori no o no*
しだり尾の	*shidario no*

長長し夜も   *naganagashi yo mo*
明けてけるかな   *akete keru kana*

After the long, long night
as long as
the dragging tail of the copper pheasant
morning finally dawns!

Ashibiki no here is a pillow word that means "mountain;" originally it may have referred to the tiring process of climbing a mountain. *Yamadori* literally means mountain bird, but this word refers specifically to the copper pheasant (*Syrmaticus soemmerringii*), which has chestnut-colored plumage and a long tail. *Shidario* is the dragging tail of the bird.

The first four lines are an adaptation of a famous waka attributed to celebrated poet Kakinomoto Hitomaro (柿本人麿; d. 708 CE) and included in the famous compilation *One Hundred Poems by One Hundred Poets* (百人一首; Jp. *Hyakunin isshu*). Dōgen borrowed the first four lines of his waka from Hitomaro's but changed the last line: "*Ashibiki no / yamadori no o no / shidario no / naga-nagashi yo wo / hitori ka mo nemu*" (Must I sleep alone through the long night, as long as the tail of the copper pheasant?) It is said that male and female copper pheasants sleep separately, so Hitomaro's waka is about the loneliness of a couple or family living separately.

In Dōgen's waka, the "long night" refers to life-and-death—transmigration in the six realms of saṃsāra. Beings have been living a long time in the darkness of ignorance. Yet even such a long night driven by ignorance within saṃsāra ends with dawn, thanks to the study and practice of the Dharma and faith in Buddha's compassion. This is the common understanding of the phrase "long night" in Buddhism. It seems this waka expresses the surprise of seeing the morning beginning to dawn after the long night and the joy of the brightness of the sun. This is the turning point of our lives from the first and second noble truths to the third and fourth.

In *Dōgen's Extensive Record* (永平広録; Jp. *Eihei kōroku*) volume seven, "Dharma Discourse 479," Dōgen quotes a saying by the Buddha: "Life-and-death is long; life-and-death is short. If we rely on greed, anger, and foolishness, then [the cycle of suffering of] life-and-death is long. If we rely on precepts, samadhi, and wisdom, then this life-and-death is short."[405]

According to this saying, the dark night of ignorance need not be long. When we change the foundation of our lives from the three poisonous minds to the three basic practices (precepts, samadhi, and wisdom), then the transformation from night to day is actualized here and now.

In the *Shōbōgenzō* fascicle "Arousing the Mind of Awakening" (發菩提心; Jp. "Hotsu bodaishin"), Dōgen writes:

> Arousing the mind of awakening is first arousing the mind of ferrying others before oneself. . . . Having aroused this mind, we meet with innumerable buddhas and make offerings to them, we see buddhas and hear Dharmas, and further arouse the mind of awakening. It is like adding frost on snow. . . . When we compare *anuttara-samyak-sambodhi* (supreme awakening) with first arousing the mind of awakening, they are like the *kalpāgni* and the light of a firefly. However, when we arouse the mind of ferrying others across before ourselves, these two are not at all different. . . . This mind is neither one's self nor others; it does not come [from somewhere else]. However, after having aroused this mind, when we touch the great earth, everything becomes gold, and when we stir the great ocean, it becomes sweet dew.

Kalpāgni is a Sanskrit compound of the words for "aeon" (*kalpa*) and "fire" (*agni*); it refers to the fire that burns down the entire world at the end of the so-called *kalpa* of dissolution, the third of four *kalpas* in traditional Indian cosmology. There are four *kalpas* that comprise a full cyclic age: (1) the *kalpa* of creation, (2) the *kalpa* of abiding, (3) the *kalpa* of dissolution, and (4) the *kalpa* of nothingness. The *kalpāgni* is an unfathomably large fire on a universal scale, while the light of a firefly is tiny. Our first aspiration for awakening is as tiny as the flash of a firefly, whereas the Buddha's ultimate awakening is vast like *kalpāgni*, and yet the nature of these two is the same.

In the same text Dōgen adds, "Within this swiftness of the arising and perishing of transmigration in each *kṣaṇa*, if we arouse one single thought of ferrying others before ourselves, the eternal longevity [of the Tathagata] immediately manifests itself."[406]

These sayings show both sides of Dōgen's teaching—long, continuous practice on the one hand and immediate transformation on the other.

29

六つの道	*mutsu no michi*
遠近迷ふ	*ochikochi mayou*
輩は	*tomogara wa*
わが父ぞかし	*waga chichi zo kashi*
わが母ぞかし	*waga haha zo kashi*

Those fellow beings
who wander in delusion
here and there
within the six realms
are actually my mothers and fathers

The twentieth minor precept in the *Brahmā Net Sutra* (Ch. 梵網經, *Fànwǎng jīng*; Jp. 梵網経, *Bonmō kyō*) says the following:

My disciples, you should compassionately engage in the practice of releasing captive animals into the wild. All men have been our fathers, and all women our mothers. . . . If we were to slaughter and eat them, it would be the same as slaughtering and eating my own parents, as well as slaughtering [and eating] my own former body.[407]

Dōgen might have resonated personally with this understanding of all beings as one's family because of the sadness and loneliness of losing his mother when he was very young.

In *Shōbōgenzō zuimonki*, he wrote:

Filial piety and obedience are most important to carry out. Yet there is a difference between laypeople and home-leavers when it comes to performing filial piety. Laypeople keep the teachings in the *Classic of Filial Piety*, and so on, serve their parents while they are alive, and hold services after their deaths. All worldly people know this. Home-leavers abandon their debts of gratitude and enter the realm of nondoing. Within the family of nondoing, the manner [of paying off debts of gratitude] must not be limited to one particular person. Considering that we have debts of gratitude to all living beings just as we do to our own fathers and mothers, we must transmit all the merits of our good deeds throughout the [entire] Dharma world. We do not limit [the dedication of merit] specifically to our own parents and in this [one] lifetime. This is how we do not violate the Way of nondoing. In our continuous day-to-day practice and moment-to-moment study, simply following the Buddha Way is the true fulfillment of filial piety. . . .[However,] we should see that our debts of gratitude to all living beings are as important [as the debt to our parents].[408]

Although Dōgen said in *Zuimonki* that monks do not hold memorial services for their parents, in *Dōgen's Extensive Record* we find that Dōgen gave memorial Dharma discourses for his mother and father in his later years.[409]

30

賤士の	*shizunowo no*
垣根に春の	*kakine ni haru no*
立ちしより	*tachishi yori*
古せに生ふる	*furuse ni ouru*
若菜をぞつむ	*wakana o zo tsumu*

Even to the hedges
of humble gardens
spring has come
people gather young greens
in the ancient field

In the East Asian lunar calendar, spring begins on New Year's Day,
which corresponds to about February 10 in the Gregorian calendar.
This is the biggest celebration of the year for Japanese people. In Japan,
people used to count their age differently. At birth, they were already
considered one year old. On New Year's Day everyone became one
year older. In a sense, New Year's Day was everyone's birthday. Spring
and the new year come without discrimination even to humble homes.

"Gather young greens" refers to the custom of eating rice gruel
with seven kinds of young greens (春の七草; Jp. *haru no nana kusa*)
growing at that time of year. This custom still continues in Japan.

"The ancient field" is a translation of *furuno* (古野), which appeared
in Menzan's version of this poem instead of "ancient shallows" or
"ancient rapids" (古瀬; *furuse*) which appears in the Shunjusha text
and earlier manuscripts. To me, it makes more sense to gather greens
from a field rather than from a stream, but it is possible that *furuse* was
a specific place, or that he meant, "by the stream." Anyway, in inter-
preting this poem as an expression of Dharma, the contrast between
"young" and "ancient" is important.

In chapter fifteen of the *Lotus Sutra*, "Spring Up out of the Earth"
(従地湧出; Jp. "Jūchi yushutsu") there is a parable in which numberless old bodhisattvas rise from the earth. Shakyamuni Buddha says

these old bodhisattvas are his disciples. People wonder how the disciples can be so much older than Shakyamuni, like children older than their father. In the following chapter, Shakyamuni explains that his life span is eternal.

In the *Shōbōgenzō* fascicle titled "The Dharma Flowers Turn the Dharma Flower" (法華轉法華: Jp. "Hokke ten hokke"), Dōgen wrote: "In general, at the time of the Dharma flower, without fail the father is young and the son is old. It is not that the son is not the son, or that the father is not the father. We should just learn that truly the son is old and the father is young."

In this case, Dōgen likens the young father to our moment-by-moment practice, which gives birth to, or manifests, an old son, representing the eternal life of Shakyamuni's Dharma body. Shakyamuni said in the *Sutra on the Teachings Bequeathed by the Buddha* (佛遺教經; Ch. *Fóyíjiào jīng*; Jp. *Butsuyuikyō gyō*), "From now on all of my disciples must continuously practice. Then the Thus Come One's Dharma body will always be present and indestructible."[410]

31
早苗とる　　　*sanae toru*
春の始めの　　*haru no hajime no*
祈りには　　　*inori ni wa*
広瀬龍田の　　*hirose tatsuta no*
政をぞする　　*matsuri o zo suru*

At the beginning of spring
before transplanting rice seedlings
farmers hold festivals
praying to the gods of Hirose and Tatsuta shrines
for a fine harvest

This is another waka about Shinto practice. Hirose and Tatsuta shrines are both near one of the oldest and most famous temples in Japan, Hōryū-ji (法隆寺) in Nara. Suijin (水神; god of water) is enshrined in Hirose, and Fūjin (風神; god of wind) in Tatsuta. These are the guardian gods of agriculture. In early spring farmers would organize festivals to pray for a good harvest of rice. At these festivals, they performed plays about growing rice.

Following Menzan Zuihō's *Commentary on the Verses on the Way from Sanshō Peak* (傘松道詠聞解; Jp. *Sanshō dōei monge*), a commentary on Dōgen's waka collection, commentators in the Sōtō Zen tradition interpreted this waka as the bodhisattvas' prayer to the gods and buddhas for protection until their ultimate awakening (harvest) after arousing the mind of awakening (planting seedlings). The most important prayer for a bodhisattva is to pray for support from all beings to continue practicing and fulfill one's vows.

32

大空に	*ōzora ni*
心の月を	*kokoro no tsuki o*
ながむるも	*nagamuru mo*
闇に迷ひて	*yami ni mayoi te*
色にめでけり	*iro ni medekeri*

Despite beholding
the moon of the mind
in the great sky,
deluded in darkness
I praise its shape and color

"The moon of the mind" (*kokoro no tsuki*) is the key phrase in this waka. What is the meaning of "mind" here? As I discussed regarding the theme of the moon in waka number seventeen, the fascicle of the *Shōbōgenzō* called "Moon" (都機; Jp. "Tsuki") is helpful for understanding what Dōgen might have meant. In that fascicle, Dōgen quotes Zen Master Panshan Baoji's saying:

The mind-moon is alone and completely round. Its light swallows the myriad phenomenal things. The light does not illuminate objects. Nor do any objects exist. Light and objects simultaneously vanish. Then what is this?

The moonlight swallows all things; there is nothing outside it. This is what "alone and completely round" means.

In the *Shōbōgenzō* fascicle "The Mind Is Itself Buddha" (即心是仏; Jp. "Sokushin ze butsu"), Dōgen wrote the following:

The mind that has been authentically transmitted is "one mind is all Dharmas; all Dharmas are one mind." For this reason an ancient said, "When we understand the mind, there is not an inch of soil on the great earth." We should know that when we understand the mind, the entire sky is struck down and the whole earth is ripped apart.

Ōzora (大空) is literally the "great sky," but it also can mean "great emptiness." In the conception of mind discussed above, all things, both subject and objects, are included in it. "Great" means absolute, before separation between subjects (sense organs) and their objects. *Iro* (色) is "shape and color," but this kanji can also mean "form," as in "form and emptiness" in the *Heart Sutra*. We commonly appreciate the moon in the sky as an object of our eyes and entertainment for our mind, and we may feel joy or sadness. However, Dōgen says this perception is merely delusion in the darkness.

We can interpret this waka in two ways. It could be an admonishment to people who see the moon merely as an object of their minds, and an expression of Dōgen's regret for his own limited perception. Most commentators interpret the waka in this way. The other possibility is to understand the poem as a reflection of Dōgen's appreciation of the beautiful moon as an object of his mind, as it is expressed in many other of his waka poems.

In this case, "deluded in darkness" is not really negative. It is like returning to delusion from great realization, as in the fascicle of the *Shōbōgenzō* "Great Realization" (大悟; Jp. "Daigo"). Great realization is seeing the ultimate truth of emptiness, equality, and oneness beyond discrimination. Yet being caught up and staying there is not our practice. We return to delusion and function by embracing the conventional and relative reality as our daily lives.

Waka number thirty-nine also supports both of these interpretations:

花紅葉	*hana momiji*
冬の白雪	*fuyu no shirayuki*
見ることも	*miru koto mo*
思へばくやし	*omoeba kuyashi*
色にめでけり	*iro ni medekeri*

Seeing flowers in spring
crimson leaves in autumn
and white snow in winter
I regret having appreciated them
as objects of my feelings

In this waka, Dōgen changes "mind-moon" to the beauty of spring, autumn, and winter. Yet as in waka number thirty-two, I do not feel he sincerely regrets appreciating the many beauties of the seasons as objects. Waka number fifty-three, Dōgen's final waka—about the harvest moon shortly before his death—is the same.

Both interpretations might be true: although Dōgen felt some regret for objectifying the world's beauty in his perception and his poetry, he was also deeply grateful that he could appreciate it. As long as human beings live, we naturally interpret the world as an object of our senses, and this kind of perception, which is our delusion, leads us both to further delusion and to joy. This is one aspect of awakening to the human nature of bodhisattvas, who are ordinary human beings even though they are living by bodhisattva vows.

33

安名尊	*ana touto*
七の仏の	*nana no hotoke no*
ふる言は	*furu kotoba*
学ぶに六つの	*namabu ni mutsu no*
道に越えたり	*michi ni koetari*

How venerable
the seven buddhas'
ancient words!
Studying them
we go beyond the six realms

"Seven buddhas" refers to Shakyamuni and the six buddhas prior to him. The idea of seven buddhas (Skt. *saptatathāgata*) appears in the Pali *Nikāyas* and Chinese *Āgamas* and thus probably pre-dates Mahāyāna Buddhism. *Furu kotoba* ("ancient words") refers to the admonitions that were taught by the seven buddhas. The most well-known of these is by Kāśyapa Buddha, the sixth buddha: "Do not what is evil. Do what is good. Keep your mind pure. This is the teaching of Buddha."[411] This verse also appears in the *Dhammapada*.

The *Dhammapada* includes another verse: "Some people are born on this earth; those who do evil are reborn in hell; the righteous go to heaven; but those who are pure reach Nirvana."[412] The traditional understanding of these verses is that the first two lines on not doing evil and doing good are about transmigration within saṃsāra based on cause and effect, and the third line about keeping one's mind pure is the teaching of going beyond saṃsāra and entering nirvana.

Dōgen wrote a fascicle of the *Shōbōgenzō* titled "Not Doing Evil" (諸悪莫作; Jp. "Shoaku makusa"). At the very beginning, he quotes this verse and comments:

This teaching, as the general precept of the ancestral school from the seven buddhas, has been authentically transmitted from former buddhas to later buddhas, and later buddhas have received its transmission from former buddhas. It is not only of the seven buddhas: it is the teaching of all buddhas.

He continues,

This being so, when we study the supreme unsurpassable true awakening (*anuttarā-samyak-sambodhi*), when we hear the teachings, practice, and verify the results, it is profound, far-reaching, and wondrous. We hear of this supreme awakening, sometimes following a teacher and sometimes following the sutras. At the beginning, it sounds like, "Do not do any evil." If we do not hear "Do not do any evil," it is not the true Dharma of buddhas; it must be the suggestion of demons. We should know that which says "Do not do any evil" as the true Dharma of buddhas.

In this passage, we see that Dōgen interprets the teachings in the verse as an integration of two sets of teachings: the worldly Dharma (Skt. *laukika*) of causality based on good and evil actions, and the ultimate awakening beyond the six realms (Skt. *lokottara*). Bodhisattvas go beyond saṃsāra yet they do not escape from saṃsāra, just as a lotus flower blooms beyond the surface of the muddy water while its roots are still in that water.

34
本末も   *moto sue mo*
皆偽の   *mina itsuwari no*
つくもがみ   *tsukumo gami*
思ひ乱るる   *omoi midaruru*
夢をこそ説け   *yume o koso toke*

> From beginning to end
> everything is unreal
> as white tangled hair shows
> even while confused by conflicting emotions
> we should clarify this as a dream

Itsuwari means false, untrue, or fictitious. I translate this word here as "unreal." This means that everything is without any fixed self-nature, and therefore everything is changing all the time.

Tsukumogami is old people's white, tangled hair, which symbolizes impermanence and emptiness. This word is written in kanji as 九十九髪. This is a play on words. 髪 (*kami*; here "*gami*" due to the compound causing a sounds shift) is hair. 九十九 means "ninety-nine," signifying very old people. In kanji, "one hundred" is 百. Ninety-nine is one hundred minus one. When we remove the character that means "one" (一) from the top of the character that means "hundred" (百), the result is the character for "white" (白).

Our lives change just as the color of our hair changes. We cannot naturally have our original hair color again or become young again. When we look back, our youth seems as unreal as a dream. Within our dream-like lives, we are always confused by conflicting emotions and various thoughts coming and going. We worry about so many things as if they were real. Particularly in our old age, what we did when we were young seems like a dream, and often we feel sad reflecting on it. We may even think we are no good anymore.

The end of the *Diamond Sutra* includes the following:

> All conditioned things are
> like a dream, a phantom, a bubble, a shadow,
> like a dewdrop,
> and also like a flash of lightning.
> We should see them thus.[413]

In *Verses on the Way from Sanshō Peak* (傘松道詠; Jp. *Sanshō dōei*), the collection of Dōgen Zenji's waka compiled and edited by Menzan Zuihō, the title of this waka is "Clarifying the Dream within the Dream" (夢中説夢; Jp. "Muchū setsumu"). Dōgen composed a fascicle of the *Shōbōgenzō* with this same title, where he wrote, "This place of clarifying the dream within the dream is the homeland of buddhas and ancestors and the assemblies of buddhas and ancestors." When we dream, we believe that what we see and think is real. However, when we awaken to the reality of impermanence and no fixed self, or emptiness, we can clearly see everything is like a dream.

35

夏冬も	*natsu fuyu mo*
思ひに分ぬ	*omoi ni wakanu*
越の山	*koshi no yama*
降る白雪も	*furu shirayuki mo*
鳴るいかづちも	*naru ikazuchi mo*

Whether summer or winter
Koshi's mountain
is free of discrimination
it sees equally
the falling of white snowflakes
and the roaring of thunder

The mountain of Koshi (越の山) may refer to the sacred Mt. Hakusan (白山; literally "white mountain"). Koshi was the old name of the large area in the Hokuriku region (北陸地方; *Hokuriku chihō*) that included the provinces of Echizen, Kaga, Etchū, and Echigo. In ancient times, the mountain was called Koshi no Shirane (越白嶺; meaning "the white peak of Koshi") because this mountain peak turned white earlier than the lower mountains and remained white even after snow disappeared elsewhere. Since the Nara period (eighth century CE), Hakusan has been considered a sacred mountain in *shugendō* (修験道), the Japanese mountain tradition of asceticism and shamanism, which incorporates both Shinto and Buddhist concepts. Near Eihei-ji, a temple named Heisen-ji (平泉寺) was one of the three starting points of a trail to climb Hakusan.

There is a story in Dōgen's biography, the *Record of Kenzei* (建撕記; Jp. *Kenzei ki*), regarding the god enshrined on Hakusan called Myōri Daigongen (白山妙理大権現). The day before Dōgen returned to Japan from China, he tried to copy the *Blue Cliff Record* (Ch. 碧巌録, *Bìyán lù*; Jp. 碧巌録, *Hekigan roku*). Because it was a large text, he did not have enough time to finish it. In the night, Myōri Daigongen appeared and helped Dōgen copy the text. Later in Sōtō Zen tradition, Myōri Daigongen was taken to be the guardian god of Eihei-ji.

The sacred mountain Hakusan does not discriminate between summer and winter. The mountain is immovable, accepting all the different conditions of the four seasons, including roaring thunder in summer and snow in winter.

This waka reminds me of what Dōgen wrote in *Instructions for the Cook* (典座教訓; Jp. *Tenzo kyōkun*): "As for what is called magnanimous mind, this mind is like the great mountains or like the great ocean; it is not biased or contentious mind. . . . The four seasons cooperate in a single scene; regard light and heavy with a single eye."[414]

36
都には	*miyako niwa*
紅葉しぬらん	*momiji shinuran*
奥山は	*okuyama wa*
こよいも今朝も	*koyoi mo kesa mo*
霰ふりけり	*arare furikeri*

The capital city
must still blaze with tinted autumn leaves;
in this deep mountain
hailstones this morning
hailstones this evening

This waka might have been composed in the tenth lunar month (which can begin anywhere from late October to early November) of 1243, the beginning of the first winter after Dōgen and his disciples moved from Kōshō-ji in Kyoto to Echizen province. Just like waka number six, this poem may express the surprise he felt due to the different weather.

In Japanese, a small hailstone is called *arare*. Such hailstones often appear in early winter or spring when the temperature hovers around freezing, that is, not too cold. Along the coast of the Sea of Japan, these small hailstones were a precursor to a long, dark, snowy winter. Particularly for Dōgen, who had lived in Kyoto most of his life, this must have been a change.

Kōdō Sawaki Rōshi interpreted Dōgen's contrast between his experience in the capital city and the deep mountains as the mundane world versus the world of zazen. In the everyday world, all kinds of different things are happening rapidly inside and outside of us, and we run this way and that without a decisive direction. In zazen, when we turn our light inward and illuminate our selves, everything is equally one color—"white" like the hailstone—and each moment is eternity. As in waka number six, Dōgen uses white to symbolize reality beyond discrimination or multiplicity. White can also represent purity. In Chinese Zen texts, black or darkness is more often used to refer to nondiscriminatory reality.

37

我が庵は	*waga io wa*
越の白山	*koshi no shirayama*
冬籠り	*fuyu gomori*
氷も雪も	*koori mo yuki mo*
雲かかりけり	*kumo kakari keri*

My grass hermitage
in the white mountains of Echizen
during winter retreat
ice and snow are covered in clouds

As previously noted, Koshi is another name for the area that included Echizen province, where Eihei-ji is located. This poem probably describes the middle of the first winter after Dōgen moved from Kyoto, a little after the time when the previous poem was composed.

When the wind coming from Siberia crosses the Sea of Japan and strikes the mountains, it then rises, freezes, and falls as snow. Thus, the regions facing the Sea of Japan receive heavy snow every winter. Sometimes they get more than ten feet at once, which can bury entire towns.

This must have been gloomy scenery for Dōgen and his monks from Kyoto. Before Eihei-ji was built, they lived in Yoshimine-dera (吉峯寺), a small, old temple without a kitchen and located on the top of a mountain. It is said that Tettsu Gikai (徹通義介; 1219–1309 CE), later the third abbot of Eihei-ji, was the head cook (典座; Jp. *tenzo*) at that time. Even in the snow, he had to carry food up the steep hill from the house where it was cooked. In these difficult conditions Dōgen Zenji wrote about thirty fascicles of the *Shōbōgenzō* before moving into the newly built temple of Daibutsu-ji (later renamed Eihei-ji) in the autumn of 1244.

The snowy mountains of Echizen province are often hidden by thick, gray clouds. In his Dharma talk on this waka, Kōdō Sawaki Rōshi commented that "winter retreat in the white mountains" is our zazen.[415] Ice and snow refer to negative conditions of our minds, and the clouds are emptiness. Although negative mental states influenced by the three poisonous minds can become frozen and persist, they are always enveloped in a cloud of *prajñā* that knows the emptiness of all things. This zazen mountain is far from the city of saṃsāra; it can be cold and gloomy but still serene and quiet, free of the noise of delusion.

38

あづさ弓	*azusa yumi*
春暮れ果つる	*haru kure hatsuru*
今日の日を	*kyo no hi o*
引き留めつつ	*hikitodome tsutsu*
をちこちやらん	*ochikochi yaran*

> Holding this day dear
> at the end of spring
> working on this or that
> here and there

As in waka number twenty-five, the phrase *azusayumi* is used to indicate spring. This poem describes people working hard on the last day of the third month, which is the end of spring. *Hikitodomu* means to prevent something or someone from leaving. I translate this as "holding this day dear." *Ochikochi* literally means "distant and close"— "here and there" in terms of space, or "present and future" in terms of time. Dōgen Zenji compassionately thinks of everyone working hard on the final days of spring to complete things that should be done before summer comes.

The end of spring in the East Asian lunar calendar corresponds to about May 10 in the Gregorian calendar. The beginning of spring and the New Year—around February 10 in the Gregorian calendar— is the coldest time of year. Particularly in Echizen province where Dōgen Zenji lived, snow is typical until the end of March. Therefore, even though the first three months of the year are spring according to the calendar, the actual feeling of springtime is very short. The most beautiful time of year is midspring, around the equinox, with many flowers, especially cherry blossoms, in the mountains and fields. People are released from the cold weather and relax and enjoy the beauty of the season.

Right after this brief respite, in late spring, farmers have to work hard to prepare for the growing season. They have many things to take care of, including the planting of the rice fields, before the rainy season begins. Thus farmers hold the end of spring dear, wishing its days were longer.

At Zen monasteries this is also a busy time. The summer practice period begins soon, on the fifteenth day of the fourth month, around the end of May. Monks are busy preparing for ninety days of intense practice during the hot and humid summer. Since many monks change roles among departments, they have to learn new skills. New training monks begin to arrive for the practice period. Senior monks have to train the young monks to be ready to practice with everyone, following the rules, forms, and procedures.

There is another manuscript in which this waka's last line reads *ochikochi yasen*, meaning "wandering here and there." In this scenario, Dōgen Zenji, cherishing the beautiful scenery, strolls here and there to savor the last moments of spring.

39
花紅葉   *hana momiji*
冬の白雪   *fuyu no shirayuki*
見ることも   *miru koto mo*
思へばくやし   *omoeba kuyashi*
色にめでけり   *iro ni medekeri*

Seeing flowers in spring
crimson leaves in autumn
and white snow in winter
I regret having appreciated them
as objects of my feelings

See the commentary for waka thirty-two, which includes my comments on this poem.

40
草庵に   *kusa no io ni*
起きてもねても   *okite mo nete mo*
申すこと   *mōsu koto*
われより先に   *ware yori saki ni*
人を渡さん   *hito o watasan*

In my grass hut
standing or lying down
I constantly say:
I vow to ferry others
before myself

Mōsu (申す) is a humble form of the verb of "to say" or "to speak."
Dōgen is vowing this to the Three Treasures. The first three lines of
this waka are almost the same as waka number nineteen:

In my grass hut
sleeping or waking
I always recite
"I take refuge in Shakyamuni Buddha;
bestow your compassion upon us"

And the meaning of the last two lines is the same as waka 20:

Even though because I'm dull-witted
I won't become a buddha
I wish to be a monk
helping all living beings
cross over

In *Shōbōgenzō* "Arousing the Mind of Awakening" (發菩提心; Jp.
"Hotsu bodaishin"), Dōgen Zenji quotes a verse from the *Mahāyāna
Mahāparinirvāṇa Sūtra* (大般涅槃經; Jp. *Dai hatsunehan gyō*) in which
Kāśyapa Bodhisattva praises Shakyamuni Buddha:

Arousing the mind of awakening and the mind of the ultimate
stage are not different; between these two stages of mind, the
former is more difficult to arouse. It is the mind of ferrying
others across before oneself. For this reason, I respectfully make
prostrations to those who first aroused the mind of awakening.

When they first arouse the mind of awakening, they are already the teachers of human and heavenly beings. They are superior to *śrāvakas* and *pratyekabuddhas*. Arousing such a mind of awakening surpasses the triple world. Therefore, it can be called the unsurpassable.

"Arousing the mind of awakening" is one of the key phrases in Dōgen's teaching. According to his writings there are three aspects to the way the mind of awakening functions. It functions as compassion, as he writes in this poem and in *Shōbōgenzō* "Arousing the Mind of Awakening." It also functions as wisdom through the perception of impermanence. Another way it operates is by transmitting and maintaining the traditional way of practice.

In *Points to Watch in Practicing the Way* (学道用心集; Jp. *Gakudō yōjin-shū*), Dōgen writes about the mind of awakening as wisdom:

The Ancestral Master Nāgārjuna said that the mind that solely sees the impermanence of this world of constant appearance and disappearance is called bodhi-mind. . . . Truly, when you see impermanence, egocentric mind does not arise; neither does desire for fame and profit.[416]

Dōgen explained the third aspect of the mind of awakening in *Pure Standards for the Temple Administrators* (知事清規; Jp. *Chiji shingi*):

What is called the mind of the Way is not to abandon or scatter the great Way of the buddha ancestors, but deeply to protect and esteem their great Way. . . . After all, not to sell cheaply or debase the worth of the ordinary tea and rice of the buddha ancestors' house is exactly the mind of the Way.[417]

Both "mind of the Way" (道心; Jp. *dōshin*) and "mind of awakening" or "bodhi-mind" (菩提心; Jp. *bodaishin*) are translations of

Sino-Japanese terms that were originally used to translate the Sanskrit word *bodhicitta*.

41
徒らに   *itazura ni*
過す月日は   *sugosu tsukihi wa*
多けれど   *ōkeredo*
道をもとむる   *michi o motomuru*
時ぞすくなき   *toki zo sukunaki*

Though we idle away
many days and nights
the times we seek the way
are so rare

In my commentary on the previous poem, I introduced the three aspects of arousing the mind of awakening: compassion, or helping all living beings arouse the mind of awakening; wisdom in realizing impermanence and not wasting time; and maintaining the tradition by esteeming and protecting daily activities within the buddha-ancestors' great Way.

Even though we arouse the mind of awakening by witnessing the sickness, aging, or death of people close to us, or through our own experiences of facing the reality of impermanence, we often lose sight of this truth and are distracted by all of the miscellaneous things that are attractive to us. Although we understand we have no time to waste, we often want to escape facing impermanence and seek something that gives us temporary excitement and joy even when we know such things will not give us a stable foundation for our lives. On top of that, we have many responsibilities and obligations to our families, work, and society. We forget the Way, and either let ourselves become too lazy or too busy to do anything meaningful.

We need to reflect on how to build a stable foundation for our lives. In *Shōbōgenzō zuimonki* section 3-14, Dōgen instructed:

It goes without saying that you must consider the inevitability of death. . . . Even if we do not consider this [right now], we should resolve not to waste time and to refrain from doing meaningless things. We should spend our time carrying out that which is worth carrying out. Among the things we should do, the most important thing is to understand that all deeds other than those performed by buddhas and ancestors are useless.

What Dōgen addresses here is the third aspect of the mind of awakening. This is his admonition to monks practicing at his monastery. Monastic practice is designed to maintain the traditional way of life. Some practices originated from Indian Buddhist monasticism, while others are from customs in Chinese or Japanese Zen monasteries. These include zazen, various services and ceremonies, work to support community life, and the study of Dharma, among other things. Dōgen encourages monks to maintain these practices without being diverted by personal desires or ties to the mundane world.

Most American Zen practitioners do not live in monasteries. We need to consider how to spend our daily lives without wasting time. Although "not wasting time" sounds like always working hard, pursuing more and more efficiency like workaholics, in fact, being mindful and peaceful here and now with what we are doing is a practice that is deeply intimate with the Way.

42

いただきに	*itadaki ni*
鵲巣をや	*kasasagi su o ya*
つくるらん	*tsukuru ran*
眉にかかれり	*mayu ni kakareri*
蜘蛛のいと	*sasagani no ito*

On his head
a magpie might make its nest

a spider's web is
hanging from his eyebrows

Itadaki means "crown of the head" or "mountain summit." Here, it refers to the crown of the head of a person who is sitting zazen. *Kasasagi* means "magpie," a bird related to crows that is found in many parts of the world. In Europe, this bird generally has a negative association. It has been demonized in some countries. However, in China and Korea the magpie is considered a bird of good fortune. In Japan, it is said this bird was imported from Korea in the sixteenth century. Since then magpies have lived in various places in western Japan. Probably Dōgen did not have a chance to see this bird with his own eyes except when he was living in China, but its name appears in Buddhist texts.

Ran is a particle that attaches to verbs to express conjecture. In this waka, Dōgen did not actually see the bird making a nest. *Sasagani* literally means "little crab," but here it refers to a spider. A spider is called a little crab probably because it has many legs and a crab-like walk. *Kakareri* here is a statement that does not express any conjecture; Dōgen suggests that he actually sees the spider's web hanging from the eyebrow of the person sitting.

In the *Record of the Transmission of the Light* (伝光録; Jp. *Denkōroku*), Keizan Jōkin (瑩山紹瑾; 1268–1325 CE) wrote about Shakyamuni Buddha's practice after he left his father's palace:

Shakyamuni Buddha was of the Sun Race in India. At the age of nineteen he leaped over the palace walls in the dead of night, and at Mount Dantaloka, he cut off his hair. Subsequently, he practiced austerities for six years. Later, he sat on the Adamantine Seat, where spiders spun webs in his eyebrows and magpies built a nest on top of his head. Reeds grew up between his legs as he sat tranquilly and erect without movement for six years. At the age of thirty, on the eighth day of the twelfth month, as the morning star appeared, he was suddenly enlightened.[418]

In the *Record of the Hōkyō Era* (宝慶記; Jp. *Hōkyō ki*), Dōgen recorded his master Tiantong Rujing's saying about zazen and dropping off body and mind (身心脱落; Jp. *shinjin datsuraku*):

> The zazen of arhats and pratyekabuddhas is free of attachment, yet it lacks great compassion. Their zazen is therefore different from the zazen of the buddhas and ancestors; the zazen of buddhas and ancestors places primary importance on great compassion and the vow to save all living beings. . . . In buddhas' and ancestors' zazen, they wish to gather all Buddhadharma from the time they first arouse bodhi-mind. Buddhas and ancestors do not forget or abandon living beings in their zazen; they offer a heart of compassion even to an insect. Buddhas and ancestors vow to save all living beings and dedicate all the merit of their practice to all living beings.[419]

The source of both Keizan's description of Shakyamuni's practice at Mt. Dantaloka and Rujing's statement about compassion in buddhas' and ancestors' zazen seems to be the *Great Perfection of Wisdom Treatise* (Skt. *Mahāprajñāpāramitā-śāstra*; 大智度論; Ch. *Dàzhìdù lùn*; Jp. *Daichido ron*), a commentary attributed to Nāgārjuna (fl. second or third century CE) on the *25,000-line Perfection of Wisdom Sutra* (Skt. *Pañcaviṃśatisāhasrikā Prajñāpāramitā Sūtra*). Right after the statement (as repeated by Rujing above) that buddhas and ancestors do not forget compassion toward all living beings, including insects, Nāgārjuna refers to a story about a mountain sage who was Shakyamuni in one of his past lives. Shakyamuni was then called Rakei Sennin (螺髻仙人), which means "sage with hair like a conch shell." While he was sitting immovably in an upright posture like a tree, a magpie made a nest on his head and laid eggs. The sage thought that if he stopped sitting and moved, the mother bird would be frightened and not return, and the baby birds would die. Therefore, he continued to sit without moving until the mother and baby birds flew away.

This story emphasizes that the Buddha practiced with all living beings, including birds and insects, and tried not to frighten or harm them. Even while he was sitting, he considered living beings part of his life.

A modern commentator, Nanboku Ōba (大場南北), has suggested Dōgen wrote this waka when he saw a Buddha statue in an old shrine hall, probably by the roadside.[420] Perhaps since the shrine had not been cleaned for a long time, the statue was covered with dust, and Dōgen found a spider's web on its face. Then he remembered the story of Rakei Sennin and imagined a magpie making a nest on the crown of the Buddha's head.

Since waka are short, it is not possible to describe situations in detail. Readers need to use their imaginations to help interpret such poems.

43

声づから   *Koe zukara*
耳の聞ゆる   *mimi no kikoyuru*
時されば   *toki sareba*
吾が友ならん   *waga tomo naran*
かたらひぞなき   *katarai zo naki*

At the moment
my ears hear voices
as they are
everyone I speak with
is my friend

Waga tomo naran means "that which is not my friend," and *katarai zo naki* means "there is no one I talk with." This is a double negative; its literal translation is "There is no one I talk with who is not my friend." In *Shōbōgenzō* "Genjōkōan," Dōgen says:

To study the Buddha Way is to study the self. To study the self is to forget the self. To forget the self is to be verified by all things. To be verified by all things is to let the body and mind of the self, and the body and mind of others, drop off. There is a trace of realization that cannot be grasped. We endlessly keep expressing this ungraspable trace of realization.[421]

The time of dropping off body and mind of self and others is when we hear a voice or sound as it is, without our fictitious interpretation and self-centered judgment. This is when we are released from clinging to our own five aggregates (material elements, sensations, perceptions, formations, and consciousness)—that is, our body and mind. Colors and shapes are seen as they are; sounds and voices are heard as they are.

When we are not released from clinging to the five aggregates, contact with the objects of our sense organs causes pleasant, unpleasant, or neutral sensations. According to Buddhist teaching, perceptions form out of these sensations, and we consequently develop preferences, pursue what we like and flee from what we do not. This is why we perform wholesome or unwholesome actions that produce good or bad karma, eventually making our lives into saṃsāra—we are always chasing after things we want and trying to escape things we do not want. Our life goes up and down depending on whether we are successful or not—whether our desires are satisfied or not. We lose the stable foundation of our lives.

When we see the emptiness of ourselves and the objects of our sense organs, we are released from this transmigration. We discover a stable way of life. Through our eyes, we see the Buddha's Dharma body appear; through our ears, we hear the Buddha's voice. We discover that everything we encounter is the Dharma that shows us reality, rather than a mere object of our greedy desire or hatred.

"Hearing sound as it is" is not some mystical way of hearing, but rather letting go, moment by moment, of the thoughts and feelings triggered by our contact with objects. We refrain from making concepts about objects and taking action based on these concepts.

For example, in autumn we hear the chorus of insects during early morning and evening zazen. In Japanese poetry, we call such sounds

mushi-shigure (虫時雨). *Mushi* means "insect," and *shigure* is "inter-
mittent drizzling rain," particularly in autumn or early winter. The
insects' chorus is like the sound of rainfall. This reminds me of a short
phrase in a traditional Japanese song that I heard on a radio program
many years ago when I was a student. I only remember the phrase
that goes, "*Ware mo mushi naru mushi shigure*"—which means "Within
the chorus of insect sounds, I, too, am an insect." The person hearing
the insects singing feels at one with them.

When we simply hear sounds, we do not feel separation between
subject and object. There is no trace of "I" as a subject, "hearing"
as an activity, or "the sound" as an object. This is intimate hearing
before the separation between listener and sound. We are simply sitting and insects are just chirping without any interaction—we are living together as intimate friends within the network of interdependent
origination.

Not only in zazen, but when we meet people, if we hear their
voices as they are, without prejudice or judgments about them—
whether they are good or bad people, friends or enemies—we can
see the possibility of being friends on the grounds of interdependent
origination, even if we have different opinions.

44

草の庵	*kusa no io*
夏の初めの	*natsu no hajime no*
衣がへ	*koromogae*
涼しき簾	*suzushiki sudare*
かかるばかりぞ	*kakaru bakari zo*

Grass hermitage
beginning of summer
time of changing clothes
only a cool bamboo blind hangs

Io (or *iori*) is a "small hermitage," rather than a temple or monastery. This poem might have been written during Dōgen's first summer in Echizen province, in 1244. Because the temple Daibutsu-ji (later renamed Eihei-ji) had not yet been constructed, he called his simple dwelling a hermitage.

Beginning in the Heian era in Japan (794–1185 CE), people at the emperor's court changed their wardrobes from winter to summer clothes at the start of the fourth lunar month. In the Kamakura era (1192–1333 CE), when Dōgen lived, this custom became more widespread. Even today, in Japanese schools, companies, government offices, and Buddhist temples, people change to summer clothing on June 1, around the time of the fourth lunar month.

Today at Sōtō Zen monasteries, in winter a thick curtain is hung at the entrance to the monks' hall to conserve heat. In June, the curtain is changed to a bamboo blind, allowing cool breezes in. There are many other such changes the monks make to live comfortably during the hot and humid summers.

In his small hermitage, Dōgen simply hung a bamboo blind so fresh air could enter. This final line suggests little separation between inside and outside.

45

心とて	kokoro tote
人に見すべき	hito ni misubeki
色ぞなき	iro zo naki
只露霜の	tada tsuyushimo no
結ぶのみにて	musubu nomi nite

No form
to show as my mind
only dew-frost
forms

Kokoro (心) is "mind." *Iro* (色) is "color," but as discussed in waka number eight, the same character can also mean "form." It is therefore also possible to translate these lines as "There is no color to show people as my mind." *Tsuyu* is "dew," and *shimo* is "frost." Usually these are interpreted as two different things: dew is made up of water droplets condensed on a surface when the temperature falls below the dew point, usually in late summer through autumn, while frost forms when the temperature drops below freezing in late autumn and winter.

However, Keizan Jōkin (瑩山紹瑾;1268–1325 CE), the fourth-generation descendant of Dōgen and founder of Sōji-ji (總持寺), thought in this case *tsuyushimo* was one word (dew-frost). He quoted this waka by Dōgen in the Dharma words (法語; Jp. *hōgo*) he wrote to his patron, Myōjō (妙淨). Keizan said, "At the end of autumn or the beginning of winter, we see *tsuyushimo*, which is neither dew nor frost."[422] The only thing formed is something between forms.

Depending on the subtle differences in temperature during the transition from autumn to winter, water on a leaf becomes dew, frost, or frozen dew (white dew). If the temperature falls to freezing after dewdrops are formed, they become frozen dew, which is not crystallized like frost. Here are three similar yet distinct phenomena: autumn/winter, dew/frost, and halfway between them. The moment is neither autumn nor winter, and we see something that is neither exactly dew nor frost. By what name should we call this moment and phenomenon?

Dōgen Zenji says in *Shōbōgenzō zuimonki*:

Originally, the human mind is neither good nor evil. Good and evil arise depending on conditions. For example, when people arouse the mind of awakening and enter a mountain forest, they think that a dwelling in the woods is good and the human world is bad. And when their aspiration has waned and they leave the mountain forest, they think the mountain forest is bad. This is because the human mind has no fixed characteristics; it changes in this way or that, influenced by circumstances. Consequently, if we encounter good conditions, the mind becomes good. If bad conditions draw near, the mind becomes bad. Do not think that the mind is fundamentally evil. We should simply follow good circumstances.[423]

Because our minds have no fixed form but depend on our surroundings, Dōgen Zenji encourages his students to befriend good people, listen to them, and do good with them. Then our minds are influenced by them and become good. It is like walking in the mist; our clothing gets wet little by little without our noticing. Kōdo Sawaki Rōshi, my teacher's teacher, said we have both Buddha-nature and thief-nature. When we are beginner bodhisattvas, even though we have aroused the mind of awakening and taken the bodhisattva vows and precepts, our mind is not yet stable. Depending upon the situation, our mind may become frozen, and we may take actions expressing our thief-nature. However, when conditions change, our mind thaws and becomes flexible, open, and warm. It is important for us to try to put ourselves in good circumstances and with good people.

46
如何なるか   *ika naru ka*
仏と謂うと   *hotoke to iu to*
人間はば   *hito towaba*
かいやか下に   *kaiya ga shita ni*
つららいにけり   *tsurara i ni keri*

If someone asked me,
What is Buddha?
I'd say there's ice
under the *kaiya*

The first half of this waka is not difficult at all. This is a simple question asking what Buddha is. But the answer to this question is difficult to understand because it is not clear what *kaiya* refers to. It is said this is an old word from the time of the *Man'yōshū* (万葉集, literally *Collection of Ten Thousand Leaves*), the oldest collection of waka poems that was compiled in the eighth century. According to traditional commentaries, *ya* means "roof" (屋) or a structure like a hut or shack, but there are three possible meanings for the entire word: deer fire hut (鹿火屋), mosquito fire hut (蚊火屋), and silkworm hut (蚕屋). The first possible meaning is a hut used to make a fire at night to chase deer away in order to protect vegetables or grains. The second possibility refers to the fact that mosquitoes and other insects will come to a fire, as in a proverb that says, "Of their own accord, summer insects fly to their death in the flame." And the third possibility is that the word refers to a silkworm hut which needs to be kept warm with fires built by silkworm farmers.

Dōgen Zenji wrote a fascicle in the *Shōbōgenzō* called "The King Seeks *Saindhava*" (王索仙陀婆; Jp. "Ō saku sendaba"). For us, *kaiya* is like this Sanskrit word *saindhava*, which has four different meanings: water, salt, cup, and horse. The fascicle is about the story of a servant who needed to figure out exactly what his king was asking for, depending on the context. If the king asked for *saindhava* when he wanted to wash his face, the servant gave him some water. If the king asked during a meal, the servant gave him salt. After eating, the servant offered a cup to drink from. When the king wanted to go out, the servant brought a horse. The wise servant knew what the word meant depending on what the king was doing at that moment. However, we do not know what *kaiya* meant, because we do not know what Dōgen was seeing or thinking when he wrote this waka. So we need to guess.

In modern Japanese, *tsurara* refers to an icicle, but according to a dictionary of Japanese archaisms, in Classical Japanese before the Tokugawa period (1603–1868 CE), an icicle was called *taruhi* (垂氷; literally "hanging ice"), while *tsurara* referred to ice in general. However, I do not understand how ice could form underneath a hut or shack the way it is presented here.

In this waka there are two opposites that cannot exist together: fire and ice. The traditional commentaries interpreted this as showing the interpenetration of *ji* (事) and *ri* (理), or *hen* (偏) and *shō* (正), which refer to absolute and conventional reality, or principle and phenomenon. The commentaries quote a saying by Master Caoshan Benji (曹山本寂; Jp. Sōzan Honjaku; 840–901 CE): "Within fire, cold ice is formed (燄裡寒氷結)." This expression is part of Caoshan's verses on the five ranks (五位; Jp. *go i*).

A contemporary commentator, Akio Matsumoto (松本章男), who is not a Zen practitioner or scholar of Buddhism but an expert in Japanese literature, compared this waka to one composed by Fujiwara no Kinzane (藤原公実; 1043–1107 CE) from the collection of waka *One Hundred Poems from the Era of Emperor Horikawa* (堀河百首; Jp. *Horikawa hyakushū*). The waka from that collection contains almost the same expression: "Ice is formed / even underneath the *kaiya*" (かひ屋が したも／氷しにけり; *kaiya ga shita mo / koori shinikeri*).[424] According to Matsumoto, *kaiya* here is a device for catching fish, a bundle of twigs put underwater. Small fish would get caught among the twigs, and people then lifted the bundle out to get the fish. In winter, a roof was put above the trap to prevent the surface of the water from freezing. This roof was called a *kaiya* (飼屋). In his waka, Kinzane described the scenery of an exceptionally cold winter day where even the water underneath the *kaiya* was frozen and people could not catch any fish.

I prefer this interpretation over the traditional one. In his waka, when Dōgen describes the scenery of seasons, he rarely refers to phenomena we cannot see. Ice within fire is something we do not actually see in the phenomenal world. If we accept the traditional interpretation, the waka becomes an expression of a philosophical idea: the interpenetration of opposites. However, I have not found that Dōgen uses such ideas in his waka poems. His expressions of nature are always simply sketches of what he sees.

What does this waka mean if we adopt the second interpretation? A *kaiya* is a device invented by human beings to catch fish. However, it is too cold in this waka to fish. A human-made device doesn't work when conditions are different from expectations. I think Dōgen is saying Buddhadharma is something beyond anything that human beings can hold onto with their thinking minds. In the essay "Universal Recommendation of Zazen" (普勧坐禅儀; Jp. "Fukanzazengi") Dōgen says, "In doing zazen, the kōan manifests itself; it cannot be ensnared." In this case, "kōan" refers to the reality beyond human thinking. "Cannot be ensnared" literally means that there is no way to catch or cage it to make it our possession. When there is ice beneath the *kaiya*, it too cannot ensnare anything.

The Buddhadharma is something beyond our human ability to grasp because we are merely a tiny part of it. Dōgen liked the expression, "Only Buddha together with Buddha" (唯佛與佛; Jp. *yuibutsu yobutsu*) from the second chapter of the *Lotus Sutra*. This means we have to open our hands of human thinking and just let go. Then the Buddha beyond thought is revealed.

47

世の中は	*yo no naka wa*
まどより出づる	*mado yori izuru*
きさの尾の	*kisa no o no*
ひかぬにとまる	*hikanu ni tomaru*
さはり斗りぞ	*sawari bakari zo*

People of this world
are like the elephant fleeing through a window
its tail remains despite nothing holding it
such small things become obstacles
to renouncing the mundane world

An elephant escaping through a window is an unusual image. Menzan changed "elephant" (象; Jp. *kisa*) to "water buffalo" (牛; Jp. *ushi*) and added the title "A Water Buffalo Passes through a Window" to this waka, as if Dōgen Zenji were composing this poem as a commentary on case number thirty-eight of the *Gateless Barrier* (Ch. 無門關, *Wúménguān*; Jp. 無門関, *Mumonkan*). The *Gateless Barrier* was compiled in 1228, the year after Dōgen returned to Japan from China. Shinchi Kakushin (心地覚心; 1207–1298 CE), a Rinzai Zen master who received the bodhisattva precepts from Dōgen, later went to China and received *inka* from Wumen Huikai (無門慧開; Jp. Mumon Ekai; 1183–1260 CE), the compiler of the *Gateless Barrier*.[425] Kakushin returned in 1254 and introduced the *Gateless Barrier* to Japan. Dōgen had passed away the previous year, so he probably did not have the chance to read the *Gateless Barrier*.

According to the *Gateless Barrier*, this kōan ("A Water Buffalo Passes through a Window") was the saying of the Song dynasty Rinzai Master Wuzu Fayan (五祖法演; Jp. Goso Hōen; 1024–1104 CE), so Dōgen might have been familiar with it. However, he never mentioned the kōan in his writings or included it in the collection of three hundred kōans in the *Shinji Shōbōgenzō* (真字正法眼蔵). In all of the older manuscripts of Dōgen's waka that were made prior to Menzan's version, the animal in this waka is an elephant, not a water buffalo. Menzan also changed "obstacle" (障り; Jp. *sawari*) to "mind" (心; Jp. *kokoro*). As a result, the meaning of the poem was completely changed from Dōgen's original.

The eminent modern Rinzai Zen Master Zenkei Shibayama (柴山全慶; 1894–1974) said in his comments on case number thirty-eight of the *Gateless Barrier*: "This tail is nothing else than the formless form of reality."[426] Shibayama Rōshi also quotes this waka by Dōgen Zenji, albeit the version found in Menzan's compilation. The translation of the waka as quoted in his Dharma talk is as follows:

> This world is but the tail of a buffalo passing through a window.
> The tail is the mind,
> which knows neither passing nor not-passing.[427]

The last line is Shibayama Rōshi's addition to make the meaning of "mind" clear. It seems to me that Menzan revised Dōgen Zenji's waka to make it compatible with the Rinzai interpretation of case number thirty-eight of the *Gateless Barrier*. Traditional commentaries in the Sōtō Zen tradition have also been based on Menzan's revised version of this waka. This is only one example of how, until the second half of the twentieth century, the understanding of Dōgen Zenji's teachings were filtered through the interpretations of Tokugawa-period Sōtō Zen masters like Menzan.

There is, however, a tale of an elephant passing through a window that appears in a sutra titled *The Story of the Ordination of Anāthapiṇḍa-da's Daughter* (佛説給孤長者女得度因縁經; Jp. *Bussetsu gyūkochōja jō tokudo innen kyō*).[428] The story is about a king who lived in the time of Kāśyapa Buddha, the sixth of the seven past buddhas. The king had ten unusual dreams and asked Kāśyapa Buddha about their meaning. In the first dream, an elephant tried to escape a room by passing through a window, and although its body got through, it could not escape because its tail was somehow stuck in the room, even though nothing was holding it. Kāśyapa Buddha said this dream was about a time in the future, after Shakyamuni Buddha had passed away, when some monks, despite having left home, would still have minds influenced by greedy attachments to fame and profit that made them unable to attain liberation.

In this waka, Dōgen means to say many people of his time who had left home to become monks could not fully escape saṃsāra due to their attachments to money and status.

In the *Shōbōgenzō* fascicle "Sounds of Valley Streams, Colors of Mountains" (谿聲山色; Jp. "Keisei sanshoku"), Dōgen says:

> Moreover, we should not forget the aspiration we aroused when we first sought the Buddha Way. What I want to say is that when we first aroused the mind of awakening, we . . . abandoned fame and profit . . . [and] we simply aspired to attain the Way. We never expected to be venerated or receive offerings from the king and ministers. . . . We did not expect to be involved in entanglements with human and heavenly affairs. And yet foolish people, even if they have aroused the mind of awakening, soon forget their original aspiration and mistakenly

expect offerings from human and heavenly beings. And when they receive them, they are delighted, thinking the virtue of the Buddhadharma has been realized. When kings and ministers come frequently to take refuge, foolish practitioners think this is the manifestation of their own [virtue of the] Way. This is one of the demons afflicting the practice of the Way. Even though we should not forget to have a compassionate mind towards kings and ministers, we should not be delighted when such people venerate us.[429]

In this waka, Dōgen uses the story of the elephant's tail from *The Story of the Ordination of Anāthapiṇḍada's Daughter* to criticize many of the Japanese Buddhist monks of his time. In *Shōbōgenzō zuimonki*, he said something similar to what he wrote in "Sounds of Valley Streams, Colors of Mountains," for example, in section 6-21:

Even though it seems that some people of the world today have renounced the world and left their homes, if we examine their conduct, there are also those who are not yet true home-leavers. Those who are called home-leavers must first of all give up the [ego-centered] self as well as fame and profit. Unless we become free from these, even if we practice the Way as if extinguishing a fire enveloping our heads, or zealously cut off our hands or legs, it would only be a meaningless hardship that has nothing to do with renunciation.[430]

This was not solely a problem for Indian monks after Shakyamuni's death or Japanese monks in Dōgen's time. In the United States today, Buddhist institutions are not as large as they were in India or medieval Japan, so I do not think people can easily become Buddhist monks/priests for the sake of fame and profit. Still, we may make similar mistakes on a smaller scale in our practice. For example, when we compete with others and want to consider ourselves better than them, or when we want others to view us as superior practitioners, or if we study Buddhist teachings to show others that we have knowledge, our motivation is not the genuine mind of awakening. In those cases we are motivated by our ego-centered desire to win an imaginary competition. This is the way we create saṃsāra within our Buddhist practice. This is the tiny tail of the elephant that binds us to saṃsāra.

48
朝日待つ　　　　asahi matsu
草葉の露の　　　kusaba no tsuyu no
ほどなきに　　　hodo naki ni
急ぎな立ちそ　　isogina tachi so
野辺の秋風　　　nobe no akikaze

Dewdrops on blades of grass
waiting for the morning sunrise
exist only a moment
Autumn wind in the field,
don't hurry!

A dewdrop is beautiful and yet lasts for only a short time. Japanese expressions such as "a dewdrop as beautiful as a jewel" (露珠; Jp. *roshu*) and "dewdrops shining in sunlight like flowers" (露華; Jp. *roka*) show an appreciation for the dewdrop's fleeting beauty. Our lives, which are precious but without an abiding self-nature, are compared to dewdrops in the expression "dewdrop-like life" (露命; Jp. *romei*). Dōgen Zenji used this expression often; for example in "Universal Recommendation of Zazen" (普勧坐禅儀; Jp. "Fukanzazengi") he says: "Furthermore, your body is like a drop of dew on a blade of grass; your life is like a flash of lightning. Your body will soon disappear; your life will be lost in an instant."[431]

While I was living at Valley Zendo in western Massachusetts, I worked harvesting blueberries a few weeks each summer for several years. In the early mornings, the blueberry field was so beautiful. Each blueberry and each leaf were covered with dewdrops. In the morning sun, the many acres of the blueberry field looked like a carpet of bright jewels. However, soon the sun rose higher, the plants warmed, and the dewdrops disappeared.

In this waka, Dōgen describes dewdrops on a blade of grass during an early autumn morning. The dewdrops remain only until the sun rises. When the cold autumn wind blows, even the grass on which the dewdrops rest will wither. Seeing this scenery of changing seasons, we human beings feel melancholy and have some sympathy or even compassion for the dewdrops and the grass. We see that our lives are the same. Sooner or later we will all disappear, but we do not know when.

However, for Dōgen this is not a pessimistic view of life. He sees beauty and dignity in impermanence. As Dōgen wrote in *Shōbōgenzō* "Genjōkōan," each and every dewdrop reflects the boundless moonlight. Eternity lives within impermanence. He also writes in *Instructions for the Cook* (典座教訓; Jp. *Tenzo kyōkun*): "Although drawn by the voices of spring, do not wander over spring meadows; viewing the fall colors, do not allow your heart to fall."[432]

We see that spring will come again, and plants, flowers, insects, birds, and all living beings will renew their activity. We do not need to be overwhelmed by the cold autumn winds in our lives.

49

心なき	*kokoro naki*
草木も今日は	*kusaki mo kyō wa*
しぼむなり	*shibomu nari*
目に見たる人	*meni mitaru hito*
愁へざらめや	*ure-e zarameya*

Even insentient beings
such as grasses and trees
wither today;
seeing this in front of our eyes,
how can we not grieve?

In his Dharma talk on this waka, Kōdō Sawaki Rōshi emphasized the quality of our eyes—whether they are open to seeing impermanence and feeling grief about the plants' and our own lives. He compared himself with Dōgen Zenji, who deeply realized impermanence by experiencing his mother's death when he was seven years old. Seeing the incense smoke at his mother's funeral, Dōgen aspired to become a Buddhist monk. Sawaki Rōshi's mother died when he was five; his father died when he was seven. He was adopted by his aunt, but before long her husband died of a stroke right in front of Sawaki Rōshi. Although he had such painful early experiences, Sawaki Roshi said he did not really see impermanence; rather, he only worried about who would feed and raise him.

His next adoptive father, Bunkichi Sawaki, was a gambler living in a red-light district. When Sawaki Rōshi was eight, a middle-aged man died of a stroke in a prostitute's room nearby. Sawaki Rōshi saw the dead man in bed, with his wife beside him, crying, "Why did you die in a place like this, of all places?" Witnessing this miserable scene, Sawaki Rōshi was stunned, and this time impermanence and the impossibility of keeping secrets were inscribed deeply in his mind.[433] Sawaki Rōshi later said, "Dōgen Zenji was sharp-witted, so he could deeply see impermanence and arouse the mind of awakening by simply seeing the smoke of incense, or withering trees and grasses, but a dull-witted person like me could not feel the same thing until I had much more intense experiences."[434] Even though Sawaki Rōshi said he was dull-witted compared to Dōgen Zenji, I think he was probably the only person among many at the brothel who had the eyes to see the spiritual meaning of impermanence at that event.

After Sawaki Rōshi became a well-known Zen master, he was invited to give a talk for a group of priests near his hometown. He talked about his experience of realizing impermanence when he was eight. One of the priests in the audience remembered that a member of one of his temple's families had died like that several decades before. He recalled that the strict abbot of the temple at that time was furious about how the man had died, and as a result he refused to give him a Dharma name at his funeral.[435] When Sawaki Rōshi heard this, he wrote to the current abbot of the temple that the man who died was a great teacher for him, who saved him and made him a monk, and he asked the priest to give the dead man a Dharma name.

All plants know when to sprout, grow, bloom, bear fruit, and wither. Each plant has its own time and season. If we are mindful, we see that everything in nature expresses the Dharma of impermanence. Particularly when we see plants wither, if our eyes are open, we cannot help but realize the transience of our own lives. Perceiving impermanence and grieving for it is an opportunity to arouse the mind of awakening. It is important to note that this view of impermanence is fundamentally different from the ordinary sense of the fragility of life expressed by many Japanese poets. For example, the basic theme of the famous story *Tale of the Heike* (平家物語, Jp. *Heike monogatari*) is impermanence. The story begins: "The sound of the Gion Shoja bells echoes the impermanence of all things; the color of the sala flowers reveals the truth that the prosperous must decline. The proud do not endure, they are like a dream on a spring night; the mighty fall at last, they are as dust before the wind."[436]

"Gion Shōja" (祇園精舍) refers to Jetavana monastery in India where Shakyamuni practiced, and the *sala* flowers refer to the tree in Kuśinagara where Shakyamuni passed away. It is said that when Shakyamuni died, the *sala* trees bore full blossoms out of season, but these flowers faded quickly, symbolizing both gratitude and sadness for the Buddha. As students, many Japanese memorize this beautiful passage from Heike and later quote it when they speak of impermanence. This saying expresses feelings of futility, fear of change, and pessimistic resignation.

However, impermanence is not negative in Buddhism. In the *Sutra on the Teachings Bequeathed by the Buddha* (佛遺教經; Ch. *Fóyíjiào jīng*; Jp. *Butsuyuikyō gyō*), Shakyamuni said:

All of you Bhikshus! Do not be grieved or distressed. If I were to live in the world for an eon, my association with you would still come to an end. A meeting without a separation can never be. The Dharma for benefitting oneself and others is complete. If I were to live longer it would be of no further benefit. All of those who could be crossed over, whether in the heavens above or among humans, have already crossed over, and all of those who have not yet crossed over have already created the causes and conditions for crossing over. . . . Meetings necessarily have separations, so do not harbor grief. Every appearance in the world is like this; be vigorous, seek liberation right away! Destroy the darkness of delusion with the brightness of wisdom.[437]

Although the Buddha encourages his followers not to mourn, sadness about impermanence is not considered negative in Buddhism. Awakening to the truth of suffering, the first of the four noble truths, is the starting point of Buddhist study and practice. It is our opportunity to practice what the Buddha taught.

Seeing the reality that lies beyond our self-centered desires and expectations, we understand how our lives are connected with all beings. In case number twenty-seven of the *Blue Cliff Record*, a monk asks Yunmen Wenyan (雲門文偃; Jp. Unmon Bun'en; 864–949 CE), "How is it when the tree withers and the leaves fall?" Yunmen answers, "Body exposed in the golden wind."[438] The "golden wind" can be interpreted as the Buddhadharma, so this suggests that impermanence is not a negative, but rather it has something to teach us about the true nature of reality.

50
隙もなく   *hima mo naku*
ゆきはふれども   *yuki wa furedomo*
たにの戸に   *tani no to ni*
はる来にけりと   *haru kinikeri to*
うぐひすぞなく   *uguisu zo naku*

> Although it snows ceaselessly
> at the gate of the mountain valley
> the warbler is singing
> "Spring has already come"

This poem is about early spring at Eihei-ji, when it is still cold, gloomy, and snowy. After a long winter, people yearn for spring. Suddenly a warbler begins to sing, announcing that spring has arrived. This tiny bird is the only sign of spring in the world. Yet within the scenery of winter, spring is already here.

Sawaki Rōshi interpreted this poem as a metaphor for Dōgen Zenji's teaching of the unity of practice and realization, saṃsāra and nirvana. Within winter, spring already exists. Within spring, winter remains. Winter and spring permeate each other. This is how we practice as bodhisattvas. Even when we arouse the mind of awakening and practice the Buddhadharma, we are still ordinary human beings with egocentricity and delusions. Still, in our practice of the Buddha's teachings, the Dharma body of the Buddha manifests itself. Our practice here and now is the warbler's singing.

Another sign of spring amid winter is plum blossoms. In his Dharma discourse on the full moon of the first lunar month in 1247, Dōgen composed a Chinese poem:

> The family style is pure white like plum blossoms, snow, and
>   the moon.
> At the time of flowering, fortunately there is a way to pro-
>   tect the body.
> The clouds are bright, the water is delightful, and our effort
>   is totally perfect.
> Without realizing it, our entire body enters the emperor's
>   capital.[439]

As I mentioned in the commentary on waka number twelve, New Year's Day is the beginning of spring. In Echizen province, although it is actually the coldest time of year and everything is covered with snow, it is already spring. Yet the only visible sign of spring is plum blossoms. Dōgen's family style of practice is pure and undefiled, like the plum blossoms and snow illuminated by the full moon. The way to protect our body is to practice zazen. In sitting and letting go of thoughts, we are one with the plum blossoms, the snow, and the moonlight. The "clouds" and "water" refer to the assembly monks (雲水; Jp. *unsui*). The monks are refreshed with the coming of the New Year. In their continuous day-to-day practice, nothing is lacking. The "emperor's capital" refers to Chang'an (長安; in English literally "eternal peace"); like in waka number eleven, this refers to nirvana.

51

この心	*kono kokoro*
天つ空にも	*amatsu sora ni mo*
花そなふ	*hana sonau*
三世の仏に	*miyo no hotoke ni*
奉らなむ	*tatematsura namu*

With this mind
I adorn the heavenly sky
with flowers
respectfully offering them to all buddhas
in the three times

"I adorn the heavenly sky with flowers" refers to a story in the Vinaya of a bodhisattva in one of Shakyamuni Buddha's past lives. When Dīpaṃkara Buddha lived in this world, there was a bodhisattva (the future Shakyamuni Buddha) who lived as a hermit. When he heard that Dīpaṃkara Buddha was coming, he wanted to offer flowers to him. He bought five stalks of lotus, spending all the money he had. When he threw the flowers to the Buddha as an offering, they stayed in the sky and were transformed into a flower canopy that covered the Buddha wherever he went.

In the *Shōbōgenzō* fascicle "Arousing the Unsurpassable Mind" (發無上心; Jp. "Hotsu mujōshin") Dōgen refers to this offering of five stalks of lotus flowers:

> Taking it up like this, "sitting as a buddha" and "making a buddha" are called "bringing forth the mind." Generally speaking, in the cases of [those] bringing forth the mind of bodhi, rather than taking up the mind of bodhi from elsewhere, they bring forth the mind by taking up the mind of bodhi [itself]. To "take up the mind" means to take up "one blade of grass" and construct a buddha, to take up "a tree without roots" and construct a sūtra. It is to offer sand to a buddha, to offer slop to a buddha. It is to provide one ball of food to a living being, to offer five flowers to a tathāgata.[440]

In the waka, the Japanese text simply reads "mind" (心; Jp. *kokoro*) instead of "bodhi-mind," the mind of awakening. However, it is clear from the context that this is what Dōgen is thinking. As bodhisattvas, people who have aroused the mind of awakening, we exchange all our personal possessions for the lotus flowers (Dharma) and throw them into the sky (空, which also means "emptiness") as an offering to the Buddha. Our offerings remain in the sky as ornaments of the world of the Buddhadharma. They do not fall back to earth, the ground of human desire.

Inspired by this waka, Ryōkan (良寛; 1758–1831 CE) composed his own:

鉢の子に　　　　*hachinoko ni*
菫たむぽぽ　　　*sumire tamupopo*
こき混ぜて　　　*kokimazete*
三世の仏に　　　*miyo no hotoke ni*
奉りてな　　　　*tatematsuri tena*

In my begging bowl
violets and dandelions
mix together
let's respectfully offer them
to all buddhas in the three times

While Ryōkan was begging (托鉢; Jp. *takuhatsu*) on a spring day, some children in the village wanted to play with him, as was usually the case. Ryōkan started to pick violets and dandelions in the spring field with the children. He put the flowers in his begging bowl and told the children, "Let's offer these pretty flowers to the buddhas."

Possibly on the same occasion, Ryōkan composed another waka:

飯乞うと	*ii kou to*
わが来しかども	*waga koshi kadomo*
春の野に	*haru no no ni*
すみれ摘みつつ	*sumire tsumitsutsu*
時を経にけ	*toki o henikeri*

Although I came to beg for food
I spent the whole day
in a spring field
picking violets

A begging bowl is made for receiving offerings from people, but Ryōkan used it to make an offering to the buddhas. His practices of begging and playing with the children were also his offerings.

52
建長五年八月初五日、開山御上洛(中略)御上洛ノ其日
御頌・歌在之

kenchō gonen hachigatsu shōgonichi kaisangojōraku (chūryaku) gojōraku
no sono hi goju ・ ka kore ari

In the fifth year of Kencho (1253), on the fifth day of the
eighth lunar month, Dōgen Zenji went to the capital,
Kyoto. On the day he arrived, he composed a poem as
follows:[441]

草の葉に	*kusa no ha ni*
かどでせる身の	*kadode seru mi no*
木部山	*konobeyama*
雲にをかある	*kumo ni woka aru*
心地こそすれ	*kokochi koso sure*

Having left the leaves of grass,
arriving at Konobeyama Mountain
I felt I was walking in the clouds

In the first lunar month of 1253, Dōgen Zenji wrote a fascicle
of the *Shōbōgenzō* called "Eight Aspects of the Awakening of Great
Beings" (八大人覺; Jp. "Hachi dainin gaku"). This was the final year
of Dōgen's life. Most of this fascicle is a quotation from the *Sutra on the
Teachings Bequeathed by the Buddha* (佛遺教經; Ch. *Fóyíjiào jīng*; Jp. *Butsuyuikyō gyō*), but Dōgen wrote very short comments before and after.
It seems that by this time he knew he was dying. His successor, Ejō,
observed in the afterword that this teaching on awakening was both
Shakyamuni Buddha's and Dōgen Zenji's will for their descendants.

Dōgen's supporters asked him to go to Kyoto for medical treatment. In September, while the grasses were still thriving, he left
Eihei-ji. This poem is about his journey from there to Kyoto. The trip
must have been extremely hard on his body. Not far from Eihei-ji is a
steep mountain named Konobeyama (or Konomeyama). The peak of
this mountain pass separated Echizen province from Wakasa province.
There he rested. He probably knew this was his last chance to see the
mountains of Echizen province, but the peak was covered in misty

clouds. Here, the clouds symbolize the emptiness in which he traveled
with his sick body.

53
御入滅之年八月十五日夜、御詠歌に云
gonyūmetsu no toshi hachigatsu jūgonichi yoru, goeika ni iwaku
The year he passed away, on the evening of the fifteenth
day of the eighth lunar month, Dōgen composed the following poem:

また見んと	*mata min to*
思ひし時の	*omoishi toki no*
秋だにも	*aki da nimo*
今夜の月に	*koyoi no tsuki ni*
ねられやはする	*nerare yawasuru*

I wasn't sure if I could expect to see autumn again
gratefully I view tonight's full moon
How is it possible to sleep?

About ten days after arriving in Kyoto, Dōgen saw the beautiful
full moon. According to the East Asian lunar calendar, the fifteenth
day of the eighth lunar month is mid-autumn, which falls around the
September equinox. In most East Asian countries, including Japan,
people celebrate the mid-autumn harvest moon festival (Ch. 中秋節;
zhōngqiū jié; Jp. 月見; *tsukimi*).

At Eihei-ji, Dōgen usually gave a formal Dharma discourse on this
day each year. He also gathered with his disciples to compose Chinese
poems. The following is one such example found in *Dōgen's Extensive
Record* (永平広録; Jp. *Eihei kōroku*):

Although golden waves are not calm,
The moon lodges in the river.

> In refreshing air it shines on high, and all the ground is
> autumn.
> Reed flowers on the Wei River, snow on Song Peak,
> Who would resent the endlessness of the long night?[442]

In his final year, Dōgen was not sure he would live until autumn, so he was delighted to see the full moon in Kyoto, where he was born and raised. He did not want to waste the beautiful sight by sleeping.

The moon was a symbol he often used, like the image of the moon in the dewdrop in "Genjōkōan." He wrote an entire fascicle of *Shōbō-genzō* titled "Moon" (都機; Jp. "Tsuki"). In another waka (see addendum ten below) he wrote that this world is like a dewdrop splashed from a waterfowl's beak, staying in the air for only a few seconds, and yet reflecting boundless moonlight within this single drop, which shines like the entire moon itself.

Dōgen passed away on the twenty-eighth day of the eighth lunar month in 1253. His death poem translated from Chinese is recorded in the *Record of Kenzei* as follows:

> For fifty-four years
> having illuminated the highest heaven
> now leaping beyond
> breaking through the great thousand worlds
> Ha!
> with the entire body, without seeking anything
> still alive
> I jump into the Yellow Spring[443]

In Chinese, "Yellow Spring" (黄泉; Ch. Huángquán; Jp. Yomi) refers to an underground world where people go after death. It is similar to the underworld from Greek mythology.

Kishun's Postscript

右謹奉書写永平初祖大和尚之御詠歌若干首、奉附授梯公首座
禅師。伏乞洞宗大興、門派流通焉。至祝至祝、至祷至祷。

応永廿七年六月朔日　宝慶八世洞雲比丘喜舜　在判

In the above, I have respectfully copied a number of waka poems
by the Great Master, the Founder of Eihei-ji [Dōgen Zenji], and humbly offer them to Teikō Shuso Zenji. From the bottom of my heart, I
wish that the Sōtō school will greatly thrive and our lineage will widely
pervade. Sincerely congratulate, sincerely pray.[444]

The first day of the sixth month in the twenty-seventh year of Oei
(1420),

The eighth abbot of Hōkyō-ji, the monk of Tōun-ji, Kishun
(stamp)[445]

This is the postscript to the collection of Dōgen's waka poems by
the monk Kishun (喜舜; n.d.), the eighth abbot of Hōkyō-ji (宝慶寺),
who later lived at Tōun-ji (洞雲寺). Teikō Shuso Zenji refers to the
thirteenth abbot of Eihei-ji, Kenkō (建綱; 1413–1469 CE). Ostensi-
bly, Kishun copied these waka poems of Dōgen's and offered them to
Kenkō in 1420, but as I noted in my introduction, there must be some
confusion about the year or person. In 1420, Kenkō was only seven
years old. Perhaps the name Teikō Shuso Zenji refers to someone else.

補遺
Additional Waka from Later Manuscripts[446]

1

たちよりて　　　　*tachiyorite*
かげもうつさじ　　*kage mo utsusaji*
かも川に　　　　　*kamogawa ni*

みやこにいづる   *miyako ni izuru*
水とおもへば   *mizu to omoeba*

I won't stop
by the Kamo River
so my appearance isn't reflected there
because I assume
the water will flow to the capital

    I have difficulty understanding why Dōgen would have written this waka. It is the first of the thirteen additional waka in the Shunjusha text, and one of two waka that first appeared in a manuscript found at the temple Ryūgen-ji (龍源寺). It was produced at some point after the *Record of Kenzei* and contains only waka, but its exact date of composition and the sources it used are unknown. In this poem, Dōgen says he does not want his face reflected in the river because—depending on the interpretation—the water will either go into the capital city (Kyoto), or it already came from there. Bunji Takahashi (高橋文二), the scholar of Japanese literature who translated the waka into modern Japanese in the Shunjusha text, interprets *miyako ni izuru* as "came out of the capital."[447] Takahashi thought this poem was written while Dōgen was living at Kōshō-ji in Fukakusa, which is south of Kyoto. However, I do not think that is the case.

    If this waka was indeed written by Dōgen, I assume Dōgen composed it shortly after his ordination, when he was thirteen years old and living on Mt. Hiei. This mountain is located northeast of Kyoto. If my guess is correct, this phrase should be translated as "will flow into the capital." The Kamo River flows from the northwest of Kyoto and merges with the Takano River from the northeast. Then the river flows south through the city of Kyoto and eventually to Osaka Bay. If Dōgen lived north of the city on Mt. Hiei, the water flowed into the capital; if he lived at Kōshō-ji in Fukakusa, the water flowed out of the capital.

I do not believe Dōgen would have had such a negative feeling about Kyoto while living at Kōshō-ji that he did not even want his face reflected in the river because it was defiled by people in the capital. In volume eight of *Dōgen's Extensive Record* (永平広録; Jp. *Eihei kōroku*), Dōgen wrote:

> However, I do not yearn for mountains and forests, and do not depart from the neighborhoods of people. Lotus flowers blossom within the red furnace; above the blue sky there is a white elm. . . . Don't you see that the morning marketplace and battlefield are the original place of awakening for complete penetration of freedom? Why aren't taverns and houses of prostitution the classroom of naturally real tathagata? This is exactly the significance of the ancient wise one [Sakyamuni] departing from Bodhgaya, and previous worthies traveling to Chang'an.[448]

I believe this is what Dōgen thought when he established his first monastery, Kōshō-ji, in the southern suburbs of Kyoto. He did not look down on the capital and the people who lived there. Rather he wanted to practice with people in saṃsāra. Probably he had some hope that if he offered genuine Dharma and its practice to the people of Kyoto, he would be accepted and supported. Unfortunately, he later became disillusioned and moved to Echizen province.

If this poem was really written by Dōgen, he was probably expressing his determination to renounce his aristocratic family and the mundane world and devote himself to studying and practicing the Buddhadharma as a young monk on Mt. Hiei. From my own experience, I understand how Dōgen could have had such an immature but nonetheless pure resolution upon leaving home. I do not believe, however, that Dōgen would have continued to harbor such discrimination against worldly people after he came back from China and began trying to transmit the Dharma to Japan.

2

植て見よ   *uete miyo*
花のそだたぬ   *hana no sodatanu*
里もなし   *sato mo nashi*
心かようぞ   *kokoro kayou zo*
身はいやしけれ   *mi wa iyashi kere*

Plant the tree!
there's no village
where flowers don't grow
our bodhi-mind will be penetrated by the buddhas' minds
although we are of humble birth

This waka is also included only in the Ryūgen-ji manuscript, and its source is unknown. An almost identical poem (waka number 638) is in a collection of Ryōkan's waka compiled by Toyoharu Tōgō (東郷豊治), published by Tokyo Sōgensha in 1959. This poem is widely known as Ryōkan's and is included in *Great Fool: Zen Master Ryōkan; Poems, Letters, and Other Writings* by Ryuichi Abe and Peter Haskel. The waka in this collection reads:

植えて見よ   *uetemiyo*
花の育たぬ   *hana no sodatanu*
里もなし   *sato mo nashi*
心からこそ   *kokoro kara koso*
身はいやしけれ   *mi wa iyashikere*

Go ahead, plant the seed!
There isn't a village
Where flowers won't grow
The very notion of being "lowborn"
only comes from people's minds[449]

However, in the newer collection of Ryōkan's waka compiled by Toshirō Tanigawa (谷川 敏朗) and published by Shunjusha in 1996, this waka is not considered to be Ryōkan's own.[450] Ryōkan might have done calligraphy of someone else's waka and whoever came into possession of the calligraphy could have assumed it was composed by Ryōkan himself. However, according to Tanigawa's collection, the source of this waka is not Dōgen but the *Waka Collection of Ten-thousand Generations* (万代和歌集; Jp. *Mandai wakashū*), a large waka anthology compiled in 1249, while Dōgen was alive. I tried to find this waka out of the almost four thousand poems in the *Waka Collection of Ten-thousand Generations*, but I eventually gave up.

Possibly this poem is neither Dōgen's nor Ryōkan's work. However, if we assume it was composed by Dōgen, he likely wanted to say that people can surely attain the Way if they practice. In Dōgen's time, the notion that humans were living in the age of the last Dharma (末法; Ch. *mòfǎ*; Jp. *mappō*) was widespread. People believed that because they lived in that degenerate age, even if they practiced it would not be possible to attain the Way. That was one of the reasons Pure Land Buddhism became popular in medieval Japan. People believed the age of the last Dharma had begun in 1052 CE. However, Dōgen did not agree.

In *Shōbōgenzō zuimonki*, he wrote:

Many people of worldly society say, "Although I have the aspiration to study the Way, the world is in the age of the last Dharma. People's quality has been declining, and I have only inferior capabilities. I cannot bear to practice in accordance with the Dharma. I would like to follow an easier path that is suitable to me, to merely make a connection [with the Buddha] and hope to attain realization in a future lifetime."

And Dōgen expressed his counterargument:

Now, I say that this utterance is totally wrong. In the Buddha-dharma, distinguishing the three periods of time—the ages of the true Dharma, the semblance Dharma, and the last Dharma—is only a temporary expedient. The genuine teaching of the Way is not like this. When we practice, all of us should be able to attain [the Way]. Monks while [Shakyamuni] was alive were not necessarily superior. There were some monks who had incredibly despicable minds and who were inferior in capacity. The Buddha set forth various kinds of precepts for the sake of bad people and inferior people. Each and every human being has the possibility [to clarify] the Dharma. Do not think that you are not a vessel [of the Buddhadharma]. When we practice in accordance [with the Dharma], all of us should be able to attain [the Way]. Because we already have a mind, we can distinguish between good and bad. Because we have hands and feet, we do not lack anything for doing *gassho* and walking. In practicing the Buddhadharma, we should not be concerned with the quality [of people]. All beings within the human realm are all vessels. It is not possible [to practice the Buddhadharma] if we are born as animals or something else. People who study the Way should not wait for tomorrow. Only today and in this moment, we must practice following the Buddha.[451]

Dōgen's opinion is that if we arouse the mind of awakening and study and practice the teaching, we cannot fail to attain the Way. This is one of the reasons he emphasized the identity of practice and realization. When we practice, realization is manifested immediately. This agrees with what the Buddha said in the first two verses of Dhammapada:

> 1.
> What we are today comes from our thoughts of yesterday, and our present thoughts build our life of tomorrow: our life is the creation of our mind.

If a man speaks or acts with an impure mind, suffering follows him as the wheel of the cart follows the beast that
draws the cart.
2.
What we are today comes from our thoughts of yesterday,
and our present thoughts build our life of tomorrow: our
life is the creation of our mind.
If a man speaks or acts with a pure mind, joy follows him as
his own shadow.[452]

3

詠十二時中不空過之意
ei jūniji chū fukūka no i
The Meaning of Not Spending Twelve Hours in Vain

人しれず	*hito shirezu*
めでし心は	*medeshi kokoro wa*
世の中の	*yononaka no*
ただ山川の	*tada yama kawa no*
秋の夕暮れ	*aki no yūgure*

Without telling others
I've been appreciating
nothing other than mountains and rivers
in autumn twilight
in the world

As mentioned in the introduction, Dōgen's father, Minamoto no
Michitomo, was a well-known waka poet who served as one of the
six editors who compiled the *New Collection of Poems Ancient and Modern* (新古今和歌集; Jp. *Shin kokin wakashū*) commissioned by Emperor
Go-Toba (後鳥羽;1180–1239 CE). The collection was first completed
in 1210, but the selection process was extended by the emperor until

1216. Therefore, until Dōgen was at least ten years old, his father would have been working on this process of selecting almost two thousand poems from a much larger pool of available waka. Another famous poet also worked on the editing process: Michitomo's friend Fujiwara no Sadaie[453] (藤原定家; 1162–1241 CE).

In the *New Collection of Poems Ancient and Modern*, three famous waka about the beauty and subtle profundity of autumn twilight (Jp. 秋の夕暮れ; *aki no yūgure*) are included. One was composed by Sadaie:

見わたせは   *miwataseba*
花も紅葉も   *hana mo momiji mo*
なかりけり   *nakarikeri*
浦のとまやの   *ura no tomaya no*
秋のゆふくれ   *aki no yugure*

Looking around
neither flowers nor tinted leaves
only a rush-thatched cottage in the inlet
autumn twilight

It is said that an appreciation of the serene beauty of late autumn, without showy images such as flowers or brightly colored leaves, was not found in Japanese poetry before the *New Collection of Poems Ancient and Modern*. This waka by Sadaie in particular has been esteemed as a quintessential expression of subtle profundity (幽玄; Jp. *yūgen*)—or the *wabisabi* (侘び寂び) prized in later Japanese arts such as Noh theater, tea ceremony, *renga* (連歌; linked verse), and haiku. Although *wabi* and *sabi* were originally two different concepts, in modern times these came to be used as a single term. *Wabi* is the attitude of finding satisfaction in poverty or deficiency. *Sabi* is the sense of beauty in solitude and stillness.

Many people relish the luxurious beauty of spring flowers, such as cherry blossoms, or the spectacular changing leaves in the mountains in mid-autumn. Japanese often have parties to enjoy a day in nature, and many poems have been composed on these occasions. After all this exciting beauty has passed, in the late autumn when people expect the cold, snowy winter to begin at any time, no one makes an effort to enjoy the scenery. However, in the quiet, rather lonely scenery of late autumn twilight people can find a much more profound beauty. This beauty is not something we proclaim loudly and enthusiastically with other people. Rather, we quietly savor it within ourselves.

If this waka was composed by Dōgen, I think he wanted to express more than an appreciation of such serene beauty. I believe this waka expresses what he called "turning the light inward and illuminating the self" (回向返照; Jp. *ekō henshō*) in the "Universal Recommendation of Zazen" (普勧坐禅儀; Jp. "Fukanzazengi") Although this translation works in the context of the "Universal Recommendation of Zazen," it is actually not a literal translation. A more literal translation would be "turning light, returning illumination"—that is, a description of the sky after sunset. The sun has already set below the horizon, but its light "returns" and illuminates the entire sky, making it glow. This is the time of transition between day (when people think and act) and night (when people rest and sleep). Zazen is like evening twilight; the time of thinking is already gone, but we do not have the complete darkness of nonthinking either. Evening twilight in late autumn expresses the beauty of zazen. Settling down in this quiet tranquility and illuminating the self is the way to avoid wasting time.

4

詠坐禅工夫意
ei zazen kufū i
Wholehearted Practice of Zazen

しづかなる　　　*shizuka naru*
心の中に　　　　*kokoro no uchi ni*
栖む月は　　　　*sumu tsuki wa*
波もくだけて　　*nami mo kudakete*
光とぞなる　　　*hikari to zo naru*

>   Illuminated by the moon dwelling
>   in the quiet mind
>   even the waves are dissolving
>   into light

The "quiet mind" is the mind in zazen. In the fascicle of the *Shōbō-genzō* called "Eight Aspects of the Awakening of Great Beings" (八大人覺; Jp. "Hachi dainin gaku"), Dōgen Zenji quotes the *Sutra on the Teachings Bequeathed by the Buddha* (佛遺教經; Ch. *Fóyíjiào jīng*; Jp. *Butsuyuikyō gyō*) on the third aspect: "The third is to enjoy serenity. Departing from crowds and noise, and staying alone in a quiet place is called enjoying serenity."

"Serenity" is a translation of *jakujō* (寂静), which means quiet, tranquil, serene, or solitary. This does not simply mean silent or without external noise. When our minds are torn, there is always dispute, conflict, or anxiety. Such conditions make our minds unsettled and agitated. Often when we sit in the quiet zendo, we begin to hear noise from inside ourselves. Our zazen of letting go of thoughts enables us to sit imperturbably, without being pulled around by internal or external conditions.

In this waka, Dōgen describes zazen using the scenery of a rocky coast where the waves incessantly hit the rocks and break into tiny drops of water. In each and every drop, the moonlight is reflected. In our zazen, thoughts, images, emotions, and memories are like waves constantly coming and going, but when we let go of them they cease to be *our* thinking. Thoughts are coming and going, but we do not think. We are not deceived or controlled by thoughts. We do not take any action based on the waves. Within zazen, each thought coming and going without being grasped becomes simply the scenery of our zazen.

This waka is the fourth of the thirteen supplementary poems in the Shunjusha text. It appears only in two versions of the *Record of Kenzei*. A waka that is almost the same is included in Menzan's *Verses on the Way from Sanshō Peak* (傘松道詠; Jp. *Sanshō dōei*), as the sixth supplementary waka, entitled "Zazen":

にごりなき	*nigori naki*
こころのみずに	*kokoro no mizu ni*
すむ月は	*sumu tsuki wa*
なみもくだけて	*nami mo kudakete*
ひかりとぞなる	*hikari to zo naru*

Illuminated by the moon dwelling
in the mind-water without cloudiness,
even the waves are dissolving
into light

Only the beginning is slightly different. I think these are not really two separate waka, but rather two versions of the same poem. There is no evidence to judge which is Dōgen's original, or even whether either was composed by Dōgen. However, if these poems were written by Dōgen they are surely connected with what he wrote in *Shōbōgenzō* "Genjokoan":

When a person attains realization, it is like the moon's reflection in water. The moon never becomes wet; the water is never disturbed. Although the moon is a vast and great light, it is reflected in a drop of water. The whole moon and even the whole sky are reflected in a drop of dew on a blade of grass. Realization does not destroy the person, as the moon does not make a hole in the water. The person does not obstruct realization, as a drop of dew does not obstruct the moon in the sky. The depth is the same as the height. [To investigate the significance of] the length and brevity of time, we should consider whether the water is great or small, and understand the size of the moon in the sky.[454]

The *Flower Adornment Sutra* (華嚴經, Ch. *Huáyán jīng*; Jp. *Kegon kyō*; Skt. *Avataṃsaka-sūtra*) describes what it calls "ocean-seal *samādhi*" (海印三昧; Jp. *kaiin zanmai*; Skt. *sāgara-mudrā-samādhi*). According to this teaching, water is the original mind-nature, peaceful and quiet, reflecting everything as it is, like a clear mirror. However, when the wind of ignorance begins to blow, the water's surface is agitated and waves arise. Then the ocean's surface can no longer reflect things as they are. In this teaching, meditation practice is a method of restoring the original calmness by stopping the wind of ignorance, which is discriminative thinking, so the mind can reflect all things as they are once again. The ocean water thus becomes like a seal or stamp, which copies an image just as it is. Devotees of the *Flower Adornment Sutra* called this sort of meditation "contemplation for eliminating delusory thoughts and returning to the source" (妄尽還源観; *mōjin kangen kan*).

However, Dōgen criticizes this interpretation in the *Shōbōgenzō* fascicle "Acupuncture Needle of Zazen" (坐禪箴; Jp. "Zazenshin"):

> Their writings seem only to discuss *going back to the source or returning to the origin, and vainly endeavoring to stop thinking and become absorbed in tranquility. . . .* How could such people have received the single transmission of zazen of the buddhas and ancestors? Since the chroniclers of the Song dynasty have mistakenly included these writings, students in later ages should discard them without reading them.[455]

In another fascicle of the *Shōbōgenzō* called "Ocean-Seal Samādhi" (海印三昧; Jp. "Kaiin Zanmai"), Dōgen wrote further about his understanding of this term, which is quite different from the traditional interpretation:

> To be the buddhas and ancestors is always the ocean-seal samadhi. As they swim in this samadhi, they have a time to teach, a time to verify, a time to practice. Their virtue of walking on the ocean goes to its bottom: they walk on the ocean as

"walking the floor of the deepest ocean." To seek to cause the currents of birth and death to return to the source is not "What are you thinking?"[456]

Here Dōgen says his practice of zazen is not a method of stopping the winds of ignorance, that is, renouncing thinking and making the ocean's surface completely quiet so it can reflect things as they are. Rather, in this waka Dōgen says that even the waves of thought and delusion themselves turn into moonlight.

5

鏡清雨滴声
kyōsei uteki sei
Jingqing's Sound of Raindrops

聞ままに	*kiku mama ni*
また心なき	*mata kokoro naki*
身にしあれば	*mi ni shi areba*
おのれなりけり	*onore nari keri*
軒の玉水	*noki no tamamizu*

Just hearing them
without grasping mind
raindrops like jewels
dripping from eaves
are myself

This waka does not appear in any of the manuscripts of the *Record of Kenzei*. It first appears in Menzan's collection of Dōgen's waka, *Verses on the Way from Sanshō Peak*. We do not know where Menzan found this poem. There is a similar poem in a later collection of Dōgen's waka found at a temple called Yūkon-zan (湧金山), but the first three lines are different:

耳に見て　　　　　*mimi ni mite*
目に聞くならば　　*me ni kiku naraba*
うたがはじ　　　　*utagawaji*
おのれなりけり　　*onore nari keri*
軒の玉水　　　　　*noki no tamamizu*

Seeing with ears and hearing with eyes[457]
There's no doubt
the jewel-like raindrops
dripping from the eaves
are myself

In the Rinzai tradition, this waka is attributed to Shuhō Myōchō (宗峰妙超; 1282–1338 CE). However, the final line of Shuhō Myōchō's waka is a little different: seeing with ears and hearing with eyes / there is no doubt that the jewel-like raindrops / dripping from the eaves / *are as they simply are* (おのずからなる; *onozukara naru*). As in some other cases, we have no evidence to judge whether this is really Dōgen's waka or not.

The title of this waka, "Jingqing's Sound of Raindrops," refers to the kōan in case forty-six of the *Blue Cliff Record*, which includes the following the conversation between Zen Master Jingqing Daofu (鏡清 道怤; Jp. Kyōsei Dōfu; 863–937 CE) and a monk:

Jingqing asked a monk, "What sound is that outside the gate?"

The monk said, "The sound of raindrops."

Jingqing said, "Sentient beings are inverted. They lose themselves and follow after things." (衆生顚倒、迷己遂物)

Then the monk said, "What about you, Teacher?"

Jingqing said, "I almost don't lose myself."

The monk said, "What is the meaning of 'I almost don't lose myself?'"

Jingqing said, "Though it still should be easy to express oneself, to say the whole thing has to be difficult."[458]

In this kōan, the Zen Master Jingqing and his student are inside a building and hear a sound. This kōan is about the relation between the six sense organs and their objects, in this case, *ear* and *sound*. Because it was raining outside, the monk answered his teacher that the sound was raindrops. Then Jingqing responds that sentient beings view things in an upside-down manner. They lose themselves chasing after this and that. This response is based on a teaching of the *Śūraṅgama Sūtra* (大佛頂首楞嚴經; Ch. *Dà fódǐng shǒulèngyán jīng*; Jp. *Dai butchō shuryōgon kyō*):

一切衆生從無始來迷己爲物。失於本心爲物所轉。

From the time without beginning, all beings have *mistakenly identified themselves with what they are aware of*. Controlled by their experience of perceived objects, they lose track of their fundamental minds.[459]

In this version, *meiko imotsu* (迷己爲物; a literal translation might be "being deluded in the self, they consider [the self] to be an objective thing") is rendered as "mistakenly identify themselves with what they are aware of." After this, beings are affected and controlled by the perceived objects. This is like a person who paints a demon and then feels threatened by their painted image.

"Their fundamental minds" refers to the terms One Mind (一心), Mind Nature (心性), and Original Mind (本心)—the mind source as noumenon. In this section of the *Śūraṅgama Sūtra*, the fundamental mind (本妙明浄心; Jp. *honmyō meijō shin*; literally "the originally pure and wondrous mind") is compared to an innkeeper. In contrast, the thinking mind, which arises due to encountering objects and is thus based on a dichotomy between subject and object, is likened to the visitors of the inn. The thinking mind is conditioned, impermanent, and ever changing, but the innkeeper is always present and therefore permanent.

The *Śūraṅgama Sūtra* claims that when we lose sight of the true essence of the self (the fundamental mind), we identify ourselves as the subject facing the objects we encounter. We discriminate among those objects, evaluate them, and try to chase after or escape from them, and thus we begin to transmigrate within saṃsāra. Being deluded by the discriminative mind and losing our connection with the fundamental mind is the cause of suffering within saṃsāra.

However, Dōgen did not always appreciate the *Śūraṅgama Sūtra*, probably because it promoted this concept of an "original fundamental mind" as noumenon. Jingqing says people are deluded and lose themselves chasing after external things, which causes subject and object to become separate. When these are separate and interact, something arises in our minds. In the kōan, a thought comes up in the student's mind and he says, "That was the sound of raindrops." He grasps onto himself as the subject that is hearing the sound of raindrops. According to this master's teaching, at that moment the student loses his fundamental self, chases after an object (sound), and becomes the subject (hearer) performing an action (hearing).

According to the *Śūraṅgama Sūtra*, this means that all discriminative thinking caused by interactions between the sense organs and their objects is delusion. We should therefore stop thinking, restore our calmness, and simply awaken to our pure and bright fundamental mind, free of all duality and defilements. Based on this teaching, Jingqing is saying that as soon as the monk hears the sound of the raindrops and tries to answer his teacher's question, he has fallen into the duality between subject and object. When the monk's mind is divided into subject and object, he has lost his original self.

Similarly, in the *Shōbōgenzō* fascicle "One Bright Jewel" (一顆明珠; Jp. "Ikka myōju") Dōgen writes: "The 'entire ten-directions' means the ceaseless activity of chasing after things and making them into the self, and chasing after the self and making it into things." Dōgen uses an expression similar to Jingqing's, but he uses it in a more positive way. If this waka was written by Dōgen, I think he wanted to express that our life consists of endless interactions between the self and myriad things, but that the self and myriad things do not exist only within the dichotomy of subject and objects. Rather, they work together as a part of the total function (全機; Jp. *zenki*) of the entire network of interdependent origination. In *Instructions for the Cook* (典座教訓; Jp. *Tenzo kyōkun*), Dōgen writes, "All day and all night things come to mind and the mind attends to them; and at one with them all, diligently carry on the Way."[460]

In this case, "mind" means the *tenzo* or the self. Things come to the self, and the self attends to them. This is the way the self and myriad things work together as one reality. The important point here is being attentive. We need to intimately work with myriad things in a way that expresses our awakening to the reality of impermanence, selflessness, and interconnection.

6

坐禅
zazen

にごりなき	*nigori naki*
こころのみずに	*kokoro no mizu ni*
すむ月は	*sumu tsuki wa*
なみもくだけて	*nami mo kudakete*
ひかりとぞなる	*hikari to zo naru*

Illuminated by the moon dwelling
in the mind-water without muddiness,
even the waves are dissolving
into light

This waka is almost the same as supplementary poem number four. Only the second line of the English translation is slightly different: "in the quiet mind" appears in supplementary poem number four, as opposed to "in the mind-water without muddiness" here. See my comments on supplementary poem number four.

7

礼拝
raihai
Prostration

ふし草も	*fushikusa mo*
みえぬ雪のの	*mienu yukino no*
白さぎは	*shirasagi wa*
おのがすがたに	*ono ga sugatani*
身をかくしけり	*mi o kakushi keri*

Grasses lie unseen
in the field under snow
the white egret hides itself
in its own appearance

This is the scenery of a midwinter's day. All kinds of grasses, short
and tall, are buried under deep snow. This scene is very different from
snow on the bright leaves of autumn. The entire world is covered in
snow, and it is still snowing continually. The bird is also white, so we
cannot distinguish it from its environment. It seems the bird is hiding
within its own color.

The practice of making prostrations is the same. We are part of
the network of interdependent origination and by offering prostrations, we hide ourselves within the world of interdependent origination. We disappear into this world and become one with all beings.

In the *Record of the Hōkyō Era* (宝慶記; Jp. *Hōkyō ki*), Dōgen recorded
one of his dialogues with his teacher Tiantong Rujing (天童如浄; Jp.
Tendo Nyojō; 1163–1228 CE). When Dōgen made a prostration,
Rujing said, "As for their nature, the person who makes a prostration
and the person who receives it are empty and serene. The correspon-
dence and interpenetration of the Way between them is beyond com-
prehension."[461] Not only the giver and receiver of a prostration but all

beings in the entire Dharma world are hidden within this prostration. Everything disappears into the deep, white snow of the Dharma.

8

とどまらぬ	*todomaranu*
日影の駒の	*hikage no koma no*
ゆくすへに	*yukusue ni*
のりの道うる	*nori no michi uru*
人ぞすくなき	*hito zo sukunaki*

In the future of
the horse of sunlight
that never stops
those who attain the Way
are rare

The meaning of this waka is essentially the same as waka number five in the main collection. Please see my comments there.

9

山のはの	*yama no ha no*
ほのめくよひの	*honomeku yoi no*
月影に	*tsukikage ni*
光もうすく	*hikari mo usuku*
とぶほたるかな	*tobu hotaru kana*

The moon begins to rise
above the mountain's brow
in glimmering evening moonbeams
fireflies take flight
glowing softly

From mid-June to early July, we see fireflies on the grounds of San-shin-ji here in Bloomington, Indiana. The tiny lights floating around trees and bamboo are very pretty.

A Japanese proverb says, "*Hotaru hatsuka ni, semi mikka*" (蛍二十日に蝉三日)—meaning, "a firefly lives only twenty days, a cicada only three." As beings with brief life spans, both of these insects symbolize impermanence.

In Buddhist sutras, a firefly's glow is often compared with the light of the sun or moon.[462] The light of a firefly symbolizes narrow and con-ditioned human thought, whereas the sunlight and moonlight represent Buddha's boundless wisdom. This waka is about early evening in summer. The sun has already set, but the sky is not yet dark. The moon emerges behind a mountain ridge, but its radiance does not dominate the sky.

This is a beautiful time of transition from day to night, from the time of discrimination and activity to the time of nondistinction and rest. The fireflies are like human beings who have aroused the mind of awakening. The light of such ordinary bodhisattvas is tiny and glows only briefly, and yet this light is the same as the vast moonlight of Buddha's wisdom.

10

無常
mujō
Impermanence

世中は　　　　　*yononaka wa*
何にたとへん　　*nani ni tatoen*
水鳥の　　　　　*mizudori no*
はしふる露に　　*hashi furu tsuyu ni*
やどる月影　　　*yadoru tsukikage*

To what can this world be compared?
Moonlight reflected in drops
splashed from the beak of a waterfowl

This waka appears only in Menzan's collection *Verses on the Way from Sanshō Peak* (傘松道詠; Jp. *Sanshō dōei*). Again it is not clear where he found this poem. If it was composed by Dōgen, he likely was expressing the beauty of impermanence and the interpenetration of transience and eternity.

A waterfowl dives into a pond and surfaces. It shakes its bill; the water drops fall. In each and every drop, the boundless moonlight is reflected. The drops stay in the air less than a moment before returning to the pond. Each drop is as bright as the moon itself. Dōgen believes our lives in this world are the same: as impermanent as water drops and yet, as he wrote in "Genjokoan," reflecting the boundless moonlight.

From the end of the Heian era (1185) to the beginning of the Kamakura era (1192), Japan experienced a transition in social structure and political power. The emperor's court was losing power, while the samurai were gaining it. During this growth of the warrior class, there were countless battles between the Heike and Genji clans, including in Kyoto, the capital. Finally, at the end of the twelfth century, the shogunate government was established in Kamakura by Minamoto no Yoritomo (源頼朝; 1147–1199). During this societal transition, Japan also endured many natural disasters. People saw piles of dead bodies on the banks of the Kamo River in Kyoto due to the various battles and natural catastrophes. There was a widespread belief that the age of the last Dharma (末法; Ch. *mòfǎ*; Jp. *mappō*) had begun in 1052 CE, and the world was falling deeper into degeneracy. People clearly recognized the impermanence of individual lives and society.

Dōgen's contemporary Kamo no Chōmei (鴨長明; 1155–1216 CE) wrote a collection of essays entitled *Hōjōki* (方丈記; *The Ten-Foot Square Hut*) in 1212, one year before Dōgen became a monk at Enryaku-ji on Mt. Hiei. Chōmei wrote about the situation in Kyoto. He recorded disasters, such as great fires, whirlwinds, typhoons, and earthquakes, in addition to the devastation caused by the civil wars between the Heike and Genji clans:

[1] Though the river's current never fails, the water passing, moment by moment, is never the same. Where the current pools, bubbles form on the surface, bursting and disappearing as others rise to replace them, none lasting long. In this world, people and their dwelling places are like that, always changing. . . . [3] Nor is it clear to me, as people are born and die, where they are coming from and where they are going. Nor why, being so ephemeral in this world, they take such pains to make their houses pleasing to the eye. The master and the dwelling are competing in their transience. Both will perish from this world like the morning glory that blooms in the morning dew. In some cases, the dew may evaporate first, while the flower remains—but only to be withered by the morning sun. In others, the flower may wither even before the dew is gone, but no one expects the dew to last until evening.[463]

These are well-known examples of people's sense of transience and the vanity of life in the mundane world during Dōgen's time. However, Dōgen's insight into impermanence is very different from these pessimistic views of the fleeting world. In this waka, although realizing impermanence is sad and painful, it is also how we arouse the mind of awakening and come to perceive eternity within impermanence.

11

山居二首
sankyo nishu
Two Poems on Mountain Dwelling

立よりて	*tachiyorite*
かげもうつさじ	*kage mo utsu sa ji*
溪川の	*tanigawa no*
ながれて世にし	*nagarete yo ni shi*
出でんとおもへば	*iden to omoeba*

I won't stop by
the banks of the valley stream
so my appearance isn't reflected
because I think the water will flow
into the world of saṃsāra

Supplementary poems 11 and 12, both titled "Mountain Dwelling" (山居; Jp. *sankyo*), are taken from the collection *Ryakugebon* (略解
本), a commentary on Menzan's collection of Dōgen's waka, *Verses
on the Way from Sanshō Peak*. The author of the *Ryakugebon* was a monk
named Kakugan (覚巖), who was the abbot of Entsu-ji (円通寺) in
Kurashiki City in Okayama Prefecture in the nineteenth century. We
do not know where Kakugan found these poems. Entsu-ji is the temple where the famous monk-poet Ryōkan practiced with his master,
Dainin Kokusen (大忍国仙; 1723–1791).

This waka is very similar to supplementary poem number one, and
its meaning is the same. Please see my comments there.

12

山ずみの	*yama zumi no*
友とはならじ	*tomo towa naraji*
峯の月	*mine no tsuki*
かれも浮世を	*karemo ukiyo o*
めぐる身なれば	*meguru mi nareba*

The moon on the mountain's brow
no friend
to this mountain dweller
because it moves also
in the floating world

The meaning of this poem is similar to supplementary poems one
and eleven. It seems Dōgen is saying he does not want to interact
with the valley stream or the moon, because they are connected to the

mundane world. It is difficult for me to think Dōgen had such a negative attitude toward everyday life and people in the world. It is true that as a Zen Buddhist monk Dōgen emphasized the renunciation of fame and profit so he would not need to rely on political or economic power. However, his practice in the mountains was not an escape from the world. He also cherished the sounds of valley streams as Buddha's voice and the moon as the boundless, radiant light of all interdependent origination.

If Dōgen really composed this waka, I would like to read it as follows:

> The moon on the mountain's brow
> cannot always accompany
> this mountain dweller
> because it needs to move on
> and illuminate those in the world of saṃsāra

The moon and the valley streams illuminate and expound the Dharma not only for monks practicing in secluded mountains but also for people living their everyday lives.

13

にほの海や　　　*nio no umi ya*
矢橋のおきの　　*yahashi no oki no*
渡し舟　　　　　*watashi bune*
おしても人に　　*oshitemo hito ni*
あふみならばや　*afumi naraba ya*

On Nio Lake
a ferryboat is sailing
off Yabase's shore
I'd like to push it
to meet the person

Nio is an old word for *kaitsuburi* (鷉鷉; Little Grebe, *Tachybaptus ruficollis*), a species of waterfowl. The largest freshwater lake in Japan, Lake Biwa, which is located in Shiga Prefecture, was formerly called Nio no Umi (Nio Lake) because many grebes and other waterbirds live there. Today the Little Grebe is the prefectural bird of Shiga. Lake Biwa can be seen from Mt. Hiei, where Dōgen practiced for several years as a novice.

Yabase is a town on the eastern coast of Lake Biwa, in what is now Kusatsu City. In ancient times, Yabase was well known as the port of a ferry between Kusatsu and Ōtsu, the city that is now the capital of Shiga Prefecture and which lies on the western coast of the lake. This boat ride was a major shortcut to get to Kyoto as it was much faster than walking all the way around the lake. *Afumi* in the last line is a pun on the old name for Shiga (Ōmi province; 近江国) and "to meet the person." *Afu* can mean "to meet" (Modern Japanese 会う; *au*), and *mi* (身) means a "body" or "person."

The first three lines of this waka depict the scenery of Lake Biwa. A ferryboat is sailing offshore of Yabase. Then the poet says that even though the boat is already taking the quickest route, he wishes to hurry to meet the person as soon as possible.

This poem was found by the scholar Dōshū Ōkubo (大久保道舟) in the *Wistera Leaves Waka Collection* (藤葉和歌集; Jp. *Tōyō wakashū*), a collection of waka compiled by Ogura Sanenori (小倉実教; n.d.) in the Nanbokuchō period (1336–1392 CE). Ōkubo included this poem in the collection of Dōgen's waka as part of *Dōgen Zenji zenshū*, published by Chikuma Shobō in 1970. Ōkubo wrote in his *Dōgen Zenji den no kenkyū* that this waka might be evidence that, while he lived in Fukakusa, Dōgen attended gatherings of aristocrats for the purpose of composing waka.

In the *Wistera Leaves Waka Collection*, this waka is included in the section of love poems, so people considered this a poem about a person who wishes to meet their lover as soon as possible by pushing the boat. Because of this reading, some hesitate to consider this to be a poem written by Dōgen. However, it is possible that it is not necessarily a love poem and the compiler of the waka collection merely thought it was about a lover's sentiments.

I have no basis for deciding whether this waka was written by Dōgen Zenji. All I can suggest is that in the fascicle of the *Shōbōgenzō* titled "Continuous Practice" (行持; Jp. "Gyōji") Dōgen wrote about his encounter with his late master Rujing (Jp. Nyojō): "I saw my late master with my own eyes; this is [truly] meeting with a person" (まの あたり先師をみる、これ人にあふなり; Jp. *Manoatari senshi wo miru kore hito ni afunari*).

If this waka was written by Dōgen, I think the expression *hito ni afu* ("to meet a person") could mean to meet a true person of the Way. In *Shōbōgenzō zuimonki*, Dōgen talked about meeting many such people who completely dedicated their lives to the Buddha Way.

As Dōgen wrote in *Shōbōgenzō* "Being Time" (有時; Jp. "Uji"):

我逢人なり、人逢人なり、我逢我なり、出逢出なり

Ware hito ni au nari; hito ware ni au nari; ware ware ni au nari; shutsu shutsu ni au nari.

I encounter a person; a person encounters a person; I encounter myself; going forth encounters going forth.

Notes to Part 1

1   See, for example, sections 1-10, 1-14, 2-13, 3-3, 3-15, 4-6, 5-6, and 5-8.

2   Although *The Record of the Deeds of the Three Great Venerable Masters*, *The Record of the Deeds of the Three Ancestors of Eihei-ji*, and the *Record of Kenzei* have his name as Ryōken (良顕), the *Record of the Transmission of the Light* records it as Ryōkan (良観).

3   Translated from Kawamura, *Shohontaikō*, 158, 161.

4   *The Record of the Deeds of the Three Great Venerable Masters*, *The Record of the Deeds of the Three Ancestors of Eihei-ji*, and the *Record of Kenzei* all say that Kōin instead encouraged Dōgen to go to China, but the *Record of the Transmission of the Light* says Kōin encouraged him to go first to study with Eisai and *then* to go to China.

5   See, for example, sections 1-12, 2-1, 2-4, 2-14, 3-2, 3-5, 5-8, and 6-6.

6   According to Ōkubo (in *Dōgen Zenji den no kenkyū*, 143–46), Dōgen visited Wanshou temple (Ch. 萬壽寺; Jp. 万寿寺, Manju-ji) on Mt. Jing (Ch. 徑山; Jp. 径山, Kin zan); Wannian temple (Ch. 萬年寺; Jp. 万年寺, Manen-ji) on Mt. Tiantai (天台山; Jp. Tendai san); and Husheng temple (護聖寺; Jp. Goshō-ji) on Mt. Damei (大梅山; Jp. Daibai san). As with Mt. Tiantong, all of these locations are in modern Zhejiang province.

7   This text can be found in English translation in Tanahashi, *Enlightenment Unfolds*, 30–31.

8   My translation made from the Japanese text in Foulk, *Record of the Transmission*, 563–64.

9   My translation made from the Japanese text in Foulk, *Record of the Transmission*, 565.

10 Takeuchi, *Eihei-niso koun*, 102.

11 Okumura and Leighton, *Wholehearted Way*, 32.

12 The relevant passage of *The Record of the Hōkyō Era* can be found in English translation in Tanahashi, *Enlightenment Unfolds*, 7, as well as

Kodera, *Dogen's Formative Years*, 121. Note that Tanahashi mistranslates the *Śūraṅgama Sūtra* as the *Laṅkāvatāra Sūtra*, likely due to their similar names in Sino-Japanese (楞嚴經; Jp. *Ryōgon kyō*—and 楞伽經; Jp. *Ryōga kyō*). The passage from *Dōgen's Extensive Record* is Dharma discourse number 383 in Okumura and Leighton, *Dōgen's Extensive Record*, 341.

13   A few selections of this text related to zazen are translated in Okumura, *Shikantaza*, 78–82.

14   No English translation of this book yet exists; see Uchiyama Rōshi, *Jiko*, in the bibliography for information on the Japanese text.

15   Mizuno, *Shōbōgenzō zuimonki*, 208.

16   Azuma, "Shōbōgenzō zuimonki," 298.

17   Ikeda, *Gendaigoyaku shōbōgenzō zuimonki*, 190.

18   This was translated into English by Steve Bein as "Purifying Zen." See bibliography for full details.

19   "Preceptor Jing" (Ch. 淨和尚, Jìng *héshàng*; Jp. 浄和尚, Jō *oshō*) refers to Dōgen's teacher Tiantong Rujing (Ch. 天童如淨; Jp. 天童如浄, Tendō Nyojō; 1163–1228 CE). "Venerable Gen" (元子; Ch. Yuán *zǐ*; Jp. Gen *su*) refers to Dōgen. Dōgen went to Song dynasty China together with his teacher Myōzen (明全; 1184–1225 CE) in 1223. In 1225 Dōgen began to practice under the guidance of Rujing, a Dharma heir of Xuedou Zhijian (雪竇智鑑; Jp. Setchō Chikan; 1105–92 CE). During his two and a half years with Rujing, Dōgen recorded some of their conversations in *The Record of the Hōkyō Era* (宝慶記; Jp. *Hōkyōki*). Rujing had become the abbot of Tiantong monastery in 1224 at the age of fifty-eight. Dōgen received Dharma transmission from Rujing in 1227 and returned to Japan shortly thereafter. Rujing died in the same year.

20   In the *Rules of Purity in the Chan Monastery* (Ch. 禪苑清規, *Chányuàn qīngguī*; Jp. 禅苑清規, *Zen'en shingi*), the following is said about the position of abbot's attendant (侍者; Ch. *shìzhě*; Jp. *jisha*): "If an abbot's attendant needs to be appointed, he should be young and physically strong, his words should be precise and clear, he should be righteous in the observance of the precepts, and he should be especially quick-witted; then everything in the abbot's office will be accomplished with natural ease. . . . Although the abbot's attendants are appointed by the rector, they must first be selected by the abbot" (Yifa, *Origins of Buddhist Monastic Codes*, 173).

21   "My own practice of the Way" is a translation of the Japanese *gakudō no keiko* (学道の稽古). *Gaku* is "study" or "practice," *dō* is "the Way," and

keiko literally means "to consider the ancient." This phrase is still used to refer to the practice of the martial arts, the tea ceremony, and other traditional Japanese arts.

"Great monastery" here translates *dai sōrin* (大叢林; Ch. *dà cónglín*). *Dai* means great, and *sōrin* literally means a "grove and a forest," symbolizing monks practicing together harmoniously like trees in a peaceful grove.

The scholar Yaoko Mizuno has suggested that this talk was given when Dōgen appointed Ejō as his abbot's attendant (Mizuno, *Shōbōgenzō zuimonki*, 10). In the section on Ejō in Keizan's *Record of the Transmission of the Light* (伝光録; Jp. *Denkōroku*), it is said that Ejō continued to serve as abbot's attendant until Dōgen's death and that he wanted to continue in this role even after his death. It says, "After [Ejō] received formal approval, he followed [Dōgen] without leaving him for a single day. He was like a shadow following the form for twenty years. Although he was given many duties, he remained [Dōgen's] attendant, assuming the position when his other tasks were completed. . . . Not only that, but during the fifteen years when he was continuing the teaching at Eihei-ji, he kept his master's portrait beside him in his quarters. He greeted it each morning with, 'Good morning,' and said, 'Good night' every evening, never forgetting for a single day. He wanted to be the master's attendant in life after life, as Ananda was to the Venerable Shakyamuni. Moreover, in order that his illusory body would not be separated [from his master], he had his own remains installed next to his master's memorial marker as if he were still his attendant, without a separate marker, fearing that a marker [for himself] would indicate reverence [for himself]." (Cook, *Record of Transmitting the Light*, 269–70)

22 "A vessel" in this case means having the capacity to receive and maintain the Buddhadharma. Such statements were based on the assumption that the age of the last Dharma (末法; Ch. *mòfǎ*; Jp. *mappō*) had begun in 1052 CE, as was the common belief in Japan at the time, and it was therefore not possible to truly study or practice the Dharma and attain awakening. This was the last of the so-called three periods (三時; Ch. *sānshí*; Jp. *sanji*) following the Buddha's death. During the age of the true Dharma (正法; Ch. *zhèngfǎ*; Jp. *shōbō*), lasting five hundred (or one thousand) years, the Buddha's teaching is properly practiced and awakening can be attained. During the period of the semblance Dharma (像法; Ch. *xiàngfǎ*; Jp. *zōhō*), lasting another five hundred (or one thousand) years, the teaching is practiced, but awakening is no longer possible. During the period of the last Dharma, lasting ten thousand years, the teaching exists, but it is not practiced and there can be no awakening.

Belief in this concept greatly influenced Japanese Buddhism in the Heian period (794–1185 CE) and Kamakura period (1192–1333 CE). Dōgen did not accept this theory. In fact, his famous teaching equating practice and enlightenment (修証一如; Jp. *shūshō ichinyo*) was probably a criticism of the popular idea that it is of no use to practice in the degenerate age of the last Dharma. In *Zuimonki*, Dōgen discusses this concept often, for example, in sections 2-13 and 5-8.

23   "Dharma gates" (法門; Ch. *fǎmén*; Jp. *hōmon*) are the Buddhist teachings through which we can enter the Dharma. It is said that there are eighty-four thousand Dharma gates. In other words, they are numberless. Because people's problems are numberless, the teachings as medicine for healing the sicknesses caused by each problem are also numberless.

24   "Golden bones" (金骨; Ch. *jīngǔ*; Jp. *kinkotsu*) refers to the Buddha's relics; the meaning of the full statement here is that not all of the ancient practitioners were as strong and capable as the Buddha.

25   "Mind of awakening" (道心; Ch. *dàoxīn*; Jp. *dōshin*) is literally "mind of the Way." The more common word for this is *bodaishin* (菩提心; Ch. *pútíxīn*), a part-transliteration, part-translation of the Sanskrit word *bodhicitta*, itself an abbreviation of *anuttarā-samyak-sambodhi-citta*. This is the mind that seeks ultimate awakening. In the case of *dōshin*, *dō* (道; Ch. *dào*) is an older translation of *bodhi*. Sometimes this mind is also called *gudōshin* (求道心; Ch. *qiúdàoxīn*): "Way-seeking mind."

26   Not being greedy for food, clothing, possessions, or fame and profit is one of the main topics of *Zuimonki*. If the monks who formed the audience of Dōgen's talks had stayed within the structure of an established Buddhist institution like the Tendai monastery where Dōgen had first studied, their lives would have been supported by the government. Because they had thoroughly renounced institutions connected with the power of the mundane world, the question of how to support their practice apparently became a concern. Dōgen repeatedly says that they should not worry about such things and instead devote themselves to practice based on the Dharma.

27   The meaning of this sentence in this version of the text (the Chōen-ji version) is not clear. The scholar-priest Rosan Ikeda interprets it as meaning that receiving food from benefactors is easier than receiving food only by daily begging (Ikeda, *Gendaigoyaku shōbōgenzō zuimonki*, 10). Yaoko Mizuno believes it means that receiving food from benefactors is different from ordinary begging in the mundane world (Mizuno, *Shōbōgenzō zuimonki*, 17). Menzan's version reads, "[The food obtained through] daily begging would never be exhausted."

28 "Wrong livelihood" (邪命; Ch. *xiémìng*; Jp. *jamyō*; Skt. *mithyâjīva*) is the opposite of "right livelihood" (正命; Ch. *zhèngmìng*; Jp. *shōmyō*; Skt. *samyag-ājīva*), the fifth part of the eightfold noble path. If monks supported their lives through one of the four occupations listed in this passage, this was considered wrong livelihood and was prohibited by the Vinaya precepts. In the *Sutra on the Teachings Bequeathed by the Buddha* (佛遺教經; Ch. *Fóyíjiào jīng*; Jp. *Butsuyuikyō gyō*), Shakyamuni said, "Those of you who uphold the pure precepts should not buy, sell or trade. You should not covet fields or buildings, or keep servants or raise animals. You should stay far away from all kinds of agriculture and wealth as you would avoid a pit of fire. You should not cut down grass or trees, plow fields or dig the earth. Nor may you compound medicines, prophesize good and evil, observe the constellations, cast horoscopes by the waxing and waning of the moon, or compute astrological fortunes. All of these activities are improper. Regulate yourselves by eating at the appropriate time and by living in purity. You should not participate in worldly affairs or act as an envoy, nor should you become involved with magical spells and elixirs of immortality, or with making connections with high ranking people, being affectionate towards them and condescending towards the lowly" (Buddhist Text Translation Society, *Sutra on the Buddha's Bequeathed Teaching*).

29 This story appears in the twenty-fifth volume of the *Continued Biographies of Eminent Monks* (續高僧傳; Ch. *Xù gāosēng zhuàn*; Jp. *Zo kukōsō den*). It was compiled by Nanshan Daoxuan (南山道宣; Jp. Nanzan Dōsen; 596–667 CE), the founder of the South Mountain Vinaya school (南山律宗; Ch. nánshān lùzōng; Jp. nanzan risshū). This thirty-volume collection includes the biographies of monks from the Liang dynasty (502–57 CE) to the beginning of the Tang dynasty (618–907 CE). Daoxuan and his school are also remembered for adopting the precepts of the Dharmaguptaka school (法藏部; Ch. fǎzàng bù; Jp. hōzō bu) as the standard Vinaya for Chinese Buddhism, something that remains the case today.

King Yama (Ch. 閻羅王, Yánluó wáng; Jp. 閻魔王, Enma-ō) is a *dharmapāla*, a wrathful Dharma-protecting god, who is the lord of death and king of hell in Buddhist mythology. He makes judgments as to where the dead should go, depending on their wholesome and unwholesome karma.

30 "Single whorl of white hair" is a translation of *byakugō* (白毫; Ch. *báiháo*; Skt. *urnakesa*), one of the thirty-two major marks of a buddha. It is described as a spiral of hair of infinite length located between the eyebrows and endowed with magical powers. In some sutras, such as

the *Lotus Sutra*, the Buddha emits a ray of light from his *urnakesa*. In the *Buddha Treasury Sutra* (Ch. 佛藏經, *Fózàng jīng*; Jp. 仏蔵経, *Butsuzō kyō*), it is said that the Buddha will offer a small part of his *urnakesa* to his disciples, which will be enough to support all future monks even if all human beings become Buddhist monks. It is also said that the Buddha was to live for one hundred years, but he died when he was eighty years old in order to offer twenty years of his life to his descendents. Therefore, Dōgen says we should not worry about food and clothing.

31   "Pure practices" is a translation of *bongyō* (梵行; Ch. *fànxíng*), which is the Sino-Japanese translation of the Sanskrit *brahma-caryā*. This expression was adopted from Brahmanism, where it refers to students dedicating themselves to studying the teachings and carrying out the holy religious life. In Buddhism, this word refers to a monk's life of practice following the precepts, free from the defilement of the three poisons of greed, anger, and delusion.

32   "The exoteric and esoteric teachings" refer to the teachings of the Shingon school (Ch. 眞言宗, Zhēnyán zōng; Jp. 真言宗, Shingon shū), in the latter case, and those of all other schools, in the former case. Shingon, the East Asian representative of Vajrayāna Buddhism, uses teachings said to be "esoteric" (密教; Ch. *mìjiào*; Jp. *mikkyō*; literally "secret teaching"), while all other schools use teachings that are "exoteric" (Ch. 顯教, *xiǎnjiào*; Jp. 顕教, *kengyō*; "revealed teachings"). Zen considers itself to be outside of both categories because it is claimed it fundamentally does not rely on scripture.

33   Sichuan is a province in the southwestern part of China, just east of Tibet. It is over 1,800 kilometers (just over 1,100 miles) away from Tiantong monastery, which is located near the modern coastal city of Ningbo.

34   The founder of Xuefeng monastery was Xuefeng Yicun (雪峰義存; Jp. Seppō Gison; 822–908 CE). "Weedy legumes" (緑豆; Ch. *lǜdòu*; Jp. *rokuzu*) refers to green-colored beans that were unintentionally harvested along with rice and were usually discarded later. In *Instructions for the Cook* (典座教訓; Jp. *Tenzo kyōkun*), Dōgen wrote, "First, take out any insects in the rice. And carefully winnow out any weedy legumes, rice bran, or tiny stones."

35   Devadatta was a cousin of Śākyamuni Buddha and a brother of Ānanda. He became a disciple of the Buddha together with Ānanda and other young people of the Śākya clan. Later, Devadatta was supported by King Ajātaśatru, who built a monastery for him and sent daily offerings of five hundred cartloads of provisions. Devadatta asked

Śākyamuni to retire in an attempt to become the head of the Buddhist Sangha. When the Buddha declined, Devadatta attempted to kill him. He is also said to have encouraged Ajātaśatru to kill his father, Bimbisāra, the king of Magadha.

36 "Physical behavior" is a translation of *mi no igi* (身の威儀). *Mi* means "body." *Igi* (威儀; Ch. *wēiyí*) can be translated as "comportment" or "dignified conduct," as, for example, in the fascicle of the *Shōbōgenzō* entitled "The Dignified Conduct of the Practice-Buddha" (行佛威儀; Jp. "Gyōbutsu-Igi"). Dōgen's title of this fascicle represents his unusual alternative understanding of this phrase, which would normally be read as "practicing the Buddha's dignified conduct." The bodily actions of walking, standing still, sitting, and lying down are also called the "four comportments" (四威儀; Ch. *sìwēiyí*; Jp. *shi igi*).

37 "Moral codes and forms" is a translation of *ritsugi* (律儀; Ch. *lǜyí*), literally "regulations and forms." It is, in turn, a translation of the Sanskrit word *saṃvara*, meaning "restraint." This refers to the fact that by following moral codes, one can restrain one's unwholesome behavior.

38 See note 25.

39 "Ancient practices" is a translation of *kojitsu* (故実; Ch. 故實, *gùshí*), meaning the way certain things have been done in a certain tradition and the directions that people must follow in order to continue that tradition.

40 "A good teacher" translates *zen chishiki* (善知識; Ch. *shàn zhīshí*), literally "good friend." In Buddhism, there are three kinds of good friends: teachers, copractitioners, and supporters.

41 This refers to a story that can be found, for example, in *Shinji shōbōgenzō* (真字正法眼蔵), case 121. The story involves Liangsui Shouzhou (壽州良遂; Jp. Jushū Ryōsui; n.d.) visiting the teacher Magu Baoche (麻谷寶徹; Jp. Mayoku Hōtetsu; n.d.):

> The lecturer Liangsui visited Magu for the first time. Upon seeing Liangsui coming, Magu took a hoe and began hoeing up weeds. Although Liangsui went to where Magu was working, Magu paid no attention to him, but rather immediately went back to the abbot's quarters and shut the gate. The next day, Liangsui visited Magu again. Magu shut the gate again. Liangsui then knocked on the gate. Magu asked, "Who is this?" "Liangsui!" Upon calling out his own name, the lecturer suddenly attained realization. He said, "Master, do not deceive Liangsui. If I had not come and made obeisance to you, I would have been deceived by the sutras

and commentaries for my entire lifetime." When Liangsui went back to his lecture hall, he gave a speech, saying, "All you know, Liangsui knows. What Liangsui knows, you do not know." Then he quit giving lectures and had the people leave. (Adapted from Okumura, *Realizing Genjokoan*, 185)

42   "Repentance ceremony" translates *fusatsu* (布薩; Ch. *bùsà*; transliterated from Skt. *poṣadha*). It is a gathering of sangha members on the evening of the full moon and the new moon, where the monastic rules in the Vinaya are recited and individual violations are repented. In today's Sōtō Zen tradition, the officiant recites the *Brahmā Net Sutra* (Ch. 梵網經, *Fànwǎng jīng*; Jp. 梵網経, *Bonmō kyō*) or Dōgen's "Comments on Teaching and Conferring the Bodhisattva Precepts" (教授戒文; Jp. "Kyōjukaimon") instead of the Vinaya precepts.

43   The ten major precepts and forty-eight minor precepts mentioned in the *Brahmā Net Sutra* are called "the bodhisattva precepts." In the Tendai tradition, in which Dōgen began his practice, these precepts were given upon ordination. However, in Dōgen's Sōtō tradition only sixteen precepts are given—the three refuges, the threefold pure precepts, and the ten major precepts.

44   The "four gross elements" (四大種; Ch. *sìdàzhǒng*; Jp. *shidaishu*; Skt. *cattāro mahābhūta*) include earth (solidity), water (the flowing together of all things), fire (heat), and wind (mobility).

45   This is a quotation from the end of the well-known Zen poem "Merging of Difference and Unity" (參同契; Ch. "Cāntóngqì"; Jp. "Sandōkai") composed by Shitou Xiqian (石頭希遷; Jp. Sekitō Kisen; 700–790 CE).

46   According to the Vinaya precepts, Buddhist monks are only allowed to own three robes and one begging bowl.

47   In the sixteenth chapter of the *Lotus Sutra*, there is a verse that reads, "And when the living have become faithful, / Honest and upright and gentle, / And wholeheartedly want to see the Buddha, / Even at the cost of their own lives" (Reeves, *Lotus Sutra*, 296). In Chinese this reads, "生既信伏 / 直意柔 / 一心欲佛 / 不自惜身命." The expression Dōgen uses here is similar to the last line, but he added, "We should not fail to take care of our lives."

48   Moxibustion (灸; Ch. *jiǔ*; Jp. *kyū*) is a traditional Chinese medical treatment that involves burning moxa, or dried mugwort leaves, on particular areas of the skin. It is still used in East Asia today.

49   The Dragon Gate (龍門; Ch. *lóngmén*; Jp. *ryūmon*) is the name of a waterfall along China's Yellow River. There is a legend that if a fish is able

to swim up the waterfall, it becomes a dragon. Here, Dōgen says that, rather than being a specific waterfall along a river, the Dragon Gate is in the ocean, and further any fish can become a dragon simply by passing through a particular place in the ocean. Instead of stating that only strong fish capable of ascending the waterfall are able to become dragons, Dōgen writes that all fish are able to become dragons simply by passing through the gate. The Dragon Gate is thus a metaphor for the monastery, where anyone can come and practice.

50   "A square robe" refers to a *kesa* (袈裟; Ch. *jiāshā*), the robe Buddhist monks wear over one shoulder. The word is a transliteration of the Sanskrit *kāṣāya*, which literally means "turbid colored." In India, Buddhist monks collected abandoned, soiled cloth before selecting clean parts to wash and dye a saffron-like color. They would then make their own robes by sewing these pieces together. "Patch-robed monks" thus refers to Buddhist monks who wear such a dyed and patched square robe.

51   Dōgen wrote in the *Shōbōgenzō* 's "Arousing the Mind of Awakening" (發菩提心; Jp. "Hotsu bodaishin"), "In the one moment in which a young and strong man snaps his finger, there are sixty-five *kṣaṇas*. Although [in each *kṣaṇa*] the five aggregates arise and perish, ordinary people never sense it or know it. Ordinary people can [only] recognize a length of time larger than a *tatkṣaṇa*. Within one day and night, there are 6,400,099,980 *kṣaṇas*. [In each *kṣaṇa*] all five aggregates arise and perish. However, ordinary people never sense or know it. Because they do not know it, they do not arouse the mind of awakening."

52   "The Director of Monks Eshin" (惠心僧都; Jp. Eshin *Sōzu*) is Genshin (源信; 942–1017 CE), a Japanese Tendai scholar-monk. He lived at a temple called Eshin-in (惠心院) and held the governmental rank of director of monks (僧都; Ch. *sēngdū*; Jp. *sōzu*), the second highest such rank. He wrote many texts on Tendai and Pure Land teachings and is considered to be the founder of the "Eshin branch" of the Tendai school. For many years, Genshin lived at a secluded temple in Yokawa (横川) on Mt. Hiei, where Dōgen later lived while he was a novice. Also see note 135.

53   See note 23 from section 1-2.

54   "Hīnayāna" means "lesser vehicle" or "inferior vehicle"; it has historically been used in Mahāyāna Buddhism to criticize practices perceived to be focused on personal gain among non-Mahāyāna monks. There was never a school that identified itself as "Hīnayāna," and it is important to note that most monks of Dōgen's time did not have any interactions with non-Mahāyāna monks, so the idea of the Hīnayāna

was mostly used as a sort of straw man. The word is now considered derogatory toward non-Mahāyāna Buddhists.

55 The "provisional teachings" (Ch. 權教, *quánjiào*; Jp. 権教, *gonkyō*) and the "genuine teachings" (Ch. 實教, *shíjiào*; Jp. 実教, *jikkyō*) are a Chinese method of classifying the Buddhist teachings. In the Tendai school, the teachings taught before the Buddha expounded the *Lotus Sutra* were considered to be temporary expedients, while those in the *Lotus Sutra* were believed to be his real teachings. Historically speaking, we now know that Mahāyāna teachings significantly postdate the death of the Buddha.

56 The sentences of this paragraph are difficult to interpret. Menzan's version instead reads, "When you see a person, value his true virtue. Do not judge him on his outward appearance or superficial characteristics." In his version, this paragraph is clearly the introduction to the paragraphs that follow about Confucius and the emperor's chief advisor, while in the Chōen-ji version it seems more like an independent paragraph.

57 The "emperor's chief advisor of Uji" (Jp. 宇治の関白殿, Uji *no kanpaku*) at this time was Fujiwara no Yorimichi (藤原頼通; 992–1074 CE), who served in this position under three emperors, totaling over fifty years. He had a villa in Uji outside of Kyoto, where he constructed the temple Byōdō-in (平等院), which is still famous for its beautiful buildings and statues, and a garden inspired by the Pure Land teachings.

58 This is a quotation from a Chinese treatise called the *Classic of Filial Piety* (孝經; Ch. *Xiàojīng*; Jp. *Kōkyō*), which was likely written between 350 and 200 BCE.

59 This expression also comes from the *Classic of Filial Piety*. This text predates the arrival of Buddhism in China, so "Way" here is not the "Buddha Way" in the sense that Dōgen usually uses it.

60 The deeds of body, speech, and thought are also called the *three activities* (三行; Ch. *sānxíng*; Jp. *sangō*); these are the source of wholesome or unwholesome karma. For "dignified conduct," see note 36.

61 This saying is a paraphrase of a saying from the *Classic of Filial Piety*.

62 Taizong (太宗; Jp. Taisō; 598–649 CE) was the second emperor of the Tang dynasty. He reigned for twenty-three years, from 626 to 649 CE, and was considered a great and wise emperor. This story is from the *Essentials of Government of the Zhenguan Period* (貞觀政要; Ch. *Zhēnguānzhèngyào*; Jp. *Jōkanseiyō*), a ten-volume collection of discussions on politics between Taizong and his ministers. In the *Essentials*, however, the

emperor who returned the horse was not Taizong but Wen of the Han dynasty (漢文帝; Ch. Hànwéndì; Jp. Kanmontei). This text was studied by students belonging to families of the nobility and the samurai class in Japan. Dōgen probably studied this text before he became a Buddhist monk, as a part of his education to become a government officer.

63 Wei Zheng (Ch. 魏徵; Jp. Gi Chō; 580–643 CE) was Taizong's chancellor and the lead editor of the official history of the Sui dynasty.

64 "Dharma bridge" (法橋; Jp. *Hōkyō*) is a rank in the government ministry system that is responsible for overseeing Buddhist orders. "Director of monks" in note 52 from section 1-7 is another such rank. Chisō (地相) might be the person's name, but nothing is known about him.

65 "The late superintendent of monks" here refers to Eisai (栄西; 1141–1215 CE), the founder of Rinzai Zen in Japan. Eisai was a well-known Tendai (天台; Ch. Tiāntái) master before he went to China to study Rinzai Zen. He was already considered to be the founder of the Yōjō lineage (用祥) within the esoteric tradition in the Tendai school before practicing Zen. He founded several Zen temples in Kyoto and Kamakura, including Kennin-ji (建仁寺) where Dōgen practiced with Eisai's disciple Myōzen (see note 19 from section 1-1) from 1217 to 1223.

The term "superintendent of monks" translates *sōjō* (僧正; Ch. *sēngzhèng*), another government rank like "Dharma bridge" in the previous note; Eisai is often referred to by this title in *Zuimonki*. The superintendent of monks was the highest position within the governmental system that oversaw Buddhist temples and monks, a system that was first established in the year 760 in Japan. There were two lower positions called "director of monks" (僧都; Ch. *sēngdū*; Jp. *sōzu*; see note 52 from section 1-7) and "preceptor" (律師; Ch. *lùshī*; Jp. *risshi*). Within each of these three ranks there were also additional subranks. By the time of the Kamakura era, these positions had become largely honorific titles, without actual administrative power, given by the government.

66 "Patron" translates *dan'na* (檀那; Ch. *tán-nà*), which is a transliteration of the Sanskrit word *dāna* ("donation") or *dānapati* ("a generous donor"). Although *dāna* usually refers to generosity, in Japan it also came to refer to patrons who would occasionally invite the abbot or priests to perform ceremonies or give talks, and in return they would offer food or other necessities such as cloth for making robes.

67 For information on the *Continued Biographies of Eminent Monks*, see note 29 from section 1-3.

68 "Relics" translates *shari* (舎利; Ch. *shèlì*; a transliteration of Skt. *śarīra*). After Shakyamuni died, his relics were divided into eight portions and

enshrined in stupas erected by his students in various parts of India. Several hundred years after Shakyamuni's death, Indian Buddhists also began to make images of the Buddha to enshrine in temples. Visiting these stupas and temples to worship relics and Buddha statues became a common Buddhist practice, and it remains so.

69   "Study hall" translates *shūryō* (衆寮; Ch. *zhōngliáo*), which today is a hall for studying, having tea, or taking a rest in a Zen monastery. The layout of this hall is similar to a monks' hall (僧堂; Ch. *sēngtáng*; Jp. *sōdō*). Study halls traditionally have the bodhisattva Avalokiteśvara enshrined. In Dōgen's "Regulations for the Study Hall" (衆寮清規; Jp. "Shūryō shingi"), it states that "it is impolite for a person in the study hall to put a Buddha or bodhisattva image at their own desk. Also, do not hang any pictures."

70   "Heavenly demon Pāpīyas" is from *tenma hajun* (天魔波旬; Ch. *tiānmó bōxún*). *Tenma* (Skt. *deva-māra*) literally means "heavenly demon" and refers specifically to the king of the *Paranirmita-vaśavartin* heaven (他化 自在天; Ch. *tāhuà zìzài tiān*; Jp. *take jizai ten*), who attempts to hinder those who follow the Buddhist way. He is one of four or five *māra*s, and he is the *māra* said to be responsible for tempting the Buddha while he sat under the Bodhi Tree. "Pāpīyas," meaning *demon*, is synonymous with *māra*. The Sino-Japanese *hajun* is a transliteration of the Sanskrit rather than a translation.

71   The Sanskrit word Tathāgata (如来; Ch. *rúlái*; Jp. *nyorai*) is a common epithet of the Buddha. Literally it means "thus-come" or "thus-gone."

72   "Happiness" here is *fukubun* (福分; Ch. *fúfēn*), which refers to the causes that bring about happiness in the human and heavenly worlds, i.e., in saṃsāra. *Fukubun* is contrasted with *dōbun* (道分; Ch. *dàoēn*), the causes for awakening that transcend saṃsāra. What Dōgen is saying here can be compared to Bodhidharma's encounter with Emperor Wu, who asks how much merit he will receive as a result of his lavish patronage of Buddhism. Bodhidharma famously answers, "No merit."

73   We become the "Buddha's children" by receiving the Buddha's precepts and taking the vows of a bodhisattva. "Buddhahood" translates *butsui* (仏位; Ch. 佛位, *fówèi*), literally "the rank of a Buddha." Dōgen wrote about this term in the fascicle of the *Shōbōgenzō* entitled the "Thirty-Seven Elements of Training to Realize Awakening" (三十七品菩提 分法; Jp. "Sanjūshichihon bodai bunpō"):

> The great teacher Shakyamuni abandoned succeeding to his father's rank of king not because it was ignoble, but because he was to succeed to the rank of a Buddha, which is incomparably

precious. The rank of Buddha is the rank of a homeless monk. This is the rank venerated by all heavenly and human beings. This is the rank of ultimate awakening. (Okumura and Wright, *Shōbōgenzō zuimonki*, 22)

74 "Just sitting" is a literal translation of *shikantaza* (只管打坐; Ch. *zhǐguǎndǎzuò*). In Dōgen's "Talk on the Wholehearted Practice of the Way" (辨道話; Jp. "Bendōwa"), he quotes his teacher Rujing (see note 19 in section 1-1) as follows:

> According to the tradition handed down without mistake, this Buddhadharma, which has been singularly and directly transmitted, is supreme beyond comparison. From the time you begin to practice under a teacher, incense burning, bowing, *nenbutsu*, as well as the practices of repentance or of reading the sutras, are unnecessary. Simply practice zazen (*shikantaza*), dropping off body and mind.

75 During the Kamakura period (1192–1333 CE) in which Dōgen lived, some monks eschewed the precepts, while others put heavy emphasis on observing them. The former group included the Pure Land Buddhists, especially Shinran (親鸞; 1173–1263 CE), while an example of the latter was Eisai (栄西; 1141–1215 CE). It seems that Dōgen sought a middle way: keeping the precepts without clinging to them and with no expectation of any reward for observing them.

76 "Family style" translates *kafū* (家風; Ch. *jiāfēng*). In China, Buddhists were said to be of the *bukke* (仏家; Ch. 佛家, *fójiā*), "the Buddha family"; Confucians were from the *juke* (儒家; Ch. *rújiā*), "the Confucian family"; and Daoists were from the *dōke* (道家; Ch. *dàojiā*), "the Dao family." Each had its own "family style."

77 This statement is similar to the opening of the fascicle of the *Shōbōgenzō* entitled "True Reality of All Things" (諸法實相; Jp. "Shohō jissō"). There, Dōgen wrote, "The manifestation of the buddhas and ancestors is the completely penetrated true reality." The "completely penetrated true reality" is how Dōgen understands zazen.

78 In Menzan's version of the text, this monk's name is given as Gogenbō (五眼房). This might be another name of Eisai's disciple Ryūzen (隆禪), who went to China before Dōgen. In Dōgen's *Record of the Hōkyō Era* (宝慶記; Jp. *Hōkyōki*), we find, "'When the body and mind are confused, chant the beginning of the text called "the bodhisattva precepts."' Then I [Dōgen] asked, 'What text is that?' Rujing said, 'It's what the Japanese monk Ryūzen has been chanting'" (Tanahashi, *Enlightenment Unfolds*, 6).

79   "The late Superintendent of Monks Yōjō" refers to Eisai (see note 65 from section 1-12).

80   "The *Precepts Sutra*" refers to the *Brahmā Net Sutra* (Ch. 梵網経, *Fànwǎng jīng*; Jp. 梵網経, *Bonmō-kyō*), which was thought to have been translated from Sanskrit into Chinese by Kumārajīva in the early fifth century. It presents the Mahāyāna precepts for bodhisattvas, which are called "bodhisattva precepts" or "fundamental precepts," consisting of ten major precepts and forty-eight minor precepts. Today's scholars generally believe this sutra was written in China.

81   "Pure standards" (清規; Ch. *qīnggūi*; Jp. *shingi*) are the regulations that students observe when practicing in Zen monasteries. The oldest pure standards text was said to have been compiled by Baizhang Huaihai (百丈懷海; Jp. Hyakujō Ekai; 720–814 CE), who was thus thought of as the founder of Zen monasteries. This putative *Pure Standards of Baizhang* (百丈清規; Ch. *Bǎizhàng qīnggūi*; Jp. *Hyakujō shingi*) is not extant, and today's scholars believe it probably never existed. In the later *Pure Standards of the Zen Monastery* (禪苑清規; Ch. *Chányuàn qīnggūi*; Jp. 禅苑清規, *Zen-en shingi*), the oldest surviving pure standards text, the first chapter is on receiving the precepts, and the second chapter is on maintaining them. The first chapter states, "In learning Zen and seeking the Way, the precepts are of primary importance. If you do not depart from evil deeds and protect yourself from wrong, how is it possible to be a Buddha or an ancestor?"

82   "Fundamental precepts" is a translation of *konponkai* (根本戒; Ch. *gēnběnjiè*), which refers to the bodhisattva precepts. In the *Brahmā Net Sutra*, it is said that the fundamental precepts are "the source of all buddhas, the origin of all bodhisattvas, the seed of buddha-nature" (Muller and Tanaka, *Brahmā's Net Sutra*, 40).

83   The thirty-fourth minor precept of the *Brahmā Net Sutra* begins with the following: "My disciples, you should uphold the precepts when walking, standing, sitting, or lying down. You should chant these precepts throughout the six periods of the day and night" (Muller and Tanaka, *Brahmā's Net Sutra*, 62).

84   After this section, Menzan's version includes an additional talk (section 1-3 in his version) as follows:

> On one occasion Dōgen said: "In the assembly of Zen master Fuzhao, there was a monk who, when he was sick, wanted to eat meat. The master allowed him to do so. One night the master himself went to the infirmary and saw the sick monk eating meat in the dim lamplight. Although the monk thought he was putting

it into his own mouth, it was not him, but the demon who was eating. After that whenever a sick monk wanted to eat meat, the master allowed him to do so because he knew such a monk was possessed by a demon.

Thinking about this story, we must carefully consider whether to allow [such a thing], or not. There was also an instance of eating meat in the assembly of Wuzu Fayan. Whether allowing or prohibiting it, all the ancient masters surely had their own deep considerations." (Okumura and Wright, *Shōbōgenzō zuimonki*, 26)

The individuals mentioned in this section are Fozhao Deguang (佛照德光; Jp. Busshō Tokkō; 1121–1203 CE), a student of Dahui and transmitter to Dainichibō Nōnin (大日房 能忍; fl. 1190s), and Wuzu Fayan (五祖法演; Jp. Goso Hōen; 1024–1104 CE), a prominent Zen master of the early Song dynasty and the teacher of Yuanwu Keqin (圓悟克勤; Jp. Engo Kokugon; 1063–1135 CE), author of the *Blue Cliff Record* (Ch. 碧巖録, *Bìyánlù*; Jp. 碧巖録, *Hekiganroku*).

85 In section 1 of Dōgen's *Points to Watch in Practicing the Way* (学道用心集; Jp. *Gakudō yōjin shū)*, he writes the following:

Though there are many names for bodhi mind [the mind of awakening], they all refer to the one-mind. The Ancestral Master Nāgārjuna said that the mind that solely sees the impermanence of this world of constant appearance and disappearance is called bodhi mind. Therefore, [for now I think it would be appropriate to talk about] bodhi mind as the mind that sees impermanence. Truly, when you see impermanence, egocentric mind does not arise, neither does desire for fame and profit. Out of fear of time slipping away too swiftly, practice the Way as if you are trying to extinguish a fire enveloping your head. Reflecting on the transiency of your bodily life, practice as diligently as the Buddha did when he stood on tiptoe for seven days. Even when you hear the melodious music of *kinnara* or the sound of the *kalaviṅka* bird flattering you, it is only the evening breeze blowing in your ears. Even when you see such a beauty as Maoqiang and Xishi, it is merely a drop of morning dew passing before your eyes. (Okumura, *Heart of Zen*, 6)

The *kinnara* and *kalaviṅka* of Indian mythology are both half-bird, half-human hybrids with beautiful voices; Maoqiang (毛嬙; Jp. Mōshō) and Xishi (西施; Jp. Seishi) are legendary Chinese women famous for their extraordinary beauty.

86 This is a quotation from a famous dialogue between Baizhang Huaihai (see note 81) and a former Zen master who had been reborn as a fox in retribution for stating that accomplished Zen practitioners are not subject to cause and effect. Taking the form of an old man, he asks for Baizhang's teaching on the matter. Baizhang tells him that a Zen master is "not blind to cause and effect." Upon hearing this, the fox is awakened and dies. This story appears in two major kōan collections: case 8 of the *Book of Serenity* (Ch. 從容録, *Cóngróng lù*; Jp. 従容録, *Shōyōroku*) and case 2 of the *Gateless Barrier* (Ch. 無門關, *Wúménguān*; Jp. 無門関, *Mumonkan*). Dōgen made additional comments on this story in two fascicles of the *Shōbōgenzō*: "Great Practice" (大修行; Jp. "Daishugyō") and "Profound Faith in Cause and Effect" (深信因果; Jp. "Jinshin inga").

87 In Menzan's version of the text, this passage has only "Cause and effect are clearly manifested" (因果歴然; Jp. *inga rekinen*). The Chōen-ji version thus transitions into the next sentence more clearly due to the former version's omission of "together at one time."

88 This refers to another famous story, this time about Nanquan Puyuan (南泉普願; Jp. Nansen Fugan; 748–834 CE), the monks in his assembly, and his student Zhaozhou Congshen (趙州從諗; Jp. Jōshū Jūshin; 778–897 CE). There is an unspecified argument among the monks about a cat when Nanquan appears and says he will cut the cat unless his students can say something. No one speaks, and he cuts the cat in two. Nanquan later tells Zhaozhou what happened, and in response Zhaozhou takes off his sandals, puts them on his head, and leaves. Nanquan then says that if Zhaozhou had been there, he could have saved the cat. This story appears in case 9 of the *Book of Serenity*, and case 14 of the *Gateless Barrier*.

89 Menzan's version has "Speaking is not possible" (道不得) instead of "We have already spoken."

90 This is a quotation from Yuanwu's introduction to case 3 of the *Blue Cliff Record* (see also the end of note 84, which briefly mentions Yuanwu and some of the individuals connected to him).

91 "Pivotal words" translates *itten go* (一転語; Ch. 一轉語, *yīzhuǎn yǔ*), which are powerful expressions that are supposed to be capable of transforming a person's fundamental understanding of the self.

92 "The mountains . . . are . . . mind" is taken from a conversation between Guishan Lingyou (Ch. 潙山靈佑; Jp. 潙山霊佑, Isan Reiyū; 771–853 CE) and his disciple Yangshan Huiji (仰山慧寂; Jp. Kyōzan Ejaku; 807–83 CE). It appears as case 168 in Dōgen's *Shinji Shōbōgenzō* as follows:

Guishan asked Yangshan, "How do you understand the wondrous, pure, and bright mind?"

Yangshan replied, "Mountains, rivers, the great earth, the sun, the moon, and the stars." (Tanahashi and Loori, *True Dharma Eye*, 225)

This expression is mentioned by Dōgen in the fascicle of the *Shōbōgenzō* entitled "The Mind Is Itself Buddha" (即心是仏; Jp. "Sokushin ze butsu"), where he wrote, "It should be clearly understood that the Mind is mountains, rivers, and the great earth, the sun, the moon and the stars." This is likely part of Dōgen's attempt to reform Ejō's understanding of "mind," or Buddha-nature. Ejō's previous teacher taught that Buddha-nature is something hidden that we must find within us, whereas Dōgen taught that it is nothing other than ordinary reality prior to our concepts and ideas.

93   "The mind is itself Buddha" is a famous saying of Mazu Daoyi (馬祖道一; Jp. Baso Dōitsu; 709–88 CE). As mentioned in the previous note, Dōgen dedicated a fascicle of the *Shōbōgenzō* to this expression.

94   Here, Dōgen is employing one of his common teaching techniques where he equates two things (in this case, the "cutting of the cat" and the "action of a Buddha") but then states that each is fundamentally just that thing itself (i.e., cutting the cat is just cutting the cat). He does this to pull the student away from conceptualization and dualism and instead bring their attention to reality as it is. This is famously found in two fascicles of the *Shōbōgenzō*: in "Great Perfection of Wisdom" (摩訶般若波羅蜜; Jp. "Maka hannya haramitsu") where he equates form and emptiness but then writes that "form is nothing but form; emptiness is nothing but emptiness," and in "The Samadhi That Is King of Samadhis" (三昧王三昧; Jp. "Zanmai ō zanmai") where he equates sitting zazen with the Buddhadharma but then states that we must let sitting just be sitting and the Buddhadharma just be the Buddhadharma.

95   *Pratimokṣa* is Sanskrit for the list of rules contained in the Vinaya. These are recited in the repentance ceremony (see note 42 from section 1-6). The Sino-Japanese translation of *pratimokṣa* used by Ejō is *betsu gedatsu kai* (別解脱戒; Ch. *biéjiětuō jiè*), literally "separate liberation precepts," indicating that by keeping each precept, monks can attain the liberation corresponding to each precept. In *The Sutra of the Last Discourse* (Ch. 佛遺教經, *Fóyíjiào jīng*; Jp. 仏遺教経, *Butsuyuikyō gyō*), Shakyamuni says, "Monks, after my death, respect and follow the *pratimokṣa*. If you do so, you will be like a person who has been given a light in the dark, or like a pauper who has acquired a great treasure."

96   The remainder of this section is a fairly technical discussion between
     Ejō and Dōgen about the prohibitions of the *Brahmā Net Sutra*. Through-
     out the exchange, Ejō's questions follow a literal understanding of the
     text, while Dōgen's answers are based on his own unique and much
     freer interpretation. This discussion may have been part of Ejō's prepa-
     ration to have the precepts transmitted to him from Dōgen; this pre-
     cepts transmission is called *denkai* (Jp. 伝戒; Ch. 傳戒, *chuánjiè*), which
     happens shortly before Dharma transmission (嗣法; Ch. *sìfǎ*; Jp. *shihō*)
     and is distinct from receiving the precepts at the time of ordination.
     This tradition still exists today.

97   The *Brahmā Net Sutra's* forty-first minor precept says:

> If [the one requesting precepts] has broken one of the ten pre-
> cepts, you should teach him or her how to repent: they should go
> before an image of a buddha or bodhisattva and recite the ten
> grave and forty-eight minor precepts throughout the six periods
> of the day and night. (Muller and Tanaka, *Brahmā's Net Sutra*, 62)

This would seem to suggest a precept can be broken even if it has not
yet been received, which is the thrust of Ejō's line of questioning.

98   Repentance is a Buddhist practice that stretches back to India. At a
     repentance ceremony (see note 42 from section 1-6), as well as at the
     time of receiving the precepts at ordination, all unwholesome deeds
     committed in the past are repented. Dōgen's teaching emphasizes the
     power of sincere repentance, no matter what violation was committed
     or when, as we see in this exchange with Ejō.

99   In the beginning of the forty-second minor precept it is said, "My dis-
     ciples, you should not, with the intent of gaining some kind of personal
     advantage, discuss the Mahāyāna precepts of the thousand buddhas
     before those who have not yet received them, nor in front of evil
     non-Buddhists" (Muller and Tanaka, *Brahmā's Net Sutra*, 70).

100 Ejō is alluding to a section of the *Brahma Net Sutra* about the fifth minor
     precept. It reads, "My disciples, if you see any sentient beings violating
     the eight precepts, the five precepts, or the ten precepts, or who are
     defying the prohibitions by way of the seven heinous acts or the eight
     difficult circumstances, or any other kind of violation of the precepts,
     you should encourage them to repent" (Muller and Tanaka, *Brahmā's
     Net Sutra*, 49).

101 Here Dōgen is referring to the fortieth minor precept in the *Brahma Net
     Sutra*. It states the following:

When someone wishes to receive the precepts, the preceptor should inquire, "In this life, have you ever committed one of the seven heinous acts?" A bodhisattva preceptor should not confer the precepts on anyone who has committed one of the seven heinous acts in this life. The seven heinous acts are wounding a buddha, killing one's father or mother, killing one's teacher, killing one's preceptor, disrupting the sangha, and killing an arhat. If someone has committed any one of these seven heinous acts, he or she cannot receive the precepts in this lifetime. Anyone else can receive the precepts. (Muller and Tanaka, *Brahmā's Net Sutra*, 68)

Despite the apparent finality of this precept, in Dōgen's interpretation this is merely meant as a deterrent against someone committing these offenses, and it should not actually disqualify someone from receiving the precepts. Perhaps because in Dōgen's time Japan was a relatively violent society run by a military government, Dōgen may have thought it important to put strong emphasis on the forgiveness of past misdeeds.

102 "Evening talk" translates *yawa* (夜話; Ch. *yèhuà*). These were informal talks given in the evening in the abbot's chamber. At the time that this text was being recorded, Dōgen's temple did not yet have a Dharma hall, and he therefore could not give formal Dharma hall discourses (上堂; Ch. *shàngtáng*; Jp. *jōdō*).

103 "To scold" translates *kashaku* (呵嘖; Ch. *hēzé*), a word used in Vinaya texts for the formal public blaming and assignment of penalties to monks that had violated the precepts. Here, Dōgen is not referring to this formal monastic practice, but, instead, he is cautioning his senior monks regarding their treatment of junior monks who may have misbehaved.

104 Vinaya texts state that four or five monks are the minimum required to form a sangha, depending on the tradition. Saichō (最澄; 767–822 CE), the founder of the Japanese Tendai school in which Dōgen first became a monk, wrote in the beginning of his *Regulations for the Student of the Mountain Monastery* (山家学生式; Jp. *Sanke gakushō shiki*), "What is the treasure of the nation? Truly it is the mind of awakening (*bodhicitta*). Those who have aroused the mind of awakening are national treasures."

105 "Parental heart" is a translation of the Japanese expression *rōbashin* (老婆心), which literally means "heart/mind of an old woman." Another translation might be "grandmotherly heart." In Dōgen's *Instructions for the Cook* (典座教訓; Jp. *Tenzo kyōkun*), he discusses three minds: joyful mind (喜心; Jp. *kishin*), parental mind (老心; Jp. *rōshin*), and magnanimous

mind (大心; Jp. *daishin*). Of "parental mind," he writes, "*Rōshin* is the mind or attitude of a parent. In the same way that a parent cares for an only child, keep the Three Treasures in your mind."

106 For biographical information on Rujing, see note 19 from section 1-1.

107 Minamoto no Yoritomo (源頼朝; 1147–99 CE) was the first shōgun (military dictator) of the Kamakura period (1192–1333 CE). He was the third child of Minamoto no Yoshitomo (源義朝; 1123–60 CE). Yoritomo was appointed general of the Right Imperial Guard (右大将; Jp. *udaishō*) in 1190 and became the shōgun in 1192. He was the first samurai who fully seized political power from the emperor's government.

108 The Middle Palace Guard (abbreviated in the text as 兵衛府; Jp. *hyōe-fu*) was the office of the samurai class that guarded the imperial court and the emperor when he was traveling. Yoritomo was appointed to be the assistant secretary of the headquarters of the Middle Palace Guard in 1159 when he was twelve years old. Soon after, his Minamoto clan was defeated by the Taira clan, his father was killed, and Yoritomo was exiled to Izu (伊豆), near Kamakura.

109 "Minister of the interior" translates *daifu* (内府). In 1160, the year after this story takes place, Dōgen's maternal grandfather, Fujiwara no Motofusa (藤原基房; 1144–1230 CE), became the minister of the interior. The scholar Yaoko Mizuno has surmised that Dōgen may have heard this story from his grandfather (Mizuno, *Shōbōgenzō zuimonki*, 96). Dōgen's paternal grandfather (or, less likely, father), Minamoto no Michichika (源通親; 1149–1202 CE) also held this position.

110 "Major councilor" translates *dainagon* (大納言), a relatively high-ranking position in the imperial government.

111 Rokuhara (六波羅) is the name of the place in Kyoto where the Taira clan (平氏; Jp. Heishi) had their estate; it was an ancient Japanese custom to replace a person's name with the place where they live. The Taira clan was the rival of the Minamoto clan and was the more powerful of the two at the time this story takes place. These clans continued to fight until Yoritomo established the Kamakura shogunate.

112 Lu Zhonglian (魯仲連; Jp. Ro Chūren; 305–245 BCE) was a famous Chinese political advisor and scholar (not in fact a general as stated in the text) during the Warring States period (475–221 BCE). Lord Pingyuan (平原君; Ch. píngyuán jūn; Jp. heigen kun) was a son of King Wuling of Zhao (趙武靈王; Ch. Zhào Wǔlíng wáng; Jp. 趙武霊王, chō burei ō; d. 295 BCE). This particular story appears in volume

83 of the *Records of the Historian* (史記; Ch. *Shǐjì*; Jp. *Shiki*). The larger story relates to the siege of the capital of the State of Zhao (趙; Jp. Chō) by the powerful State of Qin (秦; Jp. Shin). Lu Zhonglian prevented an advisor from the neighboring State of Wei (魏; Jp. Gi) from convincing the king of Zhao to surrender to the Qin army. Soon after, an army from Wei came to the rescue and the siege was lifted. However, the State of Qin would ultimately go on to conquer these other states, unifying China under the Qin dynasty.

113 "Impermanence is swift. Life-and-death is the great matter" translates the famous phrase *mujō jinsoku shōji jidai* (無常迅速生死事大; Ch. *wúcháng xùnsù shēngsǐ shìdà*). The phrase comes from a conversation between Dajian Huineng (大鑒惠能; Jp. Daikan Enō; 638–713 CE), the semi-legendary Sixth Ancestor of Zen, and his putative disciple Yongjia Xuanjue (Ch. 永嘉玄覺; Jp. 永嘉玄覚, Yōka Genkaku; 665–713 CE), who is the author of the well-known *Song of Enlightenment* (證道歌; Ch. *Zhèngdào gē*; Jp. *Shōdōka*). The dialogue appears in volume 5 of *The Record of the Transmission of the Lamp* (景德傳燈錄; Ch. *Jǐngdé chuándēnglù*; Jp. *Keitokudentōroku*), an important collection of biographies of Zen monks that dates from 1004. The phrase is also a part of a verse commonly written on the percussive woodblock called a *han* (板; Ch. *bǎn*), used in Zen monasteries to alert residents to the start and end of activities. "Life-and-death" is hyphenated because the phrase is understood as a compound that fully includes both concepts as one thing without separation.

114 "Teaching schools" (教家; Ch. *jiàojiā*; Jp. *kyōgaku*) refers to all non-Zen schools of Buddhism. While most schools of East Asian Buddhism were centered on particular scriptures, the Zen school claimed not to rely on written teachings. However, in the fascicle of the *Shōbōgenzō* entitled "Buddha's Teachings" (仏教; Jp. "Bukkyō"), Dōgen negates this idea of a transmission outside the teachings. For an explanation of exoteric and esoteric scriptures, see note 32 from section 1-4.

115 In *Points to Watch in Practicing the Way* (学道用心集; Jp. *Gakudō yōjin shū*), Dōgen wrote, "Neither intelligence nor broad knowledge is of primary importance. Intellect, volition, consciousness, memory, imagination and contemplation are of no value. Without resorting to these methods, enter the buddha-way by harmonizing body and mind" (Okumura, *Heart of Zen*, 22).

116 "Zen Master Zhijue" (Ch. 智覺禪師; Jp. 智覚禅師, Chikaku *Zenji*) is the honorific title of Yongming Yanshou (永明延壽; Jp. Yōmyō Enju; 904–75 CE), an eminent scholar known for his work the *Record*

of the Source Mirror (宗鏡録; Ch. *zōngjìng lù*; Jp. *Sugyō roku*). His teacher's teacher was Fayan Wenyi (法眼文益; Jp. Hōgen Buneki; 885–958 CE), the founder of the Fayan school (法眼宗; Jp. Hōgen shū) of Zen. Yanshou has been studied in English; see, for example, Albert Welter, *Yongming Yanshou's Conception of Chan in the Zongjing Lu: A Special Transmission within the Scriptures* (New York: Oxford University Press, 2011).

117 "Climb to the top of a hundred-foot pole . . ." references the following verse by the Chinese Zen Master Changsha Jingcen (長沙景岑; Jp. Chōsa Keishin; 788–868 CE), a disciple of Nanquan Puyuan (see note 88 from section 2-4); it is recorded in the tenth volume of *The Record of the Transmission of the Lamp* (景德傳燈録; Ch. *Jǐngdé chuándēnglù*; Jp. *Keitokudentōroku*):

> The immovable person at the top of the hundred-foot pole,
> Although he has entered [the Way], he is not truly [a person of the Way],
> [He should] advance one step further from the top of the hundred-foot pole.
> The ten-direction world is the whole body [of the person].

118 Tiantong is the name of the mountain where Dōgen's teacher's temple was located. It was customary for a teacher to take the mountain name of their temple as part of their name. Thus, Dōgen's teacher was known as Tiantong Rujing. For biographical information, see note 19 from section 1-1.

119 "Authentic" is a translation of *nyohō* (如法; Ch. *rúfǎ*), which literally means "being in accordance with the Dharma" or "like the Dharma," referring to any form that manifests or expresses the Dharma. This expression is known to many American Zen Buddhists through the term *nyohō-e* (如法衣; Ch. *rúfǎyī*), which refers to a style of Buddhist robes that are sewn by hand.

120 The sixteenth minor precept in the *Brahmā Net Sutra* says, "You should fully offer your body to hungry tigers, wolves, and lions, as well as to all hungry ghosts, including the flesh from your arms and legs" (Muller and Tanaka, *Brahmā's Net Sutra*, 53).

121 "Robes made of abandoned rags" is a translation of the Sino-Japanese word *funzō-e* (糞掃衣; Ch. *fènsǎo yī*; Skt. *pāṃsu-kūla*). In India, the kesa (袈裟; Ch. *jiāshā*; Skt. *kāṣāya*), the robe of Buddhist monks, was made of abandoned rags found in garbage heaps, graveyards, and other waste places. In the *Shōbōgenzō* fascicle "Virtues of the Kāṣāya" (袈裟功徳; Jp.

"Kesa kudoku"), Dōgen wrote, "As the unchanging way of the buddhas, *funzō-e* are best [for monks' clothing]."

122 In early Chinese Zen, monasteries owned land and communal property called *jōjū motsu* (常住物; Ch. *chángzhù wù*) in order to be self-sufficient. They quickly came to be supported by the emperor, the government, or the nobility, and they received all of their provisions from them.

123 "Wrong livelihood" translates *jamyōjiki* (邪命食; Ch. *xiémìngshí*), the opposite of right livelihood (正命; Ch. *zhèngmìng*; Jp. *shōmyō*) in the eight-fold noble path. See also note 28 from section 1-3.

124 For an explanation of the "last Dharma," see note 22 from section 1-2.

125 "The three countries" (Ch. 三國, *sānguó*; Jp. 三国, *sankoku*) are India, China, and Japan.

126 This is a quotation from the fourth chapter of *The Analects* (論語; Ch. *Lúnyǔ*; Jp. *Rongo*) of Confucius.

127 Subhūti (须菩提; Ch. Xūpútí; Jp. Shubodai; referred to here by the epi-thet 空生; Ch. *kōngshēng*; Jp. *kūshō*) was one of the ten great disciples of Shakyamuni Buddha. In the Mahāyāna tradition it is said that he had a profound understanding of emptiness, while in Theravada Buddhism he is associated with loving-kindness; he is also the student to whom the Buddha speaks in the *Diamond Sutra*.

128 Mahākāśyapa (大迦葉; Ch. Dàjiāyè; Jp. Daikashō) was also one of the ten great disciples. According to the Zen tradition, he received Dharma transmission from the Buddha and became the First Ancestor of India.

129 Xishi (西施; Jp. Seishi) and Maoqiang (毛嬙; Jp. Mōshō) are legendary Chinese women of extraordinary beauty. They are also mentioned in note 85 relating to section 2-2.

130 Feitu (飛兔; Jp. Hito) and Lu'er (緑耳; Jp. Ryokuji) were famous horses in China.

131 "Dragon's liver" and "leopard's embryo" were used in Chinese litera-ture to refer metaphorically to rare delicacies.

132 A certain king invited the Buddha and his five hundred disciples to spend a ninety-day summer practice period in his country. The Buddha and his assembly went to the country, but the king was so absorbed in pleasure that he forgot to make daily offerings of food, so they suffered from malnutrition. There was a man who owned five hundred horses who offered half of his horse fodder to the Buddha and his disciples. The Buddha received the offering in order to continue the practice

period. Variants of this story appear in many texts, both in Pali and Chinese sources.

133 The *Selections of Refined Literature* (文選; Ch. *Wénxuǎn*; Jp. *Monzen*) is an anthology of classical Chinese works compiled around 530 CE. It was popular in Japan as a text for students of literature.

134 "Seven or eight years" from the time Dōgen returned to Kyoto from China would suggest this talk was given in 1234 or 1235. See also note 19 from section 1-1.

135 This saying is from the *Essentials of Rebirth in the Pure Land* (往生要集; Jp. *Ōjōyōshū*), written by the Japanese Tendai monk Genshin (源信; 942–1017 CE). The work is famous for its vivid depictions of the hell realms, and it influenced both Hōnen (法然; 1133–1212 CE) and Shinran (see note 75 in section 2-1), contemporaries of Dōgen and the founders of the two major schools of Japanese Pure Land Buddhism.

136 "Unseen deities" refers to guardian deities of Indian origin such as Brahmā or Indra. It was commonly believed in China and Japan that these unseen deities were responsible for rewarding or punishing human actions.

137 For example, the twenty-eighth minor precept in the *Brahmā Net Sutra* states the following:

> My disciples, if there is a renunciant bodhisattva, a householder bodhisattva, or a patron who wishes to invite a monk in order to gain merit, then at the time of making the invitation he should go to the monastery and speak to a monastery officer, saying, "I now wish [to make a request to invite a monk," to which the officer should respond,] "Invitations are distributed in order of seniority, which means that you will be gaining access to all enlightened monks in the monastery." Even though, [as recounted in some scriptures,] secular people gave private invitations to the five hundred arhats and bodhisattva monks, this is not as good as following the protocol of seniority and you may end up with an unenlightened monk. Giving personal invitations to monks is a custom of non-Buddhists. In the tradition of the Seven Buddhas there is no such custom as giving personal invitations, and it does not accord with the way of filial piety. If you intentionally make an invitation to a monk, this constitutes a minor transgression of the precepts. (Muller and Tanaka, *Brahmā's Net Sutra*, 59–60)

138 This alludes to a commentary on the *Lotus Sutra* by Zhiyi (智顗; Jp. Chigi; 538–97 CE) known as *The Profound Meaning of the Lotus Sutra* (法

華玄義; Ch. *Fǎhuā xuányì*; Jp. *Hokke gengi*). These phrases mean that although causality cannot be doubted, we cannot always know the effect of any given cause.

139 In the fascicle of the *Shōbōgenzō* entitled "The Karma of the Three Periods of Time" (三時業; Jp. "Sanjigō"), Dōgen writes, "In learning and practicing the Way of buddhas and ancestors, from the outset, we should study and clarify this principle of karma and its effects in the three periods of time. Otherwise, we will fall into inverted views. Not only that, we will also fall into the painful realms and suffer for a long time."

140 The phrase Dōgen uses here is *shidai kotsujiki* (次第乞食; Ch. *cìdì qǐshí*; Skt. *paiṇḍapâtika*), literally meaning "begging in order." When monks begged, they needed to do so at each and every house on the street, one after the other, without discriminating on the basis of the wealth of the inhabitants.

141 The points made in this section are similar to those made in section 6-21.

142 "Regulate" translates *jōbuku* (調伏; Ch. *diàofú*), which is literally "harmonize and subdue." As a Buddhist term it means to control our body and mind in order to avoid unwholesome deeds. The same compound is used to translate the Sanskrit word *vinaya*, which—in addition to referring to the rules of conduct for monks—literally means "discipline" or "removal."

143 "Worldly sentiment" translates *sejō* (世情; Ch. *shìqíng*), and "human sentiment" translates *ninjō* (人情; Ch. *rénqíng*). These are natural functions of the mind in the mundane human world. Typically, Zen teaching is understood to be going beyond good and bad, but here Dōgen says even if we are acting based on worldly or human sentiments, we should still refrain from unwholesome acts and instead perform wholesome actions. Going beyond the dichotomy of good and bad should never be understood to mean that it is acceptable to act in an unwholesome way.

144 For biographical information on Eisai and an explanation of the rank "superintendent of monks," see note 65 from section 1-12.

145 "Medicine Buddha" translates Yakushi (薬師; Ch. *Zhuóshī*; Skt. Bhaiṣajyaguru; literally "medicine master"), the Buddha of healing. He is often depicted holding a pot of medicine in his left hand, and sometimes his skin is colored blue. When he was a bodhisattva, he is said to have made twelve vows, one of which was to save those subject to starvation, even if they had committed a crime to obtain food.

146 According to the Vinaya, property offered to a stupa belongs to the Buddha, and property given to the sangha belongs to the monks. In this case, the copper was a material donated to construct the Buddha statue; therefore, in accordance with the Vinaya, it should not have been used for any other purpose.

147 In the *Jātaka* tales, a collection of stories on the previous lives of the Buddha, there is one in which he offered his own body to feed a starving tigress and her cubs. Many similar tales are found in the collection.

148 "Evil rebirth" (惡趣; Ch. *èqù*; Jp. *akushu*; Skt. *durgati*) refers to rebirth as a hell dweller, an animal, or a hungry ghost. Sometimes the list includes rebirth as an *asura*, an antigod jealous of and at war with the gods. Of the six realms of saṃsāra, only rebirth as a human or god was typically considered desirable.

149 Kennin-ji was located by the east side of the Kamo River (鴨川). Because Kyoto is surrounded by steep mountains, heavy rainstorms would often cause serious flooding.

150 Jetavana monastery (祇園精舍; Ch. qíyuán jīngshè; Jp. gion shōja) was a major Buddhist monastery near Śrāvastī, one of the largest cities in India in the Buddha's time. It was donated by Anāthapiṇḍika (給孤独; Ch. Gěigūdú; Jp. Kyūkotoku), a wealthy merchant. Jeta was the name of a prince who owned the property before Anāthapiṇḍika purchased it from him. It is traditionally held to be the first permanent center of Buddhism. Its archaeological remains were rediscovered in the nineteenth century, and today it is a historical park.

151 For biographical information on Emperor Taizong and Wei Zheng, see notes 62–63 in relation to section 1-10.

152 Emperor Wen (文帝; Ch. Wéndì; Jp. Montei; 541–604 CE) was the founder of the Sui dynasty.

153 "The heavenly demon Pāpīyas" is explained in note 70 in relation to section 2-1.

154 "Demon" (魔; Ch. *mó*; Jp. *ma*) is often used to refer to Māra, the demon who tried to tempt the Buddha as he sat beneath the Bodhi Tree.

155 As explained in note 125, "the three countries" (Ch. 三國, *sānguó*; Jp. 三国, *sankoku*) are India, China, and Japan.

156 "Hīnayāna nature" means the attitude of practicing only for the sake of the emancipation of one's own self or of escaping from saṃsāra through one's own efforts. The spirit of a bodhisattva is, instead, a vow to save all living beings. In Dōgen's fascicle of the *Shōbōgenzō* entitled

"Arousing the Mind of Awakening" (發菩提心; Jp. "Hotsu bodaishin"), he wrote, "To arouse the mind of awakening is to vow to work for the salvation of all living beings before saving oneself." The word *Hīnayāna* is also discussed in note 54 from section 1-8.

157 For an explanation of "teaching schools," see note 114 from section 2-8.

158 "Life-and-death" here means saṃsāra; also see note 113 from section 2-8 for an explanation of this term.

159 Minamoto no Harukane (源顯兼; d. 1215 CE) practiced as a "lay monk," which translates *nyūdō* (入道; Ch. *rùdào*; literally "one who has entered the Way"). This meant a person had received a monk's ordination, shaved their head, and put on a Buddhist robe, yet lived at home with a family. "Middle councilor" is a translation of *chūnagon* (中納言), a court ranking below major councilor (大納言; Jp. *dainagon*). Other Japanese imperial government ranks also come up in section 2-6.

160 Kōin (公胤; 1145(?)–1216 CE) is discussed on page 10 of the introduction.

161 "The three thousand worlds in a single moment of thought" (一念三千; Ch. *yīniàn sānqiān*; Jp. *ichinen sanzen*) is a central teaching in the Tendai tradition. It states that all phenomena in the universe are included in any one thought-moment.

162 When monks traveled, they wore bamboo hats called *kasa* (笠; Ch. *lì*). This saying means that for a monk to wander without studying or practicing is misguided. *Tengu* are supernatural creatures associated with Japanese religion. In Dōgen's time, they were usually viewed as disruptive demons, though later they were also viewed as protective deities. They are typically depicted with a mixture of avian and human characteristics, and today usually with extremely long noses.

163 Hongzhi Zhengjue (宏智正覺; Jp. Wanshi Shōgaku; 1091–1157 CE) is a famous Chinese Caodong (曹洞; Jp. Sōtō) Zen master who served as the abbot of Tiantong monastery, where Dōgen later practiced when he went to China. Hongzhi was well known for his poetry, and he composed verses on one hundred kōan stories. Wansong Xingxiu (萬松行秀; Jp. Banshō Gyōshu; 1166–1246 CE) later wrote a commentary on these verses and created the *Book of Serenity* (從容錄; Ch. *Cóngróng lù*; Jp. *Shōyōroku*), one of the most important texts in Sōtō Zen.

164 Here Dōgen refers to Hongzhi as *chōrō* (長老; Ch. *chánglǎo*), translated as "Elder." This is a title of respect for an accomplished Buddhist teacher. Dōgen frequently praises Hongzhi in his writings.

165 For an explanation of "Shakyamuni's legacy," see note 30 in section 1-3.

166 "Arhat" translates ōgu (応供; Ch. 應供, *yìnggōng*), which literally means "worthy to receive offerings," and it is one of several Chinese words that refers to an arhat. Here, Dōgen is specifically referring to the Sixteen Arhats (十六羅漢; Ch. *shíliù luóhàn*; Jp. *jūroku rakan*) who were asked by Shakyamuni not to enter nirvana, in order to protect the Dharma and the people who study and practice the Dharma, until the appearance of the future Buddha Maitreya.

167 For an explanation of "last Dharma," see note 22 in section 1-2.

168 "Evil destinies" (惡道; Ch. *èdào*; Jp. *akudō*) here has the same meaning as "evil rebirth" commented on in note 148 of section 3-2.

169 The text here literally has "eight catties and half a tael" (八両と半斤; Jp. *hachiryō to hankin*). A tael is a measurement of weight equal to about forty grams, and there are sixteen catties in one tael. These units are still used for certain applications in the Chinese-speaking world. The same expression is also still used in modern Chinese.

170 A famous example of a small cause having a great result is a young boy's sincere offering of sand to the Buddha that resulted in his later rebirth as the great King Aśoka of the Mauryan dynasty. This story comes from the *Chronicle of Aśoka* (阿育王傳; Ch. *Āyùwáng zhuàn*; Jp. *Aikuō den*). Dōgen specifically cites this story elsewhere, for example, in the fascicle of the *Shōbōgenzō* entitled "The Bodhisattva's Four Embracing Actions" (菩提薩埵四摂法; Jp. "Bodaisatta shishōbō"): "Offering sand, a child gained the throne. These people did not covet rewards from others. They simply shared what they had according to their ability" (Okumura, "28th Chapter of Shōbōgenzō," 11).

171 In this passage, Dōgen is distinguishing the activities of laypeople and the activities of monks, as well as the results of their respective activities. He does not negate the notion that laypeople can receive tangible benefits from giving to the Buddhist community, but he says that this alone cannot cause people to awaken. Instead, only sincere practice can do this.

172 Dōgen wrote an appeal letter in the twelfth lunar month of 1235 to raise funds to construct the first formal monks' hall (僧堂; Ch. *sēngtáng*; Jp. *sōdō*) in Japan. Construction was completed the next year. It is possible that the monks' hall and the Dharma hall (法堂; Ch. *fǎtáng*; Jp. *hattō*) were built at the same time. Dōgen gave the first formal Dharma hall discourse in the tenth month of 1236.

173 The Sino-Japanese word *dōjō* (道場; Ch. *dàocháng*) has entered the English language and refers to a place where Japanese martial arts are

practiced. Originally, however, it translated the Sanskrit *bodhi-maṇḍa*, the "place of awakening," referring to the ground under the Bodhi Tree where the Buddha awakened. In *Zuimonki* it has the intermediate meaning of "place of Buddhist practice."

174 Kantō (関東) is a large flat area in eastern Japan, dominated today by Tokyo and its suburbs. In this case, it refers to the city of Kamakura, the seat of the shogunate that ruled Japan in Dōgen's time. The person referred to in this passage encourages Dōgen to go there and gain the support of powerful samurai in order to fund his temple construction project. Many Buddhist masters, including Eisai, moved to Kamakura to gain the support of the samurai class. Dōgen did end up visiting Kamakura later on, from 1247 to 1248.

175 "Dharma words" (法語; Ch. *fǎyǔ*; Jp. *hōgo*) are brief lectures, often in poetic form, that express something about the Dharma and are usually delivered by an abbot.

176 As mentioned previously, the *Selections of Refined Literature* (文選; Ch. *Wénxuǎn*; Jp. *Monzen*) is a sixth-century Chinese compilation of about seven hundred well-known poems and prose writings by about 130 important writers. In Japan, this collection was regularly studied as part of an aristocratic education. According to the *Record of Kenzei* (建撕記; Jp. *Kenzei ki*), one of Dōgen's biographies, he read a collection of Chinese poems when he was only four years old and continued to receive the best education available at his time.

177 In Menzan's version of the text there is an additional exchange before this reply. To the first question, Dōgen replies, "I want to understand the deeds of the ancients," after which the monk repeats the same question.

178 "Principle of mind" (心の理; Jp. *shin no ri*) describes the nature of "mind" as it is understood in East Asian Buddhism, but this mind should not be confused with the human brain or the limited psychology of the individual. In Dōgen's teaching, "mind" includes all beings in the here and now, but it is not an abstract, unchanging, permanent thing like a soul or an essence. In his "Talk on the Wholehearted Practice of the Way" (辨道話; Jp. "Bendōwa"), Dōgen criticizes the notion of a permanent, unchanging mind, explaining that all beings in the ever-changing phenomenal world are nothing other than one mind (一心; Ch. *yīxīn*; Jp. *isshin*).

179 "Restraining precepts" translates *kai ritsugi* (戒律儀; Ch. *jièlǜyí*; Skt. *śīla-saṃvara*). *Kai* translates the Sanskrit word *śīla*, which means "morality." *Ritsugi* was used to translate *saṃvara*, a word adapted into Buddhism

from Jainism that means "restraint." Together, they refer to the precepts that aim to prevent unvirtuous deeds of body and speech.

180 These various scriptural categories are explained in note 32 from section 1-4.

181 In classical Chinese poetry, tones are often prescribed in a set structure similar to meter, or rhythmic structure, in English poetry. In Chinese, these structures are called *píngzè* (平仄; Jp. *hyōsoku*).

182 Ku Amidabutsu (空阿弥陀仏) is the name that the monk Myōhen (明遍; 1142–1224 CE) used to refer to himself after he became a Pure Land Buddhist. He extensively studied both East Asian Mādhyamaka (三論宗; Ch. Sānlùn-zōng; Jp. Sanron-shū) and East Asian Esoteric Buddhism (密教; Ch. Mìjiào; Jp. Mikkyō) and was an eminent scholar. Originally a monk of the esoteric Shingon school headquartered on Mt. Kōya (高野山), he later became a student of Hōnen (法然; 1133–1212 CE) and his Pure Land school (Ch. 浄土宗; Ch. Jìngtǔ-zōng; Jp. 浄土宗, Jōdo-shū), which is referred to as the "Nenbutsu school" later in the text in reference to the school's practice of *nenbutsu* (念仏; Ch. 念佛, *niànfó*), i.e., reciting the name of the buddha Amitābha.

183 "Renounced the world" here is *tonsei* (遁世; Ch. *dùnshì*), which normally refers to the act of becoming a Buddhist monk. In this passage, however, this phrase actually refers to him "renouncing" his Shingon temple, which was part of the Buddhist establishment, in favor of a Pure Land temple, which was not. For a broader discussion of this term, see the introduction, pages 9–10.

184 "Formal discourses" translates *jōdō* (上堂; Ch. *shàngtáng*), which literally means "ascend the hall," probably referring to the abbot taking a high seat in the Dharma hall before delivering the talk. Dōgen's formal discourses, also loosely translated as "Dharma hall discourses," are collected in *Dōgen's Extensive Record* (永平広録; Jp. *Eihei kōroku*).

185 This same phrase ("impermanence is swift and life-and-death is the great matter") is also quoted in section 2-8; it is explained in note 113.

186 *Nāgá* (龍; Ch. *lóng*; Jp. *ryū*; literally "dragon" in Sino-Japanese) is the Sanskrit word for a snake-like deity from ancient Indian mythology. Nāgás were found in pre-Buddhist Indian traditions but came to be one of the eight classes of deities who protect the Buddhist faith. There are many specific nāgás discussed in Buddhist texts; in East Asian Buddhism the "eight great dragon kings" (八大龍王; Ch. *bā dàlóng wáng*; Jp. *hachi dairyū ō*) are especially popular, for example. Although originally conceived of as snake-like, when Buddhism traveled to China, the nāgá

was conflated with preexisting dragon myths; thus, in East Asia they are generally thought of as more dragon-like than snake-like.

187 As in note 126, this is a quotation of Confucius from chapter 4 of his *Analects* (論語; Ch. *Lúnyǔ*; Jp. *Rongo*).

188 "Repaying our debts of gratitude" translates *hō'on* (報恩; Ch. *bàoēn*). *Hō* means "repayment," and *on* means "kindness." The phrase can thus be translated as to "repay a kindness" or, in this case, "repay a debt of gratitude."

189 "Filial piety and obedience" is a translation of *kōjun* (孝順; Ch. *xiàoshùn*). Filial piety is one of the most important virtues in Confucian thought in China, Korea, and Japan. In the *Brahmā Net Sutra*, which was likely produced in China, we find the following: ". . . [the Buddha's] first act was to establish the *Prātimokṣa*, [encouraging his followers] to piously obey their fathers and mothers, honored monks, and the Three Treasures. Pious obedience is the principle of the ultimate path" (Muller and Tanaka, *Brahmā's Net Sutra*, 42).

190 The *Classic of Filial Piety* (Ch. 孝經, *Xiàojīng*; Jp. 孝経, *Kōkyō*) mentioned here is one of the most important Confucian texts. In it, Confucius insists that filial piety is the foundation of all virtues and social morality.

191 As a Buddhist term, "nondoing" (Ch. 無爲, *wúwéi*; Jp. 無為, *mu'i*) is a translation of the Sanskrit word *asaṃskṛta*, which means "unconditioned" and is usually synonymous with nirvana. However, the Chinese compound was borrowed from Daoism, where it already had the meaning of "effortless doing." In Zen Buddhism, the Buddhist and Daoist concepts blended together. It does not necessarily mean inactive; rather it means to act freely for the sake of Dharma or all living beings—that is, without a narrow purpose, one example of narrow purpose being when children make offerings exclusively for their parents. Bodhidharma's "no merit" and Dōgen's *shikan* (只管; "just doing") refer to the same attitude.

192 In a bodhisattva practice, we do not do things in order to get a good result for us alone, but we vow to do beneficial things for the sake of the awakening of all beings. In early Buddhism, it was believed that when one chanted sutras, the individual received good karma from the activity. In later Mahāyāna Buddhism, the notion of taking good karma for oneself was rejected, and merit from the activity was instead always dedicated to all beings or certain people in need.

193 "The period between death and rebirth" translates *chūin* (中陰; Ch. *zhōngyīn*), in turn, a translation of the Sanskrit word *antarabhāva*, meaning

"intermediate state" or "transitional existence." The Tibetan term *bardo* is more commonly used in English than the Sino-Japanese or Sanskrit words. In Mahāyāna Buddhism, the state is believed to last forty-nine days, during which time meritorious activities performed by the deceased's family may help the transitional being to be born in a better realm.

194 The twentieth minor precept in the *Brahmā Net Sutra* states, "On the day of the death of your father, mother, or elder or younger siblings you should request a Dharma teacher to deliver a lecture from the *Bodhisattva Vinaya Sutra* in order to convey blessings on the deceased that they may attain a vision of the buddhas and be reborn as a human being or as a celestial" (Muller and Tanaka, *Brahmā's Net Sutra*, 55).

195 Cūdapanthaka (Ch. 周利盤特, Zhōulìpántè; Jp. 周利槃特, Shūri-handoku) was one of the Buddha's disciples. He was dull-witted and unable to memorize even one verse of teaching in four months. Shakyamuni Buddha gave him the job of cleaning the monks' sandals, and this enabled him to attain realization. In another version of the story, the Buddha instructed him to sit facing east while repeating the phrase "cleaning off the dirt" and wiping his face with a clean cloth. As Cūdapanthaka noticed the cloth getting dirty from wiping off his sweat, he gained insight into the reality of impermanence and immediately became an arhat.

196 This refers to a famous story in which Nanyue Huairang (南嶽懷讓; Jp. Nangaku Ejō; 677–744 CE) approaches his student Mazu Daoyi (馬祖道一; Jp. Baso Dōitsu; 709–788 CE), who is sitting in zazen. Nanyue asks him what he hopes to become by sitting zazen, and Mazu responds that he intends to become a buddha. Nanyue then picks up a clay roof tile and begins to attempt to polish it. When Mazu asks why he is doing so, Nanyue says he intends to polish it into a mirror (a mirror being a common Buddhist symbol for the Buddha's wisdom). Mazu asks how it is possible to polish a tile into a mirror, and Nanyue, in turn, asks him how it is possible to become a buddha by sitting zazen. Dōgen discusses this story extensively in the *Shōbōgenzō* fascicle entitled "Acupuncture Needle of Zazen" (坐禪箴; "Zazenshin").

197 "Not-doing" is a translation of *fui* (不為; Ch. *bùwéi*). This is essentially the same as the phrase *mu'i* discussed in note 191 in section 3-15.

198 "Self" is capitalized here because it translates *jiko* (自己; Ch. *zìjǐ*), which Dōgen consistently uses to denote the Self that includes all beings, not the limited self or ātman of the ignorant individual.

199 Qu Yuan (屈原; Jp. Kutsugen; ca. 339–ca. 278 BCE) was a famous politician and poet who lived in ancient China during the Warring States

period. Here, the text states that Qu Yuan died in the Canglang River (滄浪; Jp. Sōrō), but, in fact, that is the name of a river that appeared in one of his poems. He actually is said to have died in the Miluo River (汨羅江; Jp. bekira kō) in northern Hunan province.

200 Eating one meal is one of the twelve austerities (十二頭陀行; Ch. *shíèr tóutuó xíng*; Jp. *jūni zuda gyō*; Skt. *dvādaśa dhūta guṇāḥ*), but according to Dōgen's "Instructions to the Kitchen Staff" (示庫院文; Jp. "Ji kuin mon"), Dōgen and his disciples seem to have eaten three meals per day (Nishijima and Cross, *Shōbōgenzō*, 4:143).

201 "Great peace and joy" (Ch. 大安樂, *dà ānlè*; Jp. 大安楽, *dai anraku*) ultimately translates the Sanskrit *mahā-sukha*, which in turn is usually equated with "nirvana." See also note 305 in relation to section 6-2.

202 The "will of heaven" refers to an important historical Chinese belief that an emperor can only rule with the "mandate of heaven" (天命; Ch. *tiānmìng*; Jp. *tenmei*). If a rebellion or natural disaster occurred, this was seen as an indication that the mandate of heaven had been lost, and the emperor could justifiably be overthrown.

203 In ancient times, the night was divided into five watches, and each watch was divided into five parts. The third part of the third watch was around 1:00 a.m.

204 "The four dignified actions" (四威儀; Ch. *sìwēiyí*; Jp. *shi igi*) are walking, standing still, sitting, and lying down. Also see note 36 from section 1-5.

205 About 11:00 p.m.

206 About 2:30 or 3:00 a.m.

207 The "illuminated hall" (照堂; Ch. *zhàotáng*; Jp. *shōdō*) was a hall behind the monks' hall where the head monk gave talks on behalf of the abbot. The hall developed from what was originally a walkway between the monks' hall and the washroom. It had a skylight in order to brighten it, hence the name "illuminated hall." It seems that Rujing sometimes gave informal talks in this hall.

208 The logic here is that while we really attain the Way with the mind, because the mind and body are one, the body also attains the Way.

209 Dōgen here refers to Lingyun Zhiqin (靈雲志勤; Jp. Reiun Shigon; n.d.) and Xiangyan Zhixian (香嚴智閑; Jp. Kyōgen Chikan; d. 898 CE), respectively. They were both disciples of Guishan Lingyou (Ch. 潙山靈佑; Jp. 潙山靈祐, Isan Reiyū; 771–853 CE; see also note 92 in relation to section 2-4). Lingyun was said to have awakened after seeing peach blossoms in the spring, when he realized the impermanence of

all things. Xiangyan was said to have been a great scholar who had memorized many Buddhist texts. He was asked to explain how things were, from the perspective of when he was an infant unable to use language. After being unable to find an answer in his books, he burned them all and ceased studying texts. Later, while sweeping the grave of a Zen master, he hit a piece of tile into a stalk of bamboo and attained awakening upon hearing the sound that was produced. Dōgen also discusses Lingyun and Xiangyan in the fascicle of the *Shōbōgenzō* entitled "Sounds of Valley Streams, Colors of Mountains" (谿聲山色; Jp. "Keisei sanshoku").

210 Dōgen's logic is essentially the opposite of the teaching schools: his logic is that because we attain the Way with the body, the mind also attains the Way. On this point, in the *Shōbōgenzō* fascicle "Zanmai ō zanmai," Dōgen wrote, "Full lotus sitting is the straight body, the straight mind, the straight body-and-mind. This is buddhas and ancestors themselves, and practice-enlightenment itself."

211 "Cast away" translates *hōge* (放下; Ch. *fàngxià*), meaning "throw away," "give up," "abandon," or "discard." It appears, for example, in a conversation between Zhaozhou (see note 88 in section 2-4 for biographical information) and Yanyang Shanxin (嚴陽善信; Jp. Genyō Zenshin; n.d.) in the *Book of Serenity* (Ch. 從容錄, *Cóngróng lù*; Jp. 從容錄, *Shōyōroku*):

> Yanyang asked Zhaozhou, "When not a single thing is brought, then what?"
> Zhaozhou said, "Cast it away."
> Yanyang said, "If I don't bring a single thing, what should I cast away?"
> Zhaozhou said, "Then carry it out."
> (Modified from Cleary, *Book of Serenity*, 241)

212 For an explanation of the "hundred-foot pole," see note 117 from section 2-10.

213 The image of practicing as if attempting to extinguish a fire engulfing one's head can be found in *The Rules of Purity in the Chan Monastery* (Ch. 禪苑清規, *Chányuàn qīngguī*; Jp. 禅苑清規, *Zen'en shingi*), which was compiled in 1103. It is part of a chant that was to be performed three times per month:

> . . . Another day has passed, / And our lives have been reduced commensurately; / We are like fish trapped in water that is slowly dwindling. / How can there be any pleasure at all in such an

existence? / One must live vigorously, / As if one's head were on fire and needed to be extinguished immediately. / Simply contemplate the impermanence of all things / And take care to avoid idle delay . . . (Yifa, *Origins of Buddhist Monastic Codes*, 137)

214 For the source and significance of this phrase, see note 113 from section 2-8.

215 "Fortune" here translates *kahō* (果報; Ch. *guǒbào*), which is a Buddhist term referring to the results of past karmic actions. It literally means the "fruit" of one's past action, whereas the "seed" would be the past action itself. It translates the Sanskrit *phala*, which also has the metaphorical sense of a "fruit."

216 "Transcendent world" translates *shusseken* (出世間; Ch. *hū shìjiān*). It can also be translated as "supramundane" or "transmundane," and it is used to translate the Sanskrit *lokôttara*. In the context in which it is used here, it refers to the monastic world as opposed to the world of laypeople.

217 "Battle" (合戦; Jp. *kassen*), as in a military engagement, is meant literally here. In Dōgen's time, warfare frequently took place among the wealthy ruling classes.

218 Dōgen entered Kennin-ji (建仁寺) and began to practice with his first Zen teacher, Myōzen (see note 326 in section 6-13), in 1217 when Dōgen was seventeen years old. He stayed there until he went to China with Myōzen in 1223. Myōzen died while they were abroad. After returning from China in 1227, Dōgen resided at Kennin-ji again until 1230.

219 "The forms of greeting one another" translates *monjin* (問訊; Ch. *wènxùn*). It refers to bowing to others in greeting with the palms of the hands pressed together (合掌; Ch. *hézhǎng*; Jp. *gasshō*). In Dharma hall discourse 133 from *Dōgen's Extensive Record*, Dōgen said of these greetings:

> Whenever brother monks meet each other in the hall, on the walkway, by the stream, or under the trees, lower your head and bow in *gasshō* to each other in accord with Dharma. Then start to speak. Before bowing it is not permissible to speak to each other on great or minor matters. We should always make this a constant rule. (Okumura and Leighton, *Dōgen's Extensive Record*, 159)

220 Haimen Shizhai (海門師斎; Jp. Kaimon Shisai; n.d.) was a disciple of Fozhao Deguang (佛照德光; Jp. Busshō Tokkō; 1121–1203 CE). Haimen's Dharma brother Wuchi Liaopai (無際了派; Jp. Musai Ryōha;

1149–1224 CE) was the abbot of Tiantong monastery when Dōgen first began to practice there in 1223.

221 Further details on the identity of the head monk, Yuan (元; Jp. Gen), are unknown.

222 "Head monk of the rear hall" is a translation of *godō shuso* (後堂首座; Ch. *hòutáng shǒuzuò*). In large monasteries, the monks' hall was divided into two parts: a front half (前堂; Ch. *qiántáng*; Jp. *zendō*) and a rear half (後堂; Ch. *hòutáng*; Jp. *godō*). Each half had its own head monk to lead the other monks. At Sōtō Zen monasteries today, only the position of *zendō shuso* remains, and that person is now simply called the *shuso*; the term *godō* evolved to refer to the disciplinary instructor of all the monks, including the *shuso*.

223 For biographical information about Taizong, see note 62 in section 1-10.

224 This relates to a passage in the third chapter of the *Lotus Sutra*:

> Now, this threefold world
> Is all my domain,
> And the living beings in it
> Are all my children.
> (Reeves, *Lotus Sutra*, 126)

225 "Wheel-turning king" is a translation of *rin ō* (輪王; Ch. *lún wáng*), which is an abbreviation for *tenrin jō'ō* (轉輪聖王; Ch. *zhuǎnlún shèngwáng*; Skt. *cakra-vartin*). In Indian Buddhism this refers to an ideal king who would rule the world according to the Buddhadharma. When the Buddha was born, a hermit named Asita predicted that the baby would become a wheel-turning king if he stayed in the mundane world or the Buddha if he left home. Despite the apparent assertion in this passage, the Buddha's father is not normally considered to be a wheel-turning king himself.

226 For "the age of the last Dharma," see note 22 in section 1-2.

227 For "teaching schools," see note 114 in section 2-8.

228 Zen monasteries are traditionally held to have been established around the time of Baizhang Huaihai (720–814 CE; for biographical information, see note 81 from section 2-1). It was said that before that time, Zen monks lacked their own monasteries and stayed in the temples of other schools, or otherwise wandered.

229 Dōgen says here that he had inherited wealth and lands from his family. It is possible that he might have used this wealth to fund his trip to

China, but whatever the case may have been, it seems that Dōgen had parted with it by the time he gave these talks.

230 Buddhist sutra scrolls were usually made of yellow paper rolled around a red rod. The key descriptor here is "coarse"; because yellow paper and the red rod were standard, they themselves do not indicate inferior quality.

231 Danxia Tianran (丹霞天然; Jp. Tanka Tennen; 739–824 CE) was a Dharma heir of Shitou Xiqian (see note 45 in section 1-6). The story about him burning a wooden Buddha statue appears in the fourteenth volume of *The Record of the Transmission of the Lamp* (景德傳燈錄; Ch. *Jǐngdé chuándēnglù*; Jp. *Keitokudentōroku*). According to the story, while Tianran was staying at a monastery, it was extremely cold, so he took a wooden Buddha statue and burned it. When he was criticized, he claimed he was doing so to obtain relics. When asked how this was possible, Tianran said, "If it is not [possible], why do you blame me?" When Shakyamuni passed away, people divided his relics into eight portions and housed them in eight stupas in various regions. Visiting those stupas and worshiping the Buddha's relics became an important practice for early Buddhists.

232 In Sōtō Zen, the *shashu* (叉手; Ch. *chāshǒu*) hand position is made by first putting the thumb of the left hand in the middle of the palm and making a fist around it. The fist is then placed on the chest and covered with the right hand. The elbows are kept away from the body such that the forearms form a straight line.

233 Dōgen uses the same simile of caring for temple property as if it were one's own eyes in *Instructions for the Cook* (典座教訓; Jp. *Tenzo kyōkun*). That text was produced in 1237, near the end of the period when Ejō was recording the talks that make up *Zuimonki*. The section reads as follows:

> First, following the midday meal, go to the offices of the prior and comptroller and get the ingredients for the next day's meals: rice, vegetables, and so on. Having received them, protect and be frugal with them, as if they were your own eyes. Chan Master Yong of Baoning [Monastery] said, "Protect and be frugal with monastery property, which is [like] your own eyes." Respect and value them as if they were ingredients for an imperial repast. These cautions apply to fresh and cooked things alike. (Foulk, "Instructions for the Cook," 22)

234 "Nest" (Jp. 窠臼, *kakkyū*; Ch. *kējiù*) refers to an incorrect view to which we constantly return, like birds returning to their nests.

235 "The pail of lacquer" (漆桶; Ch. *qītǒng*; Jp. *shittsū*) refers to a container for black lacquer, a liquid so dark that whatever it covers cannot be seen through it. It is a metaphor for delusions, ignorance, and ego-attachment. "Breaking the bottom of the pail of lacquer" means to become free from these delusions.

236 Although monks are actually allowed to own three robes and one bowl, Dōgen specifically says "one robe and one bowl" here. The Japanese Sōtō Zen monk and poet Ryōkan (良寛; 1758–1831 CE) used this same expression in his poetry.

237 Pang Yun (龐蘊; Jp. Hōun; ?–808 CE), more commonly called Layman Pang (龐居士; Ch. Páng Jūshì; Jp. Hōkoji), was a famous Buddhist lay practitioner whose example served as a model for ideal lay practice. Although Dōgen here says that Layman Pang threw his family's possessions into the ocean, in the introduction to his recorded sayings it states that he threw them into the Xiang River (湘江) near Lake Dongting (洞庭湖).

238 This question is similar to one asked by a monk in section 2-13, where the presence of communal property (常住物; Ch. *chángzhù wù*; Jp. *jōjū motsu*) in Chinese monasteries is also brought up, in that case as a reason for seeking out provisions from wealthy donors.

239 Dōgen gave this talk in 1236; ten years prior would have been around the time he had returned from China, in 1227.

240 For details about the legacy of the Tathāgata, see note 29 in section 1-3.

241 Dōgen gives a similar answer to a different question in section 3-11.

242 "The Sixth Ancestor of Caoxi" is Dajian Huineng (大鑒惠能; Jp. Daikan Enō; 638–713 CE), one of Zen's most famous figures; Caoxi (曹溪; Jp. 曹渓, Sōkei) is the mountain in what is now northern Guangdong province, where Huineng is supposed to have taught. Xinzhou (新州; Jp. Shinshū), today called Xinxing (新興), is regarded as his birthplace. Huineng's hagiography is recorded in *The Platform Sutra of the Sixth Ancestor* (六祖壇經; Ch. *Liùzǔ tánjīng*; Jp. *Rokuso dankyō*).

243 Huangmei (黃梅; Jp. Ōbai) is the name of the mountain where the monastery of Huineng's teacher, Daman Hongren (大満弘忍; Jp. Daiman Kōnin; 601–674 CE), was located.

244 In *The Platform Sutra of the Sixth Ancestor*, Huineng receives ten ounces of silver instead of the thirty ounces recorded here.

245 "Truly fulfilling your debt of gratitude" translates *shinjitsu hō'onsha* (真実報恩者; Ch. 眞實報恩者, *zhēnshí bàoēnzhě*). This is a part of the "Head-Shaving Verse" (剃髪偈; Ch. "Tìfǎ jié"; Jp. "Teihatsu ge") chanted during Buddhist ordination ceremonies in East Asian traditions when the ordinee's head is shaved. The verse is the following: "Within the karmic life of the triple world / The bonds of attachment are hard to break / Leaving them behind is to enter the Truth / Truly this fulfills your debt of gratitude" (流転三界中、恩愛不能断、棄恩入無為、真実報恩者).

246 *The Recorded Sayings of Zen Master Dongshan Liangjie* (瑞州洞山良价禪師語錄; Ch. *Ruìzhōu dòngshān liángjiè chánshī yǔlù*; Jp. *Zuishū tōzan ryōkai zenji goroku*) mentions this notion: "A sutra says that if one child leaves home [to become a monk], families of nine generations will be born in heaven." I have been unable to locate the sutra to which Dongshan alludes. Note also that Dongshan mentions nine generations, whereas Dōgen is recorded here as having said seven.

247 The "imperial attendant monk" (供奉; Ch. *gōngfèng*; Jp. *kubu*) was a monk who served at the Buddhist shrine hall in the imperial court.

248 National Teacher Zhong (Ch. 忠國師, Zhōng *guóshī*; Jp. 忠国師, Chū *kokushi*) refers to Nanyang Huizhong (南陽慧忠; Jp. Nanyō Echū; 675–775 CE) who, according to Zen tradition, was a disciple of Huineng (see note 242 in section 4-10). Zhong was said to have lived for more than forty years in the Dangzi valley (黨子) of Baiya Mountain (白崕) in Nanyang (南陽), Henan province (河南). In 761 CE, his renown caught the attention of the Tang Emperor Suzong (唐太宗; Ch. Táng Sùzōng; Jp. Tō Taisō), who invited him to the capital and gave him the high-ranking title of "national teacher."

249 This story about National Teacher Zhong is found in the section on him in the *Compendium of the Successive Lamp of the Chan School* (宗門聯燈會要; Ch. *Zōngmén liándēng huìyào*; Jp. *Shūmon rentō eyō*), which dates from 1189. In Menzan's version of *Zuimonki*, this story is recounted quite differently. It reads as follows:

> The National Teacher Zhong of Nanyang asked the imperial attendant monk Lin [who received] the purple [robe from the emperor], "Where did you come from?"
> The attendant monk replied, "I came from south of the city."
> The Master said, "What is the color of the grass there?"
> The attendant monk replied, "It is yellow."
> The Master inquired of his attending boy, "What is the color of the grass south of the city?"
> The boy said, "It is yellow."

The Master said, "Even this boy can receive the purple robe and talk about the profound truth to the emperor at the court."

[The Master] meant here that the boy could be a teacher of the emperor since he answered [with] the true color. The attendant monk's view did not go beyond common understanding.

250 "Personal views" (我見; Ch. *wǒjiàn*; Jp. *gaken*) can mean either one's personal views generally or the specific view that the self (我; Skt. *ātman*) has essential existence.

251 For "the provisional or genuine teachings," see note 55 in section 1-8. For "exoteric or esoteric scriptures," see note 32 in section 1-4.

252 In section five of *Points to Watch in Practicing the Way* (学道用心集; Jp. *Gakudō yōjin shū*), Dōgen wrote something much the same regarding scholars: "Day and night they counted the wealth of others; yet, not even a half penny could be called their own" (Okumura, Heart of Zen, 18). This expression is, in turn, taken from *The Flower Adornment Sutra* (華嚴經, Ch. *Huáyán jīng*; Jp. *Kegon kyō*; Skt. *Avataṃsaka-sūtra*). It comes from a section in which a variety of similes are used to describe people with extensive Buddhist knowledge who fail to put it into practice.

253 In section 1 of *Points to Watch in Practicing the Way*, written around the same time that Ejō recorded *Zuimonki*, Dōgen wrote:

> The sixty-two views are based on ego. When egocentric views arise, sit quietly, illuminate them and consider the following. What is the substance of all things inside and outside your body? You received all parts of your body from your mother and father. Your parents' red and white droplets are empty and are in no way substantial. Therefore your body is not "I." The mind and its functions, such as consciousness, thoughts and knowledge, bind your life moment by moment while you are alive. When inhaling and exhaling ceases, what on earth happens to your mind? Therefore, the mind is not "I" either. You should not be attached to your body or mind. A deluded person clings to body and mind, while an awakened person is unattached. And yet, you assume the existence of the ego though there is no ego, and you cling to life though it is unborn. You should practice the Buddha Way, but you don't. You should cut off worldly sentiments, but you don't. You dislike reality and seek after illusions. How can you avoid mistakes? (Okumura, *Heart of Zen*, 7)

254 The "eighteen elements" (十八界; Ch. *shíbā jiè*; Jp. *jūhachi kai*; Skt. *aṣṭadaśa dhātu*) are the six sense organs (eye, ear, nose, tongue, body,

mind), the six objects of the sense organs (visible objects, sounds, smells, tastes, touch, objects of mind), and the six consciousnesses (eye consciousness, ear consciousness, nose consciousness, tongue consciousness, body consciousness, mind consciousness).

255 For "the teaching schools," see note 114 from section 2-8.

256 This is a quotation from *Guishan's Admonitions* (潙山警策; Ch. *Guīshān jǐngcè*; Jp. *Isan keisaku*) written by Guishan Lingyou (Ch. 潙山靈祐; Jp. 潙山靈祐, Isan Reiyū; 771–853 CE), a Dharma heir of Baizhang Huai-hai (百丈懷海; Jp. Hyakujō Ekai; 720–814 CE). Guishan is also discussed in note 92 in relation to section 2-4.

In Menzan's version of *Zuimonki*, this line instead reads: "Associating with a good person is like walking through mist and dew; though you will not become drenched, gradually your robes will become damp."

257 "Master Juzhi" is Jinhua Juzhi (金華俱胝; Jp. Kinka Gutei), a Tang dynasty Zen master and the third generation descendent of Mazu Daoyi (馬祖道一; Jp. Baso Dōitsu; 709–788 CE). The story referenced here is case 245 in the *Shinji shōbōgenzō*. The story goes that whenever Juzhi was asked a question, he did not answer but instead just raised a finger. One day, someone asked Juzhi's attendant about his master's teaching, and the boy mimicked his master's action of raising a finger. When Juzhi heard this, he cut off the boy's finger. The boy ran away crying. Juzhi called after him, and when the boy turned his head, Juzhi raised his finger. The boy suddenly attained realization.

258 In December 1235, Dōgen began raising funds to build a Chinese-style monks' hall (僧堂; Ch. *sēngtáng*; Jp. *sōdō*) at Kōshō-ji (興聖寺), which would be the first of its kind to be built in Japan. A Dharma hall (法堂; Ch. *fǎtáng*; Jp. *hattō*) was completed around the same time. According to *Dōgen's Extensive Record* (永平広録; Jp. *Eihei kōroku*), Dōgen gave the first Dharma hall discourse (上堂; Ch. *shàngtáng*; Jp. *jōdō*) on the fifteenth day of the tenth month in 1236, just a few weeks before Ejō became head monk (首座; Ch. *shǒuzuò*; Jp. *shuso*). See note 222 in section 4-5 for more information on head monks.

259 "Informal gathering" translates *shōsan* (小参; Ch. *xiǎocān*), literally a "small meeting." These were usually held in the abbot's quarters. A Dharma hall discourse (上堂; Ch. *shàngtáng*; Jp. *jōdō*), in contrast, was called *daisan* (大参; Ch. *dàcān*), or "big meeting." *Shōsan* are only informal compared with *jōdō*, and they still have elements of formality. They are also distinct from the talks recorded in *Zuimonki* that Dōgen gave before the Dharma hall was completed. *Shōsan* began with a short Dharma talk followed by a question and answer session with the

students. In the eighth volume of *Dōgen's Extensive Record* (永平広録; Jp. *Eihei kōroku*), Dōgen said, "This informal meeting is [where are given] the family instructions of all buddhas and ancestors. In our country of Japan, in previous generations the name of this [shōsan] had not been heard, much less has it ever been practiced. Since I, Eihei, first transmitted this, twenty years have already passed" (Okumura and Leighton, *Dōgen's Extensive Record*, 484).

260 "Take up the whisk" translates *hinpotsu* (秉払; Ch. 秉拂, *bǐngfú*). It refers to the head monk or another senior monk giving a Dharma discourse in place of the abbot. It is so called because the person who gives the discourse holds the flywhisk of the abbot.

261 "The First Ancestor" (初祖; Ch. *chūzǔ*; Jp. *shoso*) is Bodhidharma (菩提達磨; Ch. Pútídámó; Jp. Bodaidaruma), the semi-legendary transmitter of Zen from India to China. According to traditional accounts, he sat in meditation at Shaolin temple continuously for nine years.

262 "Shenguang" (神光; Jp. Shinkō) is the birth name of Dazu Huike (大祖慧可; Jp. Taiso Eka; 487–593 CE), who became the Second Ancestor after becoming Bodhidharma's disciple. Dōgen extensively discusses stories about Huike and Bodhidharma in the fascicle of the *Shōbōgenzō* entitled "Continuous Practice" (行持; Jp. "Gyōji").

263 "The supreme vehicle" translates *saijō jō* (最上乘; Ch. 最上乘, *zuìshàng chéng*). In the Zen tradition, Bodhidharma's teaching was called the supreme or highest vehicle.

264 "Fenyang" refers to the place in Shanxi province where the temple of Master Fenyang Shanzhao (汾陽善昭; Jp. Funyō Zenshō; 947–1024 CE)—a Dharma descendent of Linji Yixuan (臨濟義玄; Jp. Rinzai Gigen; d. 866 CE)—was located. "Yaoshan" is the mountain in Hunan province where Yaoshan Weiyan (藥山惟儼; Jp. Yakusan Igen; 745–828 CE), a disciple of Shitou Xiqian (石頭希遷; Sekitō Kisen; 700–790 CE), was abbot. In the *Pure Standards for the Temple Administrators* (知事清規; Jp. *Chiji shingi*), Dōgen wrote:

> Yaoshan was an ancient buddha, but there were not as many as ten monks in his assembly. Zhaozhou also was an ancient buddha, but there were not as many as twenty monks in his assembly. Fenyang's assembly was as small as seven or eight monks. Just see that Buddha ancestors together with great [awakened] dragons are not limited by [the size of] their assembly. They only value having the Way, not whether there is a crowded assembly. Now and hereafter, [many] having the Way and having virtue are under [the lineage of] Yaoshan and descendants of Fenyang. We must value

Yaoshan's family style and must venerate the excellent example of Fenyang. You should know that even if there are one hundred, one thousand, or ten thousand monks, without the mind of the Way and without practice of contemplating the ancients, [the assembly] is inferior to toads and lower than earthworms. Even an assembly of seven, eight, or nine monks who have the mind of the Way and contemplate the ancients is superior to dragons and elephants and excels the wisdom of the sages. (Leighton and Okumura, *Dōgen's Pure Standards*, 156)

265 Xiangyan Zhixian and Lingyun Zhiqin and the stories about their respective awakening experiences are discussed in note 209 from section 3-20.

266 In Menzan's version of *Zuimonki*, this sentence instead reads, "Although the sound of bamboo is wondrous, it does not make sound of itself; it cries out with the condition of a piece of tile [hitting it]."

267 Dōgen also quotes this line in section 1-6; see note 45 for a brief discussion. It is also quoted in section 6-9.

268 Ānanda (阿難; Ch. Ānán; Jp. Anan) was one of the ten great disciples of Shakyamuni Buddha. He was the Buddha's attendant for more than twenty years and was said to have committed all his sermons to memory. It was said that after the Buddha's death Ānanda recited all of the sermons he had memorized at the First Buddhist Council, and these were later compiled into the collection of sutras (Skt. Sūtra Piṭaka).

269 The "three pounds of hemp" story refers to a dialogue involving Dongshan Shouchu (洞山守初; Jp. Tōzan Shusho; 910–90 CE), a disciple of Yunmen Wenyan (雲門文偃; Jp. Unmon Bun'en; 864–949 CE). It appears as case 172 in Dōgen's *Shinji shōbōgenzō* (真字正法眼蔵) and case 12 of the *Blue Cliff Record* (Ch. 碧巖錄, *Bìyánlù*; Jp. 碧巖録, *Hekiganroku*). The laconic story reads:

> A monk asked, "What is the Buddha?"
> Dongshan said, "Three pounds of hemp."

270 "Get water from the river" is translated from *mizu ni aki* (水にあき), but this phrase is difficult to interpret in the Japanese. *Aki* is from the verb *aku* (飽く), meaning "to get tired of" or "to be satisfied," neither of which makes sense in this context. Menzan's version instead has *kumo ni nemuri* (雲に眠り; "sleeping under the clouds"), possibly representing his attempt to make sense of it. To me, it seems what is meant here is likely the same as what Dōgen wrote in the *Shōbōgenzō* fascicle the "Mountains and Waters Sutra" (山水經; Jp. "Sansui kyō"): "From the distant past

to the distant present, mountains have been the dwelling places of the great sages . . . since ancient times, wise men and sages have also lived by the water" (Okumura, *Mountains and Waters Sutra*, 32–34). They did so because they wanted to be separate from the mundane world and its system of values.

271 As in note 24, "golden bones" (金骨; Ch. *jīngǔ*; Jp. *kinkotsu*) refers to the Buddha's relics; this means that not all of the ancient practitioners were as strong and capable as the Buddha.

272 The Vinaya Piṭaka (Ch. 律藏, Lǜ zàng; Jp. 律蔵, Ritsu zō) is one of the "three baskets" (Tripiṭaka), or categories, of the Buddhist scriptures, along with the Sūtra Piṭaka and the Abhidharma Piṭaka. The Vinaya Piṭaka includes the rules and regulations of monastic conduct. Each rule includes a story about why it was created; therefore, the texts showcase some of the worst behavior by early monks. There is, in fact, no separate Mahāyāna version of the Vinaya Piṭaka despite what is suggested here.

273 In early Buddhism, the term *arhat* meant "a worthy one" who has destroyed all the afflictions and all causes for future rebirth and who will thus enter nirvana upon death; in the *Lotus Sutra*, all arhats received a prediction from the Buddha that they would become buddhas in the future. In the *Shōbōgenzō* fascicle "The Arhat" (阿羅漢; Jp. "Arakan"), Dōgen used this word in the latter sense.

274 In the *Shōbōgenzō* fascicle "Mind Is Itself Buddha" (即心是佛; Jp. "Sokushin ze butsu"), Dōgen writes: "Upon hearing the expression 'mind itself,' many foolish people consider that the thinking and sensing mind that has not yet aroused the mind of awakening is itself buddha." Later in the same fascicle, he writes, "We clearly understand that the mind refers to the mountains, rivers, and the great earth; the sun, the moon and the stars."

275 In Buddhist scriptures, it is said that the Buddha has thirty-two major marks and eighty minor characteristics, including a two-meter-wide (six-and-a-half-foot-wide) halo emanating from his body. In the *Shōbōgenzō* fascicle "Ancient Buddha Mind" (古佛心; Jp. "Kobusshin"), Dōgen quoted Nanyang Huizhong's dialogue with a monk (see note 248 in section 5-1 for more about Nanyang):

A monk once asked the National Teacher, "What is the old buddha mind?"

The master answered, "Fences, walls, tiles, and pebbles."

276 Menzan's version adds the following: "You should believe that tiles and pebbles are 'Buddha.'"

277 This quotation originally comes from the Chinese classic *The Masters of Huainan* (淮南子; Ch. *Huáinánzǐ*; Jp. *Enanji*), which dates from the Han dynasty (206 BCE–220 CE). As Dōgen says, it is also found in the much later *Essentials of Government of the Zhenguan Period* (貞觀政要; Ch. *Zhēnguān zhèngyào*; Jp. *Jōkan seiyō*), a ten-volume collection of discussions on politics between Emperor Taizong and his ministers that was compiled during the Tang dynasty (618–907 CE). Dōgen also quotes from the *Essentials* in section 1-10 (see note 62).

278 "Mind of a beginner" translates *shoshin* (初心; Ch. *chūxīn*). This is the same phrase that Shunryū Suzuki cites in his popular contemporary work *Zen Mind, Beginner's Mind*. The book famously begins, "In the beginner's mind there are many possibilities, but in the expert's there are few" (Suzuki, *Zen Mind*, 1). Dōgen, however, simply uses this expression synonymously with "beginner" without the same positive valence.

279 According to his biography *The Record of Kenzei* (建撕記; Jp. *Kenzei ki*), Dōgen saw impermanence when his mother died, and thereafter he became determined to seek the Dharma.

280 "Great master" (大師; Ch. *dàshī*; Jp. *daishi*) was an honorific title given by the emperor in China and Japan to the most eminent Buddhist monks. In Japan, recipients of the title included Saichō (最澄), the founder of the Tendai school, and Kūkai (空海), the founder of the Shingon school. In 1878, Emperor Meiji gave the posthumous title Jōyō Daishi (承陽大師) to Dōgen.

281 The *Biographies of Eminent Monks* (高僧伝; Ch. *Gāosēng zhuàn*; Jp. *Kōsō den*) is a collection of biographies of eminent Chinese monks compiled by Huijiao (慧皎; Jp. Ekō; 497–554 CE). It covers monks from the time of Buddhism's introduction into China up to the Liang dynasty (502–57 CE). For the *Continued Biographies of Eminent Monks*, see note 29 from section 1-3.

282 This sentence appears in the fourteenth volume of the *Precepts of the Mahāsāṃghika* (摩訶僧祇律; Ch. *Móhēsēng qílǜ*; Jp. *Makasō giritsu*).

283 The nineteenth fascicle of Xuanzang's (玄奘; Jp. Genjō; 602–64 CE) translation of the *Abhidharma Storehouse Treatise* (阿毗達磨俱舍論; Ch. *Āpídámó jùshè lùn*; Jp. *Abidatsuma kusha ron*; Skt. *Abhidharmakośa-bhāṣya*) includes an enumeration of seven kinds of arrogance; these two are among them.

284 "Lay monk" translates *nyūdō* (入道; Ch. *rùdào*). There were some who received monk ordination (得度; Ch. *dédù*; Jp. *tokudo*) but remained at home with a family.

285 "Gods" here can refer to both the guardian gods of Buddhism of Indian origin, such as Brahmā, Indra, and so forth, or to the Japanese gods of what is now known as Shintō (祈祷).

286 See note 218 in section 4-4 for information on Dōgen's time at Kennin-ji.

287 "Superintendent of monks" refers to Eisai, the founder of Kennin-ji. See note 65 in section 1-12 for biographical information on him. He died in 1215, two years before Dōgen arrived.

288 The story that follows appears in volume 81 of the *Records of the Historian*. This work is also used as the source for Dōgen's recounting of another event from China's Warring States period in section 2-7. See note 112 there for background on the conflict between the states of Zhao and Qin and the source texts. Lin Xiangru (藺相如; Jp. Rin Shōjo) is known only from the *Records of the Historian*.

289 A *bi* (璧; Jp. *heki*) is a jade disk with a hole in the center. These disks were important in Chinese culture as far back as the Neolithic period, during which time *bi* were buried with high-status individuals. They are thought to be symbols of the heavens. In later Chinese history they were used to define court ranks, among other ceremonial uses.

290 In the section entitled "Upholding the Precepts" in *The Rules of Purity in the Chan Monastery* (Ch. 禪苑清規, *Chanyuan qinggui*; Jp. 禅苑清規, *Zenen shingi*), it is said that "after a monk has received the precepts, he must always uphold them. A monk would rather die with the law (the Dharma) than live without the law (the Dharma)" (Yifa, *Origins of Buddhist Monastic Codes*, 114).

291 For an explanation of the "age of the last Dharma," as well as the other periods, see note 22 in section 1-2.

292 For further information on the precepts, see note 272 in section 5-5.

293 *Gasshō* (合掌; Ch. *hézhǎng*; Skt. *añjali*) is the familiar Buddhist gesture of pressing one's palms together in greeting, reverence, etc. See also note 219 in relation to section 4-4.

294 "The six ways of harmony" (六和敬; Ch. *liùhé jìng*; Jp. *roku wakyō*) are mentioned in the *Jeweled Necklace Sutra* (Ch. 瓔珞經, *Yīngluò jīng*; Jp. 瓔珞経, *Yōraku kyō*), a Chinese-produced text. They are the unity of the

three actions (of body, speech, and thought), keeping the same precepts, sharing the same understanding, and carrying on the same practice.

295 Yanqi Fanghui (楊岐方會; Jp. Yōgi Hōe; 992–1049 CE) was a Dharma heir of Shishuang Chuyuan (石霜楚圓; Jp. Sekisō Soen; 986–1039 CE). Fanghui was the founder of the Yanqi branch of the Linji school, and all Japanese Rinzai lineages that exist today descend through this branch. His Dharma brother Huanglong Huinan (黃龍慧南; Jp. Ōryū Enan; 1002–69 CE) was the founder of the Huanglong branch.

296 In the Chōen-ji version, the final part of this line actually reads "sigh in space" (そらに嗟嘘す; Jp. sora ni sakyo su). The same quotation is found in the Shōbōgenzō fascicle "Continuous Practice" (行持; Jp. "Gyōji"), but this part reads "sigh in the darkness." Menzan's version also has "sigh in the darkness." I am therefore following his version and assuming the Chōen-ji version is mistaken here.

297 For biographical information on Emperor Taizong, see note 62 in section 1-10. The story about Taizong deciding against the construction of a new palace is told in the first paragraph of section 4-6.

298 Longya Judun (龍牙居遁; Jp. Ryūge Koton; 835–923 CE) was a Dharma heir of Dongshan Liangjie (洞山良价; Jp. Tōzan Ryōkai; 807–69 CE).

299 Jimyōin (持明院) was the Dharma name of Ichijō Motoie (一条基家; 1132–1214 CE). "Middle councilor" is a translation of chūnagon (中納言), a court ranking below dainagon (大納言) or "major councilor." For "lay monk," see note 284 in section 5-7.

300 "The Way" in this sentence does not refer to the Buddha Way but rather the Way of ministers and retainers in Confucianism.

301 Emperor Gaozu of Han (高祖; Jp. Kōsu; 256–195 BCE) was the founder of the Han dynasty (206 BCE–220 CE). The minister discussed later in the story is Wangling (王陵; Jp. Ōryō).

302 "Dedicate" here translates ekō (廻向; Ch. huíxiàng), the usual Sino-Japanese translation for the Sanskrit pariṇāmanā. It is typically used in a Buddhist context to mean "transfer of merit," such as is done during Mahāyāna Buddhist services when the merit gained from practice is transferred to some other party or to all beings. The implication here is that in dedicating ourselves to the Three Treasures, we must completely give ourselves away.

303 For "Dharma gates," see note 23 (section 1-2); for the "mind of awakening," see note 25 (section 1-2).

304 The notion that "we should allow ourselves to be used by the Buddha-dharma" is the same point that Dōgen makes in "Genjōkōan" (現成公案) when he writes, "All things coming and carrying out practice-enlightenment through the self is realization" (Okumura, *Realizing Genjokoan*, 1).

305 "Great peace and joy" translates *dai anraku* (大安楽; Ch. *dà ānlè*). *Anraku* is the Sino-Japanese translation of the Sanskrit *sukha*, which is understood to be the opposite of *duḥkha*, or "suffering." "Great peace and joy" is often understood as a synonym for nirvana.

306 "Points to watch in practicing the way": these same characters form the title of Dōgen's work *Points to Watch in Practicing the Way* (学道用心集; Jp. *Gakudō yōjinshū*). See notes 252 and 253 in section 5-2, note 85 in section 2-2, and note 115 in section 2-8 for quotations from this text.

307 "Secretary" translates *shoki* (書記; Ch. *shūji*). This was a monastic officer whose job was maintaining correspondences, especially with government officials, and keeping records. The position still exists at the larger Sōtō Zen monasteries in Japan, although the duties are now different because the government no longer regulates religious institutions. Secretary is one of the six traditionally prescribed monastic prefect positions in a monastery (六頭首; Ch. *liù tóushǒu*; Jp. *roku chōshu*).

308 This story is from the *Book of Jin* (Ch. 晉書, *Jìnshū*; Jp. 晋書, *Shinjo*), a history of the Jin dynasty made in 648 CE during the Tang dynasty (618–907 CE). The story was later included in the *Quest of the Unschooled* (蒙求; Ch. *Měngqiú*; Jp. *Mōgyū*), an eighth-century collection of biographies and anecdotes for children. In Japan, the book was used from the Heian period (794–1185 CE) all the way into early modern times as a primer for educated children.

309 This story is also from the *Book of Jin* and *Quest of the Unschooled*. The intended meaning of this story is not entirely clear, although it seems to suggest that the father was laudable because he gave away everything that his immediate personal needs did not require.

310 "Mountain immortal" translates *sennin* (仙人; Ch. *xiānrén*). It refers here to a Daoist mountain hermit who has attained immortality and supernatural powers. It is also sometimes translated as "thaumaturge," "sage," or "wizard." It has also been used elsewhere to translate the Sanskrit word *ṛṣi*, which refers to any of a variety of sages or saints of ancient or modern India, including the Buddha.

311 "Way" in this instance is used in the sense of Daoism (i.e., "the Dao"). The exchange comes from a Daoist story that first appeared in the

Biographies of the Deities and Immortals (神仙傳; Ch. *Shénxiān zhuàn*; Jp. *Shinsen den*), which is attributed to a fourth-century author. It was also included in the *Quest of the Unschooled* mentioned in note 308.

312 In the Chōen-ji version, instead of "benevolent emperor" (仁帝; Jp. *jintei*), the text has 心帝 (Jp. *shintei*), meaning "heart emperor." "Heart emperor," which makes little sense, is assumed to be a scribal error. The other instances of "benevolent" in the passage are given with the correct character (仁).

313 This story appears in the Chinese classic *Master Lu's Spring and Autumn Annals* (呂氏春秋; Ch *Lǔshì chūnqiū*; Jp. *Roshi shunjū*), and it is quoted in the *Quest of the Unschooled* mentioned in note 308.

314 Shihuang of Qin (Ch. 秦始皇, Qín shǐ huáng; Jp. 秦の始皇, Shin no shikō) was the founding emperor of the Qin dynasty (221–207 BCE); he is also mentioned as "the king of Qin," his role before becoming emperor, in section 5-8.

315 This story appears in the *Records of the Historian* (see also note 112 in section 2-7), and it is also quoted in the *Quest of the Unschooled*.

316 This refers to Qu Yuan, who is discussed in note 199 in section 3-18.

317 This alludes to a story from the *Records of the Historian* (see also note 112 in section 2-7) about two brothers named Boyi (伯夷; Jp. Hakui) and Shuqi (叔齊; Jp. Shukusei) who were from Guzhu (孤竹; Jp. Kochiku), a vassal state of the Shang dynasty (ca. 1600–ca. 1046 BCE). Their father planned to make the younger brother, Shuqi, his successor. Learning this, the elder brother, Boyi, left home, but Shuqi did not want to push his elder brother out, so he also left home. They both ended up living in the state of Zhou (周), which had begun planning to conquer Shang. The king of Zhou consulted Boyi and Shuqi about his plans, and they pleaded with him not to proceed. The king dismissed their petition. The brothers then refused to eat grain produced in Zhou. They hid on Shouyang Mountain (首陽山; Jp. Shuyōzan), initially eating only wild plants. Realizing that these also belonged to Zhou, they chose to starve themselves to death.

318 "Superintendent of monks" is a title that refers to Eisai; see note 65 in section 1-12. Eisai is also discussed in sections 2-1, 2-4, 2-14, 3-2, 3-6, and 5-8.

319 Zhenjing Kewen (真淨克文; Jp. Shinjō Kokubun; 1025–1102 CE), also known as Baofeng Kewen (寶峰克文; Jp. Hōbō Kokubun) was a disciple of Huanglong Huinan (黄龍慧南; Jp. Ōryū Enan; 1002–69

CE), the progenitor of the eponymous Huanglong branch of the Linji school.

320 Yunfeng Taoyuan (Ch. 雲峯道圓; Jp. 雲峰道円, Unpō Dōen; n.d.) was another student of Huanglong. In the Chōen-ji version, "Yunfeng" (雲峰; Jp. Unpō) was mistakenly written as "Xuefeng" (雪峰; Jp. Seppō).

321 This is likely related to the Buddha's hesitation to teach people immediately after his awakening. According to texts such as the *Āyācana Sutta* (SN 6.1) of the Pali canon, Brahmā requests three times that the Buddha teach his Dharma, after which he accepts.

322 This quotation from the poem "Merging of Difference and Unity" appeared previously in section 1-6; see note 45. It is also quoted in section 5-4.

323 For an explanation of *shikantaza*, see note 74 in section 2-1.

324 Dadao Guquan (大道谷泉; Jp. Daidō Yokusen), who was productive somewhere between the tenth and eleventh century CE, was a Linji Zen teacher of the Song dynasty (960–1279 CE) and a Dharma heir of Fenyang Shanzhao (see note 264 from section 5-4). The quotation that follows in the text is from his poem "The Song of the Great Way" (大道歌; Ch. "Dàdàogē"; Jp. "Daidōka").

325 When Shakyamuni abandoned his practice of extreme asceticism after six years, he bathed in the river and received an offering of milk porridge from a milkmaid named Sujātā before he began to sit under the Bodhi Tree. His eating of horse fodder was mentioned in section 2-13 (see note 132).

326 Butsuju Myōzen (佛樹明全; 1184–1225 CE) was born into the Soga family. Later, he practiced Zen under Eisai (see note 65 from section 1-12) at Kennin-ji and became his Dharma heir. Myōzen went to China in 1223 with Dōgen and a few other monks but died there when he was forty-one years old. Dōgen brought Myōzen's relics back to Japan and buried them at Kennin-ji. In the *Record of the Transmission of the Relics* (舍利相伝記; Jp. *Sharisōdenki*), Dōgen briefly describes Myōzen's life. For an English translation of this text, see Tanahashi, *Enlightenment Unfolds*, 30–31.

327 Myōyu (明融; d. 1223?) was a Tendai teacher from whom Myōzen first received ordination at Shuryōgon-in (首楞厳院), a temple on Mt. Hiei. *Ācārya* is a Sanskrit word that is transliterated in Sino-Japanese as *azari* or *ajari* (阿闍梨; Ch. *āshéli*). In Sanskrit it simply meant a teacher or preceptor; ācārya was similar in meaning to the Sanskrit *upādhyāya*, which literally means "preceptor." But in the Japanese Tendai and Shingon

schools, it became a formal rank of the priesthood; it came to be a rank or a general term for an abbot in its Sino-Japanese form of *oshō* (Ch. 和尚, *héshàng*; Jp. 和尚; also read *kashō* in Tendai and *washō* in Shingon). In the Sōtō school today, it is a low-level rank given to priests who have spent over five years in a training monastery and have received Dharma transmission (嗣法; Ch. *sìfǎ*; Jp. *shihō*). It is used immediately before this in the text as "preceptor" in "Preceptor Myōzen."

328 "The dark road" translates *meiro* (冥路; Ch. *mínglù*). This is a road that leads to the Yellow Spring (Ch. 黄泉, Huángquán; Jp. 黄泉, Yomi), a mythological underworld of the dead described in early Chinese written records. Yellow is the color representing the earth in the five-element theory of Chinese philosophy. By requesting that Myōzen see him off, Myōyu may be suggesting that Myōzen perform his funeral.

329 "Released" translates *shutsuri* (出離; Ch. *chūlí*), which in turn is often used to translate the Sanskrit *niryāṇa*, meaning exit, departure, or disappearance; the term is often synonymous with nirvana.

330 Xuanzang (玄奘; Jp. Genjō; 602–64 CE) is one of the most famous of all Chinese Buddhist monks. He traveled to India, studied Yogācāra, and brought back hundreds of Sanskrit manuscripts, which he and a large team of assistants then translated into Chinese, with imperial support. He first left China in 629 and returned in 645. Along with Kumārajīva (鳩摩羅什; Ch. Jiūmóluóshí; Jp. Kumarajū; 343/344–413 CE), Xuanzang is considered one of the greatest translators of the Chinese Buddhist canon. He is also considered the founder of the Chinese Yogācāra school (唯識宗; Ch. Wéishí zōng; Jp. Yuishiki shū; later known as 法相宗; Ch. Fǎxiàng zōng; Jp. Hossō shū). "Tripiṭaka master" (三藏法師; Ch. *sānzàng fǎshī*; Jp. *sanzō hōshi*) is an honorific title for monks who have mastered Buddhist scriptures (i.e., the Tripiṭaka) and translated them into Chinese.

331 *Mahāsattva* (大士; Ch. *dàshì*; Jp. *daishi*) is literally "a great person." It is often synonymous with bodhisattva.

332 In their notes on this section, the scholars Yaoko Mizuno and Rosan Ikeda suggest that this question is related to Ejō's own situation with his dying mother, mentioned in Keizan's *Record of the Transmission of the Light* (伝光録; Jp. *Denkō roku*). According to this account, at Kōshō-ji there was a regulation that a monk could only leave the monastery twice a month and for no more than three days at a time. Ejō had already visited his mother twice, but the entire assembly encouraged Ejō to visit his mother again to be with her when she died. Ejō ultimately decided

not to go, and his mother died without him (Mizuno, *Shōbōgenzō zuim-onki*, 369; Ikeda, *Gendaigoyaku shōbōgenzō zuimonki*, 322).

333 Dōgen here uses the Confucian expression *suishuku no kō* (水菽の孝; Ch. *shuǐshū xiào*) that literally means, "filial piety of water and beans," referring to children taking care of their sick and aged parents even if they can only provide water and beans.

334 "The mind of the past, present, and future," which translates *sanze no kokoro* (三世の心; Ch. *sānshì xīn*), refers to deluded human values, perceptions, and prejudices formed by worldly experiences. It is not certain which sutra Dōgen is quoting from.

335 This saying comes from a biography of a prince of Huainan (淮南王; Ch. *Huáinán wáng*; Jp. *Wainan ō*) from the *Records of the Historian* (see note 112 in section 2-7). The original sentence reads, "Although good advice sounds harsh to the ear, it is beneficial to our actions."

336 *Great Treatise* (大論; Ch. *Dàlùn*; Jp. *Dairon*) usually refers to the *Great Perfection of Wisdom Treatise* (Skt. *Mahāprajñāpāramitā-śāstra*; 大智度論; Ch. *Dàzhìdù lùn*; Jp. *Daichido ron*), a commentary attributed to Nāgārjuna (fl. second or third century CE) on the *25,000-line Perfection of Wisdom Sutra* (Skt. *Pañcaviṃśatisāhasrikā prajñāpāramitā sūtra*), which is popularly called the *Great Perfection of Wisdom Sutra* (Skt. *Mahāprajñāpāramitā sūtra*). The commentary was translated into Chinese by Kumārajīva. However, I cannot locate the story Dōgen references in that text.

337 The same simile of mist is used in section 5-3; see note 256 for further details.

338 The source of this story is not certain. According to Mizuno and Ikeda, "Zen Master Dahui" refers to Dahui Zonggao (大慧宗杲; Jp. Daie Sōkō; 1089–1163 CE), the same person who appears in section 6-18 (Mizuno, *Shōbōgenzō zuimonki*, 383; Ikeda, *Gendaigoyaku shōbōgenzō zuimonki*, 332).

339 "Thoroughly devoted" translates *tettokukon* (徹得困; Ch. *chèdékùn*), which appears, for example, in case 44 of *Shinji shōbōgenzō*:

> Guishan sat on the teaching seat.
>   A monastic came up and said, "Master, please expound the dharma for the assembly."
>   Guishan said, "I have already thoroughly devoted myself to you."
>   The monastic bowed. (Modified from Tanahashi and Loori, *True Dharma Eye*, 60)

In Menzan's version, this sentence is instead the following: "People who have penetrated the bones and penetrated the marrow (徹骨徹髓; Jp. *tekkotsu tetsuzui*) can attain this." This refers to a famous story about Bodhidharma and his students, who attempt to demonstrate their understanding of his teaching. The final student prostrates himself rather than saying anything, and Bodhidharma says that student has "attained the marrow [of his teaching]."

340 "Strings of coins" translates *kansen* (貫錢; Ch. *guànqián*). A *kan* (貫) denotes a thousand coins with holes in their centers tied together on a string. A *sen* (錢) was historically a coin-based unit of currency.

341 This saying appears in volume 23 of *The Recorded Sayings of Zen Master Dahui Pujue* (大慧普覺禪師語錄; Ch. *Dàhuì pǔjué chánshī yǔlù*; Jp. *Daie fukaku zenji goroku*).

342 The "Inscription on Faith in Mind" (信心銘; Ch. "Xìnxīn míng"; Jp. "Shinjin mei") is a famous Zen poem attributed to the Third Ancestor of Zen, Jianzhi Sengcan (鑑智僧璨; Jp. Kanchi Sōsan; d. 606 CE).

343 This section is absent from Menzan's version of the text.

344 *The Spring and Autumn Annals* (春秋; Ch. *Chūnqiū*; Jp. *Shunjū*), a chronicle of the State of Lu (魯; Ch. *Lǔ*; Jp. Ro) from 722 to 481 BCE, is one of the Five Classics (五經; Ch. *Wǔjīng*; Jp. Gokyō) of Confucianism.

345 Xuansha Shibei (玄沙師備; Jp. Gensha Shibi; 835–908 CE) was a disciple of Xuefeng Yicun (雪峰義存; Jp. Seppō Gison; 822–908 CE).

346 The story here relates to one told about Xuansha in Dahui's collection of kōans, the *True Dharma-Eye Treasury* (正法眼藏; Ch. *Zhèngfǎyǎnzàng*; Jp. *Shōbōgenzō*), not to be confused with Dōgen's later writings of the same name. In it, Xuansha was sick but took the wrong medicine, resulting in his entire body becoming red and festered. The "Dharma body" (法身; Ch. *fǎshēn*; Jp. *hōshin*; Skt. *dharmakāya*), in a Mahāyāna context, usually refers to absolute reality and is more or less synonymous with emptiness. However, the monk asks about the Dharma body as "indestructible" (堅固; Ch. *jiāngù*; Jp. *genko*). Xuansha answers by emphasizing the impermanent nature of the Dharma body in order to correct the monk's mistaken conception of it as permanent or unchanging. He also corrects the monk's conceptualization of the Dharma body as a lofty and abstract concept by instead tying it to the very mundane phenomenon of pus secretion.

347 The meaning of this sentence in the Chōen-ji version is not clear because no subject is specified. Menzan's version of the text instead

gives "the abbot" as the subject of the sentence (while the Chōen-ji text makes no mention of the abbot). Menzan's version reads:

> An ancient said, "Regarding properties and grain supplies that belong to the monastery storage, let the officers who understand cause and result administer the various tasks, dividing the monastery into departments and distributing the work." This means that the abbot of the monastery should not take charge of any major or minor matter whatsoever; rather he should concentrate only on practicing zazen, teaching, and encouraging the great assembly.

348 "Fundamental point" translates *watō* (話頭; Ch. *huàtóu*). In kōan practice, this refers to a kōan's essential point, which is the focus of investigation by the student.

349 This saying of the monk Changsha Jingcen also appears in sections 2-10 (see note 117) and 4-1.

350 For the source of the image of practicing as if one's head were aflame, see note 213 in section 4-1.

351 This can refer to a number of stories involving practitioners who cut off limbs out of devotion to their practice, but the story of Dazu Huike (see note 262 in section 5-4), who cut off his arm to prove to his teacher Bodhidharma the seriousness of his intention to practice, is one of the most famous. The word "zealously" translates *shōjin* (精進; Ch. *jīngjìn*; Skt. *vīrya*), which is the fourth of the six perfections or *pāramitās*, where it is usually translated as "diligence" or "effort." In modern Japanese it also appears in the word for Buddhist vegetarian cuisine, *shōjin ryōri* (精進料理).

352 This phrase begins with *go sendai tō* (五闡提等). There are two possible interpretations: either "five *sandhilā*" or "five *icchantika*." The five *sandhilā* (usually 五闡提羅; Ch. *wǔ chǎntíluó*; Jp. *go sendaira*) were five monks who claimed they had achieved awakening in order to receive donations from laypeople. As a result, they fell into hell and were later reborn as neutered males. *Icchantika* (usually 一闡提; Ch. *yīchǎntí*; Jp. *issendai*; often abbreviated as just 闡提) are people who are supposed to have forever lost the potential to attain awakening. Most Mahāyāna Buddhists, probably including Dōgen, rejected this was a possibility, so Dōgen would be using the phrase rhetorically if it is what he meant. The difficulty in interpretation arises from the fact that the "*sandhi*" in *sandhilā* and the "*chantí*" in *icchantika* are transliterated with the same Chinese characters (闡提). The final character in the compound (等) is a pluralizing suffix.

353 This is a saying of Zhaozhou (see note 88 in section 2-4) from *The Recorded Sayings of Zhaozhou* (趙州錄; Ch. *Zhàozhōu lù*; Jp. *Jōshū roku*). The section reads:

> A monk asked Zhaozhou, "I'm leaving for the south, and want to leave with a little knowledge about the Buddha-Dharma. What about it?"
>
> The master said, "You are leaving for the south. If you come to a place where there is a Buddha, quickly move on. At a place where there is no Buddha, do not tarry."
>
> The monk said, "In that case, I am dependent on nothing."
>
> The master said, "Willow catkins, willow catkins." (Green, *Recorded Sayings*, 96)

Willow catkins are ephemeral flowers that are pollinated by the wind, emphasizing the need to not stay in one place.

"No-buddha" (Jp. 無仏, *mubutsu*; Ch. 無佛, *wúfó*) is hyphenated because it could be interpreted as "the Buddha that is emptiness." Dōgen made at least two similar interpretative moves: in the fascicle of the *Shōbōgenzō* entitled "The Dignified Conduct of the Practice-Buddha" (行佛威儀; Jp. "Gyōbutsu-igi"), in which he interprets the titular phrase as such instead of the standard "practicing the Buddha's dignified conduct"; and in the fascicle "Buddha-Nature" (佛性; Jp. "Busshō"), in which he interprets the phrase "without Buddha-nature" (無佛性; Ch. *wú fóxìng*; Jp. *mu busshō*) to mean "Buddha-nature is emptiness" (Nishijima and Cross, *Shōbōgenzō*, 2:10).

354 Traditionally, monks were not allowed to store the food they received from begging.

355 For "wrong livelihood," see note 28 from section 1-3.

356 The first chapter of *The Analects* (論語; Ch. *Lúnyǔ*; Jp. *Rongo*) contains a similar saying: "When poor, never fawning; when rich, never arrogant" (Hinton, *Analects*, 7).

357 See note 218 in relation to section 4-4 for Dōgen's dates at Kennin-ji. Here, he is talking about the experiences he had during his second stay at Kennin-ji. Because he had recently returned from China and received Dharma transmission from a Chinese Zen master, many people visited Dōgen to inquire about what he had learned. Ejō, the recorder of these talks, was one such person.

358 Here, as in note 348, "fundamental points" translates *watō* (話頭; Ch. *huàtóu*). In kōan practice, this refers to a kōan's essential point that is to be investigated by the student.

359 The phrase "following and heard record" is the most literal possible translation of *Zuimonki* (随聞記). Because this title does not translate well into English, I have elected to keep it untranslated elsewhere as *Zuimonki*. A clearer but looser and more cumbersome translation would be "the record of things heard in the order in which they were heard."

360 *The Record of Profundity* (玄記; Ch. *Xuán jì*; Jp. *Gen ki*) refers to part of the third volume of *The Extensive Record of Yunmen Kuangzhen* (雲門和尚廣錄; Ch. *Yúnmén héshàng guǎnglù*; Jp. Unmon oshō kōroku), a collection of the teachings of Yunmen Wenyan (雲門文偃; Jp. Unmon Bun'en; 864–949 CE).

361 *The Record of the Hōkyō Era* (宝慶記; Jp. *Hōkyōki*) is described in note 19 in section 1-1.

362 *Kana shōbōgenzō* (仮名正法眼蔵) refers to what is typically regarded as Dōgen's magnum opus, usually simply called *Shōbōgenzō* in English. The text was written in vernacular Japanese instead of Classical Chinese—that is, using kana, the Japanese syllabary. Dōgen also compiled a collection of kōans called *Shōbōgenzō*, which is in Classical Chinese, so *Kana shōbōgenzō* is sometimes used to differentiate the two, in which case the kōan collection is called *Shinji shōbōgenzō* (真字正法眼蔵).

363 The bath manager (浴主; Ch. *yùzhǔ*; Jp. *yokusu*) is the monk in charge of the bathhouse at a monastery. It is not clear if the person who copied the text was actually the bath manager or if they merely used that room for their work.

364 Hōkyō-ji (宝慶寺) is a temple near Eihei-ji that was founded in 1279 by Jakuen (寂円; 1207–99 CE), a Chinese disciple first of Dōgen's teacher Rujing and later of Dōgen himself. After Dōgen's death, Jakuen became a student of Eihei-ji's second abbot, Ejō. When Ejō died in 1280, there was apparently a succession dispute, known as the *sandai sōron* (三代相論), involving Jakuen and others. What exactly transpired is unclear, but Jakuen's disciple Giun (義雲; 1253–1333 CE) became the fifth abbot of Eihei-ji in 1314, and Jakuen's lineage continued to hold Eihei-ji's abbacy until 1468.

365 Hazu district (幡豆郡) is now part of Nishio city (西尾市). "Sanshu" (三州) was the abbreviated name for Mikawa province (三河国). It now forms the eastern half of Aichi Prefecture (愛知県).

Notes to Part 2

366 Strictly speaking, the units of Japanese poetry are not syllables, but rather morae, which are known in Japanese as *haku* (拍). A word like

"tan," for example, would be one syllable in English, but two morae in Japanese because the "ta" and the "n" each count as a mora.

367 The *Selections of Refined Literature* (文選; Ch. *Wénxuǎn*; Jp. *Monzen)* is a sixth-century Chinese compilation of approximately seven hundred well-known poetry and prose writings by about 130 prominent writers. In Japan, this collection was regularly studied as part of an aristocratic education. See section 3-6 in part 1, and also notes 133 and 176.

368 See section 5-8 in part 1.

These are from my translation of the Chōen-ji version (長円寺本; Jp. *Chōenji-bon)* of *Zuimonki* in part 1.

369 Abe and Haskel, *Great Fool: Zen Master Ryōkan*, 108.

370 Abe and Haskel, *Great Fool: Zen Master Ryōkan*, 26.

371 A few lineages derived from different emperors took the family name Minamoto. For example, the family of Emperor Seiwa was called Seiwa Genji and included Minamoto no Yoritomo (源頼朝; 1147–99 CE), who established the first shogunate government in Kamakura. *Gen* in Genji is another pronunciation of the same Chinese character, 源, and *ji* means "family." The family name Koga came from the name of the place near Kyoto where the family had an estate.

372 Traditionally, according to Menzan's version of *Record of Kenzei*, people thought that Dōgen's father was Minamoto no Michichika (源通親; 1149–1202 CE), Michitomo's father. However, these days most Sōtō Zen scholars think Michitomo was Dōgen's true father.

373 Okubu, *Dōgen Zenji den no kenkyū*, 26.

374 There must be some confusion about either the year or the person to whom Kishun offered the copy. In 1420, Kenkō was only seven years old.

375 Funatsu, "Sanshō dōei shu no meisho."

376 Maruyama, "Dōgen no shiika," 98; Maruyama, "Dōgen Zenji no goshinei."

377 Bein, *Purifying Zen*, 83.

378 This quotation is my translation of an excerpt from *The Profound Meaning of the Lotus Sutra* (法華玄義; Ch. *Fǎhuā xuányì*; Jp. *Hokke gengi)*, a commentary on the *Lotus Sutra* by Tiantai Zhiyi (天台智顗; Jp. Tendai Chigi; 538–597 CE). Zhiyi is an exceptionally important figure in East Asian Buddhism. He is considered to be a pioneer in attempting to systematize all Buddhist teachings and to elaborate a uniquely Chinese

style of practice. He is also held to be one of the primary ancestors in the Tiantai (天台; Jp. Tendai) tradition of Buddhism, which takes its name from the mountain where he practiced. Also see note 138 for a reference to this text in *Zuimonki*.

379 Alan Senauke, *The Bodhisattva's Embrace*, 213. *Dāna-pāramitā* is the Sanskrit for "perfection of generosity," the first of six (according to Mahāyāna sources) or ten (according to Pāli sources) perfections that Buddhists should practice.

380 Okumura and Leighton, *Dōgen's Extensive Record*, 9:582.

381 Along with the *Dao de jing* (道德經), the *Zhuangzi* (莊子) is a foundational Daoist classic. It is believed to have been composed in the third century BCE, but scholars have found it difficult to date precisely.

382 This is my unpublished translation.

383 Waddell and Abe, *The Heart of Dōgen's Shōbōgenzō*, 65.

384 I have re-translated this here, but I previously translated this full work in Okumura, *Sōtō Zen: An Introduction to Zazen*, 93–98.

385 Modern people interpret the crow as a sunspot.

386 See section 5-4 in part 1.

387 The Chinese characters for *shoshōgen* (初生眼; "the eyes received at birth") in this title corresponds to *shoshōgen* (所生眼; "the eyes being born") in the chapter of the *Lotus Sutra* discussed below. The meaning is similar, but the different character used in Dōgen's waka may represent a scribal error.

388 Reeves, *Lotus Sutra*, 321.

389 Green, *Recorded Sayings*, 116.

390 Cleary, *Book of Serenity*, 4.

391 Broughton, *Zongmi on Chan*, 109–10. Text in parentheses is mine, text in brackets in original.

392 In the Shunjusha text, the last line is *ukistu shiranami* ("floating white waves"), which is based on one of the available manuscripts for *Record of Kenzei*. Another manuscript of the *Record of Kenzei* has the text I have included here. See Kawamura, *Shohontaikō: Eihei kaizan Dōgen Zenji gyōjō Kenzei ki*, 89.

393 Okumura and Leighton, *Dōgen's Extensive Record*, 292–93.

394 The "black dragon's pearl" comes from a Daoist story at the end of chapter thirty-two of the *Zhuangzi*. In it, a boy finds an extremely

valuable pearl under a sleeping dragon. In a Buddhist context the black dragon's pearl functions as a symbol for Buddha-nature, i.e., something that is normally understood to be hidden and valuable. Dōgen, however, tells us that such pearls are in fact common and not hidden, i.e. Buddha-nature is all-pervasive. The translation is from Leighton and Okumura, Dōgen's Pure Standards, 43.

395 Waka 19–51 are miscellaneous poems without titles. There are actually thirty-three poems in this category rather than thirty as the title suggests.

396 Nishijima and Cross, Shōbōgenzō: The True Dharma-Eye Treasury, 4:304.

397 Uchiyama, Opening the Hand of Thought, 87. In this passage Uchiyama uses the more popular namu Amida butsu (南無阿彌陀佛; literally "homage to Amitabha Buddha") instead of namu Kanzeon bosatsu.

398 See section 1-13 in part 1.

399 This is a paraphrase of the teaching. For a full translation, see Nishijima and Cross, Shōbōgenzō: The True Dharma-Eye Treasury, 4:170–71.

400 See Murcott, The First Buddhist Women: Translations and Commentary on the Therigatha, 32–33. The same story appears in Thera and Hecker, Great Disciples of the Buddha: Their Lives, Their Works, Their Legacy, 293–300.

401 Heine, Zen Poetry of Dōgen, 185.

402 Heine, Zen Poetry of Dōgen, 119.

403 Matsumoto, Dōgen no waka, 65. See the comments on waka number twenty-one for some background on these shrines.

404 Okumura and Leighton, Wholehearted Way, 33.

405 See Leighton and Okumura, Dōgen's Extensive Record, 426.

406 This is my unpublished translation. A kṣaṇa is considered the shortest possible division of time, or 1/4,500th of a minute.

407 Muller and Tanaka, The Brahmā's Net Sutra, 55. Brackets are in the original.

408 See section 3-15 in part 1.

409 See Dharma discourses 363, 409, 478, and 524 in Leighton and Okumura, Dōgen's Extensive Record.

410 Buddhist Text Translation Society, "Sutra on the Buddha's Bequeathed Teaching."

411 Mascaro, The Dhammapada, 62.

412 Mascaro, The Dhammapada, 53.

413 This is my own translation.

414 Leighton and Okumura, *Dōgen's Pure Standards*, 49.

415 Sawaki, *Sawaki Kōdō zenshū*, 13:128.

416 Okumura, *Heart of Zen*, 6.

417 See Leighton and Okumura, *Dōgen's Pure Standards*, 156.

418 Cook, *Record of Transmitting the Light*, 29.

419 Okumura, *Realizing Genjokoan*, 85–86.

420 Oba, *Dōgen Zenji wakashū shinshaku*, 261.

421 Okumura, *Realizing Genjokoan*, 2.

422 Etō, *Shōbōgenzō josetsu*, 342.

423 See section 6-15 in part 1.

424 Matsumoto, *Dōgen no waka: Haru wa hana natsu hototogisu*, 107–8.

425 *Inka* (印可) is a formal certification of a student's awakening. It is still given today in the Rinzai school to those who complete the entire kōan curriculum, although very few manage to do so. A small number of lineages in the Sōtō school that descend from Harada Sogaku Rōshi (原田祖岳; 1871–1961) also give *inka*.

426 Shibayama, *Zen Comments on the Mumonkan: The Authoritative Translation, with Commentary, of a Basic Zen Text*, 267.

427 Shibayama, *Zen Comments*, 267.

428 Anāthapiṇḍika (給孤独; Ch. Gěigūdú; Jp. Gyūkotoku) was a wealthy financier who donated the land to establish Jetavana monastery for Shakyamuni. This sutra is grouped together with the *Numerical Discourses* (增壹阿含經; Jp. *Zōitsu agon kyō*; Skt. *Ekottara Āgama*) in the *Taishō Tripiṭaka*, where it has the catalog number T 130. It does not seem to have a parallel in the Pali *Numerical Discourses* (Pali *Aṅguttara Nikāya*).

429 This is my unpublished translation. For an alternative translation, see Nishijima and Cross, *Shōbōgenzō: The True Dharma-Eye Treasury*, 1:115.

430 See section 6-21 in part 1.

431 This is my unpublished translation.

432 Leighton and Okumura, *Dōgen's Pure Standards*, 49.

433 See Uchiyama, *The Zen Teaching of Homeless Kodo*, 235.

434 Tanaka, *Kono koshin no hito*, 47.

435 Japanese Buddhist funerals involve ordaining the deceased as if they were becoming a monk or nun, and as such they receive a Dharma name in the process. In this case, the abbot withheld a Dharma name because he disapproved of the manner in which the person died.

436 McCullough, *The Tale of the Heike*, 23.

437 Buddhist Text Translation Society, "Sutra on the Buddha's Bequeathed Teaching."

438 Cleary and Cleary, *The Blue Cliff Record*, 176.

439 This is his Dharma discourse number 219; see Okumura and Leighton, *Dōgen's Extensive Record*, 226.

440 This is an unpublished translation by Carl Bielefeldt that will appear in a forthcoming translation of the *Shōbōgenzō* as part of the Sōtō Zen Text Project.

441 The previous fifty-one waka poems were added as a supplement to the description of Dōgen Zenji's life in the *Record of Kenzei* (建撕記; Jp. *Kenzei ki*). However, waka numbers fifty-two and fifty-three appear within the biography itself.

442 Okumura and Leighton, *Dōgen's Extensive Record*, 629.

443 This is my translation.

444 This expression (至祝至祝、至祷至祷; Jp. *shishuku shishuku shitō shitō*) is a traditional phrase used at the conclusion of a text or recitation, similar to a dedication of merit. There is no subject or object indicated, so it is difficult to translate into English.

445 This indicates where Kishun would have stamped his seal onto the manuscript.

446 This section includes waka that appear only in a subset of the manuscripts of the *Record of Kenzei* or in other later collections of Dōgen's poetry. In contrast, the preceding fifty-three waka are found in all manuscripts of the *Record of Kenzei*.

447 Takahashi, *Dōgen Zenji zenshū*, 17:52.

448 Okumura and Leighton, *Dōgen's Extensive Record*, 498.

449 Abe and Haskel, *Great Fool*, 211.

450 Tanigawa, *Ryōkan zenwakashū*, 409.

451 See section 5-8 in part 1.

452 Mascaro, *The Dhammapada*, 35.

453 The final two characters of his name may also be read as "Teika" instead of "Sadaie."

454 Okumura, *Realizing Genjokoan*, 3.

455 Italics indicate where the term in question appears.

456 Bielefeldt and Radich, "Treasury of the Eye of the True Dharma, Shobogenzo, Book 13, Ocean Seal Samadhi, Kaiin zanmai," 17.

457 The expression "Seeing with ears and hearing with eyes" came from the verse by Dongshan Liangjie (洞山良价; Jp. Tōzan Ryōkai) about nonsentient beings expounding the Dharma:

> How marvelous! How marvelous!
> The Dharma expounded by nonsentient beings is inconceivable.
> Listening with your ears, no sound.
> Hearing with your eyes, you directly understand.

This translation is found in Taigen Dan Leighton, *Just This Is It: Dongshan and the Practice of Suchness* (Boston: Shambhala Publications, 2015), 26.

458 Cleary and Cleary, *Blue Cliff Record*, 275. The Chinese characters from the original text were inserted by me for comparison with the quotation that follows.

459 Buddhist Text Translation Society, *The Śūraṅgama Sūtra*, 65. Italics and bold text are mine.

460 Leighton and Okumura, *Dōgen's Pure Standards*, 36.

461 This is my translation.

462 See the commentary on waka number twenty-eight for one example of the symbolism of the light of a firefly.

463 Lawson, "The Hojoki (My Ten-Foot Hut)."

BIBLIOGRAPHY

Part One. *Shōbōgenzō Zuimonki*

Azuma, Ryūshin (東隆真). "Shōbōgenzō zuimonki" (法眼蔵随聞記). In *Dōgen Zenji zenshū* (道元禅師全集), Vol. 16. Tokyo: Shunjūsha, 2003.

Bein, Steve, trans. *Purifying Zen: Watsuji Tetsurō's Shamon Dōgen*. Honolulu: University of Hawaii Press, 2011.

Buddhist Text Translation Society. "Sutra on the Buddha's Bequeathed Teaching." Talmage, CA: Dharma Realm Buddhist University. Accessed May 15, 2019. http://cttbusa.org/bequeathed_teaching/sutra.htm.

Cleary, Thomas, trans. *Book of Serenity*. Hudson, NY: Lindisfarne Press, 1990.

———, trans. *Record of Things Heard: From the Treasury of the Eye of the True Teaching*. Boulder: Prajna Press, 1980.

Cook, Francis Dojun, trans. *The Record of Transmitting the Light*. Somerville, MA: Wisdom Publications, 2003.

Foulk, T. Griffith, trans. "Instructions for the Cook." In *Nothing Is Hidden: Essays on Zen Master Dōgen's Instructions for the Cook*, edited by Jisho Warner, Shōhaku Okumura, John McRae, and Taigen Dan Leighton, 21–40. New York: Weatherhill, 2001.

———. *The Record of the Transmission of Illumination by the Great Ancestor, Zen Master Keizan*, Vol. 1. Tokyo: Sōtōshū Shūmuchō, 2017.

Funeoka, Makoto (船岡誠). *Dōgen to shōbōgenzō zuimonki* (道元と『正法眼蔵随聞記』). Tokyo: Hyōrinsha, 1980.

Green, James, trans. *The Recorded Sayings of Zen Master Joshu*. Boston: Shambhala, 1998.

Hinton, David, trans. *The Analects*. Washington, DC: Counterpoint, 1998.

Ikeda, Rosan (池田魯参), trans. *Gendaigoyaku shōbōgenzō zuimonki* (現代語訳 正法眼蔵随聞記). Tokyo: Daizō Shuppan, 1993.

————, ed. *Shōbōgenzō zuimonki no kenkyū* (正法眼蔵随聞記の研究). Tokyo: Keisuisha, 1989.

Kawamura, Kōdō (河村孝道). *Shohontaikō: Eihei kaizan Dōgen Zenji gyōjō Kenzei ki* (諸本対校:永平開山道元禅師行状建撕記). Tokyo: Daishūkan Shoten, 1975.

Kodera, Takashi James. *Dōgen's Formative Years in China: An Historical Study and Annotated Translation of the Hōkyō-ki*. Abingdon-on-Thames, UK: Routledge, 1980.

Leighton, Taigen Daniel, and Shōhaku Okumura, trans. *Dōgen's Pure Standards for the Zen Community*. Albany: State University of New York Press, 1996.

Masunaga, Reihō (増永霊鳳), trans. *A Primer of Sōtō Zen: A Translation of Dōgen's Shōbōgenzō Zuimonki*. Honolulu: East-West Center Press, University of Hawaii, 1971.

Mizuno, Yaoko (水野弥穂子). *Shōbōgenzō zuimonki* (正法眼蔵随聞記). Tokyo: Chikuma Shobō, 1992.

————. *Shōbōgenzō zuimonki no sekai* (『正法眼蔵随聞記』の世界). Tokyo: Daizō Shuppan, 1992.

Muller, A. Charles, ed. *Digital Dictionary of Buddhism*. Accessed May 15, 2019. http://buddhism-dict.net/ddb.

Muller, A. Charles, and Kenneth K. Tanaka, trans. *The Brahmā's Net Sutra*. Moraga, CA: Bukkyō Dendō Kyōkai and BDK America, 2018.

Nishijima, Gudō Wafu (愚道和夫), and Chodo Cross, trans. *Shōbōgenzō: The True Dharma-Eye Treasury*, Vol. 2. Berkeley, CA: Numata Center for Buddhist Translation and Research, 2008.

————, trans. *Shōbōgenzō: The True Dharma-Eye Treasury*, Vol. 4. Berkeley, CA: Numata Center for Buddhist Translation and Research, 2008.

Ōkubo, Dōshū (大久保道舟). *Dōgen Zenji den no kenkyū* (道元禅師傳の研究). Tokyo: Chikuma Shobō, 1966.

Okumura, Shōhaku. *Heart of Zen: Practice without Gaining-Mind*. Tokyo: Sōtōshū Shūmuchō, 2006.

————. *The Mountains and Waters Sutra*. Somerville, MA: Wisdom Publications, 2018.

————. *Realizing Genjokoan: The Key to Dōgen's Shōbōgenzō* . Somerville, MA: Wisdom Publications, 2010.

————. *Shikantaza: An Introduction to Zazen*. Tokyo: Sōtōshū Shūmuchō, 1985.

————. "The 28th Chapter of Shōbōgenzō: Bodaisatta-Shishobo, The Bodhisattva's Four Embracing Actions." Edited by Shōryū Bradley. *Dharma Eye* 15 (February 2005): 10–14.

Okumura, Shōhaku, and Taigen Dan Leighton, trans. *Dōgen's Extensive Record: A Translation of the Eihei Koroku*. Boston: Wisdom Publications, 2010.

————, trans. *The Wholehearted Way: A Translation of Eihei Dōgen's Bendowa, with Commentary by Kosho Uchiyama Roshi*. North Clarendon, VT: Tuttle Publishing, 1997.

Okumura, Shōhaku, and Tom Wright, trans. *Shōbōgenzō zuimonki*. Tokyo: Sōtōshū Shūmuchō, 1988.

Reeves, Gene, trans. *The Lotus Sutra: A Contemporary Translation of a Buddhist Classic*. Somerville, MA: Wisdom Publications, 2008.

Suzuki, Shunryū. *Zen Mind, Beginner's Mind*. Boston: Shambhala Publications, 2006.

Tajima, Ikudō (田島毓堂), and Yōko Kondō (近藤洋子). *Shōbōgenzō zuimonki goi sōsakuin* (正法眼蔵随聞記語彙総索引). Kyoto: Hōzōkan, 1981.

Takeuchi, Dōyū (竹内道雄). *Eihei-niso koun ejō zenji den* (永平二祖孤雲懐奘禅師傳). Tokyo: Shunjūsha, 1982.

Tanahashi, Kazuaki, trans. *Enlightenment Unfolds: The Essential Teachings of Zen Master Dōgen*. Boston: Shambhala Publications, 2000.

Tanahashi, Kazuaki, and John Daido Loori, trans. *The True Dharma Eye: Zen Master Dōgen's Three Hundred Kōans*. Boston: Shambhala, 2005.

Uchiyama Roshi, Kōshō (内山興正). *Jiko—Shūha denai shūkyō* (自己—宗派でない宗教). Tokyo: Hakujūsha, 1965.

Welter, Albert. *Yongming Yanshou's Conception of Chan in the Zongjing Lu: A Special Transmission within the Scriptures*. New York: Oxford University Press, 2011.

Yifa (依法). *The Origins of Buddhist Monastic Codes in China: An Annotated Translation and Study of the Chanyuan Qinggui*. Honolulu: University of Hawaii Press, 2002.

Part Two. *A Collection of Dōgen Zenji's Waka*

Abe, Ryūichi (阿部龍一), and Peter Haskel, trans. *Great Fool: Zen Master Ryōkan*. Honolulu: University of Hawaii Press, 1996.

Bein, Steve, trans. *Purifying Zen: Watsuji Tetsurō's Shamon Dōgen*. Honolulu: University of Hawaii Press, 2011.

Bielefeldt, Carl, and Michael Radich, trans. "Treasury of the Eye of the True Dharma, Shōbōgenzō, Book 13, Ocean Seal Samadhi, Kaiin zanmai." *Dharma Eye* 14, (2004): 17-23, accessed May 25, 2021. https://www.sotozen.com/eng/dharma/pdf/14e.pdf.

Broughton, Jeffrey. *Zongmi on Chan*. New York: Columbia University Press, 2009.

Buddhist Text Translation Society. *The Śūraṅgama Sūtra*. Ukiah, CA: Buddhist Text Translation Society, 2009.

———. "Sutra on the Buddha's Bequeathed Teaching." Talmage, CA: Dharma Realm Buddhist University. http://cttbusa.org/bequeathed_teaching/sutra.htm. Accessed May 15, 2019.

Cleary, Thomas, trans. *Book of Serenity*. Hudson, NY: Lindisfarne Press, 1990.

Cleary, Thomas, and J. C. Cleary, trans. *The Blue Cliff Record*. Boulder: Shambhala, 1977.

Cook, Francis Dojun, trans. *The Record of Transmitting the Light*. Somerville, MA: Wisdom Publications, 2003.

Etō, Sokuō (衛藤即応). *Shōbōgenzō josetsu* (正法眼蔵序説). Tokyo: Iwanami Shoten, 1959.

Funatsu, Yōko (船津洋子). "Sanshō dōei no meisho, naritachi, seikaku" (傘松道詠の名称・成立・性格). In *Dōgen shisō taikei* (道元思想大系), Vol. 6. Kyoto: Dōhōsha Shuppan, 1995), 259–86.

Green, James, trans. *The Recorded Sayings of Zen Master Joshu*. Boston: Shambhala, 1998.

Heine, Steven, trans. *The Zen Poetry of Dōgen: Verses from the Mountain of Eternal Peace*. Mount Tremper, NY: Dharma Communications, 2005.

Kakugen, Shinryō (覚巖心梁). "Eiheikōso sanshō dōei ryakuge" (永平高祖傘松道詠略解). In *Sōtōshū zensho shūgen* (曹洞宗全書宗源) Tokyo: Sōtōshūshūmuchō, 1929–1935.

Kasama, Ryūchō (笠間龍跳). *Jōyō daishi sanshō dōei shū kōjutsu* (承陽大師傘松道詠集講述). Nagoya, Japan: Bunkodo, 1882.

Kawamura, Kodo (河村孝道). *Shohontaikō: Eihei kaizan Dōgen Zenji gyōjō Kenzei ki* (諸本対校：永平開山道元禅師行状建撕記). Tokyo: Daishūkan Shoten, 1975.

Lawson, Robert N., trans. "The Hojoki (My Ten-Foot Hut)." Accessed April 12, 2021. https://www.washburn.edu/reference/bridge24/Hojoki.html.

Leighton, Taigen Daniel, and Shōhaku Okumura, trans. *Dōgen's Pure Standards for the Zen Community*. Albany: State University of New York Press, 1996.

Maruyama, Kogai (丸山劫外). "Dōgen no shiika" (道元の詩歌). In *Bessatsu taiyō Dōgen: Ima koko kono watashi o ikiru* (別冊太陽道元：いま、此処、このわたしを生きる), supervised by Tairyū Tsunoda (角田泰隆). Tokyo: Heibonsha, 2012, 98–104.

———. "Dōgen Zenji no goshinei wo mamotte" (道元禅師の御真詠を守って). In *Dōgen Zenji kenkyū ni okeru shomondai: Kindai no shūgaku ronsō o chūshin toshite* (道元禅師研究における諸問題：近代の宗学論争を中心として), edited by Tairyū Tsunoda (角田泰隆). Tokyo: Shunjusha, 2017, 291–312.

Mascaro, Juan, trans. *The Dhammapada*. London: Penguin Books, 1973.

Matsumoto, Akio (松本章男). *Dōgen no waka: Haru wa hana natsu hototogisu* (道元の和歌：春は花　夏ほととぎす). Tokyo: Chūōkōron Shinsha, 2005.

McCullough, Helen Craig, trans. *The Tale of the Heike*. Stanford, CA: Stanford University Press, 1988.

Menzan Zuiho (面山瑞方). *Sanshō dōei monge* (傘松道詠聞解). Obama, Japan: Eifukukai, 1968.

Murcott, Susan. *The First Buddhist Women: Translations and Commentary on the Therigatha*. Berkeley, CA: Parallax Press, 1991.

Narasaki, Ikkō (楢崎一光). *Hashi furu tsuyu: Dōgen zenji no outa* (はしふる露：道元禅師のお歌). Niihama, Japan: Zuiōji Senmon Sōdō, 1986.

Nishijima, Gudō Wafu (愚道和夫), and Chodo Cross, trans. *Shōbōgenzō: The True Dharma-Eye Treasury*, Vol. 4. Berkeley, CA: Numata Center for Buddhist Translation and Research, 2008.

Ōba, Nanboku (大場南北). *Dōgen zenji sanshō dōei no kenkyū* (道元禅師傘松道詠の研究). Tokyo: Nakayama Shobo, 1970.

———. *Dōgen zenji wakashū shinshaku* (道元禅師和歌集新釈) Tokyo: Nakayama Shobō, 1972.

Ōkubo, Dōshū (大久保道舟). *Dōgen Zenji den no kenkyū* (道元禅師傳の研究). Tokyo: Chikuma Shobō, 1966.

Okumura, Shōhaku. *Heart of Zen: Practice without Gaining-Mind.* Tokyo: Sōtōshū Shūmuchō, 2006.

————. *Realizing Genjokoan: The Key to Dōgen's Shōbōgenzō.* Somerville, MA: Wisdom Publications, 2010.

————. *Sōtō Zen: An Introduction to Zazen.* Tokyo: Sōtōshū Shūmuchō, 2002.

Okumura, Shōhaku, and Taigen Dan Leighton, trans. *Dōgen's Extensive Record: A Translation of the Eihei Koroku.* Boston: Wisdom Publications, 2010.

————, trans. *The Wholehearted Way: A Translation of Eihei Dōgen's Bendowa, with Commentary by Kosho Uchiyama Roshi.* North Clarendon, VT: Tuttle Publishing, 1997.

Reeves, Gene, trans. *The Lotus Sutra: A Contemporary Translation of a Buddhist Classic.* Somerville, MA: Wisdom Publications, 2008.

Sawaki, Kōdō (澤木興道). *Sawaki Kōdō zenshū* (澤木興道全集). Vol.13, *Sanshō dōei kōwa* (傘松道詠講話). Tokyo: Daihōrinkaku, 1964.

Senauke, Alan, trans. *The Bodhisattva's Embrace.* Berkeley, CA: Clear View Press, 2010.

Shibayama, Zenkei. *Zen Comments on the Mumonkan: The Authoritative Translation, with Commentary, of a Basic Zen Text.* New York: Harper & Row, 1974.

Takahashi, Bunji. *Dōgen Zenji zenshu.* Vol. 17, *Hogo kaju to* (法語・歌頌等). Tokyo: Shunjusha, 2010.

Tanaka, Tadao (田中忠雄). *Kono koshin no hito* (この古心の人). Vol. 1. Tokyo: Daihōrinkaku, 1990.

Tanigawa, Toshirō (谷川敏朗). *Ryōkan zenwakashu* (良寛全句集). Tokyo: Shunjusha, 1996, 409.

Thera, Nyanaponika, and Hellmuth Hecker. *Great Disciples of the Buddha: Their Lives, Their Works, Their Legacy.* Boston: Wisdom Publications, 1997.

Uchiyama, Kōshō (内山興正). *Opening the Hand of Thought.* Boston: Wisdom Publications, 2004.

————. *The Zen Teaching of Homeless Kodo.* Somerville, MA: Wisdom Publications, 2014.

Waddell, Norman, and Masao Abe. *The Heart of Dōgen's Shōbōgenzō.* New York: State University of New York Press, 2002.

Yoshida, Rosan Osamu (吉田収魯参), trans. *Limitless Life: Dōgen's World.* St. Louis, MO: The Missouri Zen Center, 1999.

INDEX

Liangsui Shouzhoua, 41, 413n41
life span, 33, 35, 79, 93, 121, 123
life-and-death
  awakening to, 332
  bondage of, 119, 433n158
  cutting, 139
  great matter of, 79, 81, 143, 157,
    165, 195, 427n113
  length of, 334
  long night of, 333–34
  rebirth and, 143, 145
limbs, cutting off, 261, 368, 460n351
Lin Xiangru, 209, 211, 213, 452n288
Lingyun Zhiqin, 197, 302, 439n208
Linji Yixuan, 448n264
Linji Zen, 453n295, 455–56n319,
  456n324
literature, Dōgen's view of, 127, 213,
  277–78, 285
livelihood
  concern with, 145
  giving up, 163, 185, 219, 221
  maintaining, 165
  orderly function of, 153, 155
  parents', concern for, 187, 189
  providing for, 91
  right, 19, 411n28
  training in, 65
  true reality and, 292
  wrong, 33, 35, 91, 265, 411n28,
    429n123
Longya Judun, 219, 453n298
Lotus Sutra, 11, 365, 464n387
  on all living beings as one's children,
    442n224
  on arhats, 450n273
  blessings and purification by, 294
  on bodhisattvas rising from earth,
    337–38
  on Buddha's *urnakesa*, 411–12n30
  on Dharma teachers, 305

on faith, 414n47
as genuine teachings, 416n55
importance of, 289–90
in Nichiren school, 23
on one vehicle, 325
Zhiyi's commentary on, 292
Lu Zhonglian, 77, 79, 426n112

M

Magu Baoche, 41, 413n41
Mahākāśyapa, 93, 429n128
Mahāyāna, 49, 245, 332, 415n54
  Buddha's death and, 416n55
  buddhas in, 319–20
  intermediate state in, 437–38n193
  lost potential for, 460n352
  merit dedication in, 437n192,
    453n302
Mahāyāna Mahāparinirvāṇa Sūtra, 324,
  325, 351–52
Mañjuśrī, 307, 308, 322
Man'yōshū, 280, 363
Māra/māras, 117, 300, 418n70,
  432n154
Maruyama, Kōgai, 284
Matsumoto, Akio, 330, 364
Mazu Daoyi, 153, 311, 313, 314,
  423n93, 438n196, 447n257
meat-eating, 420n84
Medicine Buddha, 113, 431n145
Menzan Zuihō, 24, 339. See also
  Revised and Annotated Record of Kenzei;
  Verses on the Way from Sanshō Peak
merit, 189, 247
  in Buddhadharma, 97
  dedicating, 147, 149, 225, 356,
    437n192, 453n302, 467n444
  in founding temples, 113, 115
  from just sitting, 271
  of offerings to monks, 430n137
  of others, 105

ABOUT THE TRANSLATOR

Shohaku Okumura is a Soto Zen priest and Dharma successor of Kosho Uchiyama Roshi. He is a graduate of Komazawa University and has practiced in Japan at Antaiji, Zuioji, and the Kyoto Soto Zen Center, and in Massachusetts at the Pioneer Valley Zendo. He is the former director of the Soto Zen Buddhism International Center in San Francisco. His previously published books of translation include *Dogen's Extensive Record*, *Living by Vow*, *The Mountains and Waters Sūtra*, *Opening the Hand of Thought*, *Realizing Genjokoan*, *Squabbling Squashes*, and *The Zen Teachings of Homeless Kodo*. He is the founding teacher of the Sanshin Zen Community, based in Bloomington, Indiana, where he lives with his family.

WHAT TO READ NEXT FROM WISDOM PUBLICATIONS

Dōgen's Extensive Record
A Translation of the Eihei Kōroku
Eihei Dōgen
Translated by Taigen Dan Leighton and Shohaku Okumura
Edited and introduced by Taigen Dan Leighton

"Taigen and Shohaku are national treasures."—Norman Fischer, author of *Sailing Home*

Being-Time
A Practitioner's Guide to Dogen's Shobogenzo Uji
Shinshu Roberts
Foreword by Norman Fischer

"This book is a great achievement. Articulate, nuanced, and wonderful."—Jan Chozen Bays, author of *Mindfulness on the Go*

How to Raise an Ox
Zen Practice as Taught in Zen Master Dogen's Shobogenzo
Francis Dojun Cook
Foreword by Taizan Maezumi Roshi

"Simply the best introduction to Dōgen's Zen."—Barry Magid, author of *Ordinary Mind*

Engaging Dōgen's Zen

The Philosophy of Practice as Awakening

Edited by Tetsuzen Jason Wirth, Kanpū Bret Davis, and Shūdō Brian Schroeder

"A rich and invaluable collection reflecting Dogen's unique wisdom."—Roshi Joan Halifax, Abbot, Upaya Zen Center

About Wisdom Publications

Wisdom Publications is the leading publisher of classic and contemporary Buddhist books and practical works on mindfulness. To learn more about us or to explore our other books, please visit our website at wisdomexperience.org or contact us at the address below.

Wisdom Publications
199 Elm Street
Somerville, MA 02144 USA

We are a 501(c)(3) organization, and donations in support of our mission are tax deductible.

Wisdom Publications is affiliated with the Foundation for the Preservation of the Mahayana Tradition (FPMT).